NORTH CAROLINA
STATE BOARD OF COMMUNITY COLLEGES
LIBRARIES
SAMPSON TECHNICAL COLLEGE

Automotive Air Conditioning

Automotive Air Conditioning

Paul Weissler, SAE, IMPA

Reston Publishing Company, Inc., Reston, Virginia
A Prentice-Hall Company

To my wife Arleen,
for her patience during the long period necessary to write this book

Library of Congress Cataloging in Publication Data

Weissler, Paul.
   Automotive air conditioning.

  1. Automobiles—Air conditioning. 2. Automobiles—Air conditioning—Maintenance and repair.
I. Title.
TL271.5.W44   629.2′77   80-39564
ISBN 0-8359-0261-7
ISBN 0-8359-0260-9 (pbk.)

© 1981 by
Reston Publishing Company, Inc.
A Prentice-Hall Company
Reston, Virginia 22090

All rights reserved. No part of this book
may be reproduced in any way, or by any means,
without permission in writing from the publisher.

10 9 8 7 6 5 4 3 2 1

Printed in the United States of America

Contents

Preface xi

1 Basic Theory of Heat and Heat Transfer ─────────── 1

Temperature 1
Temperature Versus Heat 2
Quantity of Heat 2
Heat Transfer and Temperature 4
Heat Transfer Blocked by Insulation 5
Maintaining a Temperature Differential 5
Heat and Its Effect on Liquids and Gases 6
Effect of Pressure on Temperature 8
Increasing Pressure 9
Decreasing Pressure 12
Evaporation and Humidity 13
Comfort and Humidity 14
Questions 15

2 A Simple Air Conditioning System ─────────── 18

The Modern Air Conditioner 20
The Mechanical System 22
Heat Exchanger 23
Refrigerant 12 Behavior 25
Compressor and Condenser 25
The Basic System Works 27
High-Pressure and Low-Pressure Sides of the System 28
Pressure-Temperature Relationship 28
Additional Parts and Controls in Modern System 30

Questions 30
Hands On 32

3 Electrical Review — 33

The Circuit 33
The Switch 33
The Motor 36
Electrical Ground 37
Series Circuit and Parallel Circuit 37
How a Circuit Fails 38
Measurements in the Circuit 39
Resistors 40
Use of Meters to Take Measurements 40
The Test Lamp 42
The Jumper Wire 43
Hands On 43

4 Modern Air Conditioning — 45

Two-Cylinder in Line 45
Compressor Valves 45
V-2 Compressor 47
Axial Five-Cylinder 48
Axial Six-Cylinder 49
Radial Four-Cylinder 51
Vane-Type Rotary Compressor 51
The Compressor Clutch 52
Receiver-Dryer 54
Thermostatic Expansion Valve 55
Valves-in-Receiver 61
Junction Block 62
Expansion Valve Calibration 62
High- and Low-Pressure Sides of the System 63
Additional Controls 63
Questions 64
Hands On 65

5 Controlling Evaporator Temperature — 67

Suction Throttling Valve 67
Pilot-Operated-Type Suction Throttling Valve 71

Positioning the Valves 73
Evaporator Pressure Regulator 76
Evaporator Temperature Regulator 78
System Function with Expansion Valve and Suction Throttling Valve or Evaporator Control 80
Questions 80
Hands On 82

6 Protecting the Air Conditioning and Engine — 83

Air Conditioning Protection 83
Engine Protection 88
Questions 89
Hands On 90

7 Cycling Clutch Systems — 91

Pressure Switch 92
Orifice Tube 94
Accumulator 95
Comparison of CCOT and Conventional Systems 96
Other Cycling Clutch Systems 96
Questions 98
Hands On 99

8 Moving Cold Air — 100

Vacuum and Vacuum Devices 100
Vacuum Diaphragms 101
Vacuum Reservoirs 104
The Duct System 105
Engine Cooling System-Heater 107
Controlling the Flow 110
Vacuum Reserve 116
Automatic Temperature Control 116
Testing the Air Control and Handling Systems 127
Questions 127
Hands On 129

9 Basic System Checkout — 130

Cooling System, The Place to Start 130
Cooling System Checkout 131

Drive Belts 133
Air Conditioning Drain Tubes 138
Air Conditioning Basic Performance Check 138
Automatic Temperature Control 143
Refrigeration System Service 143
Pressure Testing 144
Manifold and Gauges 150
The Third Gauge 151
Charging Station 152
Making the Connections 153
Taking Readings 154
Leak Checking 154
Major Leaks: When You Can Find Them and When You Can't 160
Questions 160
Hands On 163

10 Refrigerant 12 — 164

Containers 164
Handling Refrigerant 12 165
Tapping Into the Refrigerant Container 166
Liquid and Gas 168
Hands On 168

11 Discharge and Recharge — 169

Discharging the System 170
Vacuum Pumping the System 172
Recharging the System 175
Adding Alcohol to the System 178
Recharging Operation: With a Gauge Manifold into the Low Side, Engine Running and System Turned On 179
Recharging Operation: With a Gauge Manifold, Liquid into the High Side with the Engine Off 182
Use of the Sight Glass 182
Adding Alcohol to AMC Cars 183
Adding Alcohol with a Charging Station 183
Questions 184
Hands On 186

12 Air Conditioning Troubleshooting — 187

Preliminary Checkout 187
Detailed Troubleshooting 188

Step One: Pressure Testing 190
Step Two: Troubleshooting Guides 190
Step Three: Moisture and Component Testing 196
Compressor Clutch 200
Compressor 204
Expansion Valve and Orifice Tube 206
Suction Throttling Valve 208
Cycling Clutch Switch 211
Intermittent Operation 215
Excessive Noise 218
Questions 218
Hands On 221

13 Replacing Parts — 222

Components That Can Be Replaced Without Discharging the System 222
Components That Can Be Replaced Only after the System Is Discharged 223
General Guidelines to Parts Replacement 223
Expansion Valve with Capillary Tube 225
Cycling Clutch Switch: Thermostatic or Pressure Type, Except AMC 225
Cycling Clutch Switch: American Motors Cars 225
Orifice Tube 227
Evaporator Pressure Regulator 228
Receiver-Dryer Accumulator (except Valves-in-Receiver Design) 228
Servicing the Valves-in-Receiver 229
Refrigerant Hose 234
Questions 237
Hands On 238

14 Compressor Service — 239

Compressor Service Notes 239
General Motors Radial Four Compressor 240
General Motors Six-Cylinder Compressor 255
Nippondenso and Chrysler C-171 Compressors 260
Sankyo SD-5 Compressor 268
Tecumseh and York Two-Cylinder Compressors 277
Chrysler V-2 Compressor 286
York Rotary Vane Compressor 292
Questions 299
Hands On 300

15   Rotary Vane Air Cycle _____ **301**

Glossary   305

Appendix   320

Index   327

1

Basic Theory of Heat and Heat Transfer

Air conditioning is a system that deals with heat, so let's begin with a basic understanding of heat, starting with temperature and quantity.

Temperature

The temperature of air, water, or your body is heat you can feel (Fig. 1-1). You may not be able to make a precise distinction, but you certainly know if it's very hot or very cold. The *thermometer* is a device that enables us to measure exactly how hot or how cold. Several temperature scales are in use, but some have only scientific use. For our purposes, there are only two scales, *Fahrenheit* and *Celsius*.

In the Fahrenheit scale, water freezes at 32 degrees and boils at 212 degrees. You can identify a Fahrenheit reading by the F that follows the number of degrees: 212°F. Fahrenheit is the scale that was used almost exclusively in the United States until the late 1970s, when the country began to convert to the metric system.

In the Celsius scale, water freezes at zero degrees and boils at 100 degrees. Celsius also is called "centigrade" and is the scale used in the metric system. You can identify a Celsius reading by the C that follows the number of degrees: 100°C.

To convert Fahrenheit readings to Celsius, subtract 32 and then multiply by 5/9. For example, 212 minus 32 equals 180 multiplied by 5/9 equals 100.

To convert Celsius readings to Fahrenheit, multiply by 9/5 and then add 32. For example, 100 multiplied by 9/5 equals 180, plus 32 equals 212.

In either case, the measurement is made with a thermometer calibrated to read Fahrenheit, Celsius, or both (Fig. 1-2). Simple thermometers are bulbs filled with mercury, an element that expands in

2 Basic Theory of Heat and Heat Transfer

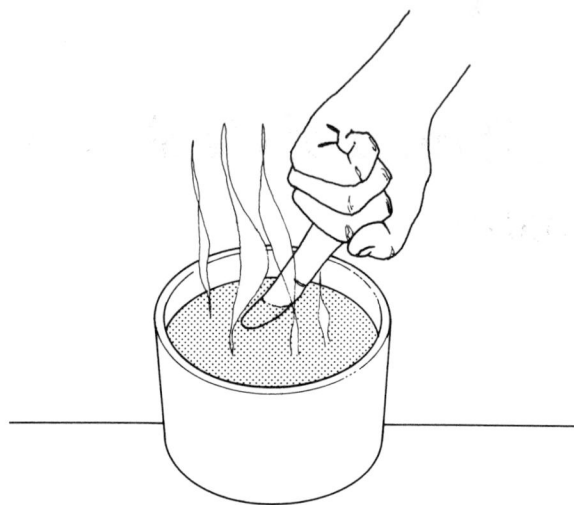

Figure 1-1 Temperature is heat you can feel.

proportion to changes in temperature. Many thermometers today are electronic devices with digital displays that are triggered by temperature-sensitive components called thermistors.

Temperature Versus Heat

Temperature is heat you can feel or measure with a thermometer. If the heat is concentrated in a small area, the temperature of that area may be high, but the amount of heat it contains may be small. A large area at a much lower temperature may actually contain more heat by virtue of its size. If you light a match, for example, and insert the end of a thermometer into the flame, the temperature reading will be very high (Fig. 1-3). You could not heat even a tiny house with the heat given off by the single match, because the amount—the quantity—is too low. Heat, therefore, also must be measured in terms of quantity.

Quantity of Heat

The quantity of heat is measured in *British thermal units* (abbreviated (Btus). The Btu is defined as the amount of heat necessary to raise the temperature of 1 pound of water by 1°F (Fig. 1-4). To raise the temperature of 10 pounds of water by 1 degree would require 10 Btu. As you can

3   Quantity of Heat

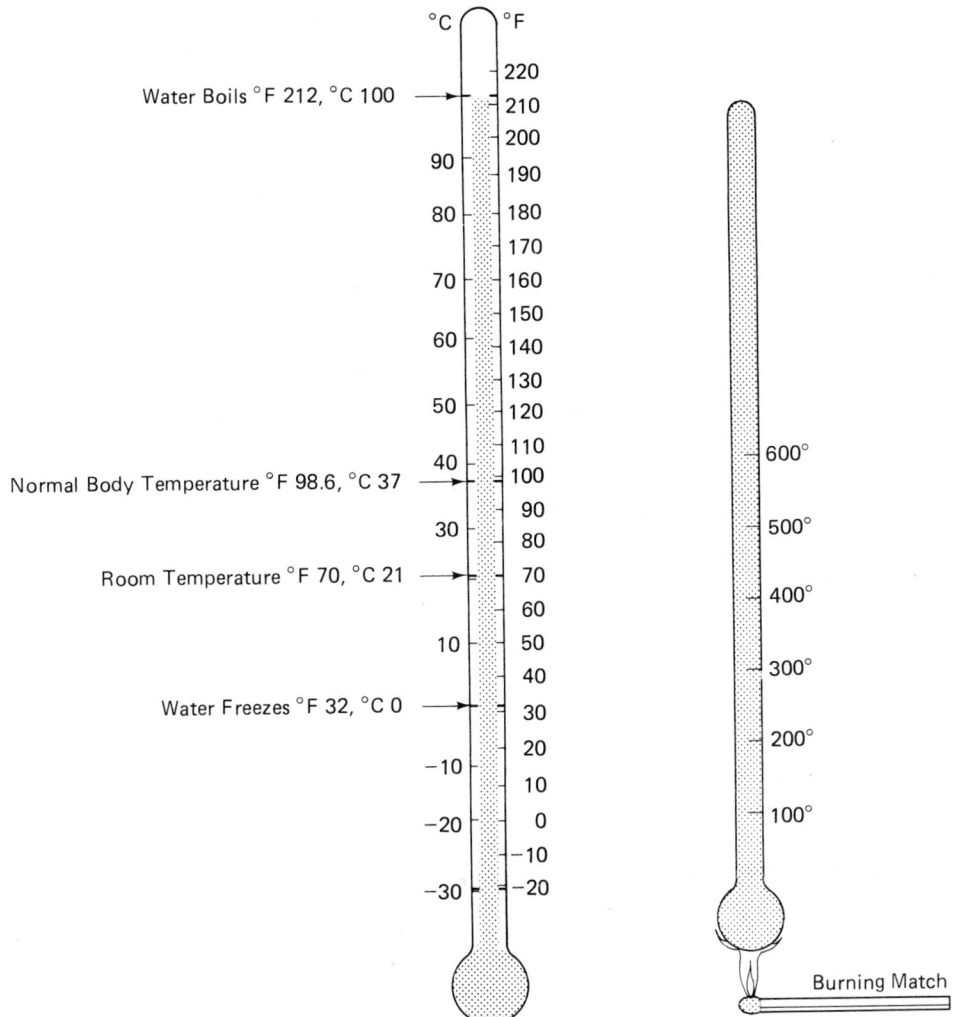

Figure 1-2 (*Left*) Comparison of Fahrenheit and Celsius (also called Centigrade) scales. The lowest temperatures shown, −21.7°F and −29.8°C, are the boilng points of fluids used in the modern automobile air conditioning system.

Figure 1-3 (*Right*) Flame of a match produces little heat, but it is concentrated, so temperature is high.

see, the temperature of the water remains the same, but the water contains more Btus and therefore a greater quantity of heat.

Although the Btu is specified to cover water, it can be extended to include anything, such as the air. Unlike the temperature scale, which does not change according to what is being measured, the Btu always refers back

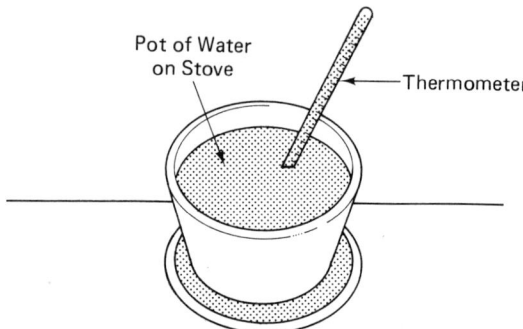

Figure 1-4 A BTU is the amount of heat necessary to raise the temperature of one pound of water one degree F.

to water, regardless of what is involved. If we add 10 Btu to a given quantity of air, for example, it means that we are adding an amount of heat that if added to 10 pounds of water would raise the temperature of that water 1°F. The Btu relationship to water temperature is always true. A similar, precise Btu relationship to the temperature of air and other gases cannot be established. The same quantity of heat in Btus on the same quantity of air may produce different temperature changes from one time to another, depending on a number of factors, including the moisture content of the air (humidity).

Heat Transfer and Temperature

Heat is a form of energy, and wherever we have two adjacent areas at different temperatures, there will be movement of the heat from the warmer to the colder. This movement is called *heat transfer* (see Fig. 1-5).

The terms warmer and colder are relative only. For example, if one area is minus 30°F and another right next to it is minus 10°F, we might call them both cold. However, the −30 is colder and the −10 is warmer. Heat would flow from the −10 to the −30 area until the temperatures of the two areas were virtually the same.

Or the temperatures of adjacent areas might be 100 and 200°F, both of which we could call very hot. However, the 200°F area is hotter than the 100, so heat would flow from the 200 to the 100, until the temperatures of both were virtually the same.

The temperature rise in the colder area in each example is proportional to its size compared with the warmer area. If both areas were the same size, the temperatures in both would change (one would go up, the other would go down) by the same number of degrees. If one area were twice the size of the other, the two areas would end up at the same temperature, but that temperature would be proportionally closer to the starting temperature of the larger area. For example, area A is twice the size of area B. Area A is at 60°F and area B is at 90°F. The temperature differential between the two is 30°F (90 minus 60). Twice the amount of heat (measured in Btus) will be required by the larger area A, and as a result the temperature rise in area A will be only one-third of the 30-degree differential, or 10°F. Both areas will end up at 70°F.

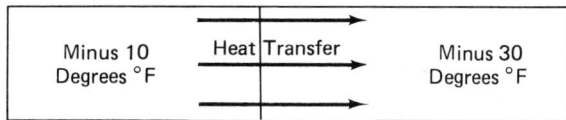

Figure 1-5 Heat flows from warmer to colder area, and in this case −10° is warm, compared with −30°.

Heat Transfer Blocked by Insulation

Heat transfer cannot be stopped completely as long as there is a temperature differential between adjacent areas. If one area is confined, such as the interior of a house or the passenger compartment of a car, the exterior of the car or house forms an insulating barrier and the heat transfer is slowed. If thick insulating material is used between the areas, such as in the walls of a house, the heat transfer is slowed still further, but, again, it can never be stopped.

The term heat transfer means just that. Heat can only be transferred, that is, moved from one place to another, never disposed of. Heat always tries to "correct" a temperature differential between adjacent areas by transferring to the cooler area.

Maintaining a Temperature Differential

In an automobile with air conditioning on a hot day, we want to create and maintain a temperature differential to make the passenger compartment cooler than the outside. To defy the natural tendency of heat to transfer to equalize temperatures in adjacent areas, a mechanical system is employed. It removes heat from passenger compartment air (thus cooling the passenger compartment) and transfers the heat to the outdoors.

The body of the car poses a barrier to the flow of heat from the outdoors back into the passenger compartment, but of course the heat gradually works its way through. The air conditioning system, therefore, must continue to operate to remove this heat. Depending on outside temperatures, it may be necessary to operate the air conditioning system only occasionally, frequently, or constantly to keep the interior of the car cool.

When air conditioning cools the passenger compartment of a car, even when millions of systems are cooling the passenger compartments of millions of cars and the interiors of millions of houses, the space that is being cooled is really tiny when compared with the outdoors. Therefore, although the passenger compartment temperatures may be lowered 20°F or more, the temperature of the outdoors does not rise by any measurable amount. The reason is that although a lot of heat has been removed from the passenger compartment, the amount (measured in Btus) is really insignificant when the size of the compartment is compared with the outdoors.

Heat and Its Effect on Liquids and Gases

To this point, we have looked at the measurement and movement of heat. Now let's see how heat behaves when it is applied to and removed from liquids and gases.

What Happens When Heat Is Added Specifically to a Liquid?

It would seem to be a simple matter to answer the question, "What happens when heat is added to a liquid?" such as water. It gets hotter, of course, and you can measure that with a thermometer. That is not a complete answer, however. When we add enough heat to bring water to a boil, its temperature rises to 212°F (100°C). We can continue to add heat, but the thermometer reading does not rise. Is the water getting hotter or isn't it?

The answer is that the water is getting hotter but the temperature is not rising. The additional heat is turning the water into vapor—a liquid into a gas—a process called *evaporation*. In the evaporation process, the water vapor is absorbed into the air. When heat does not cause a temperature rise, it is called *latent heat* or hidden heat (see Fig. 1-6). The term latent heat is not one that will help you service automobile air conditioning, but the principle it embodies is the basis for modern air conditioning: the use of a special fluid that can change to a gas and absorb a great deal of heat from the passenger compartment.

7 Heat and Its Effect on Liquids and Gases

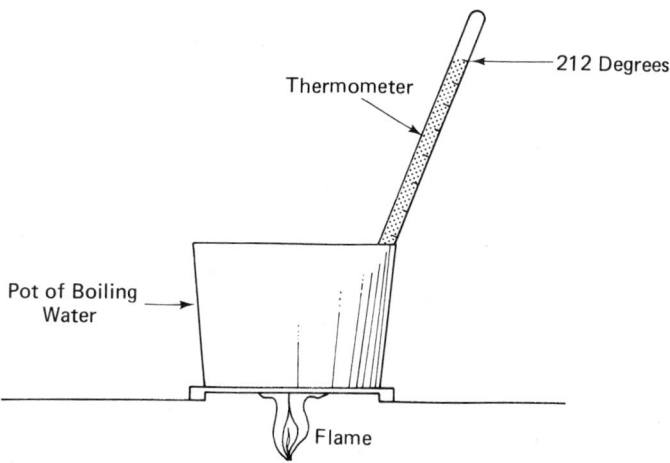

Figure 1-6 Heat is being added to water, but the temperature does not rise above 212°F.

What Happens When This Heat Is Taken Away?

As with the previous question, the answer might seem to be simply, "The temperature of the water drops." This is only partly true, however. If the water has evaporated into the air, the first effect is to convert the vapor back into liquid, a process called *condensation*. Scientists have determined by experimentation that 970 Btu must be added to change 1 pound of water at 212°F into vapor by boiling. The amount of vapor converted back to liquid, therefore, depends on the amount of heat that is taken away.

If exactly 970 Btu is removed, 1 pound of vapor will condense back to water. If 1940 Btu is removed, 2 pounds of water vapor will condense. If only 97 Btu is taken away, only 1/10 pound of water vapor will condense.

This addition or removal of heat can be spread over a day (24 hours) or made in seconds. The measurements, however, are based on changes in an hour or a day.

Just as when heat is added to turn water into vapor, the temperature may not change (in this case drop) as heat is taken away and the vapor condenses back to water. If heat is taken away only at a minimum rate, just to permit the condensation process, the temperature may remain at the boiling point, 212°F. The heat that is being removed is the latent (hidden) heat.

Water into Ice, Ice into Water

At the colder end of the thermometer scale, water freezes into ice. Just as they have determined that it takes 970 Btus to change water to vapor when the water is at 212°F, scientists have found that when water is at 32°F, taking away 144 Btu from 1 pound of water will make it solidify into ice. Add 144 Btu to 1 pound of ice and it will melt into water, a process called *fusion*. Both these acts occur with no temperature change, so the 144 Btu represents latent heat, called the *latent heat of fusion*.

Again, this won's help you service an automobile air conditioning system, but it will help you understand the reason for some of its controls to prevent the formation of ice. This information also permits the introduction of a definition of cooling capacity of an air conditioning system.

Inasmuch as the removal of 144 Btu will change 1 pound of water into ice, 2000 times that amount (288,000 Btu) will change 2000 pounds—1 ton of water—into ice. If we want an air conditioning system to have enough cooling power to change 1 ton of water into 1 ton of ice in one 24-hour day, the system must remove 288,000 Btu divided by 24 hours, or 12,000 Btu per hour to accomplish this objective.

It is common to measure air conditioning capability either in terms of tons of refrigeration (its relationship to this ice-freezing capability) or in Btus. Therefore, a system that can remove 12,000 Btu per hour is called a 1-ton system. Most automobiles have air conditioning systems rated at about 1½ tons of refrigeration, or 18,000 Btu (per hour).

Effects of Pressure on Temperature

Thus far we have looked at what happens when heat is added to or taken away from water, without considering any effect that pressure might have on the results.

Actually, pressure is always involved, because the atmosphere that contains the air we breathe always exerts pressure, which is called *atmospheric pressure*. Or you may have heard meteorologists giving the weather report refer to it as *barometric pressure*. This is atmospheric pressure as measured with a tool called a *barometer*.

Atmospheric pressure is the downward pressure exerted by the envelope of air that surrounds our planet. This air, which extends hundreds of miles outward into space, is held in place by the force of gravity. The pull of gravity is strongest at the surface of the planet, and the air is heaviest (so it exerts the greatest pressure) the closer to the earth that it is measured. At sea level, the air pressure is highest. The pressure drops off gradually at increasing altitude. It is much lower, for example, at the top of a high mountain (see Fig. 1-7). Everything and everyone on this planet is bearing up under atmospheric pressure, which is about 14.7 pounds per square inch (101 kilopascals).

Because this pressure is everywhere, our pressure gauges (tools designed to measure pressure in mechanical systems) are calibrated to

Increasing Pressure

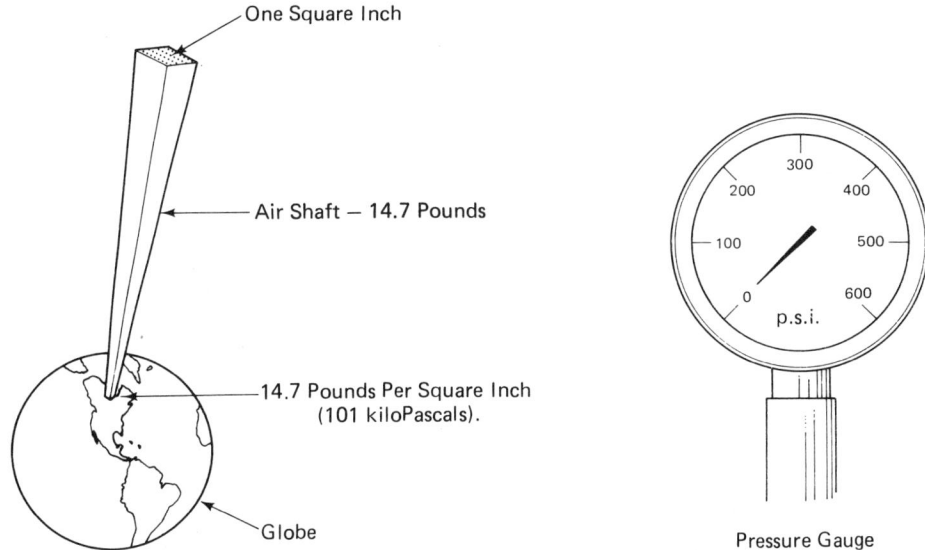

Figure 1-7 *(Left)* The atmosphere that surrounds our planet exerts a downward pressure of 14.7 pounds per square inch (100 kilopascals) at sea level.

Figure 1-8 *(Right)* Gauges are calibrated to cancel the effect of atmospheric pressure, so they read zero even though the pressure is actually about 14.7 pounds per square inch (psi) or 100 kilopascals (kPa).

cancel the effect. When a pressure gauge is unconnected, it reads zero (Fig. 1-8). Actually, of course, the pressure is about 14.7 pounds per square inch (100 kilopascals).

Atmospheric pressure is virtually constant at a given altitude;—it changes only very slightly with the weather. These slight changes have no practical effect when we measure pressure in any mechanical system. These changes are of interest only to meteorologists, because they indicate weather changes. Using a barometer, a specially calibrated gauge, the meteorologist records changes in atmospheric pressure.

Any amount of pressure, atmospheric or otherwise, changes the boiling-point of water. The familiar 212°F figure is true only at sea level. Atop a high mountain, where atmospheric pressure is much lower, the boiling point of the water also is lower.

Increasing Pressure

The greater the air pressure on the top of the water, the more difficult it is for the water to vaporize. Think of it this way. Air pressure and heat both represent energy. The air is pushing down and the heat is trying to vaporize

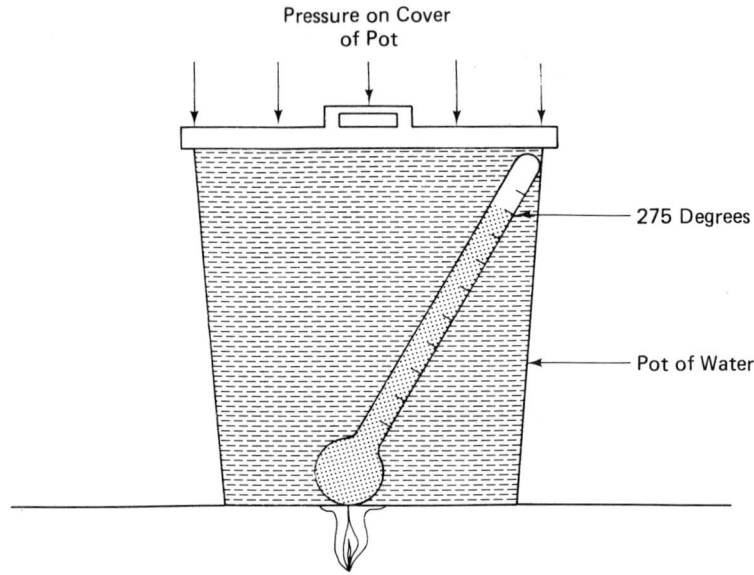

Figure 1-9 When pressure is applied to boiling water, the boiling point rises.

the water, to move it up out of the liquid into the air. The more air pressure energy pushing down, the more heat (in Btus) that must be applied to the water to vaporize it. Because more heat must be applied to the water, its temperature rises. Each pound per square inch of air pressure adds more than 2°F to the boiling point of the water (see Fig. 1-9).

This basic principle applies to other liquids and it also is used in another part of the automobile, the cooling system. Understanding the behavior of liquid under pressure in the cooling system of a car can be helpful in learning about other aspects of liquids and pressure.

In the automobile cooling system, a mixture of water and antifreeze is subject to pressure, usually 14 to 16 pounds per square inch (above the 14.7 applied by the atmosphere).

The pressure is not "applied," but the system is sealed except for a fill cap that contains a spring-loaded relief valve. The spring is calibrated so the valve will be forced open if pressure from the water and antifreeze mixture reaches the 14 to 16 pounds per square inch figure. As the water and antifreeze mixture absorbs heat from the engine, it expands and tries to boil. It exerts pressure against all parts of the cooling system, including the fill cap. If the pressure reaches the 14 to 16 pounds per square inch capability of the fill cap's spring-loaded valve, the water and antifreeze mixture will remain a liquid and stay in the cooling system of the car.

If the pressure rises above the capability of the cap, some of the water and antifreeze mixture will boil, and both vapor and some liquid will push open the spring-loaded relief valve. When enough of the water and antifreeze mixture has escaped from the system to relieve the pressure, the valve will close again (see Fig. 1-10).

11 Increasing Pressure

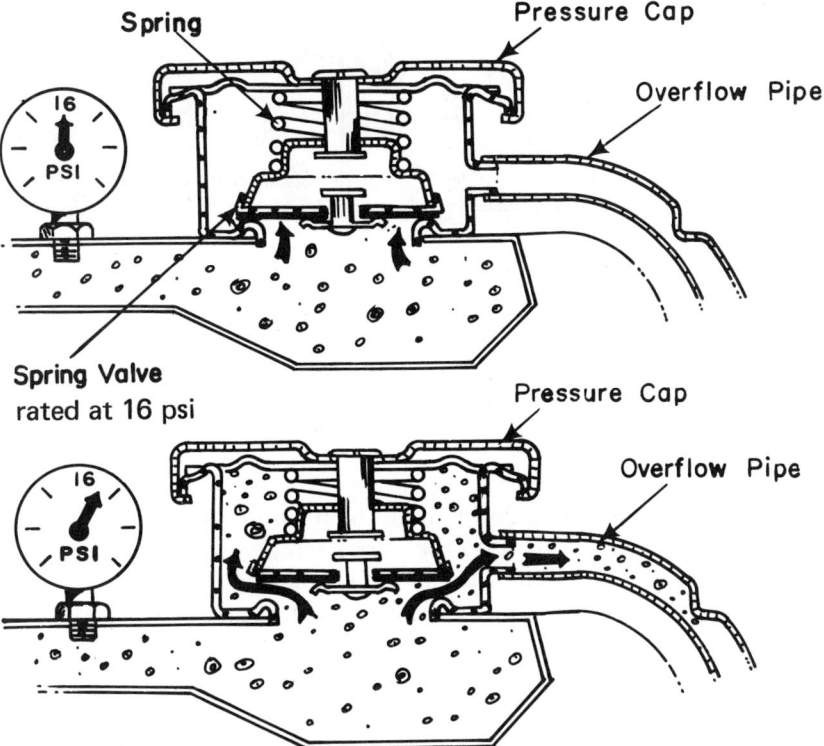

Figure 1-10 In an automotive cooling system, the coolant (water and antifreeze) expands when it is heated. As long as the pressure remains at or below the pressure rating of the spring valve in the radiator cap, the coolant remains in the system and it does not boil. If pressure builds up past 16 psi, the valve is forced open and the coolant flows out, boiling as it encounters only atmospheric pressure.

Let's now assume that the liquid level in the cooling system is somewhat low, and that the fill cap valve provides a perfect seal, capable even of preventing the escape of vapor when it is closed. Now we run the engine and the water and antifreeze mixture quickly absorbs heat and vaporizes completely. Once it is a vapor, it can continue to absorb heat without causing the pressure in the system to increase. The vapor cannot escape from the system into the atmosphere, so it continues to absorb heat. Unlike a liquid, it does not increase in pressure. Also unlike a liquid, its temperature rises as it absorbs this additional heat. This additional heat, therefore, is anything but latent (hidden). The higher temperature, above the boiling point for a liquid at the same pressure, is called *superheat*. (See Fig. 1-11.)

For example, consider a cooling system with a 14 pounds per square inch pressure cap. The system is filled with a mixture that is 50 percent water, 50 percent antifreeze, which has a boiling point in the pressurized

12   Basic Theory of Heat and Heat Transfer

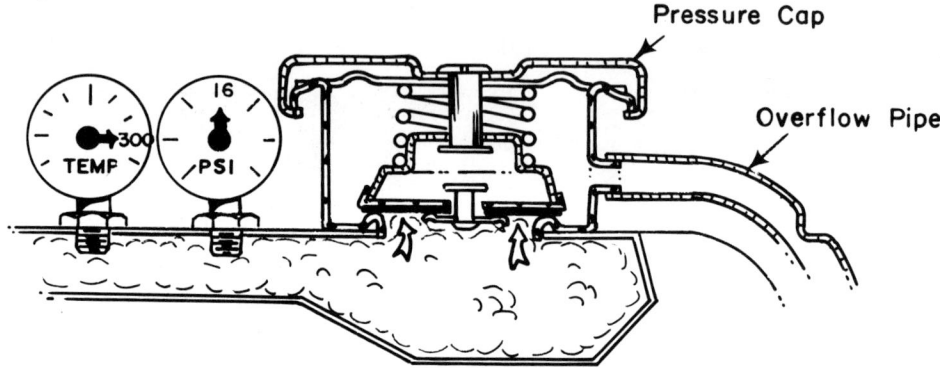

Figure 1-11   In this case, the system is filled with vapor. Once all the fluid is vaporized, adding heat will increase the vapor temperature but not the pressure in the system. The vapor is called superheated.

system of 265°F. If all the liquid is vaporized at 265°F and additional heat is added to raise the vapor temperature to 300°F, the vapor is regarded as superheated by 35°F. The vapor remains at 14 pounds per square inch pressure, however, even at the superheated temperature.

When we focus on an air conditioning system, you'll see how this principle applies.

Decreasing Pressure

Thus far we have considered the behavior of liquids and gases when pressure is increased. The opposite occurs when pressure is lowered, and some interesting things happen when pressure is lowered below atmospheric.

As explained earlier, the atmospheric pressure on top of a tall mountain is lower than that at sea level, and so the boiling point of water is lower at the top of that mountain. The car's cooling system must be designed to cope with the fact that its performance is reduced at high altitudes, but this is a relatively small application of the low-pressure principle.

Let's see what happens when pressures really drop. First, consider that, except for meteorologists with barometers, anything at atmospheric pressure is considered at zero pressure, and anything below atmospheric pressure is considered to be in a vacuum. Air or anything between the air and the vacuum that is free to move (such as liquid or solid material) rushes in to fill the vacuum. If a vacuum is to be created and maintained, it must be done in a confined area.

You are probably familiar with the vacuum cleaner, an appliance in which a motorized pump draws air from a hose, lowering the air pressure in

Figure 1-12 When the mouth sucks on the straw, it draws out air, lowering the pressure in the straw. Atmospheric pressure on the water itself remains at 14.7 psi (100 kPa), and so it pushes down on the water, forcing it up the straw.

the hose. If the hose end is held up, air rushes in to fill the vacuum. If the hose end is positioned over a dusty area, however, loose dust and outside air both flow into the hose (and the dust is collected in a bag).

Another example of vacuum is when you suck on a straw inserted into a glass of water. You draw out the air in that straw (lowering the air pressure). Atmospheric pressure pushing down on the water (as it pushes down on everything) forces water up the straw (see Fig. 1-12). Remove your lips from the open end of the straw and it immediately fills with air.

The normal measurement for vacuum is in inches of mercury; the greater the number, the more powerful the vacuum is. A "perfect" vacuum, no atmospheric pressure at all, would be measured at about 30 inches. Although some motorized pumps can come close, a perfect vacuum has not been created mechanically.

As explained earlier, in the lower pressure (vacuum) situation, the effect of heat is much different. Water would boil at 32°F in a perfect vacuum. This may not sound important, for air conditioning systems rarely have a vacuum in normal operation. However, the use of vacuum is invaluable in servicing the system, and the principle that water boils at low temperature in a vacuum is what permits removal of harmful moisture from the system.

Evaporation and Humidity

Boiling is one way to evaporate water into the air, but it is not the only way. Water may evaporate into the air without boiling, if the air can readily absorb the additional moisture. The amount of water that the air can hold varies according to air temperature.

When the air is warm, it expands and can hold more water vapor than when it is cool. You may have heard the term *relative humidity* in weather reports. The relative humidity is a ratio of the amount of water vapor in the air compared with the amount the air can hold at a given temperature. If the absolute amount of water vapor in the air is the same at 60°F as at 90°F, the relative humidity at 90 will be much lower, because the warmer air can hold more.

A combination of warm air and low relative humidity means that any water exposed to the air will evaporate into the air more readily. You have observed examples of this in such as the following:

* Wet clothing hung out on a line will give up its moisture to the air and become dry.
* After a rainstorm the relative humidity usually is lower, and the water in puddles evaporates into the air.
* Where relative humidity is low, such as in the desert, we feel cooler in spite of the temperature, because perspiration on our skin evaporates readily into the air, absorbing heat from our bodies.

The rules of heat transfer during evaporation apply to all situations, whether the water is boiling or not. A total of 970 Btu per pound of water vapor is transferred during evaporation of any kind at sea level, including perspiration from the skin.

Comfort and Humidity

If relative humidity could be kept low enough, we would be comfortable at very high temperatures because of the self-cooling mechanism of evaporating perspiration.

By contrast, even if the temperature is very low, we may be very uncomfortable when it is very humid or "muggy." At 75°F and virtually 100 percent humidity, we feel less comfortable than at 90°F with only 30 percent humidity.

An air conditioning system removes both heat and humidity from the air. The humidity removal is by condensation; the air temperature in a confined area (in a car it is the ductwork for the air conditioning) is lowered by heat transfer. The low temperatures developed in the ductwork raise the relative humidity right around the cold tubing of the air conditioning system, and water in the air condenses into liquid, which drains from the car (see Fig. 1-13).

Moisture removal is not merely an incidental occurrence. The 970 Btus of latent heat that were absorbed when 1 pound of water evaporated into the air must be removed in order for condensation to occur. As you

15 Questions

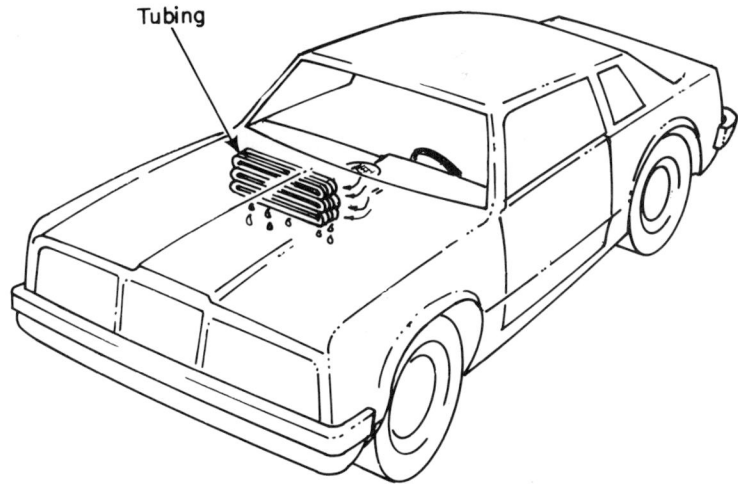

Figure 1-13 The cold vapor in the air conditioning tubing absorbs heat from the surrounding air, raising the relative humidity. As a result, just like a miniature rainstorm, moisture in the air condenses and falls on the tubing.

recall, when latent heat is added or removed, no temperature change takes place. Therefore, when the air is very humid, an air conditioning system will serve primarily to remove humidity, that is, moisture from the air. The actual temperature drop of the air will not be as great as with lower relative humidity.

The comfort of the passengers, however, is increased as effectively as if the temperature were lowered. In testing an air conditioning system on a humid day, however, you should not expect the temperature of the air blowing from the dashboard louvers to be as low as on a day with low relative humidity.

QUESTIONS

The following ten questions are about material you should have learned in Chapter 1. Read the opening statement of each question carefully; then select the statement following one of the letters that best completes it.

Example:
A reading of 140 degrees on the Fahrenheit scale is equal in the Celsius scale to
a. 50°C.
b. 60°C.
c. 70°C.

Solution and answer: To convert 140°F to Celsius, subtract 32; then multiply the remainder of 108 by 5 and divide by 9. 108 × 5 ÷ 9 = 60. Answer b, therefore, is correct.

1. A reading of 70°F is equal in the Celsius scale to about
   a. 15°C.
   b. 18°C.
   c. 21°C.
2. The following is not necessarily true of high temperature:
   a. You can feel it.
   b. It contains a lot of heat.
   c. You can measure it with a thermometer.
3. One area is 100°F (38°C), and an adjoining area is 32°F (0°C). The two areas are about the same size. When heat transfer between the two is concluded,
   a. both will be close to 32°F (0°C).
   b. both will be close to 66°F (19°C).
   c. one will be close to 80°F (27°C); the other will be close to 54°F (12°C).
4. If in question 3 we provide a thick insulation barrier between the adjacent areas, the
   a. temperature difference between the two will remain almost intact with the passage of time.
   b. the colder area will be warmed slightly with the passage of time.
   c. the results will be the same as without the insulation, with the passage of time.
5. When heat is added to a fluid in an open container (no pressure on it),
   a. the fluid vaporizes, then condenses as more heat is added.
   b. temperature rises up to a point; then the fluid vaporizes and accepts no more heat.
   c. temperature rises up to a point; then the fluid vaporizes, but keeps accepting more heat as it does.
6. When pressure is added to a fluid being heated as in question 5, the
   a. temperature at which it vaporizes will drop.
   b. temperature at which it vaporizes will rise.
   c. Btu content of the fluid is increased.
   d. Answers b and c are both correct.
7. The boiling point of water
   a. drops with increasing altitude.
   b. rises with increasing altitude.
   c. is 212°F in a perfect vacuum.
   d. Answers a and c are both correct.

8. When relative humidity is high, it means
    a. the air and temperature are close to each other and rising.
    b. there is more moisture in the air than when relative humidity is low.
    c. the air can hold more moisture than when relative humidity is low.
9. A perfect vacuum is about
    a. 14.7 pounds per square inch (100 kilopascals).
    b. 21 inches of mercury (533 millimeters).
    c. 30 inches of mercury (762 millimeters).
10. An air conditioning system
    a. causes humidity to condense in the car's air conditioning duct housing.
    b. raises the relative humidity around the tubing in the car's air conditioning duct housing.
    c. Answers a and b are both correct.
    d. Neither answer a nor b is correct.

2

A Simple Air Conditioning System

Cooling and removing humidity from the air on a hot day are the primary functions of an air conditioning system, and there are many ways in which this can be done. A very crude approach to cooling the air would be to build a duct with a holder for a block of ice, plus a fan. The ice would absorb heat from the surrounding air, chilling it, and the fan would blow this chilled air into the passenger compartment.

You know, of course, that as ice absorbs heat it melts. Each pound of water represents 144 Btu of heat, as explained in Chapter 1. Even after the water melts, it still is at 32°F (0°C), so in our simple air conditioner, it would continue to cool the surrounding air until its temperature rose to approximately the temperature of the surrounding air. Once the water had warmed up to the temperature of the surrounding air, it would be necessary to drain it and install a new block of ice.

Before modern refrigeration, a block of ice was placed in a box, which was insulated to help keep out the heat. The ice chilled the air in the box, which was filled with perishable foods. The foods, therefore, remained cool. Without the ice, the temperature would have risen to the normal room temperature of 75° to 80°F and the food would have spoiled quickly. This box, called the "ice box," was the appliance that preceded the household refrigerator (see Fig. 2-1).

Obviously, installing a fresh block of ice is not a convenient way to provide cooling. It has another disadvantage in an air conditioning system for people: moisture evaporates from the melting ice into the surrounding air, raising the relative humidity. As you learned in Chapter 1, when the relative humidity is high, it takes a lower temperature to make us feel more comfortable.

In a sense, the fan is an air conditioner even if the block of ice is not used, for the fan can be used to increase human comfort in hot weather. When the fan operates, it moves air around. The air surrounding the bodies of the passengers in the car is warm, having absorbed heat (assuming the air

19   A Simple Air Conditioning System

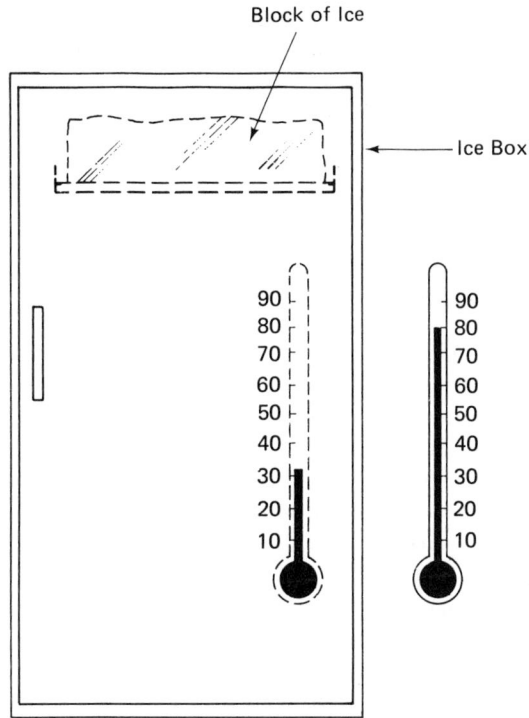

Figure 2-1 Ice box, which preceded refrigerator, used a block of ice to absorb heat from the surrounding air. Ice melts as heat is transferred to it, and so a fresh block of ice is needed to keep the interior of box cold.

temperature is below the normal body temperature of about 99°F). When this hot air is blown away from around the bodies by the fan, it is replaced by cooler air. If the air temperature is 75°F, the person could feel comfortably cool. If air temperature is 95°F, the difference may not be particularly significant.

Air movement, however, also carries away moisture, and regardless of air temperature, this may make a big difference in comfort. When it is hot, we perspire, and a layer of moisture rests on the surface of the skin. If the relative humidity is sufficiently low, this moisture from perspiration evaporates into the air. When this occurs, heat is transferred from the skin into the atmosphere—970 Btu per pound of moisture. This is the same as the heat transfer when water boils from a pot on a stove or when it evaporates from a puddle in the street.

Because heat is transferred, evaporation from the skin makes us feel cooler. When the relative humidity is low enough for rapid evaporation, operating the fan will blow away the air surrounding the body (air that has become relatively humid from the evaporation of perspiration). Dryer air will replace it, and new perspiration will evaporate into this dryer air.

On a day when the relative humidity is high, the fan will not be enough. To promote the skin-cooling effect, some of the moisture in the air must be removed, a process called *dehumidification*. This is done by the modern air conditioning system. In fact, although the modern air conditioning system also lowers temperature, its function as a dehumidifier may be nearly as important in creating human comfort.

The Modern Air Conditioner

The modern auto air conditioner is basically a pumping system that absorbs heat from air in the passenger compartment and transfers it to the outdoors. Clearly, the more heat it can absorb from the air in the passenger compartment (and get rid of outside) in a given amount of time, the more effectively it can cool. To make an air conditioning system function well, we need something that will absorb, and later give up, a great deal of heat very quickly at relatively low temperatures.

Speed is the key factor. You know from simple observation that water absorbs heat most rapidly at boiling temperatures, by recalling the examples from Chapter 1. Yes, a puddle of water will evaporate into the atmosphere and absorb heat in the process, 970 Btu for every pound of water that evaporates. But even if the humidity is relatively low, at normal air temperatures of 70° to 90°F it may take hours for that water to evaporate completely. Take that same amount of water, put it into a pot and place the pot on a stove with the burner turned on all the way. The water temperature will quickly rise to 212°F (100°C) and it will evaporate very rapidly, perhaps in a few minutes. For each pound of water at 212°F (100°C), just 970 Btu also is added to cause evaporation, but the rate of evaporation is much faster. If it took 3 hours for 3 pounds of water to evaporate at normal air temperature, the heat transfer rate would be 970 Btu per hour. If the same 3 pounds of water evaporated in 15 minutes from a pot of water boiling on a stove, the heat transfer rate would be 11,640 Btu per hour (3 pounds multiplied by 970 Btu multiplied by 4). Multiplying by 4 converts the amount boiled in 15 minutes (a quarter-hour) into an hourly figure.

Clearly, the need to transfer heat in an air conditioning system makes water at atmospheric pressure unsuitable, for air conditioning must transfer a lot of heat at temperatures of 70° to 100°F (and even below that), not at 212°F and above. Of course, the boiling point of water could be reduced by running the system in a vacuum at times. Or air could be used as the heat transfer fluid. In Chapter 15 you will learn about a system that uses air or air and a fluid chemical as heat transfer fluids, and it works rather well. This system is not yet ready for mass production, and it differs substantially from the simple pumping system that is the basis of present air conditioning systems in automobiles.

21 The Modern Air Conditioner

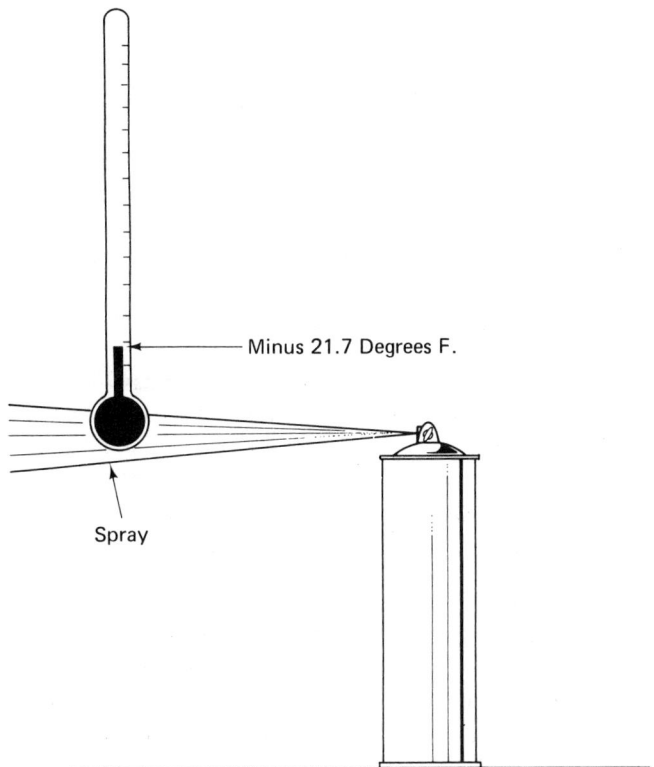

Figure 2-2 When Refrigerant 12 vaporizes, its temperature drops to –21.7°F.

The systems presently in wide use take advantage of the fact that there are many fluids that boil (and transfer a lot of heat in the process) at temperatures well below 212°F at atmospheric pressure. Ammonia, for example, boils at −28°F at atmospheric pressure, and ether at +94°F at atmospheric pressure. Although ether would pose some problems, ammonia certainly could do the job, and many air conditioning systems use ammonia, particularly stationary systems in large buildings.

The most popular choice for air conditioning in cars is a fluid called *Refrigerant 12*. It is chemically somewhat similar to carbon tetrachloride, the cleaning agent, and it has these favorable characteristics:

* It boils at −21.7°F at atmospheric pressure. This is not as low as ammonia, but it is certainly low enough (see Fig. 2-2).
* Its boiling point can be changed readily by pressure, raised by adding pressure, lowered by reducing it, just like water. This is an important factor, as will be explained later.

* It is not poisonous (ammonia is).
* It mixes readily with oil, so the mechanical parts of the air conditioning system can be lubricated properly by simply pouring an adequate amount of special refrigeration oil into the system.
* It does not affect rubber and does not combine to form a harmful compound with iron, copper, steel, or aluminum. All these materials are used in mechanical air conditioning systems.
* It can be reused. Although this is not significant now, for Refrigerant 12 is low in cost and readily available, it is possible that laws may be passed requiring reuse.

Refrigerant 12 has one known possible disadvantage: it may affect our atmosphere, just as do some propellants in aerosol containers. Those propellants (called chlorinated fluorocarbons) were banned in 1979, and it is possible that Refrigerant 12, which is also a chlorinated fluorocarbon, could be banned too. If that happened, the system that uses air instead of Refrigerant 12, described in Chapter 15, could be used in automobiles. That system, called ROVAC, is under development. Also under development is a refrigerant, R-134A, that does not contain the ingredient in Refrigerant 12 that is considered possibly harmful to the atmosphere. At present, however, Refrigerant 134A is not a suitable carrier for refrigeration oils, so it may pose compressor lubrication problems. Also, although it has been made in the laboratory, there is presently no known way to mass produce it economically.

At present, all automobile air conditioning systems except ROVAC use Refrigerant 12. The fluid is sold under many brand names, the most popular of which is Freon.

The Mechanical System

We have a fluid, Refrigerant 12, to transfer the heat from the passenger compartment to the outdoors. Now we need a mechanical system to circulate the Refrigerant 12.

A simple mechanical system features a compressor, a pump that draws fluid heated in the passenger compartment and exposes it to the atmosphere, where it gives up the heat (see Fig. 2-3). The Refrigerant 12 flows through a sealed system of tubing that runs from the passenger compartment through the compressor into tubing at the front of the engine compartment (where heat is dissipated to the atmosphere), then back to the passenger compartment.

To provide the maximum amount of heat transfer both in the passenger compartment and at the front of the engine compartment, the tubing at these two locations is formed into what are called *heat*

23　Heat Exchanger

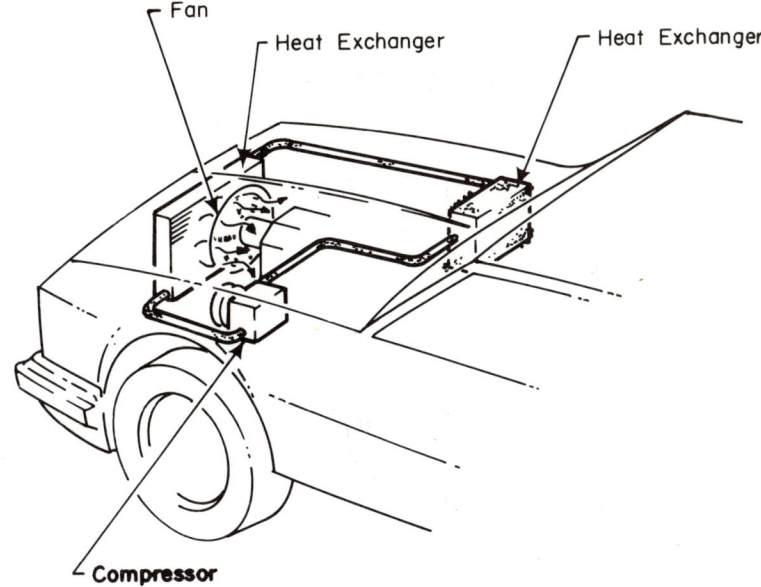

Figure 2-3 Compressor draws heated Refrigerant 12 from heat exchanger in passenger compartment and pushes it through a second heat exchanger exposed to the atmosphere. It gives up the heat to the atmosphere.

exchangers. Fans blow air by the tubing to further improve heat transfer into the surrounding air.

Heat Exchanger

An automotive air conditioning heat exchanger is a tubular structure with fins (see Fig. 2-4). In general, the larger the heat exchanger, the greater the amount of heat that can be transferred. If space is limited, some special designs are used to get more heat transfer from a smaller package.

The heat exchanger may work either of two ways: (1) it may contain a fluid that absorbs heat from the air surrounding the heat exchanger, or (2) it may contain a fluid that is very hot and must give up heat to the atmosphere.

The fins are important to the transfer of heat. If the fluid inside the heat exchanger is hot, it warms the walls of the tubing and the fins. Air flowing between the rows of tubes of the heat exchanger absorbs heat from the fins and the tubing (see Fig. 2-5).

If the fluid inside the heat exchanger is cool enough to absorb heat, the heat transfer is reversed, going from the surrounding air to the fins and tubing, and through to the fluid inside.

24 A Simple Air Conditioning System

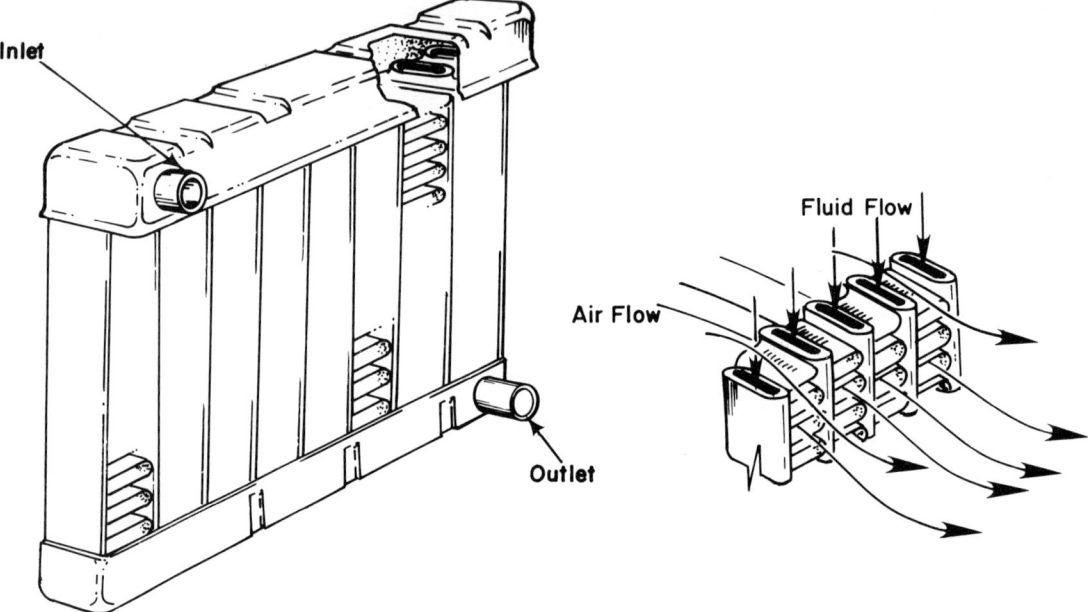

Figure 2-4 (*Left*) Heat exchanger is tubular structure with fins either attached to tubing or shaved from the tubing, the latter a process called *skivving*.

Figure 2-5 (*Right*) Heat is transferred from hot fluid to walls of tubing and to fins exposed to air flow. Or the fluid may be cold and chill the tubing and fins, and so absorb heat from the surrounding air.

In the passenger compartment, the Refrigerant 12 flows through a heat exchanger called an *evaporator*, so named because the fluid in it absorbs heat and turns to a vapor. You may wonder why it does not enter the evaporator as a vapor, considering its very low boiling point ($-21.7°F$). The reason is that the system is under pressure, and as you learned in Chapter 1, the boiling point of a fluid is raised by pressure. This pressure is applied by the compressor, as explained later.

When the Refrigerant 12 absorbs heat and vaporizes, the air surrounding the evaporator is chilled. A fan blows this cold air through ducts, which are very large diameter tubes, to circulate it through the passenger compartment of the car.

When the weather is humid, the heat absorbed from the air around the evaporator performs another function, the removal of humidity from the surrounding air.

For each 970 Btu removed from the surrounding air, 1 pound of water vapor may condense from the air. In actual practice, only a small amount of vapor is in the air immediately surrounding the evaporator, so part of the heat removed causes moisture condensation and the remainder lowers the air temperature. This less humid, colder air is blown away by the fan and in its place comes more humid, warmer air. In time, the air conditioner both removes moisture and lowers the temperature of all the air in the passenger compartment. The moisture that condenses from the air surrounding the evaporator flows through tubing from the car to the ground.

Because some of the heat absorbed by the Refrigerant 12 goes to condense moisture, the temperature reduction provided by an air conditioning system is not as great on a humid day. The lowered humidity, however, does increase evaporation of perspiration from the skin of the passengers, so physical comfort is provided.

Refrigerant 12 Behavior

When liquid Refrigerant 12 vaporizes, its temperature drops sharply. This should not be hard to believe, if you remember that temperature is determined by the amount of heat (in Btus) within a certain area. With vaporization, the fluid "spreads out" and occupies a much larger area, so the amount of heat it contains also must be spread out over this same area. As you learned in Chapter 1, when a given amount of heat (in Btus) is spread over a larger area, the temperature of the area drops.

Of course, Refrigerant 12 absorbs heat from the air surrounding the evaporator, so its temperature is well above its boiling point of $-21.7°F$ when it leaves the evaporator. In actual practice, it may leave the evaporator at close to 40°F.

Compressor and Condenser

The compressor draws the Refrigerant 12 vapor from the evaporator and squeezes it, that is, puts it under pressure. This means that the heated vapor must occupy a smaller amount of space, and so the temperature rises. In a typical automobile air conditioning system, the compressor may raise the pressure of the Refrigerant 12 to well over 200 pounds per square inch, and the temperature, as a result, will rise to more than 150°F. Raising the pressure of the Refrigerant 12 also raises the boiling point, but at this stage the Refrigerant 12 remains a vapor, although a high-pressure vapor.

At this time you may wonder, why compress the Refrigerant 12 and raise the temperature? After all, the Refrigerant 12 has absorbed heat and we want to get rid of that heat. The answer is that we cannot transfer heat to the outdoors when the temperature of the Refrigerant 12 is only about 40°F and the outdoors is perhaps 90°F. When the compressor squeezes the Refrigerant 12 and raises its temperature to 150°F, it has not added any heat (in

26 A Simple Air Conditioning System

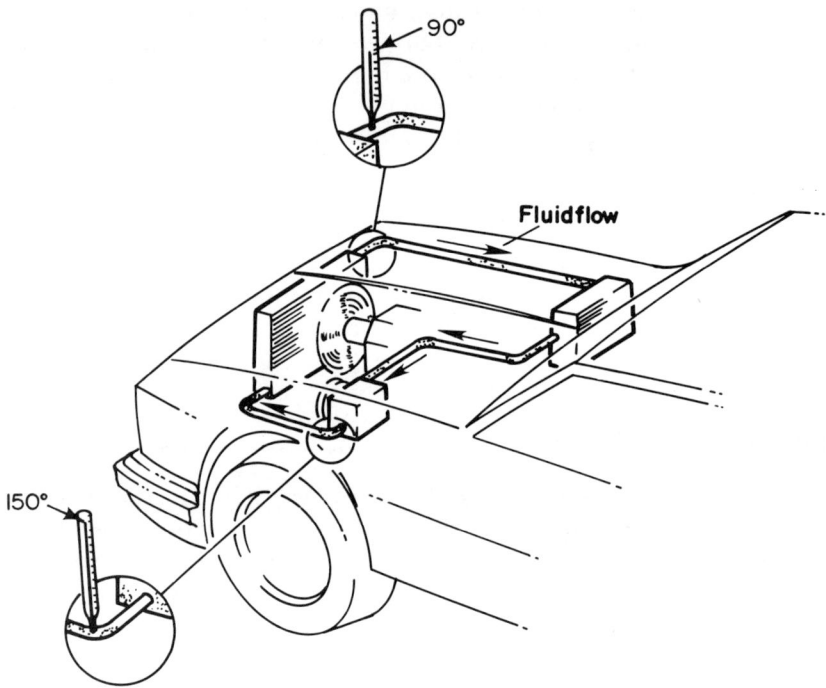

Figure 2-6 Compressor squeezes vapor from evaporator, raising its temperature to well above that of outside air. Vapor then flows into heat exchanger called condenser, where it gives up heat to outside air and condenses to a liquid.

Btus). All it has done is push the Refrigerant 12 vapors closer together, so the Btus occupy a smaller space.

The compressor pushes the high-temperature, high-pressure Refrigerant 12 vapors into the condenser. Because the Refrigerant 12 vapors now are at perhaps 150°F, heat readily flows from them to the outdoors, which is perhaps at 90°F. The Refrigerant 12 thus cools from perhaps 150° to close to the 90°F (see Fig. 2-6).

The cooling of the Refrigerant 12 may be aided by the fan, which draws fresh air between the tubes of the condenser. Or if the car is moving forward, the motion of the car rams air between the tubes even if the fan is disengaged.

As the Refrigerant 12 cools, it changes back to a liquid in the condenser. Even if Refrigerant 12 cools to only 100°F, it turns to liquid if the pressure in the air conditioning system is only 117 pounds per square inch. The typical system's compressor raises pressure to 180 pounds per square inch or more, so the Refrigerant 12 will turn back to liquid even if it is at about 131°F.

You should understand that although the liquid Refrigerant 12 temperature is high, much higher than after it has absorbed heat in the evaporator, that it contains a lot less heat (Btus) than when it came out of the evaporator. It gave up a lot of Btus to the outdoors when it passed through the condenser, and once the pressure is released, it will vaporize and its temperature will drop to well below the 40°F that it read when it came out of the evaporator.

The Basic System Works

With these three components, the evaporator, compressor, and condenser, plus the tubing that connects them and a system full of Refrigerant 12, we have a basic air conditioner, and when we add a restriction at the evaporator inlet, it will work (see Fig. 2-7). The restriction gives the compressor a partial enclosure against which to pump, so it can build up pressure and therefore temperature. The temperature buildup is necessary to permit heat transfer from the condenser at normal ambient temperatures. The restric-

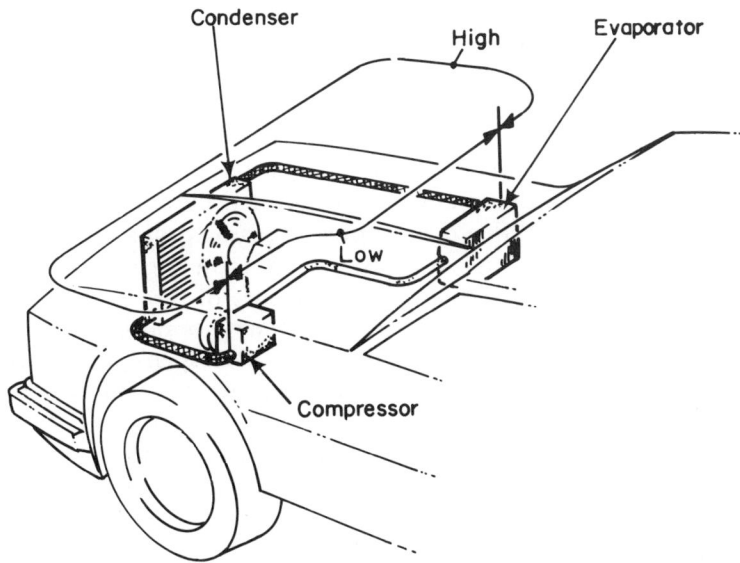

Figure 2-7 This basic air conditioning system will actually work. Note that the system from the compressor outlet through the condenser and up to the evaporator inlet contains Refrigerant 12 under high pressure and is called the high-pressure side of the system. The remainder of the system, from the evaporator itself to the compressor inlet contains vaporized Refrigerant 12 under low pressure and is called the low-pressure side of the system.

tion also limits the flow of refrigerant into the evaporator, so the refrigerant can expand, vaporize and absorb heat. A simple pinching of the inlet line at the evaporator would enable the system to work. In actual practice, as you will learn, a sophisticated device controls the restriction in many systems, and at the very least, the restriction is of a precise size.

In the evaporator the Refrigerant 12 will boil (vaporize) and absorb heat from the air surrounding this heat exchanger. The compressor will draw the heated Refrigerant 12 gases and squeeze them, raising their temperature, pressure, and boiling point. These squeezed gases will be pushed by the compressor into the condenser, where they will lose heat (in Btus) to the surrounding air and turn back to a liquid.

Still under pressure, the liquid Refrigerant 12 will flow into the evaporator, where it will vaporize, and the process begins again.

High-Pressure and Low-Pressure Sides of the System

The air conditioning system has two basic sections, which are separated in the compressor and at the restriction in the inlet to the evaporator.

When the compressor squeezes the Refrigerant 12 and pushes it out the outlet valve, the Refrigerant 12 remains under high pressure as it passes through tubing to the condenser, and then through the condenser and through more tubing to the evaporator inlet. This is called the *high-pressure side* of the system, or more simply, the *high side*. As explained, the refrigerant turns into a liquid in the condenser. The tubing that carries it back to the evaporator is called the *liquid line*.

When the compressor piston drops in the cylinder, it creates a partial vacuum, a low-pressure area. From the instant the Refrigerant 12 vaporizes in the evaporator, its pressure drops. This low-pressure condition continues as it flows through the evaporator, and then through tubing to the compressor. When the inlet valve opens, the low-pressure Refrigerant 12 is drawn into the compressor by the even-lower-pressure of the partial vacuum. From the evaporator inlet, through the evaporator and tubing to the compressor inlet is called the *low-pressure side* of the system, or just the *low side*. It also is called the *suction side* (see Fig. 2-7).

Pressure-Temperature Relationship

Earlier in this book, you learned how the Refrigerant 12 vaporizes at very low temperatures and turns to liquid at high pressures after cooling. These things happen at exactly the same temperatures and pressures every time, for there is a relationship that always holds between temperature and pressure of Refrigerant 12. Refer to Fig. 2-8, which shows the relationships.

REFRIGERANT — 12 PRESSURE — TEMPERATURE RELATIONSHIP					
(°F)	(°C)	(PSIG)	(kPa) 0(ATMOSPHERIC PRESSURE)	(°F)/(°C)	(PSIG)(kPa)
−20	−28.8C			55 12.7C	52.0 358.5
−10	−23.3C			60 15.5C	57.7 397.8
−5	−20.5C	2.4	16.5	65 18.3C	63.7 439.2
0	−17.7C	4.5	31.0	70 21.1C	70.1 482.7
5	−15.0C	6.8	46.9	75 23.8C	76.9 530.2
10	−12.2C	9.2	63.4	80 26.6C	84.1 579.9
15	−9.4C	11.8	81.4	85 29.4C	91.7 632.3
20	−6.6C	14.7	101.4	90 32.2C	99.6 686.7
25	−3.8C	17.7	122.0	95 35.0C	108.1 745.3
30	−1.1C	21.1	145.5	100 37.7C	116.9 806.0
32	0C	24.6	169.6	105 40.5C	126.2 870.2
35	1.6C	28.5	196.5	110 43.3C	136.0 937.7
40	4.4C	30.1	207.5	115 46.1C	146.5 1010.1
45	7.2C	32.6	224.8	120 48.8C	157.1 1083.2
50	10.0C	37.0	255.1	125 51.6C	167.5 1154.9
		41.7	287.5	130 54.4C	179.0 1234.2
		46.7	322.0	140 60.0C	204.5 1410.0

The table below indicates the pressure of Refrigerant — 12 at various temperatures. For instance, a drum of Refrigerant at a temperature of 80°F (26.6°C) will have a pressure of 84.1 PSI (579.9 kPa). If it is heated to 125°F (51.6°C), the pressure will increase to 167.5 PSI (1154.9 kPa). It also can be used conversely to determine the temperature at which Refrigerant — 12 boils under various pressures. For example, at a pressure of 30.1 PSI (207.5 kPa), Refrigerant — 12 boils at 32°F (0°C).

Figure 2-8 Pressure-temperature relationship of Refrigerant 12. This relationship, given in both Fahrenheit and Celsius scales, is true regardless of whether the system is operating or not. (*Courtesy General Motors Corp.*)

As you learned, the Refrigerant 12 in the low-pressure side of the system is colder than that in the high-pressure side, and the chart illustrates that. The statement that Refrigerant 12 at the evaporator outlet may be 40°F (4°C) and also is under low pressure is now confirmed. If, indeed, the temperature is 40°F, the pressure must be 37 pounds per square inch (psi). If the pressure on the high side of the system is 180 psi, the temperature of the Refrigerant 12 in that part of the system must be 131°F.

When the air conditioning system is turned off, of course, pressures equalize between the high and low sides of the system, and the pressure reading in both sides will reflect ambient temperature. For example, it is common for pressures to equalize at 70 psi. If this occurs, you know that the ambient temperature in the engine compartment of the car is just about 70°F (21°C).

The temperature-pressure relationship holds whenever the refrigerant is either a liquid or a *saturated vapor*. A saturated vapor is one that remains in contact with any liquid in the system. That is, it is not superheated. A superheated vapor, by definition, is one that has absorbed so much heat that its temperature has gone up, but without an increase in pressure. Therefore, the temperature-pressure relationship obviously cannot hold with superheated vapor.

Additional Parts and Controls in Modern System

The simple system as described will not function properly under many conditions. The modern Refrigerant 12 system, therefore, has many additional parts and controls to tailor its operation to the different conditions it encounters, and the compressor is not the simple one-cylinder design that has been illustrated. In the following chapters, you will see how clutches, switches, valves, regulators, and other controls combine with multicylinder compressors to form the modern air conditioning system.

QUESTIONS

1. When a fan blows air around people
    a. it makes the people think they feel cooler, although they actually are not.
    b. it may move hot air away from the people.
    c. it may move moist air away from the people.
    d. Answers b and c are correct.
2. Mechanic A says the air conditioning system makes the air cooler. Mechanic B says the air conditioning system removes moisture from the air to make it comfortable. Who is correct?

a. Mechanic A.
b. Mechanic B.
c. Both.
d. Neither.

3. Refrigerant 12 is used for automotive air conditioning because
   a. its boiling point at atmospheric pressure is very low.
   b. it is not poisonous.
   c. it mixes well with oil.
   d. All of the above.

4. Mechanic A says a function of the air conditioning compressor is to draw hot Refrigerant 12 from the passenger compartment. Mechanic B says the compressor pushes cooled Refrigerant 12 into the passenger compartment. Who is right?
   a. Mechanic A.
   b. Mechanic B.
   c. Both.
   d. Neither.

5. The purpose of an automotive air conditioning heat exchanger is to
   a. give up heat to the surrounding air.
   b. absorb heat from surrounding air.
   c. transfer heat to another heat exchanger.
   d. Answers a and b are correct.
   e. Answers a, b, and c are correct.

6. When Refrigerant 12 leaves the evaporator, its temperature is
   a. minus 21.7°F (minus 30°C).
   b. about 40°F (4°C).
   c. more than 150°F (66°C).

7. The compressor compresses the Refrigerant 12 to
   a. raise its temperature.
   b. be able to push it quickly through the condenser.
   c. be able to push it quickly through the evaporator.

8. Refrigerant 12 turns to a liquid in the air conditioning system at about
   a. minus 21.7°F (minus 30°C).
   b. 40°F (4°C).
   c. 131°F (55°C).

9. The pressure-temperature relationship of Refrigerant 12 means that
   a. Refrigerant 12 pressure always drops the same amount as temperature increases.
   b. the temperature is always the same at a particular pressure.
   c. the pressure always rises the same amount as temperature drops.

10. The high-pressure side of the air conditioning system is from
    a. compressor outlet to evaporator inlet.

b. evaporator inlet to compressor inlet.
   c. compressor inlet to evaporator outlet.

HANDS ON

1. Find the compressor and condenser, and because the evaporator is in the ductwork, just find the evaporator inlet and outlet necks. Identify the inlet and the outlet.
2. Observe the operation of the compressor clutch when the air conditioning control on the dashboard is turned on.

3

Electrical Review

To understand how many of the special controls in modern air conditioning function, you need a basic understanding of automotive electricity. If you already have covered this subject in other automotive shop courses, the material in this chapter may be familiar to you.

The Circuit

A circuit is a metal-to-metal connection from a source of current (the car battery in this case) to the consumer of that current (a bulb, a motorized device, and other electrical devices) and back again to the source. Copper or aluminum wire, covered by insulation to prevent the electricity from leaking out, is used to provide a metal-to-metal connection from one part to another, unless the parts are adjacent and can be connected by bolts or other fasteners (see Fig. 3-1).

The Switch

The switch is a part that breaks (opens up) the circuit when it is "off", and completes (closes) the circuit when it is "on" (see Figs. 3-2 and 3-3). The switch is a mechanical device that can be operated in any one of several ways. On air conditioning, they include the following:

* Manually by the driver pushing a button or lever.
* Automatically by a flexing diaphragm, operated by pressure, or vacuum from the engine. In some cases, when the driver pushes a button, he or she actually is operating a valve that permits vacuum to flow to a diaphragm switch.

34   Electrical Review

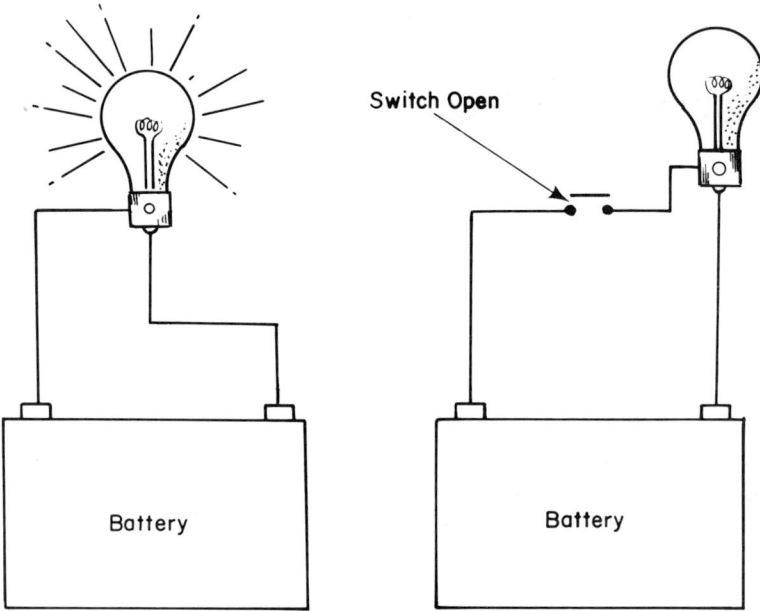

Figure 3-1 (*Left*) This is a simple direct-current circuit with a battery and bulb. Wire connects from one battery post to bottom terminal of bulb; then a second wire goes from side of bulb to second battery post.

Figure 3-2 (*Right*) With the switch placed in the circuit, there is a provision for opening the circuit when we do not want the bulb to light. The switch is nothing more than a break in the circuit and a mechanical arrangement for bridging that break.

* Automatically by flow of electricity through a second circuit.
* Automatically by a control, such as a timer, temperature sensing device or even a computer.

Electrically Operated Switch

When a switch is operated electrically, it makes use of the principles of the electromagnet. Current applied to a coil of wire wound around an iron core electrically creates a magnetic field that attracts a metal part, causing that metal part to move.

The current flowing through the coil of wire to create the electromagnetic is one circuit. The electromagnetic attraction of the metal part closes a switch to complete the second circuit, previously referred to (see Fig. 3-4.)

When the current to the electromagnetic coil is stopped (by opening a

The Switch

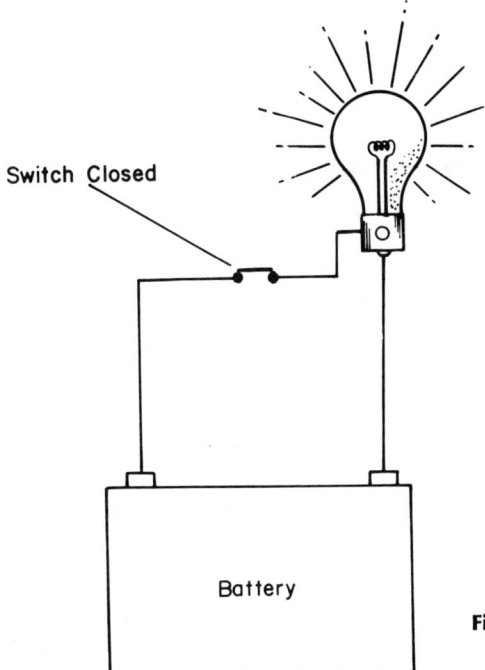

Figure 3-3 The switch is pushed to the closed position and the break is bridged. The circuit is complete and the bulb lights.

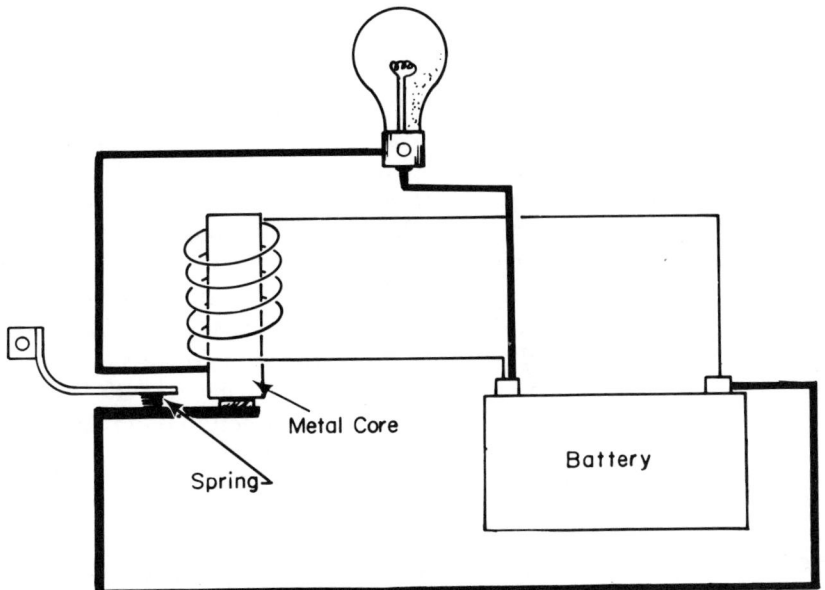

Figure 3-4 The relay is an electromagnet that when energized by electricity completes a second circuit that can carry heavy current. On some new systems, the relay is electronic, with no moving parts.

36 Electrical Review

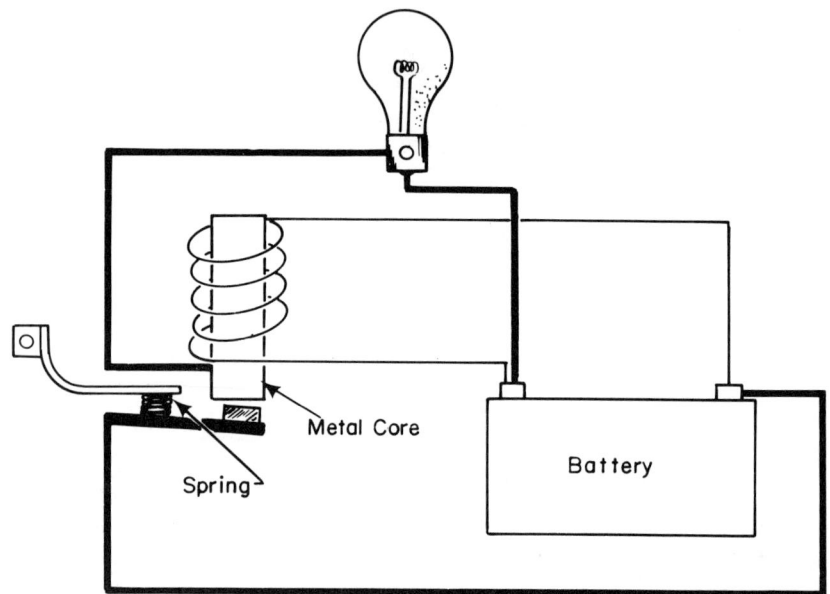

Figure 3-5 When the relay is deenergized, a spring retracts and disengages the electromagnet, breaking the second circuit, too.

switch elsewhere in the circuit), a spring retracts the metal part and opens this switch (see Fig. 3-5).

The electromagnetic switch is commonly called a *relay*. It is typically used to transfer (relay) a greater amount of current than can safely be carried by the first circuit, which needs to carry enough only to create the electromagnet. The wiring and other parts of the second circuit are made thicker to enable them to carry the greater amount of current.

In some cases the relay is called a solenoid. Actually the solenoid is an electromagnetic device that does work. For example, when the electromagnet pulls on the iron core, it may open a valve, as in a *solenoid vacuum valve*, or push a gear into position, as in a *starter solenoid*. In the starter, however, the movement of the iron core also completes a second circuit which carries a greater amount of current to the starter motor to operate it. Therefore, it is performing the function of a relay too. The term solenoid takes precedence, so even if it also does the job of a relay, it's called a solenoid.

The Motor

The motor also makes use of the principles of electromagnetism. The operating principles are covered in electrical textbooks, so they need not be repeated here. All you really need to know for air conditioning service is that the blower is operated by an electric motor, which has two terminals. Current is supplied through one; it continues through the motor itself, and leaves through the second terminal to complete the circuit.

Electrical Ground

In most cases it is inconvenient to run two wires to complete a circuit to a current consumer. Therefore, only one wire to carry current to the consumer is often used. All metals are reasonable conductors of electricity, so the engine and car body can be and are used as "master" completers of electrical circuits. All that needs to be done is to connect a short wire from the consumer to the body or engine, or just to make metal-to-metal contact with the consumer, such as with mounting screws. Either procedure is called *grounding*. The car's battery, the source, also is grounded with a short cable to both the car body and the engine (Fig. 3-6). The blower motor previously mentioned may have only one terminal (carrying current). Instead of a second terminal for a wire to complete the circuit, the motor may be grounded by a short wire from a mounting screw to car body metal.

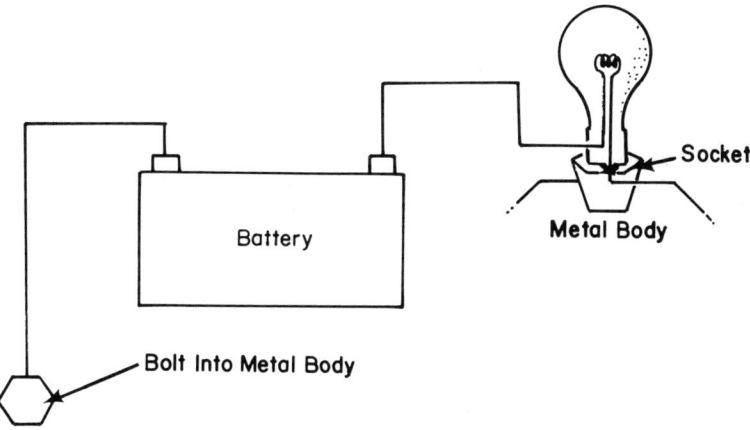

Figure 3-6 With the typical all-metal car body and the metal engine, a circuit can be completed merely by connecting one battery post to anywhere on the body and/or engine, and making similar connections to the body or engine from bulbs, motors, switches, and relays.

Series Circuit and Parallel Circuit

There are two types of circuits used in the automobile, series and parallel. In some cases, the two may be combined to form a series-parallel circuit.

38 Electrical Review

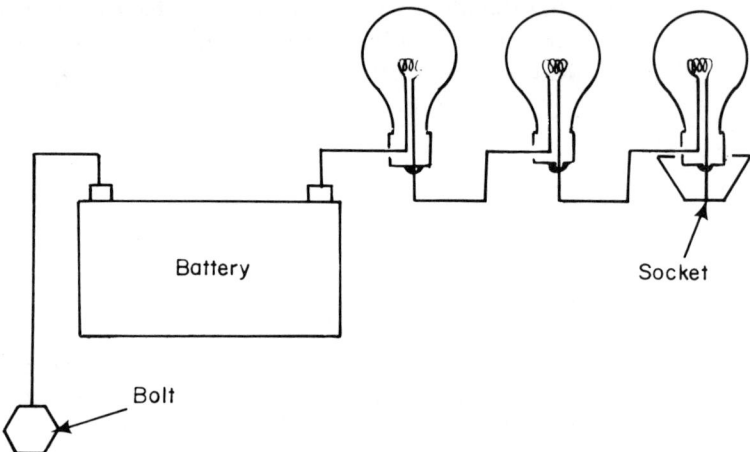

Figure 3-7 A comparison between the series and the parallel circuit. In the series circuit at left, if one bulb or other consumer of electricity fails, the entire circuit is broken and nothing will work. In the parallel circuit the wiring branches out, so that failure of any individual branch does not affect the others.

The series circuit is somewhat like Christmas tree lighting, wherein if one bulb fails, all the lights go out because a failure of just one bulb creates an open in the circuit, just as if a switch were turned off.

The parallel circuit is somewhat like the branches of a tree. The "trunk" carries the current up to the "branches," from where it divides to flow up each branch to a current consumer. Even if one current consumer fails, the circuit remains complete to all the other branches' current consumers (see Fig. 3-7).

How a Circuit Fails

A circuit may fail in either of two ways:

1. There may be an opening in the circuit. This may be a physical failure in a bulb or switch, or a break in the metal wiring, or it could be a very poor connection. The last item could be corroded grounding screws or a corroded or loose wiring terminal.
2. There may be a short circuit. A short circuit is a circuit that is completed before it gets to the current consumer. Normally, this occurs if the insulation (which holds in the electricity) is cut or worn on the wire, allowing the metal wire inside to make metal-to-metal contact with the car body or engine, or some other part that is in metal-to-metal contact with either of them (see Fig. 3-8).

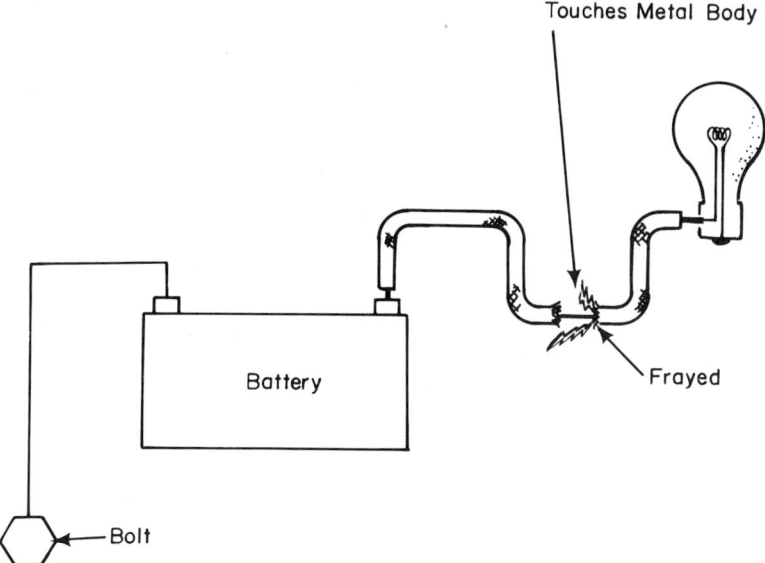

Figure 3-8 What is called a short circuit occurs if the circuit is complete before it reaches the current consumer, so the consumer does not work. The most common example is as shown, when insulation is frayed and the bare wire can touch the engine or car body. Or defective insulation can allow current to bypass a switch, keeping the current consumer on even when the switch is off. This is another type of short.

If a short is severe, it could drain a battery quickly. To prevent this, a protective device called a *fuse* is placed in many circuits. The fuse contains a piece of wire that will burn and break apart if excessive current flows. In some cases a fuse fails because of a momentary current surge. If a new fuse also fails quickly, the cause (apparently a short) must be found and corrected. A *circuit breaker* is another protective device. It opens when current flow is excessive, but unlike the fuse (which must be replaced), it closes automatically when current flow is stopped or restored to a tolerable level. Or a short may be between two wires in a harness, so that current is supplied to a device (keeping it on), even when the control switch is off.

Measurements in the Circuit

Electricity in wiring, motors, switches, and relays is subject to three measurements:

1. ***Amperes*** (called "amps"). This is a measurement of the amount of electrical current flowing in the circuit; it is made with a device called an *ammeter*. The flow itself is called *amperage*.

2. ***Volts.*** The flowing current exerts a form of pressure in the wiring or electrical devices. This pressure is called *voltage;* it is measured in volts using a device called a *voltmeter.*

3. ***Resistance.*** There is a limit to the amount of current (amperes) that can flow through wiring or electrical devices at a certain electrical pressure (voltage). This limit is imposed by an inherent resistance to current flow, which is measured in *ohms* by a device called an *ohmmeter.*

If the pressure (voltage) is increased, more current will flow through. If the resistance is decreased, current flow also will increase. The relationship between voltage, amperage and resistance is expressed by the formula:

Amperes equals volts divided by ohms, or
Volts equals ohms multiplied by amperes, or
Ohms equals volts divided by amperes.

Resistors

In the real world of the automobile, devices called resistors are commonly used to reduce current flow to levels below the 12-volt push provided by the battery and charging system of the car. Resistors may be thin wires or parts that contain special thin wiring. A common application of the resistor is in the blower (fan) circuit. When the blower switch is set at low speed, maximum resistance is in the circuit, so little current can flow to the fan. When the blower receives less current, it spins slower. The resistance is gradually reduced as the fan switch is moved to higher-speed positions.

Resistance at Connections

One type of resistance that is not intended in a circuit is that posed by a poor or corroded connection. In this case, less current can flow through the connection because of the resistance created by the corrosion or looseness. If the resistance is great enough, the current flow may be reduced so much that the electrical device it is supposed to operate (motor, switch, relay, bulb, etc.) will not work.

Use of Meters To Take Measurements

We can take measurements of amperage, voltage, and resistance in the circuit with the appropriate meters (or with one meter that takes all three measurements), as shown in Fig. 3-9. It is customary to hook up the meters

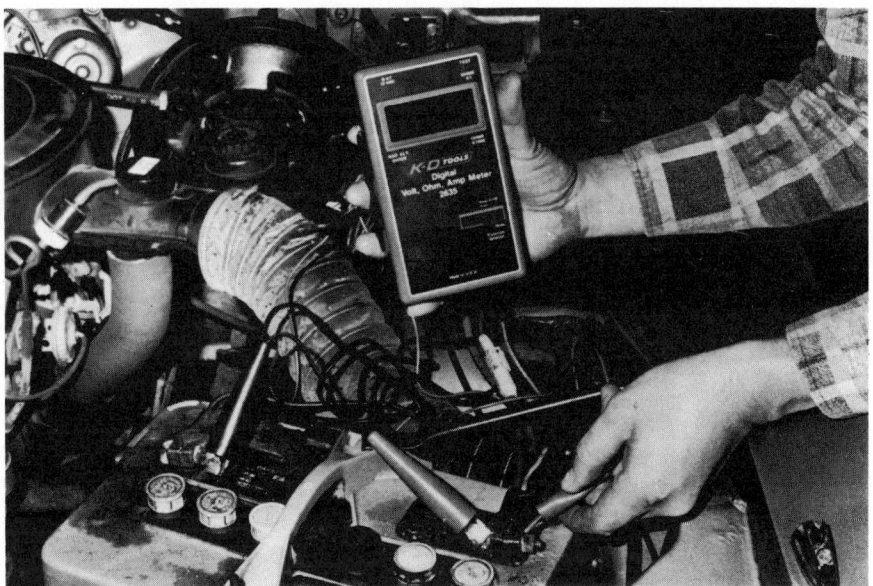

Figure 3-9 This multifunction meter can be used to measure amperes, volts, as shown, and ohms.

at wiring connections, not to cut through wiring insulation to attach them. If readings are outside specifications, repair of wiring connections, or a wire, or replacement of a part may be necessary.

The ammeter is connected "in series" with the circuit. This means that we disconnect the wiring at an appropriate connector and attach the ammeter wires to the terminals at the disconnection. This again completes the circuit, but now current also must flow through the ammeter.

The voltmeter is connected without breaking into the circuit, because it is measuring electrical pressure, not flow. One voltmeter wire is attached to a terminal of the circuit (pushing back an insulating sleeve if necessary to expose a metal part of the terminal), and the other meter wire is connected to an electrical ground.

The ohmmeter is connected to each end of the circuit. To check the resistance in just one wire, that wire is disconnected at each end and the ohmmeter wires are attached to the ends. Another common use of the ohmmeter is to make sure a wire or resistor is not internally broken. If the ohmmeter reads zero or the specification of the resistor, the wire or resistor is intact (see Fig. 3-10). If the ohmmeter reads maximum resistance (a symbol that looks like the number 8 written sideways, ∞, and called infinity), the wire is broken. Resistance is measured with the wiring disconnected, so the circuit cannot be turned on to provide current flow. The ohmmeter, therefore, is self-powered by a battery, unlike the ammeter

42 Electrical Review

Figure 3-10 Testing a resistor with an ohmmeter. If the resistor is internally intact, you will get a reading that is not zero (the reading will be whatever the resistance value of the resistor is), but it will not be infinite either (if it were, that would indicate an internal break). The resistor shown is a dual type used in some electronic ignition systems. Air conditioning systems use resistors in blower circuits.

and voltmeter. If the ohmmeter is combined with the other meters, there are additional wires to connect to the car battery to provide a source of power for the ohmmeter function.

The Test Lamp

In some cases, we do not have to measure voltage, amperage, or resistance; all we want to know is if battery current (at about 12 volts) is flowing at approximately normal levels in the circuit. This can be done with a simple test lamp, which combines a 12-volt bulb and wires with easy-to-attach clips. Just attach one alligator clip to an electrical terminal, the other to an electrical ground, turn on the switch for the circuit, and the bulb should light (see Fig. 3-11).

Battery-powered test lamps also are available, but their purpose is to check to see if wiring is not broken, as with the ohmmeter. If you have an ohmmeter, you do not need the battery-powered test lamp.

43   The Jumper Wire

Figure 3-11 The test lamp is connected as shown, one wire to the wiring connector or terminal, the other to an electrical ground. Turn on the circuit (in this case the air conditioning, for the wire is to the compressor), and the test lamp should light.

The Jumper Wire

Another wiring helper is the jumper wire, which is a length of wire with alligator clips at each end, as in Fig. 3-12. The jumper is so named because it permits the mechanic to do such things as the following:

* To connect across the terminals of a switch wiring connector ("jump" across them). If you wish to determine if a switch is defective and fails to close when it should, you can simulate a closed switch by removing the wiring connector and attaching a jumper across the terminals of the connector.

* To connect a terminal to a source of current (as the battery) or an electrical ground. If the electrical device works with a jumper, the existing connection (either a wire, or through mounting screws or other metal-to-metal connection) is defective and must be repaired.

HANDS ON

1. Using a voltmeter or multifunction meter, measure voltage at the car battery. Then trace the battery positive cable (the one from the

44 Electrical Review

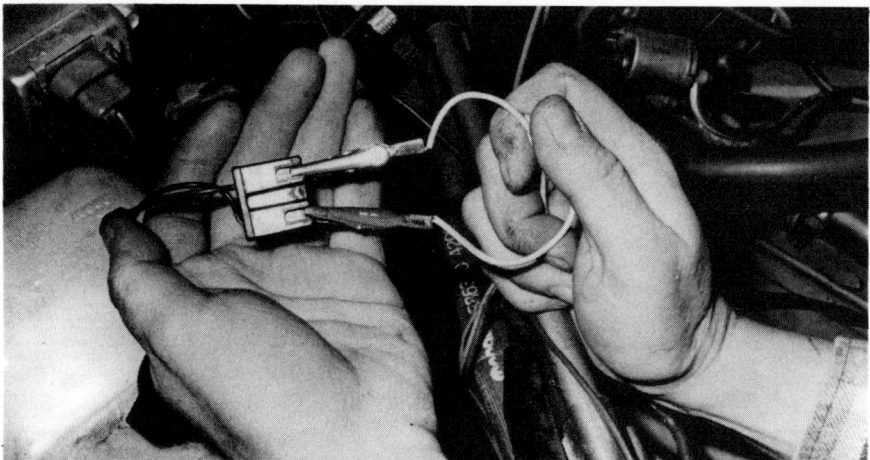

Figure 3-12 Jumper wire is used to bypass parts of an electrical circuit. In this case, it is being used across the terminals of a switch to bypass the switch. If the circuit the switch controls now works, the switch is defective.

plus terminal) to the starter, and measure voltage at the cable's starter terminal. In both cases, you should get readings of slightly over 12 volts.

2. Using an ammeter or multifunction meter, measure amperage in an automotive electrical circuit, such as a headlamp circuit.
3. Using an ohmmeter or multifunction meter, measure resistance in a spark-plug wire.
4. Connect one wire lead of a test lamp to an electrical ground and the other to the terminal of a current-carrying wire, such as at a light bulb with the switch on. The test lamp should light.
5. Use a jumper wire on an air conditioning system with just one wire to the compressor clutch and a nearby connector. Undo the connector and connect the jumper wire to the battery positive terminal at one end and to the metal terminal of the wire from the compressor clutch. The clutch should click on. Because you have not yet studied compressor clutch operation, your instructor will have to identify the connector for you.

4

Modern Air Conditioning

The modern air conditioning system is much more sophisticated than the basic type described in Chapter 2, and an important example of the differences is in the design of the compressor. No modern air conditioning system uses the one-cylinder compressor shown in Chapter 2. At the least a compressor will have two cylinders, and often four, five, or six, or it may have no cylinders. Let's begin by looking at the simplest real design, the two-cylinder with the cylinders arranged in line, that is, one behind the other.

Two-Cylinder in Line

As in a piston engine, there is a cylinder block and a cylinder head bolted to it. The two compressor pistons have connecting rods that attach to a crankshaft. The compressor, however, is a pump—an engine in reverse (see Fig. 4-1). External power is supplied to turn the crankshaft, and when the crankshaft turns, the pistons move up and down. When a piston moves down, it creates a vacuum that draws in Refrigerant 12 gas from the evaporator. When it moves up, it compresses that gas and pushes it out of the cylinder to the condenser. This contrasts with the engine, in which an air and fuel mixture burns in the cylinders above the pistons, expands, and pushes down on the pistons to turn the crankshaft.

The external source of power for the compressor is the engine's crankshaft. A pulley on the engine crankshaft is connected by a rubber drive belt to a pulley on the compressor crankshaft (Fig 4-2).

Compressor Valves

The valves that regulate the flow of Refrigerant 12 gas into and out of the compressor are much different from those in an engine. They usually are strips of spring metal attached to a metal plate in the cylinder above the

46   Modern Air Conditioning

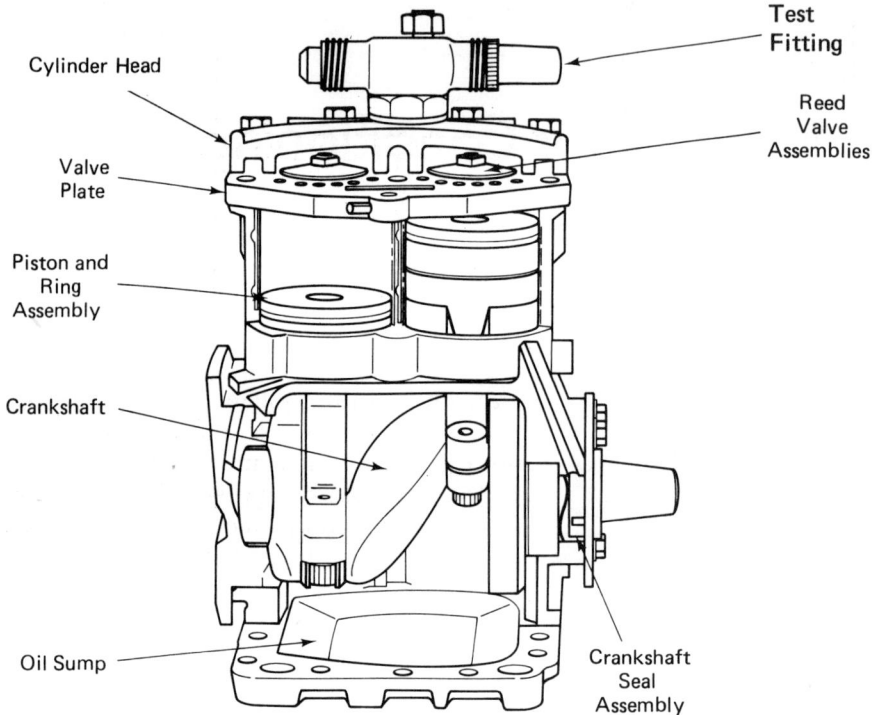

Figure 4-1 This drawing shows a two-cylinder compressor with its crankshaft, pistons, and connecting rods. As the crankshaft is turned, the pistons move up and down, either creating a vacuum that draws open an intake valve to admit vapor, or compressing the vapor and pushing it out the outlet valve. (Courtesy Ford Marketing Corp. © 1973).

piston, just under the cylinder head. The inlet valve, the valve that opens to admit Refrigerant 12 gas from the evaporator, is on the piston side of the plate. When the piston drops and creates the vacuum, the piece of spring steel flexes downward, opening the cylinder to Refrigerant 12 in the hose from the evaporator.

The outlet valve is on the opposite side of the metal plate so that when the piston goes down in the cylinder, the vacuum it creates draws down on the flap, helping to keep it closed.

Just the opposite happens when the piston rises to compress the Refrigerant 12. The gas under pressure pushes up on both valves, but only the outlet valve is forced up and open. The inlet valve is merely forced more tightly closed.

These flaps are called *reed valves*, and the plate on which they mount is called the *reed valve plate* (see Fig. 4-3). Although the triangular shape is traditional and typical, any type of spring metal flap valve, even if circular, can be considered a reed valve.

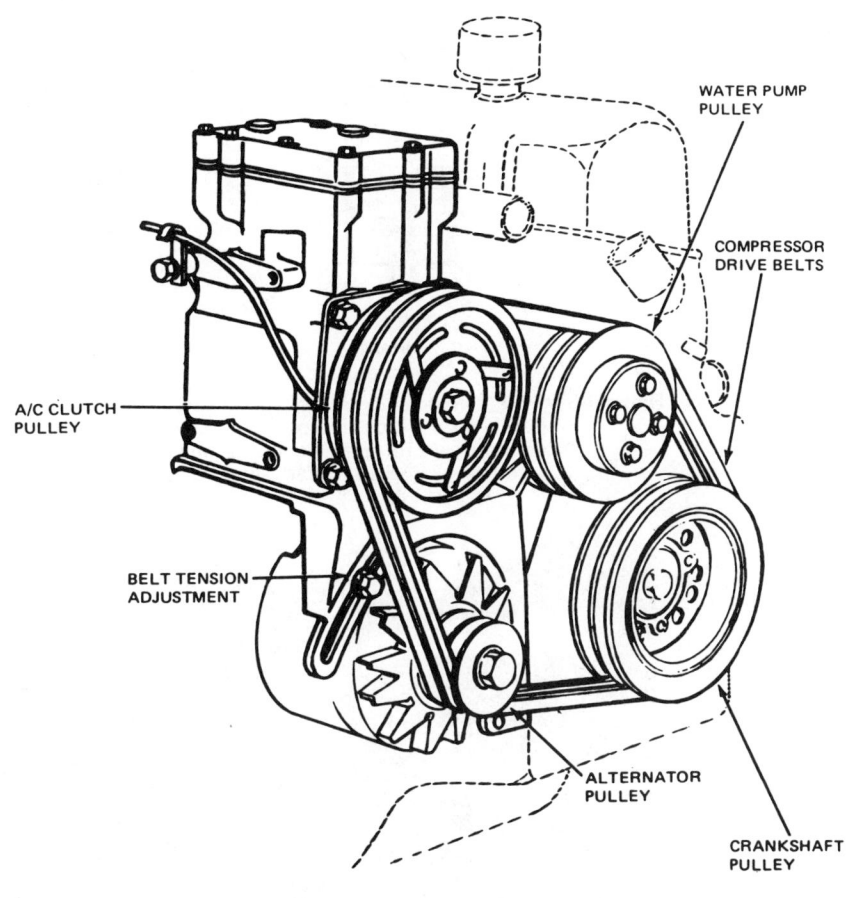

Figure 4-2 Drive belt wrapped around engine crankshaft pulley transfers power to pulley attached to compressor crankshaft. (Courtesy Ford Motor Co.)

V-2 Compressor

Just as in an engine, the cylinders can be arranged in a V form in a compressor. The typical V-type engine has four, six, or eight cylinders, the refrigeration compressor has only two, but the basic layout is similar. As with any V-type layout, there is one cylinder head for each bank of the V, and in the case of the compressor, there is a reed valve plate between the head and the compressor cylinder block (see Fig. 4-4).

48   Modern Air Conditioning

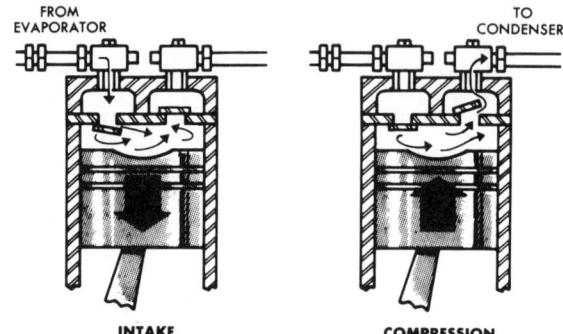

Figure 4-3 Reed valves are pieces of spring metal attached to a plate at one end. Depending on which side of the plate to which they are attached, they will be drawn down to open (suction acting on inlet valve) or pushed up to open (pressure acting on outlet valve). (Courtesy Ford Motor Co.)

Figure 4-4 This is the Chrysler V-2 compressor. The two cylinders are arranged in a V-form, like many engines, and so there are two cylinder heads.

Axial Five-Cylinder

The axial five-cylinder is a space-saving design that is quite different from the in-line or V type. The cylinders are arranged in a circle parallel to the axis of the pulley-driven compressor crankshaft (hence the term axial).

The shaft goes through the center of the circle to an inclined, eccentrically shaped bearing. When the crankshaft spins, it also turns this bearing, which causes a hexagonal plate to "wobble." At each corner of the plate are ball-socket joints, holding ball-end connecting rods from the pistons. The wobbling of the plate pushes some pistons up their cylinders and draws other pistons down, creating a pumping action that progresses smoothly from cylinder to cylinder (see Fig. 4-5).

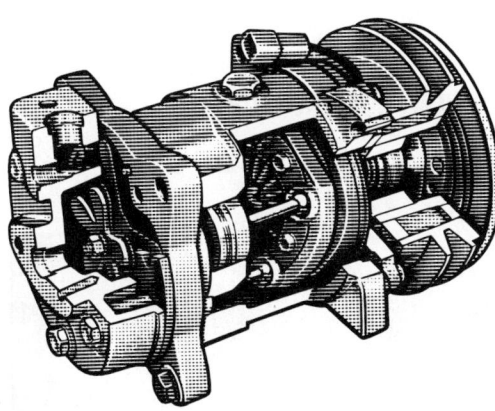

Figure 4-5 Sankyo five-cylinder compressor has "wobble" plate (called a swashplate) with ball-socket joints for connecting rods attached to pistons. As compressor shaft turns, it spins eccentric bearing, which forces swashplate to wobble, moving pistons up and down in their cylinders.

Axial Six-Cylinder

There are really just three cylinders arranged in a circle, 120 degrees apart, in the axial six-cylinder, but they extend from front to rear of the compressor, so each cylinder does double duty. Into each cylinder fits a double-ended piston with a C-shaped cutout in the center. The compressor crankshaft has an offset eccentric drive bearing, shaped like a piece of sausage cut from a loaf at an angle. The "sausage slice" is pressed into place on the shaft, and as the shaft rotates, the eccentric slice operates all the pistons. As it moves one piston toward the top of its cylinder, it is moving the opposite end of the double-ended piston toward the bottom of its cylinder (see Fig. 4-6). The double-ended piston and cylinder thus operate the same as if they each were separate parts, and so three cylinders and three double-ended pistons perform as a six-cylinder compressor.

The reference to top and bottom of the cylinder is not strictly accurate. The compressor mounting is such that the pistons are actually moving forward and backward.

This particular compressor design is probably the most popular. General Motors has built it for many years, and in recent years a Chrysler version and a Japanese-built model have emerged.

50   Modern Air Conditioning

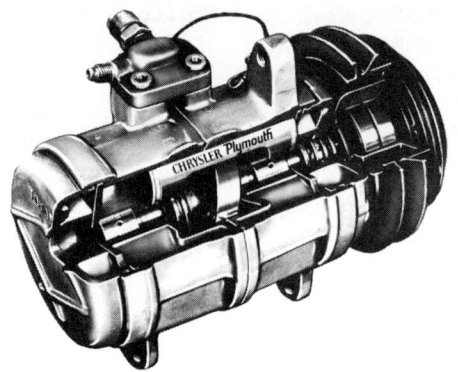

C-171 AIR CONDITIONING COMPRESSOR
(6-CYLINDER SWASHPLATE-TYPE)

(a)

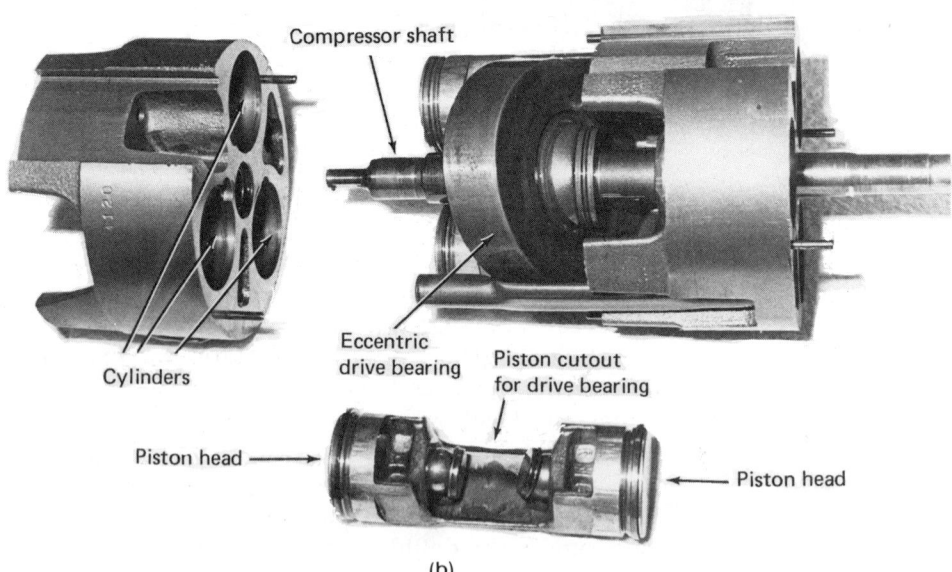

(b)

Figure 4-6 (a) Six-cylinder swashplate compressor is a very popular design. Above is a recent Chrysler version, partially cut open to show the sausage-slice shaped eccentric drive bearing. (b) Below is compressor shaft with drive bearing removed from a General Motors compressor, so that you can see how the turning of the shaft and bearing causes the double-ended piston to move back and forth. (Courtesy Chrysler Corp. and General Motors Corp.)

Radial Four-Cylinder

Even more compact than the axial six-cylinder is the radial four-cylinder. The cylinders are 90 degrees apart at one end of the compressor, perpendicular to the compressor crankshaft. The crankshaft has a U-shaped section, just as in an automobile engine, but instead of connecting rods and pistons, there is a combination assembly of two opposite pistons called a modified Scotch yoke (Fig. 4-7).

As the crankshaft turns, the U-section moves this combination assembly back and forth, pushing one piston up in its cylinder and pulling the opposite one down. There are two two-piston Scotch yokes, one behind the other, but shaped so the cylinders are in the same plane.

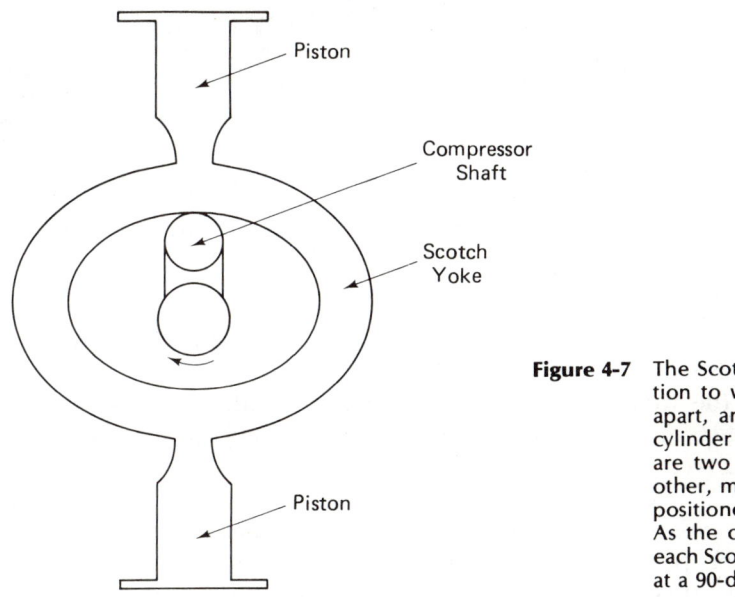

Figure 4-7 The Scotch yoke drive has a center section to which two pistons, 180 degrees apart, are attached. In the radial four-cylinder used by General Motors, there are two Scotch yokes, one behind the other, made so that four pistons can be positioned radially in a circular housing. As the compressor shaft turns, it forces each Scotch yoke to move back and forth at a 90-degree angle to the shaft.

Vane-Type Rotary Compressor

A compressor does not have to have cylinders and pistons. The compressor is a pump, and there are many other types of pumps, such as the vane type (see Fig. 4-8). The compressor shaft turns a rotor with slots into which the vanes (rectangular blades) are fitted. The vanes may slide in and out. The rotor, a cylindrical rotating member, is given an eccentric motion, as Fig. 4-8 indicates, and the vanes divide the round inner chamber into four chambers (when the rotor spins, all vanes are forced outward against the inner chamber's wall).

52 Modern Air Conditioning

Figure 4-8 Rotary vane compressor uses rotor turning in eccentric manner and sliding vanes that form low- and high-pressure chambers as a result.

Where the vane-formed chamber is large, a low-pressure area is created, drawing in refrigerant gas. As the rotor turns in its eccentric manner, the vane-formed chamber is made smaller (and the vanes are pushed back into their slots). The refrigerant gas is squeezed and pushed through a reed valve.

The Wankel, which has achieved limited production as an automobile engine, also is being produced in Japan as an air conditioning compressor. Just as the triangular rotor machine can draw in and compress an air-fuel mixture, it can do the same with refrigerant. The Wankel compressor is very light in weight compared with a piston compressor, even lighter than the typical rotary vane type.

The Compressor Clutch

If the drive belt pulley were fixed to the compressor shaft, the compressor would always be in operation, and the air conditioning would always be on. To provide a convenient way to turn off the air conditioning when desired, and also to save the power it takes to operate the compressor, an electromagnetic clutch is used (Fig. 4-8). It is a three-part component (Fig. 4-9). A coil of wire is attached to the compressor and wired through a switch

The Compressor Clutch

(or several switches) to the car's electrical system. Second, a pulley, which contains a bearing, is mounted on the compressor shaft. The pulley has a recess so it also fits over the electromagnetic coil. Third, there is a drive plate, which is rigidly attached to the end of the compressor shaft. The drive plate is made with two main sections, an outer and an inner, connected to each other by steel spring leaves. The drive plate is mounted so that it is very close (within thousandths of an inch) to the pulley. When the air conditioning is off, the belt spins the pulley, which rotates on its bearing; but because there is no rigid mechanical connection to the compressor shaft, the shaft does not turn, and so virtually no power is transferred through the belt.

When the dashboard air conditioning control is turned on, an electrical circuit is completed through the clutch's coil, creating electromagnetism in the area of the pulley that fits over it and the drive plate. The pulley attracts the outer section of the drive plate, which flexes the leaf

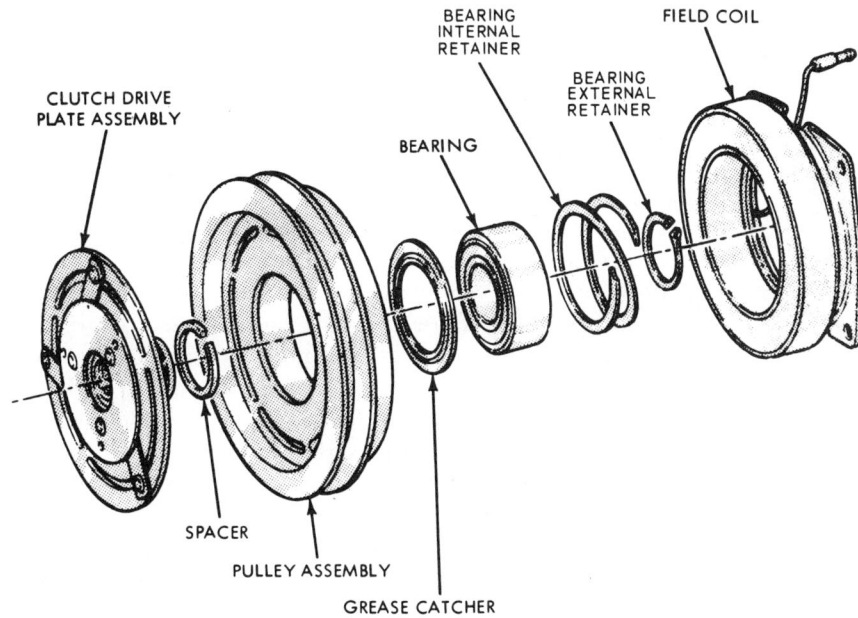

Figure 4-9 A typical compressor clutch assembly. The drive plate actually is two parts, a center section with a hub that bolts to the compressor shaft and an outer section connected to it by leaf springs. When the field coil is energized, it creates a magnetic field for the pulley assembly and the drive plate, which normally are slightly apart from each other. The magnetism locks them together, as the outer section of the drive plate flexes on its leaf springs. When the drive plate (which is attached to the compressor shaft) is locked to the pulley assembly (which is turned by a belt from the engine crankshaft), the compressor starts pumping and the air conditioning is in operation. (Courtesy Ford Motor Co.)

springs that connect it to the inner section, which is attached to the compressor shaft (see Fig. 4-8). Now there is a direct connection from the drive plate inner section through the leaf springs to the outer section, to the pulley. Power is transferred from the belt, now driving both the pulley and the drive plate, so the compressor shaft turns and the air conditioning is in operation.

On some older cars (1972 and earlier), another type of clutch was used. In this design, the clutch coil was built into the pulley assembly. Current was transferred to the coil by a pair of carbon brushes spring-mounted on the compressor and positioned so that they touched contact rings (called *slip rings*) on the coil. The coil spun with the pulley while the brushes remained rigid, even with the system off, so the tips of the brushes wore and periodic brush replacement was necessary.

Receiver-Dryer

The air conditioning system is subject to two forms of internal contamination; moisture and foreign particles. Moisture is perhaps the most critical item, for just half a drop of water is about all the average system can tolerate.

If there is more, it forms ice crystals that can stop the flow of Refrigerant 12. Of course, when the Refrigerant 12 stops flowing, heat from outside air transfers through to the refrigerant, warms it up and melts the ice, so the refrigerant flow resumes until ice crystals again form. One of the most common problems service personnel hear about is that the air conditioner cools for a while, stops, then starts cooling again. This intermittent operation is commonly caused by moisture in the system.

Moisture also can combine chemically with Refrigerant 12 to form highly corrosive hydrochloric acid, which can damage the steel parts in the system. Corrosive particles then form a muddy mixture called *sludge*, which can plug filtering screens and interfere with the control parts in the air conditioning system.

Even with carefully sealed connections, some moisture can get into the system particularly during humid weather when it can penetrate even healthy hoses.

The receiver-dryer (Fig. 4-10) has the job of preventing these problems. It contains a drying agent, also called a *desiccant*, that can remove much of the moisture taken in by a system in good condition. A few types of drying agents are in common use. A characteristic of one of the most popular is that it holds a great deal of moisture, but releases some of that moisture back into the Refrigerant 12 at very high temperatures.

In tropical climates, therefore, this desiccant is unsuitable, and instead one that releases less moisture is sold. In addition, car manu-

Figure 4-10 A typical receiver-dryer. It holds liquid refrigerant for times when system demand is high and to compensate for minor leakage.

facturers recognize that the area in which a car is used may be changed, so the hoses are designed to reduce passage of moisture.

In addition to holding moisture, the receiver-dryer has two additional functions:

1. In most cars it contains a filtering screen to remove dirt and any other impurities that may get into the Refrigerant 12 (see Fig. 4-11).
2. It also stores some extra Refrigerant 12, which the system can draw upon as needed to compensate for minor, normal leakage and in those situations when extra Refrigerant 12 is needed by the system. The need arises when the heat load is very high, that is, when the air is very hot and the evaporator must remove a lot of heat from it to reduce temperatures to comfortable levels.

Thermostatic Expansion Valve

For proper operation of the system, just the right amount of Refrigerant 12 must flow into the evaporator, and this amount varies according to ambient temperatures. Making sure the flow is correct for maximum

Figure 4-11 Cutaway look of a receiver-dryer. Note the filtering screen to remove particles from the refrigerant.

cooling is the job of the thermostatic (temperature-sensitive) expansion valve. This valve is mounted at the inlet side of the evaporator (Fig. 4-12). It is the restriction referred to in Chapter 2 (see Fig. 2-7). To understand its importance, let's see what would happen if it were not used.

On a hot day, too little Refrigerant 12 might flow through the system. The refrigerant would vaporize completely and then absorb more heat, becoming superheated. A modest amount of superheating is normal, but superheated Refrigerant 12 is not as efficient at absorbing heat from the outside air as Refrigerant 12 that has just turned from liquid to vapor. The result of too little Refrigerant 12 flow is poor cooling.

Or the flow of Refrigerant 12 might be too great, in which case there is a combined effect. First, there is not enough room for the Refrigerant 12 to vaporize, for vaporization means that the liquid becomes a gas, expanding to many times its original size. Second, pressure builds up, which raises the vaporization temperatures of a liquid. The result is that most of the Refrigerant 12 will not be able to vaporize, and inasmuch as heat absorption is greatest during vaporization, the performance of the system drops when most of the refrigerant remains a liquid.

You can now understand how important it is to supply the right amount of Refrigerant 12 to the evaporator for maximum cooling. The thermostatic expansion valve does this as follows.

A typical valve (see Fig. 4-13) contains a Refrigerant 12 passage and a

Thermostatic Expansion Valve

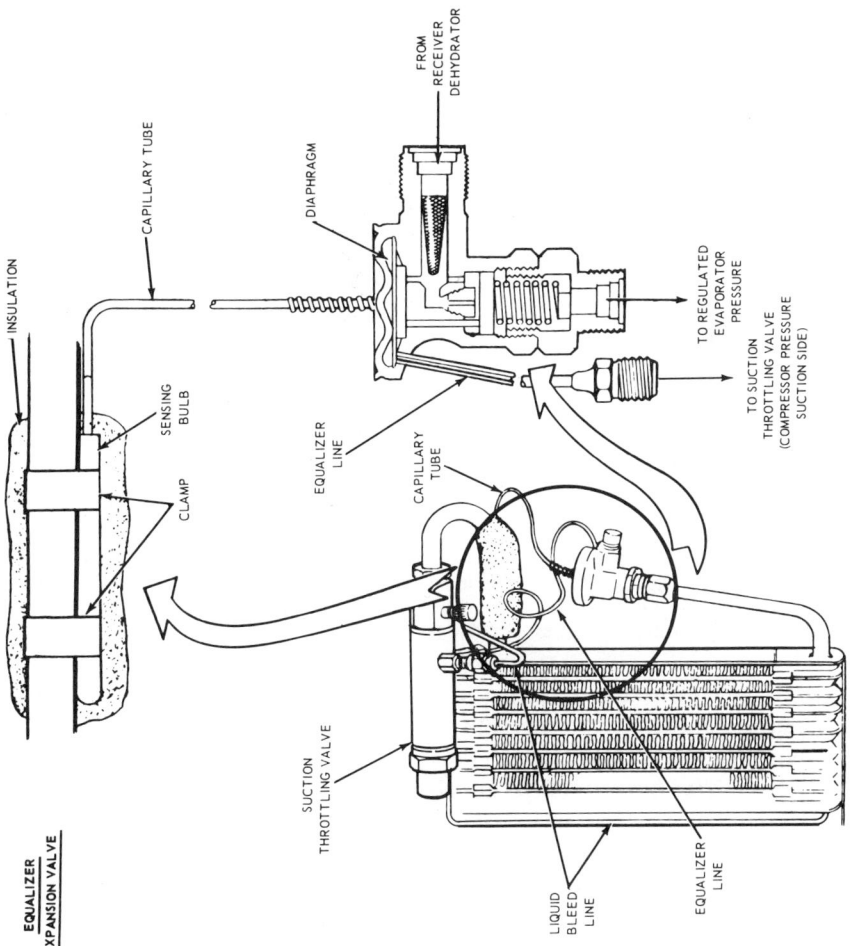

Figure 4-12 This is a thermostatic expansion valve of the external type. Note the temperature-sensing capillary tube that goes to the evaporator outlet, where it is covered with insulation. Also notice the pressure equalizing tube, which goes to a part called the suction throttling valve, covered in the next chapter. (Courtesy Ford Motor Co.)

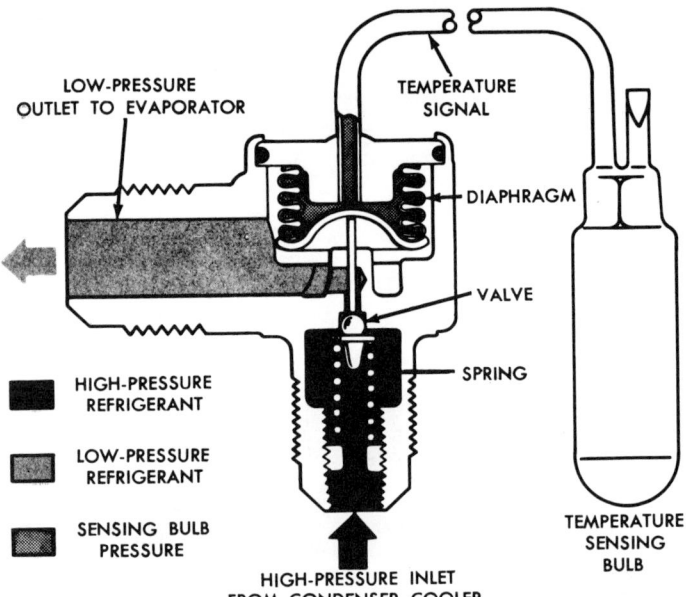

Figure 4-13 Cutaway look of a thermostatic expansion valve. As temperature in the evaporator outlet increases, it is sensed by a capillary tube bulb. Gas inside bulb and tube expands, pushing down on diaphragm in expansion valve. Diaphragm's downward movement pushes on rod and ball, opening valve against spring pressure to permit increased flow of Refrigerant 12. With more Refrigerant 12 flowing through evaporator, it does not get as hot and so is cooler when it leaves evaporator. Expansion valve bulb senses this, gas inside contracts and pressure on diaphragm is relieved somewhat, permitting valve to close. In actual air conditioning operation, the valve is never completely closed. (Courtesy Ford Motor Co.)

ball held in place by a spring underneath it. This spring pushes the ball against a part of the passage, closing it off so that Refrigerant 12 cannot flow through. The valve is closed.

A *diaphragm*, a flexible bladder, and a rod are used to open the valve. When the diaphragm flexes downward, it pushes on the rod, which pushes on the ball, opening the passage so that Refrigerant 12 can flow through. The greater the amount of downward push on the ball, the more open the passage becomes and the greater is the flow of Refrigerant 12.

The pressure of a fluid pushing down on it makes the diaphragm flex downward. A chamber above the diaphragm is filled with this fluid, which may be Refrigerant 12, carbon dioxide, or something else that increases in pressure in a stable, proportional manner as it gets warmer. Let's see how we can use this property.

Clearly, if the flow of Refrigerant 12 through the evaporator is not adequate, all of it will vaporize and become quite superheated. It will leave the evaporator much warmer than normal. If we somehow sense the temperature of the Refrigerant 12 at the evaporator outlet, we will know if the flow is inadequate, for the Refrigerant 12 will be at a higher temperature than if the flow were correct.

To sense the temperature at the outlet, the chamber atop the diaphragm is connected to the evaporator outlet pipe by very thin tubing, called a *capillary tube*, that ends with a coil of this tubing or a bulge called a *sensing bulb*. The coil or sensing bulb is clamped to the evaporator outlet tube and covered with an insulating material, so it is not affected by outside air temperatures. Inasmuch as the expansion valve is typically located in the engine compartment, the effect of engine heat could be significant if the end were not insulated.

The capillary tube and bulb, as well as the chamber above the diaphragm, are filled with temperature-sensing fluid. When the evaporator outlet temperature rises, so does the temperature of the fluid in the capillary tube and/or bulb. The heat is transferred through the fluid in the tubing into the fluid in the chamber. All this heated fluid expands and exerts downward pressure on the diaphragm, pushing on the ball to open the valve. When the evaporator outlet temperature drops, so does the temperature of the fluid in the tube and chamber. The fluid contracts and relieves the downward pressure on the diaphragm.

Two forces then work together to exert upward pressure on the diaphragm. One is the pressure of the Refrigerant 12 in the system, which is applied to the underside of the diaphragm in one of two ways: (1) through an internal passage, from the evaporator inlet or outlet; and (2) from an external capillary tube attached to the evaporator outlet (usually to a fitting on the suction throttling valve, a part covered in Chapter 5). If an internal passage is used, the expansion valve is called an internally equalized type; if an external capillary tube is used, it is called an externally equalized type. These terms merely refer to the method used—external or internal—to supply Refrigerant 12 pressure from the evaporator outlet to the underside of the expansion valve diaphragm. This pressure on the underside of the diaphragm is intended to balance (equalize) the pressure on the top of the diaphragm.

The second upward force on the diaphragm is provided by the spring under the ball; the spring is designed to close the valve a bit more than necessary. As a result, the Refrigerant 12 flow through the expansion valve is a bit less than the ideal amount. Thus, the refrigerant not only will vaporize, but it will absorb some additional heat—superheat—to positively ensure that no liquid will leave the evaporator. The Refrigerant 12 becomes about 10°F superheated. Because this is caused by the spring, it is sometimes called the *superheat spring*. Allowing under ideal Refrigerant 12 flow is called "starving the evaporator." If too much Refrigerant 12 flow is permitted, it is called "flooding the evaporator." As you can see, slight starvation is normal.

The reason it is important to ensure that no liquid leaves the evaporator is that liquid is not compressible, and if liquid Refrigerant 12 got into the compressor, the compressor could be damaged as it tried to pump it.

The superheat spring has another function; it provides a positive stop to Refrigerant 12 flow when the system is shut off. When the air conditioning is turned off, the diaphragm by itself would assume a position that would leave the expansion valve slightly open, permitting some refrigerant flow temporarily. The superheat spring exerts its pressure, however, and the valve is pushed closed, stopping the refrigerant flow.

The basic expansion valve illustrated thus far is a design still in some use. There are other designs, such as the tapered needle type. Instead of a ball in a specially shaped section of outlet passage, a tapered needle fits into a tapered section of outlet passage. The rod from the diaphragm does not bear against the needle, but against a cap on top of the superheat spring. The most common designs of this type have two or three rods, spaced equally apart, bearing against the spring cap (see Fig. 4-14). Operation is essentially the same as with the ball type. The form of operation, however, is one aspect of thermostatic expansion valve design. Physical layout is another. Common exceptions to the layout shown thus far are discussed next.

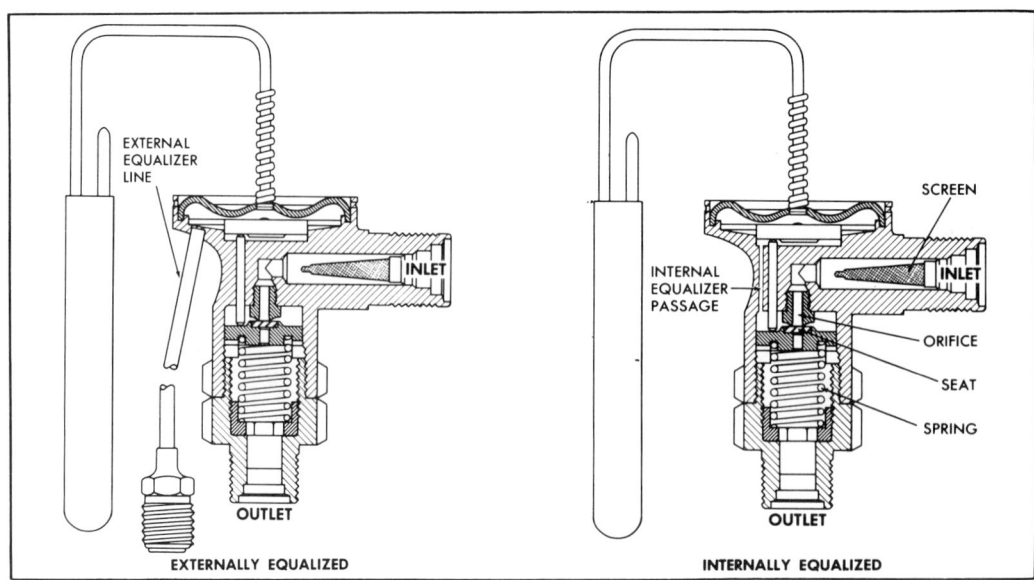

Figure 4-14 This expansion valve has two or three operating pins (only one is shown) that bear against a cap on top of the superheat spring. Both an external equalizer line and an internal equalizer passage are shown in this one drawing to illustrate the principles. In an actual expansion valve, one or the other would be used. (Courtesy General Motors Corp. © 1978)

Valves-in-Receiver

Instead of complete separation of the high- and low-pressure lines, they connect (at separate points) to a receiver that contains both the thermostatic expansion valve and a second control valve, the suction throttling valve (covered in Chapter 5). Because both the line from condenser to evaporator inlet and the line from evaporator outlet to compressor connect to this special receiver-dryer, two major differences from the physical layout shown previously can be incorporated (see Fig. 4-15).

1. There need be no external capillary tube from the evaporator outlet to the expansion valve for temperature sensing. A simple drilled passage does the job, and the question of making the capillary tube bulb secure and well insulated is eliminated.
2. The external equalizer tube can be easily replaced by an internal, drilled passage, just like the temperature-sensing tube, for greater reliability. In this case, the expansion valve is an internally equalized type. This design is called Valves-in-Receiver.

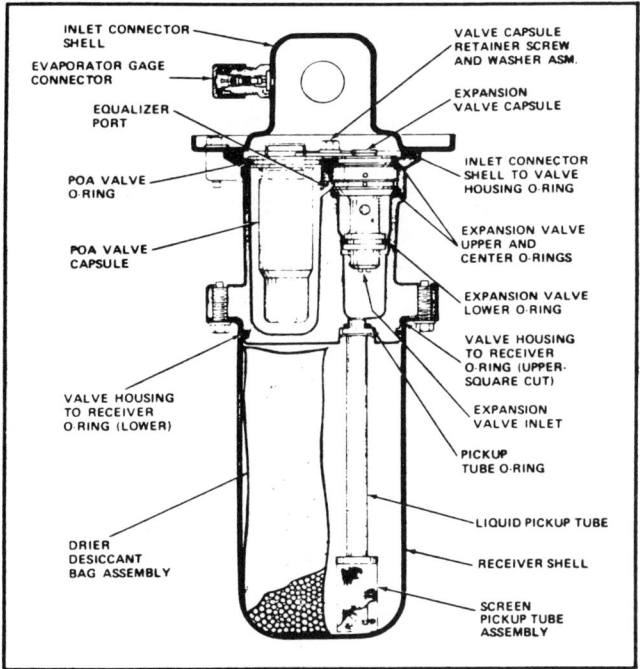

Figure 4-15 Cutaway of Valves-in-Receiver showing how all refrigeration lines connect and the locations of the thermostatic expansion valve and POA-type suction throttling valve capsules. (Courtesy General Motors Corp. © 1973)

Junction Block

The junction block is much like the Valves-in-Receiver type, except there is no receiver-dryer in the package (it remains a separate part). The block is at the evaporator, and both inlet and outlet lines connect to it. Therefore, it is simple to have both temperature-sensing and equalizer functions performed with internal drilled passages. Some junction blocks incorporate another control valve, the suction throttling valve (see Chapter 5) and are called combination valve assemblies (see Fig. 4-16). Others, which are used in systems that do not have suction throttling valves, are called H-valve assemblies. The H-valve is so named because it forms a letter H with the evaporator inlet and outlet lines.

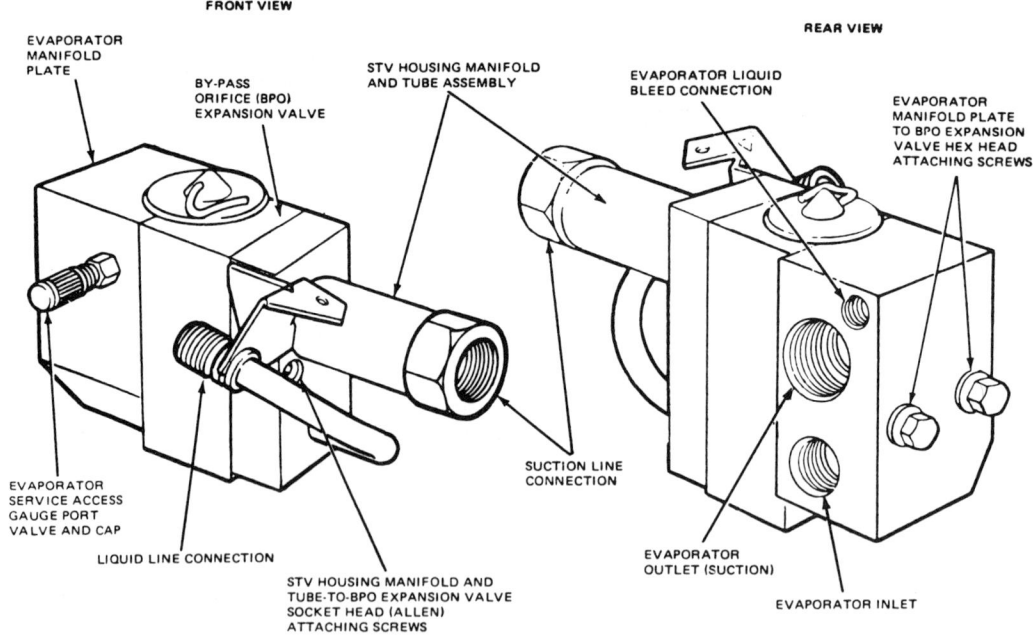

Figure 4-16 This combination valve-junction block contains the thermostatic expansion valve and the suction throttling valve, a control at the evaporator outlet, covered in the following chapter. Note the diaphragm cover at the top of the junction block. (Courtesy Ford Motor Co. 1979)

Expansion Valve Calibration

You should understand that the thermostatic expansion valve works within very narrow limits. The difference between wide open and closed is usually thousandths of an inch. For this reason, any precision that can be

63 Additional Controls

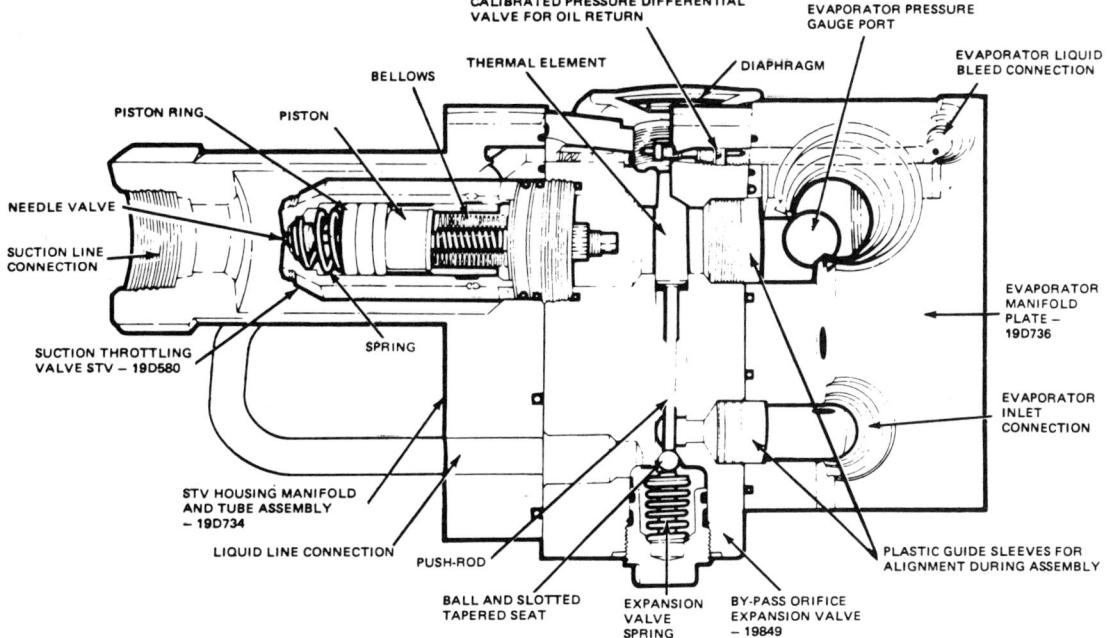

Figure 4-16 (continued)

achieved in calibration and operation is very important. Valves controlled by internal passages are generally more precise, so you will find them in greater use on late-model cars.

High- and Low-Pressure Sides of the System

In Chapter 2, the inlet to the evaporator was shown to be the dividing point between the high- and low-pressure sides of the system. Now that you have learned about the expansion valve, you should know that it is actually the expansion valve that is the dividing point. High-pressure liquid Refrigerant 12 enters the expansion valve from the compressor. The expansion valve meters the flow so that the Refrigerant 12 vaporizes (and its pressure drops) as it leaves the valve and goes into the evaporator to absorb heat.

Additional Controls

The air conditioning system described in this chapter, with its multicylinder compressor, receiver-dryer, and expansion valve, is the basic system. However, a number of special controls are required for efficient operation under certain conditions, and the system requires protection for unfavorable conditions. These additional controls are described in Chapter 5.

QUESTIONS

1. The compressor valves typically are
   a. shaped like plungers.
   b. strips of flat spring metal.
   c. a sleeve inside a cylinder, each with slits.
2. One of the following is not a typical number of cylinders in a modern compressor:
   a. two
   b. three
   c. four
   d. five
   e. six
   f. seven
3. Mechanic A says the function of a compressor clutch is to provide a way to turn off the system. Mechanic B says it is to save power used by the system. Who is right?
   a. Mechanic A.
   b. Mechanic B.
   c. Both.
   d. Neither.
4. Mechanic A says the compressor clutch coil on a late-model car is attached to the compressor. Mechanic B says the compressor clutch coil on a late-model car may be built into the pulley. Who is right?
   a. Mechanic A.
   b. Mechanic B.
   c. Both.
   d. Neither.
5. Moisture in an air conditioning system is unacceptable because it
   a. reacts with Refrigerant 12 to form a fluorocarbon.
   b. can form ice to block the system.
   c. Answers a and b are both correct.
6. Mechanic A says moisture usually gets into the system by seepage from the cooling system. Mechanic B says it gets in from the air by penetrating hoses and seeping past connections. Who is right?

a. Mechanic A.
b. Mechanic B.
c. Both.
d. Neither.

7. If the flow of Refrigerant 12 through the thermostatic expansion valve is inadequate, the Refrigerant 12
   a. cannot vaporize.
   b. will become superheated.
   c. will force the thermostatic expansion valve to close.

8. The temperature-sensing bulb of the thermostatic expansion valve is clamped to the
   a. evaporator outlet.
   b. evaporator inlet.
   c. compressor outlet.
   d. compressor inlet.

9. If we say the thermostatic expansion valve is externally equalized, it means that
   a. there is an air bleed to the atmosphere in the sensing bulb.
   b. the sensing bulb is clamped to the outside of the tubing.
   c. an external tube runs from the underside of the thermostatic expansion valve diaphragm to the evaporator outlet.

10. When a Valves-in-Receiver is used, one of the following is **not** true:
    a. The evaporator inlet and outlet lines are connected to the Valves-in-Receiver.
    b. The compressor inlet line connects to the Valves-in-Receiver.
    c. The compressor outlet line connects to the Valves-in-Receiver.
    d. The condenser outlet line connects to the Valves-in-Receiver.

HANDS ON

1. Find a thermostatic expansion valve with external tubing on a car so equipped. Check to see if its capillary tube end is clamped tight.
2. Identify the thermostatic expansion valve equalizer tubing on a car so equipped and check to make sure it is not kinked and is tightly connected.
3. On a Valves-in-Receiver system, identify all lines connecting to the receiver unit.

5

Controlling Evaporator Temperature

Suction Throttling Valve

The air conditioning system described in the previous chapter would operate satisfactorily under many conditions. However, there are some in which a problem could occur. Let's suppose it is humid and after a while the operation of the system has reduced the air temperature. The expansion valve always meters the Refrigerant 12 flow for maximum cooling, so before long the air temperature around the evaporator drops to 32°F (0°C) or lower.

Moisture in the air not only condenses, but it freezes on the evaporator coils. The fan blows, but airflow through the evaporator coils is blocked, and so the performance of the system is halted. If the system is shut off, the air temperature will rise, the frozen moisture will melt, and the air conditioning will function again if turned on. This is not acceptable, however, for the motorist expects the system to keep functioning. As a result, an additional control must be installed to prevent the freeze-up.

The control is typically the suction throttling valve, which slows down the Refrigerant 12 gas flow from the evaporator when necessary. When less Refrigerant 12 flows, less heat can be absorbed from air surrounding the evaporator, and so the performance of the air conditioner is reduced. The reduction, however, is not so much that the passenger compartment is uncomfortable, just enough to prevent moisture freeze-up and blockage of airflow between the evaporator coils (see Fig. 5-1).

It might seem that a valve that holds back pressure, which is really all the suction throttling valve is, would be a simple thing. However, as you will learn, it usually is not. The reason is that the closer the valve tolerance to the point of freeze-up, the better the air conditioning will perform, particularly in muggy weather when the extra performance is significant. As a result, car makers have developed some rather sophisticated suction throttling valves.

68 Controlling Evaporator Temperature

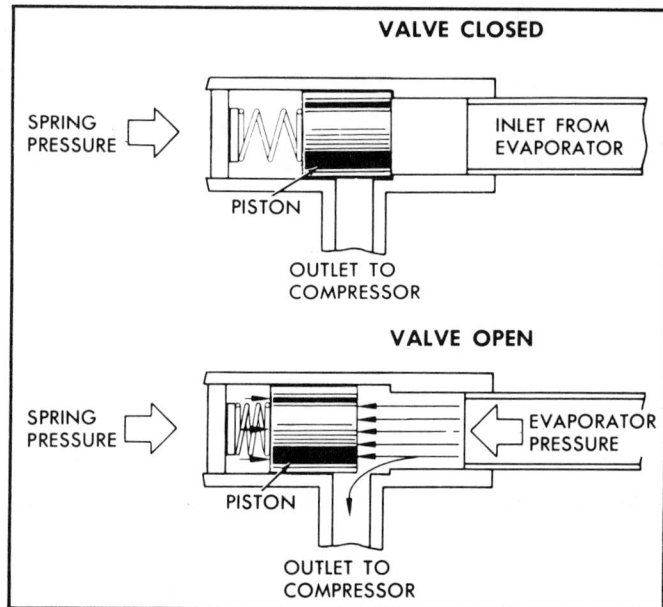

Figure 5-1 The basic function of the suction throttling valve is to hold enough back pressure in the evaporator so Refrigerant 12 temperature does not drop very low and allow condensing moisture to turn to ice on the exterior of the evaporator. On most systems, it is designed to maintain back pressure of about 30 psi (207 kPa). (Courtesy General Motors Corp. © 1978.)

The suction throttling valve is installed at the outlet of the evaporator, where a hose is connected to the inlet (suction) side of the compressor. Because this valve limits Refrigerant 12 gas flow from the evaporator, it is said to "throttle it," hence the name, suction throttling valve.

The valve contains a piston linked to a spring-loaded diaphragm. One side of the diaphragm is exposed to Refrigerant 12 under pressure from the evaporator. The other side contains the spring and is vented to the atmosphere (so atmospheric pressure bears against it).

As you learned in Chapter 2, the pressure and temperature of Refrigerant 12 are always related (see Fig. 2-8), except in a super heat situation. At 32°F (0°C), the Refrigerant 12 pressure is just about 30 pounds per square inch or 207 kilopascals (kPa). If the suction throttling valve can restrict refrigerant flow so that the pressure in the evaporator is always just about 30 psi, the system will provide maximum cooling without freeze-up of moisture in the surrounding air. In fact, the pressure can even be allowed to be somewhat lower, because the air temperature surrounding the evaporator will never come down to exactly match the Refrigerant 12 temperature inside.

Because of differences in evaporator design (which affect heat transfer through the evaporator coils) and the location of the suction throttling valve or an equivalent control (covered later in this chapter), the control pressure varies from system to system. In some cases, it is as low as 22 psi (152 kPa); in others it is as high as 31 psi (214 kPa). The pressure also varies with altitude.

The valve's spring and diaphragm are calibrated to hold the piston so as to block Refrigerant 12 flow from the evaporator to the compressor. When Refrigerant 12 pressure in the evaporator reaches the peak level (31 psi or below), it exerts a push against the piston, diaphragm, and spring, and moves the piston so the Refrigerant 12 can flow through from evaporator to compressor inlet.

Atmospheric pressure drops with increasing altitude. If you are driving in a mountainous area, you could encounter the following problem: the drop in atmospheric pressure means there is less pressure on the diaphragm and piston. As a result, less Refrigerant 12 pressure is required to push open the suction throttling valve. More Refrigerant 12 will flow through the evaporator, the temperature will drop below freezing, and the moisture in the air around the evaporator will condense and turn to ice.

In the past, to prevent this, either of two controls was added to the system with the suction throttling valve:

1. A cable from the dashboard temperature control lever to the suction throttling valve. When you move the temperature control lever from the "cold" toward the "warm" position, you also operate a link on the suction throttling valve that compresses the spring, increasing its pressure.
2. An additional diaphragm and spring assembly on the end of the suction throttling valve (see Fig. 5-2). The additional diaphragm divides the assembly into two chambers, to one of which engine vacuum is applied. The engine vacuum "sucks" on the diaphragm and keeps spring pressure from being applied to the main spring and diaphragm. When you move the temperature control lever, you not only control a flap in the duct housing (as covered in Chapter 8), you also operate linkage that closes a valve in the line from the engine vacuum to the suction throttling valve's additional diaphragm. With the vaccuum cut off, the spring against the additional diaphragm adds to the push of the main spring, increasing the Refrigerant 12 pressure that must build up before flow to the compressor can resume. *Note:* For detailed coverage of vacuum diaphragms in general, refer to Chapter 8.

The owner's manual on cars whose air conditioners were equipped with either of these arrangements advised the driver to move the temperature lever partly toward the warm position at high altitudes.

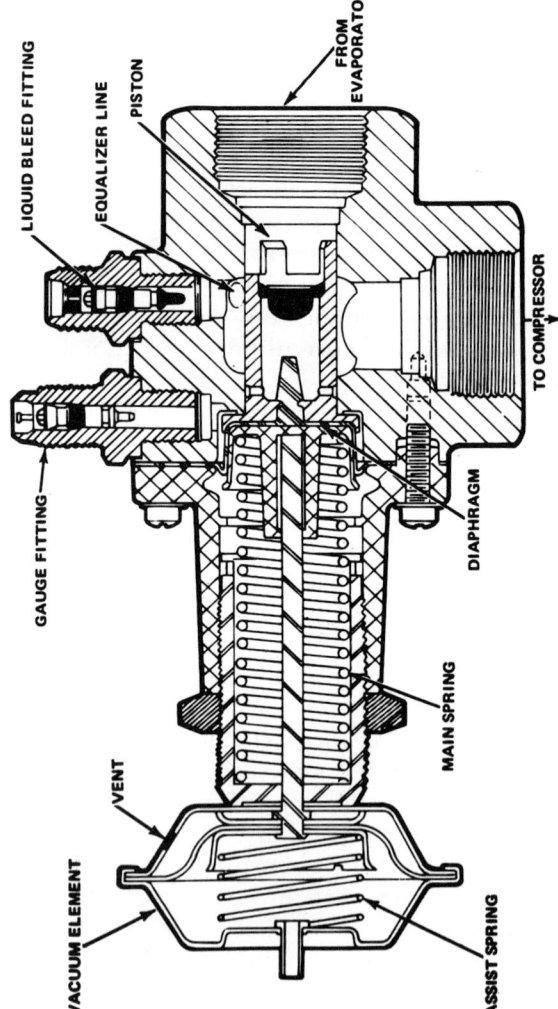

Figure 5-2 This suction throttling valve has an additional diaphragm and spring assembly attached to the (left) end. When the dashboard temperature control lever is moved toward the warm position, it closes a valve in a vacuum line to the additional diaphragm. With the vacuum shut off, the spring adds to the push of the main spring in the valve, increasing the Refrigerant 12 back pressure in the evaporator and so reducing the cooling. (Courtesy Ford Marketing Corp. © 1973.)

Both of these arrangements have been out of production for many years, so you are unlikely to have to service them, and their service is not covered in this book. On current cars with a suction throttling valve, a fully-automatic type called the pilot-operated type, is standard.

Pilot-Operated-Type Suction Throttling Valve

The possibility of high-altitude icing on the evaporator is one reason why the suction throttling valves previously described were not wholly satisfactory. Another was their lack of accuracy. The pilot-operated valve eliminates these problems (see Fig. 5-3). The term "pilot" refers to a spring-loaded needle with an arrowhead tip that is used to seal a passage to the compressor inlet. This pilot is controlled by a bronze bellows from which air is almost perfectly evacuated (virtually absolute zero air pressure inside). Because the bellows is close to absolutely zero interior pressure (or a near-perfect vacuum) the valve is called a pilot-operated-absolute type, or simply a POA. Because the bellows contains so close to a perfect vacuum and sits in a valve in which there is Refrigerant 12, the atmospheric pressure has no effect, so the valve is not altitude sensitive.

The basic idea of the valve is to use the response of the vacuum-filled bellows to changes in Refrigerant 12 pressure to control only a tiny part, the pilot valve. Then a large piston, which is more properly sized to regulate refrigerant flow, is controlled by the pilot valve. The piston is spring loaded to establish its basic positions, but the spring (which is not the most precise part) does not actually control the valve.

The POA-type valve is a sealed assembly and is nonadjustable, so if it does not work, you must replace it. For those who are interested, a more precise description of how it works follows.

When the air conditioning is on, the compressor is running and drawing Refrigerant 12 gas from the evaporator outlet line. This lowers the pressure in the outlet part of the POA valve. As long as evaporator outlet pressure is above the control pressure (let's use 30 psi as an example), the bellows is contracted and the pilot needle is held open by a spring. The Refrigerant 12 pressure above the control point is high enough to push the piston away from its seat and allow maximum Refrigerant gas flow through to the compressor. The piston has drilled holes in it, so gas also flows through them into an enclosed section around the bellows (called the bellows chamber) and then out the pilot valve.

If the system starts to overcool, the compressor will be drawing Refrigerant 12 from the evaporator so fast that the pressure will drop and reach the control point (30 psi in our example). At this lowered pressure, the bellows will expand and close the pilot needle. The Refrigerant 12 continues to flow through the holes in the piston, but it cannot get out past

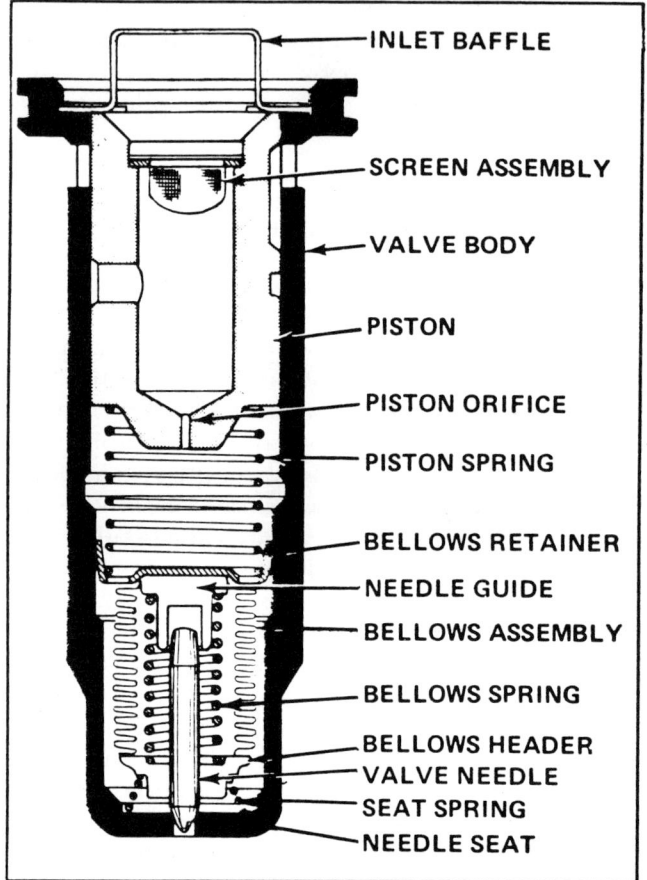

Figure 5-3 This is the pilot-operated-absolute (POA) form of suction throttling valve, Movement of the needle valve, which is regulated by expansion and contraction of the bronze bellows, controls the operation of a piston-type valve. (Courtesy General Motors Corp. © 1973.)

the now-closed pilot needle, so it exerts back pressure against the piston. When the pressure equals that of the Refrigerant 12 flowing out of the evaporator, the piston spring then becomes the deciding factor. It is located on the compressor side of the piston, and it pushes the piston back to stop Refrigerant 12 flow.

With the flow stopped, the evaporator pressure builds up again over the control point (30 psi in the example). At this pressure there is no danger of moisture in the air around the evaporator freezing up after condensing.

In the meantime, the pressure against the bronze bellows has built up and forced the bellows to contract. A spring then pushes the pilot needle open. The compressor (which is running of course) pulls down Refrigerant

12 pressure in the valve. The pressure soon drops below the Refrigerant 12 pressure at the evaporator outlet, so the Refrigerant 12 pressure at the evaporator outlet pushes open the piston against the spring pressure, and the flow of Refrigerant 12 begins again. To see the entire sequence in detail, refer to Figs. 5-4 to 5-9.

The POA may appear to be an overly complex way of regulating evaporator outlet pressure, and it is. However, the use of a bellows and pilot valve to control a main valve (the spring-loaded piston) is very accurate, and the system develops maximum cooling without freeze-up at all times.

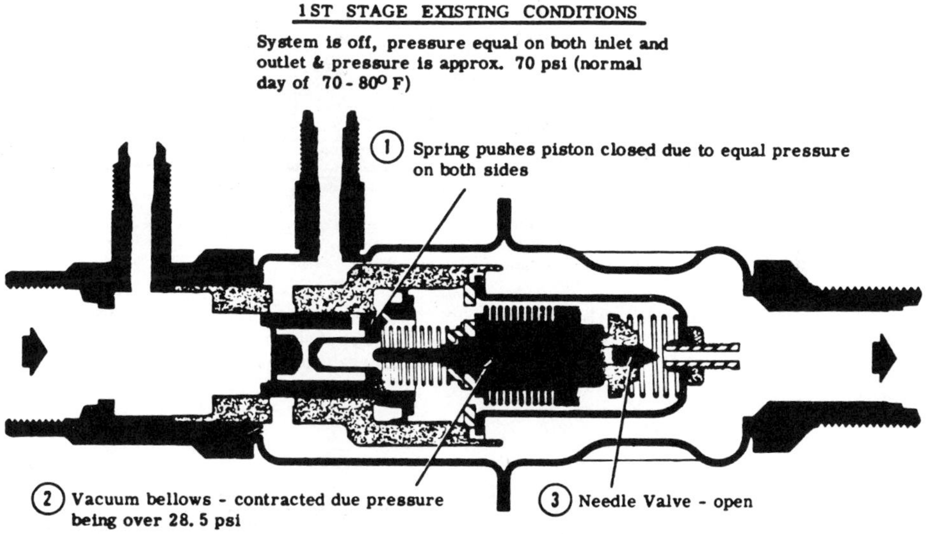

1ST STAGE EXISTING CONDITIONS

System is off, pressure equal on both inlet and outlet & pressure is approx. 70 psi (normal day of 70 - 80° F)

① Spring pushes piston closed due to equal pressure on both sides

② Vacuum bellows - contracted due pressure being over 28.5 psi

③ Needle Valve - open

Figure 5-4 A closeup look at the POA valve. In this view, the system is off and pressure on both inlet and outlet sides is equal (typically about 70 psi or 483 kPa on a 70°F day). (Courtesy General Motors Corp. © 1973.)

Positioning the Valves

In a basic system, the suction throttling valve is installed alone, in the evaporator outlet line. In this installation, it will often have connected to it an external tube that goes back into the evaporator. This tube, called an oil bleed or liquid bleed line, permits oil in the Refrigerant 12 to bypass a closed suction throttling valve to flow to the compressor to provide lubrication. The suction throttling valve also may have connected to it an equalizer line from the thermostatic expansion valve (see Chapter 4).

On many systems, the thermostatic expansion valve and the POA type suction throttling valve are physically located side by side in either of two ways:

74   Controlling Evaporator Temperature

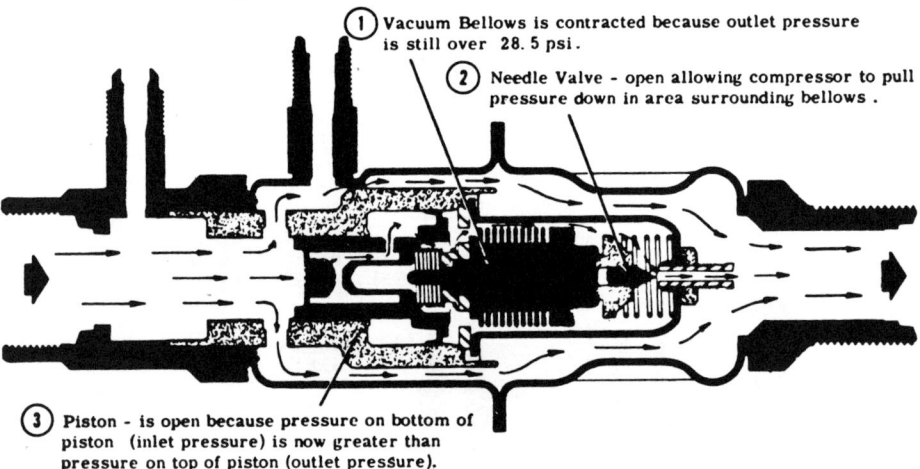

Figure 5-5   The system is on, the compressor is drawing Refrigerant 12 in and so lowering the pressure on the outlet side. The piston valve is open so Refrigerant 12 can flow. (Courtesy General Motors Corp. © 1973.)

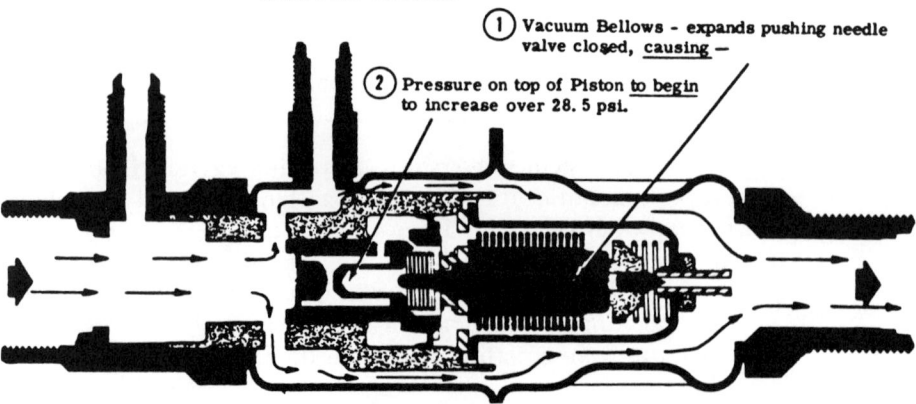

Figure 5-6   The bellows closes. The compressor has lowered the pressure on the outlet side to a control point, in this case 28.5 psi or 197 kPa. (Courtesy General Motors Corp. © 1973.)

Positioning the Valves

4TH STAGE EXISTING CONDITIONS
- PISTON CLOSES -

The pressure surrounding bellows and on top of piston has now increased sufficiently over 28.5 psi to become nearly equal (within 1.3 psi) of inlet pressure. Since —

① Pressures on both sides of piston nearly equal - spring takes over and pushes piston closed.

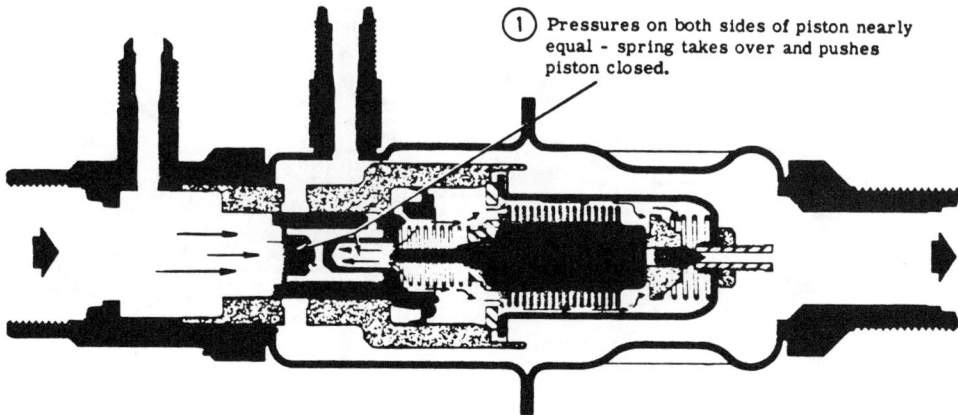

Figure 5-7 The pressure surrounding the bellows and on top of the piston is now more than 28.5 psi and is very close to the valve's inlet pressure. Inasmuch as the pressures on both sides of the piston are virtually equal, the spring pushes the piston closed. (Courtesy General Motors Corp.)

5TH STAGE EXISTING CONDITIONS
- BELLOWS OPENS -

The pressure surrounding bellows and on top of piston is now sufficiently over 28.5 psi - The result is that —

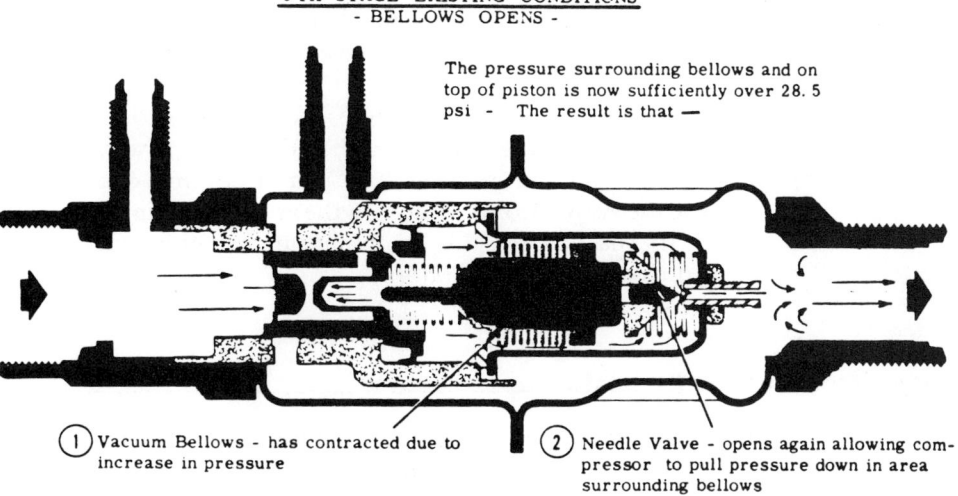

① Vacuum Bellows - has contracted due to increase in pressure

② Needle Valve - opens again allowing compressor to pull pressure down in area surrounding bellows

Figure 5-8 The bellows has contracted from the increased pressure as shown. As a result, the needle valve opens, also as shown. (Courtesy General Motors Corp.)

76 Controlling Evaporator Temperature

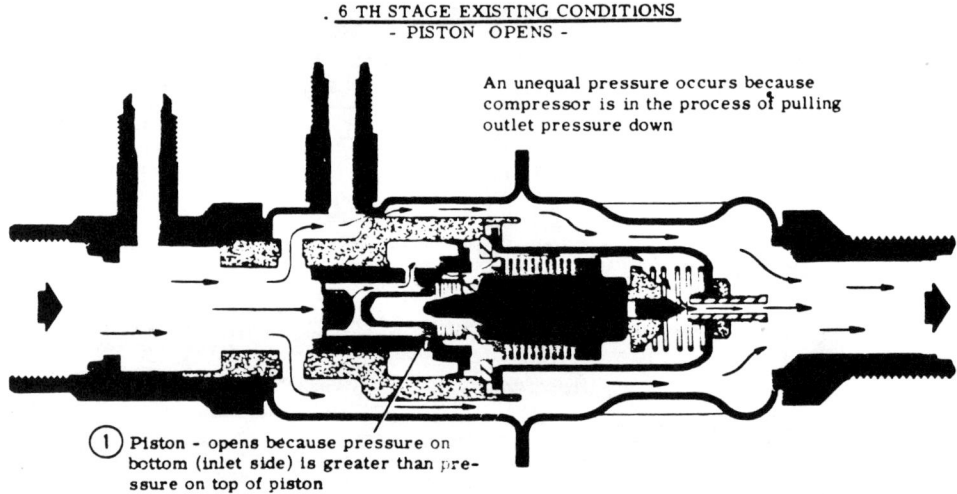

Figure 5-9 With the needle valve open, the compressor once again draws Refrigerant 12 from the outlet side. With pressures once again unequal and greater on the inlet side, the piston valve is pushed open. (Courtesy General Motors Corp.)

1. The two valves are in a single block at the evaporator. All pressure-equalizing tubing and temperature-sensing tubing are internal drilled passages. Many Ford products have such a block (see Fig. 4-16).
2. The two valves are placed in an assembly with the receiver-dryer (Fig 4-15). This design, called valves-in-receiver, was used on General Motors cars for several years.

Putting both valves in a single assembly does not change the fact that one is at the evaporator inlet and the other at the evaporator outlet. Each side of the block or receiver has separate tubing connections. In fact, because the evaporator is located in the air-distribution ductwork that goes under the dashboard, the combination assembly can be conveniently located close to the evaporator.

Evaporator Pressure Regulator

The evaporator pressure regulator (EPR) used on Chrysler Corporation cars over a period of many years, is basically a suction throttling valve that is located in the compressor inlet port, rather than at the evaporator outlet. The location of the regulator changes the calibration (control point) somewhat compared with a suction throttling valve, but the regulator does the same job despite the different location, and in some respects there is a resemblance in the way the two control devices work.

The original evaporator pressure regulator, used through the early 1970s, was a spring-loaded valve controlled by a diaphragm. The valve consisted of a rigid outer shell with slits and a close-fitting inner sleeve, also with slits. When evaporator outlet pressure was high, it pushed against the diaphragm to move the sleeve so that the slits in both the sleeve and rigid outer shell were aligned and Refrigerant 12 could flow through. When evaporator outlet pressure (actually compressor inlet pressure because of the location of the regulator) dropped to the control point (somewhere in the 22 to 26 psi or 152 to 179 kPa range), the spring pushed the sleeve back and the valve was closed (see Fig. 5-10).

This design was not too precise and was trouble prone. The close-fitting sleeve often stuck when the regulator was contaminated with foreign particles.

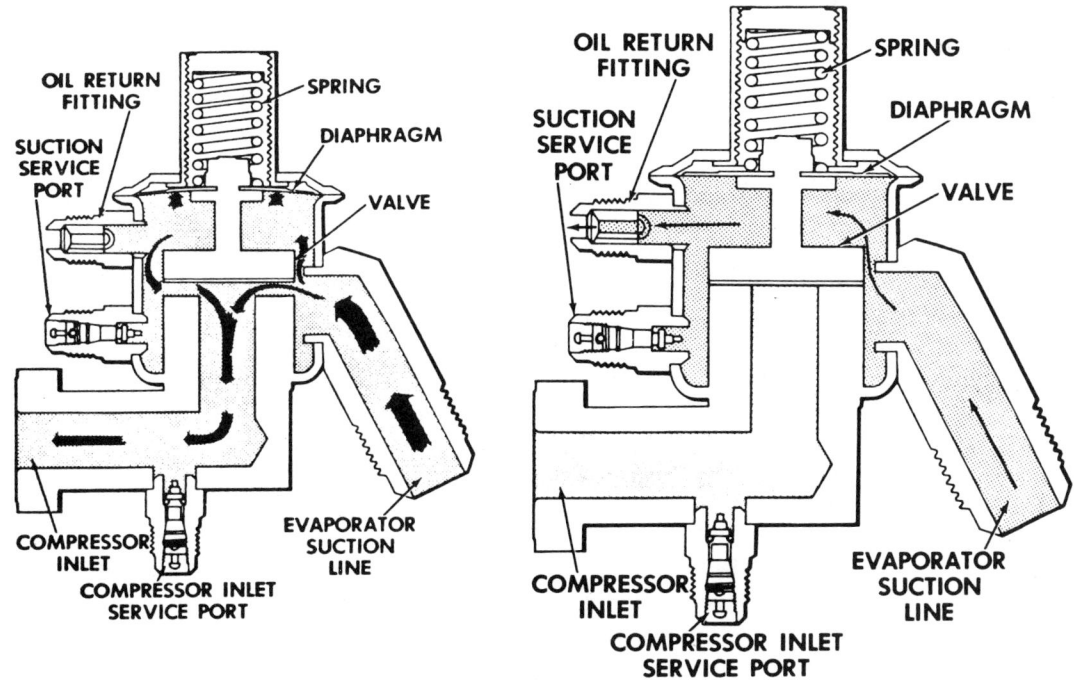

Figure 5-10 This is a cutaway of the first Chrysler evaporator pressure regulator, mounted at the compressor inlet. Later models were actually installed in the compressor inlet. At left you see how evaporator pressure above the control point pushes on the spring-loaded diaphragm valve, opening it and permitting Refrigerant 12 to flow into the compressor. At right, the evaporator pressure has dropped and the spring-loaded diaphragm pushes the valve closed. (Courtesy Chrysler Corp.)

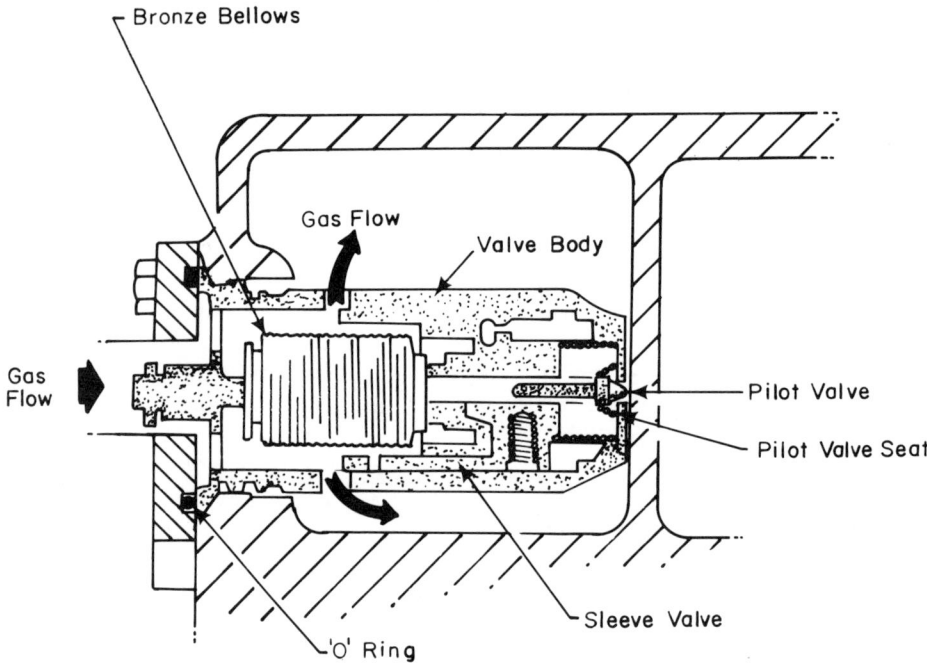

Figure 5-11 This evaporator pressure regulator, used through 1978, was controlled by a bronze bellows and a pilot valve. As evaporator pressure rises, the bellows contracts and the pilot valve retracts and opens. The higher Refrigerant 12 pressure from the evaporator forces the piston to the right, against spring pressure.

A second evaporator pressure regulator, with a pilot-operated spring-loaded piston, was introduced to replace EPR-I. It had a bronze bellows filled with a special gas (instead of being evacuated to close to zero pressure), but the operation was basically similar to the POA-type suction throttling valve (see Fig. 5-11).

A simpler, although somewhat less precise design, was introduced in 1978, the EPR-III (Fig. 5-12). It has a gas-filled bronze bellows that directly controls a cone-head valve, pushing it against or drawing it away from its seat as the bellows expands and contracts.

Evaporator Temperature Regulator

The evaporator temperature regulator, instead of the EPR, was used on Chrysler Corporation cars with automatic temperature control through the early 1970s. It was an electromagnetic valve, also in the compressor inlet,

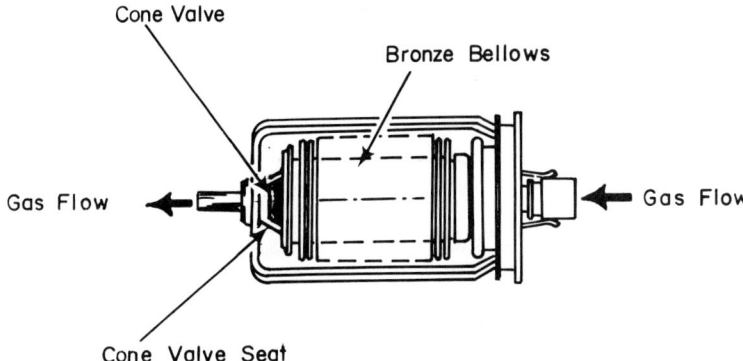

Figure 5-12 This evaporator pressure regulator uses a bronze bellows operating against a simple valve. When evaporator pressure rises and causes the bellows to contract, the valve (called a poppet type) retracts and opens to permit flow of Refrigerant 12.

but it was not self-contained. It was connected by a wire to a temperature-sensitive switch with a capillary tube bulb clamped to the evaporator. This switch contained a spring-loaded diaphragm and an electric switch controlled by the diaphragm.

When the capillary tube bulb sensed high temperature (above the control number), the diaphragm flexed and opened the switch, stopping current flow to the electromagnetic regulator. A spring opened the regulator valve and refrigerant flowed into the compressor.

When the capillary tube sensed low evaporator temperature (at the freezing point or slightly below), the pressure against the diaphragm was reduced, and the diaphragm spring closed the switch, completing the circuit to the electromagnetic regulator. Activated by the current, the regulator would close and block refrigerant flow into the compressor (see Fig. 5-13).

The evaporator temperature regulator, as you can see, was just an off-on switching arrangement that reacted to temperature changes at the evaporator coils, rather than pressure changes (although the difference is really academic because of the pressure-temperature relationship).

In any case, the evaporator temperature regulator system involved two completely separate parts, one partly buried in the duct housing against the evaporator, and both subject to electrical problems. It was an unnecessary complication that worked no better (and often worse) than the evaporator pressure regulator. When the evaporator temperature regulator failed, the wiring was disconnected and taped over, and the regulator itself was replaced with an evaporator pressure regulator.

All evaporator pressure regulators have been interchangeable among themselves, and when service is required, the latest model is used.

80 Controlling Evaporator Temperature

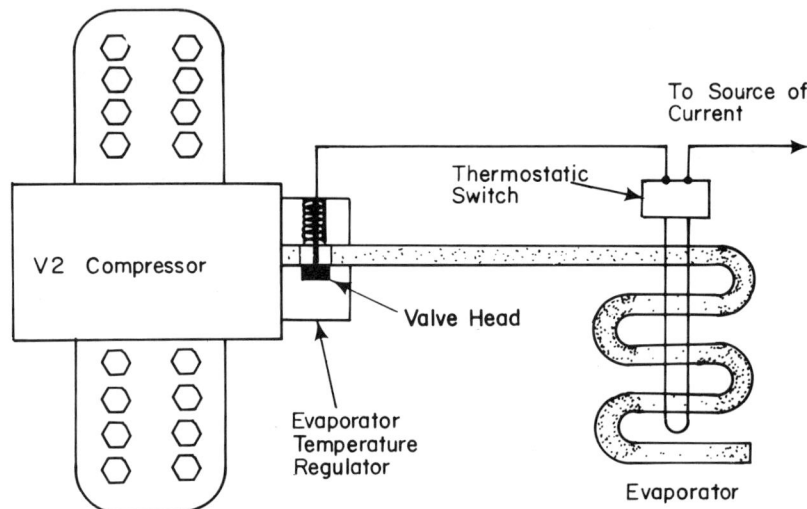

Figure 5-13 The evaporator temperature regulator was used on some Chrysler Corporation cars with automatic temperature control. It is either on or off, operated by an electromagnetic switch (solenoid), which is activated (receives current) from a switch mounted at the evaporator to sense evaporator external temperature. When evaporator external temperature drops to the freezing point, this switch closes, completing the circuit to the solenoid-operated evaporator temperature regulator. The evaporator temperature regulator is pulled closed by the solenoid, stopping the flow of Refrigerant 12. When evaporator temperature rises, the switch opens, breaking the circuit, and a spring pushes the evaporator temperature regulator valve open, permitting Refrigerant 12 flow to resume.

System Function with Expansion Valve and Suction Throttling Valve or Evaporator Control

Incorporating evaporator pressure or temperature control, we now have a system that can function effectively under just about all operating conditions. However, there are times when it is important that the system not be allowed to function to protect it from failure or to assist the engine that is powering it. Depending on the system, many protective devices may be incorporated. They are described in Chapter 6.

QUESTIONS

1. The normal location of a suction throttling valve is at the
    a. evaporator outlet.
    b. evaporator inlet.
    c. condenser outlet.
    d. condenser inlet.

2. The basic function of a suction throttling valve is to
   a. slow the change of Refrigerant 12 from vapor to liquid.
   b. control Refrigerant 12 flow from the evaporator.
   c. meter the flow of Refrigerant 12 into the evaporator.
3. The purpose of the suction throttling valve is to
   a. permit slowing the refrigeration cycle to prevent overcooling the passenger compartment.
   b. prevent ice formation inside the evaporator.
   c. prevent ice formation on the exterior of the evaporator.
4. Back pressure provided by the suction throttling valve may be varied according to altitude and
   a. location of the device in the system.
   b. design of the evaporator.
   c. Answers a and b are both correct.
   d. Neither answer a nor b is correct.
5. Currently no longer in use on suction throttling valves is
   a. a cable control to the suction throttling valve.
   b. an auxiliary diaphragm on the end of the valve.
   c. Answers a and b are both correct.
   d. Neither answer a nor b is correct.
6. On the POA-type suction throttling valve, a
   a. piston moves to control a bronze bellows.
   b. pilot needle moves to control a bellows, which contracts or expands against a piston valve.
   c. bellows contracts or expands to control a pilot needle, which controls a piston valve.
7. The POA valve is
   a. adjustable by turning a threaded nut on the outside of the valve.
   b. adjustable by disassembly and installing or removing spacers.
   c. not adjustable.
8. The chief difference between the suction throttling valve and an evaporator pressure regulator is
   a. location in the system.
   b. the evaporator pressure regulator does not have a bronze bellows.
   c. the evaporator pressure regulator controls at much higher pressure.
9. When a thermostatic expansion valve and a POA valve are in the Valves-in-Receiver or a combination valve assembly,
   a. both are in the high-pressure side of the system.
   b. both are in the low-pressure side of the system.
   c. Neither answer a nor b is correct.
10. A difference between the evaporator pressure regulator and the evaporator temperature regulator is

a. location.
b. control of the evaporator temperature regulator by a remote thermostatic switch.
c. control of the evaporator temperature regulator by an external capillary tube and bulb.

HANDS ON

1. Locate a suction throttling valve on a system so equipped and identify the external oil bleed line if used.

6

Protecting the Air Conditioning and Engine

Every mechanical system is designed to work within certain limits. If it is forced to work above or below them, the system may operate inefficiently or fail prematurely. Air conditioning and the engine that powers it are no exceptions. As a result, protective devices are used.

Air Conditioning Protection

Ambient Switch

The air conditioning has a switch that opens to prevent current from reaching the magnetic clutch if ambient air temperatures are very low (typically below 40°F or 4°C). You may have heard that the air conditioner should be turned on during the winter to circulate the Refrigerant 12 and the oil droplets in it so as to lubricate the compressor seals. This is partly true, but if the ambient temperature is below 40°F, attempting to operate the compressor could result in damage before the oil could circulate and lubricate it. In fact, the safest procedure is not to operate the air conditioning in winter, although on balance, a few minutes of operation on a "winter thaw" day, when ambient temperatures are in the forties (above 4°C) should be helpful to the compressor. On many systems (including General Motors), the dashboard control is wired to activate the air conditioning compressor for windshield demisting whenever the dash lever is on defrost. With the ambient switch in the circuit, however, the compressor comes on only when ambient temperature is in the forties (above 4°C).

The ambient switch is particularly important on cars in which the heater and air conditioner are automatically controlled (the system called automatic temperature control) to regulate temperature to a level preset by the driver. With this system, there are situations in which the air conditioner could otherwise automatically come on, even in cold weather.

Low-Pressure Protection

Previously, you learned about the pressure-temperature relationship of Refrigerant 12. Clearly, if the system contained a pressure-sensitive switch (Fig. 6-1) designed to deny current to the compressor clutch if Refrigerant 12 had leaked out of the system, that switch also could protect if ambient temperatures were very low. The switch merely would have to be calibrated for about 35 psi (241 kPa). If pressure were lower than that because of Refrigerant 12 leakage, the switch would open and deny current to the compressor clutch. If there were no leakage, but ambient temperatures were below 38°F (3°C), the Refrigerant 12 pressure also would drop to the control point for the switch. One switch would serve two purposes. Such a switch is used and is called an ambient-low pressure switch.

You should understand that it is not just the loss of Refrigerant 12 that poses a danger to the system. Rather, when a lot of Refrigerant 12 has leaked out, it is possible that it has carried out a lot of oil with it. If this has happened, the compressor could be damaged if operated with inadequate lubrication. Also, a moderate amount of refrigerant is necessary to circulate the oil.

Thermal Limiter

Another type of low-pressure protection that has been used (on some General Motors cars) is the *superheat switch and thermal limiter*. This arrangement, which has been superseded by the pressure-sensitive switch previously described, operated this way:

The superheat switch, located close to the compressor inlet port, is a temperature-sensitive switch. Superheat is a temperature increase without a corresponding rise in pressure. In this case, when refrigerant is lost, the pressure drops and the remaining refrigerant superheats in the evaporator. When the switch senses this increased temperature and low pressure it closes, completing an electrical ground (see Chapter 3).

The circuit also includes a part called the thermal limiter, which contains a fuse that is in series with the air conditioning dashboard control (and an ambient temperature protection switch if used) and the compressor's clutch coil. The normal current flow is through the air conditioning and ambient switches, then through the fuse in the thermal limiter, and finally to the magnetic clutch (see Fig. 6-2).

When the superheat switch closes to provide an electrical ground, it completes a second circuit through the thermal limiter. This second circuit is through a tiny electric heater in the limiter, and when the heater is

Air Conditioning Protection

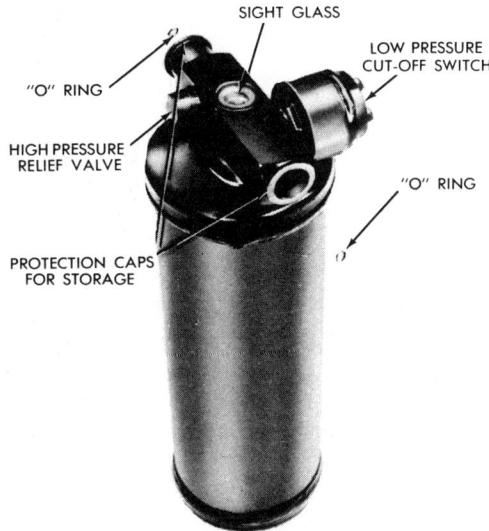

Figure 6-1 This is a common receiver-dryer. Note the valve and switch threaded into it. This switch, wired into the compressor clutch circuit, opens to break the circuit and stop the system if Refrigerant 12 pressures are too low. The valve is called the high-pressure cutout; it opens to relieve high pressure, then resets. (Courtesy Chrysler Corp.)

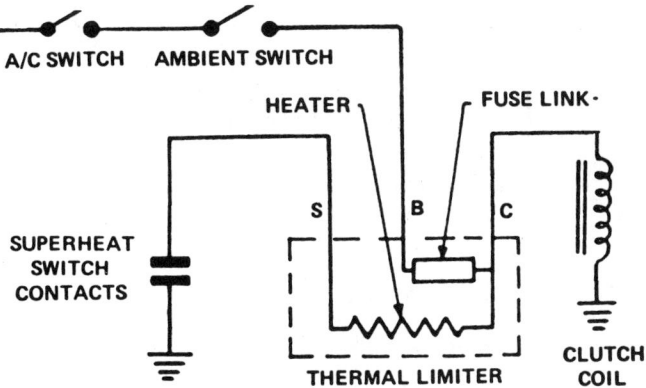

Figure 6-2 This is a typical circuit with a thermal limiter and ambient temperature switch. When the dashboard air conditioning switch is closed, current flows through the ambient switch if it also is closed, then into the thermal limiter. If the superheat switch is open, the current flow is only through the fuse link to the compressor clutch coil. If Refrigerant 12 pressure is very low, the superheat switch contacts close, completing a second circuit through the heater. The heater melts the fuse link and the current flow to the compressor clutch coil is stopped.

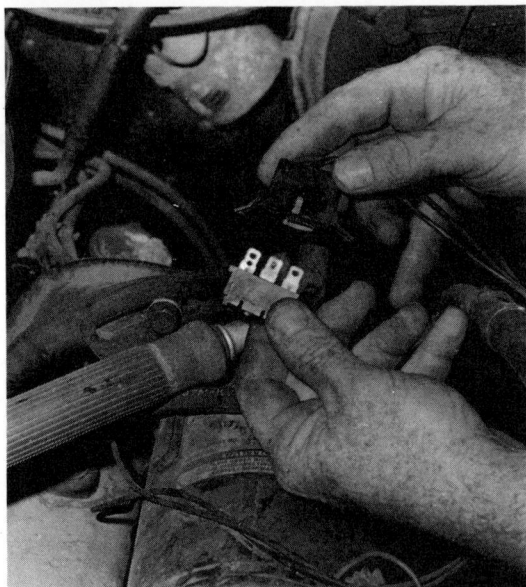

Figure 6-3 If the thermal limiter blows, it can be replaced, like a fuse, simply by removing it from its holder and installing the new one. Although the limiter can blow because of an abnormal underhood heat condition, the Refrigerant 12 pressure in the system should be checked before the car is returned to service.

energized, the fuse soon melts. This interrupts the circuit and the compressor cannot operate. The thermal limiter is an easily replaced part, much like any fuse (Fig. 6-3). However, it also has been a problem part, for it fails if placed in too hot a location, and, in practice, what the engineer who positioned it thought was a cool spot often was not. As a result, thermal limiters would blow even without a major refrigerant loss.

The superheat switch and thermal limiter were first installed on late-1971 model GM cars and were used on all models but Chevrolet Corvette, Vega, and Chevette through 1976. In 1977–1978, the arrangement was used only on Oldsmobile Toronado and Cadillac Eldorado, as GM began a changeover to a new air conditioning system, described in Chapter 7.

High-Pressure Relief Valve

If Refrigerant 12 pressures build up to too high a level, they can force leaks and cause other damage. Therefore, the typical system has a spring-loaded pressure relief valve threaded into the compressor or a high-pressure line. This valve is set for somewhere between 350 and 550 psi (2413 to 3792 kPa), depending on the system; it is forced open and allows refrigerant to escape until the pressure drops to within an acceptable range. Then the valve automatically closes (see Fig. 6-3). The causes of excessively high pressure and the cures are covered in Chapter 12.

Figure 6-4 Although this part resembles a receiver-dryer, it is an accumulator and is installed on the low-pressure (suction) side of the system with some Ford compressors to prevent the possibility of liquid reaching the compressor and causing damage to the valves.

Accumulator or Suction Accumulator

The accumulator (Fig. 6-4) is a cylindrical can that resembles the receiver-dryer, but it is installed on the low-pressure (suction) side of the system on some Ford products. The accumulator separates and holds liquid, and because it is on the low-pressure side, it is positive protection against any liquid from reaching the compressor, even if the air conditioning system's control valves malfunction.

Most compressors can tolerate a fair amount of liquid Refrigerant 12 before the attempt to compress liquid (which is incompressible) causes damage. The York compressor on whose systems the accumulator has been installed, was considered in need of the antiliquid protection the accumulator afforded.

Note: The accumulator, also called a suction accumulator, is not a replacement for the receiver-dryer on Ford products with suction throttling valves. It is an addition. As you will learn in Chapter 7, there are other forms of air conditioning (without suction throttling valves or their equivalent) that have an accumulator on the low-pressure side, but it is used instead of the receiver-dryer. Do not become confused.

Muffler

Also, do not confuse the accumulator with the muffler, a small cylindrical can installed to reduce compressor noises. The muffler is often found on the compressor outlet line and occasionally on the inlet line, too.

Engine Protection

Time-Temperature Delay Relay

This device prevents air conditioner operation (including blower operation in some cases) when coolant temperatures are very high (typically 260°F or 127°C, or above). It also contains a circuit that delays the start of the air conditioning compressor for about half a minute when the engine first is started to permit engine operation to stabilize.

Acceleration Cutout Switch

This is a switch designed to break the circuit to the compressor clutch when the car is accelerated hard. In most original equipment installations, the switch is operated by linkage or a cable from the gas pedal, so when the gas pedal is floored, the switch opens and the air conditioning cuts out. This eliminates the power draw of the air conditioning compressor at a time when all the engine power is needed for acceleration. On small engines, which have limited performance, the cutout switch is used almost universally. It usually is located at the carburetor or fuel injection throttle body.

Many motorists have installed another type of acceleration cutout switch, one that is operated by engine vacuum (Fig. 6-5). When engine vacuum is in a certain range, the switch is closed and current flows to the compressor clutch. During heavy acceleration, engine vacuum drops, and a spring pushes on a flexible diaphragm to open the switch and break the circuit to the compressor clutch. When acceleration is reduced and vacuum builds up, it moves the diaphragm to close the switch and again complete the circuit to the clutch. This second type is designed to cut out the clutch more often than the original equipment type and in some installations eliminates the air conditioning at idle. As a result, this type is normally installed to automatically reduce air conditioning operation to improve fuel economy.

Figure 6-5 This vacuum-operated switch, wired into the compressor clutch circuit, breaks the circuit to the clutch to turn off the air conditioning whenever the car is accelerated sharply. It is installed as an add-on device to improve acceleration and fuel economy on any engine.

QUESTIONS

1. The ambient switch
   a. opens if ambient temperatures are high.
   b. closes if ambient temperatures are low.
   c. opens if ambient temperatures are low.
2. The ambient switch also
   a. opens a relief valve to allow the system to discharge into the atmosphere to relieve high pressures.
   b. opens to protect the system against low pressure.
   c. closes to protect the system against very high or very low pressures.
3. The thermal limiter is a fuse that blows if a switch at the compressor inlet senses
   a. very low pressure and high temperature.
   b. very high temperature and high pressure.
   c. very low temperature.
   d. very high pressure.

4. A low-side device called an accumulator is used to
   a. protect the compressor.
   b. hold extra refrigerant for use on hot days.
   c. protect the evaporator from excessive superheat.
5. A time-temperature delay relay may shut off the air conditioning when
   a. passenger compartment temperatures drop too low.
   b. engine coolant temperature is very high.
   c. the exterior of the evaporator coils ices up.

HANDS ON

1. Locate an ambient-low pressure switch on a system so equipped. Remove the wiring connector to simulate an open switch and confirm that the system does not work.
2. Connect a jumper wire across the terminals of the ambient-low pressure switch's wiring connector to bypass the switch. Turn on the system and it should work.

7
Cycling Clutch Systems

What we call a "conventional" system, with its receiver-dryer, suction throttling valve, and expansion valve, is actually not the system that today represents the greatest percentage of air conditioning production. The most widely-produced system today is called *cycling clutch orifice tube*, or CCOT (see Fig. 7-1).

The cycling clutch is the clutch on the compressor. In the conventional air conditioning system, the clutch is energized whenever you turn the dashboard control to maximum, high, normal, or some other air-conditioning-on position. It stays energized until you move the control to the off position. This is a well-proved approach, capable of providing very precise operation. However, it means the compressor is always drawing power, even when the suction throttling valve or evaporator pressure regulator is restricting refrigerant flow to prevent evaporator freeze-up. The power draw is less than when the system is in full operation (suction throttling valve or evaporator pressure regulator open), but it still is considerable.

Instead of a suction throttling valve (or any of the variations), we can prevent evaporator freeze-up another way by simply deactivating the compressor, by shutting off current to the clutch. The effect of chopping current to the clutch is that the flow of Refrigerant 12 is virtually halted; the smaller amount in the evaporator therefore absorbs more heat and its temperature rises, and the freeze-up danger is eliminated.

If the compressor clutch is deactivated by breaking the current flow to the clutch only for very brief periods, the driver and passengers will never notice it, and the cycling (versus continuous operation) will reduce compressor power draw and so improve fuel economy. To ensure that the clutch is deactivated in a rational way, the clutch cycling is controlled by a special type of switch.

The original type of switch, still in some use, is a thermostatic type. It resembles the thermostatic expansion valve in that it has a capillary tube

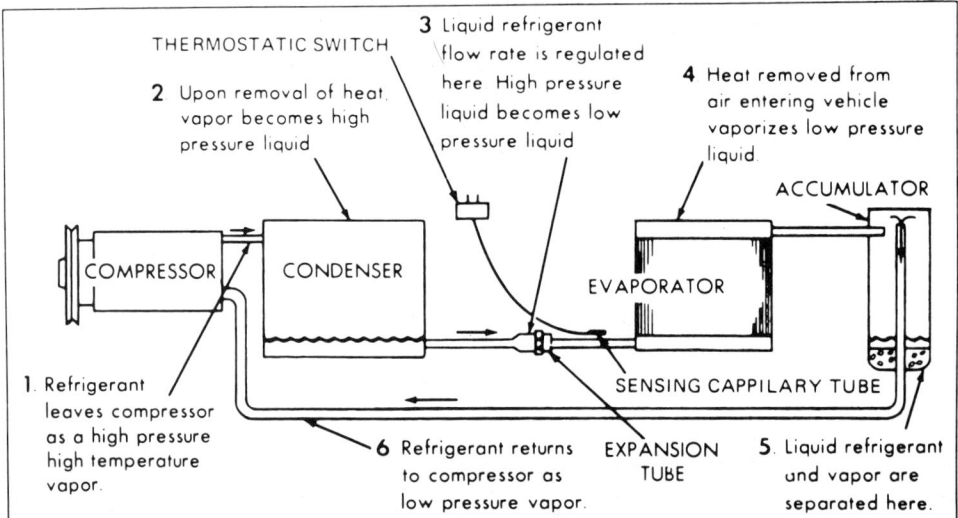

Figure 7-1 Thermostatic-type cycling clutch switch has capillary tube filled with gas and clamped to evaporator inlet. As long as the temperature the capillary senses is above a control point, the switch remains closed and current flows to the compressor clutch. If Refrigerant 12 temperature drops to the point where evaporator freeze-up could occur, the gas inside the capillary contracts and relieves pressure on the diaphragm-type electric switch. A spring then moves the diaphragm to open the switch, breaking the circuit to the compressor clutch. The switch's capillary also may be positioned to sense temperature somewhere around the middle of the evaporator, in which case the switch is calibrated differently. (Courtesy General Motors Corp.)

filled with refrigerant, and it is clamped to the evaporator inlet line, where it can sense and react to evaporator temperature.

When the evaporator temperature drops, the refrigerant in the capillary tube contracts and relieves pressure on a spring-loaded diaphragm. The spring moves the diaphragm and opens a set of switch contacts, breaking the electrical circuit to the compressor clutch (see Fig. 7-1). When evaporator temperature rises, the refrigerant gas expands and exerts pressure on the diaphragm, closing the switch and completing the circuit to the compressor clutch.

Pressure Switch

The switch presently in widest use is the pressure switch (Fig. 7-2). As you learned in Chapter 2, the relationship between the temperature and pressure of Refrigerant 12 is always the same (except in a superheat situation). Therefore, if evaporator pressure is at a certain number, the evaporator

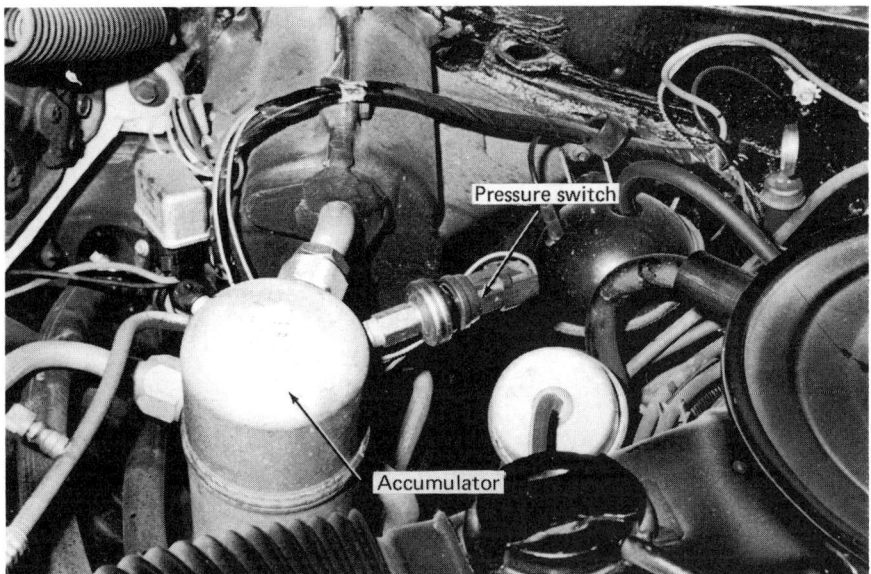

Figure 7-2 This pressure-sensitive switch, threaded into a part called the accumulator, senses low-side (suction) pressure and reacts accordingly on a diaphragm. If accumulator pressure, which is evaporator outlet pressure, is below the control point, the diaphragm switch opens and breaks the circuit to the compressor clutch. When accumulator pressure is above the control point, there is no danger of freeze-up on the evaporator coils, and the switch closes to turn on the air conditioning once more.

temperature can be determined by looking at the temperature-pressure chart (Fig. 2-8). A switch that opens to stop the flow of current to the compressor clutch when evaporator pressure is, for example, 31 psi (214 kPa) is doing the same job as a thermostatic switch that is set to open at 33°F (1°C).

The pressure switch is threaded into the low-pressure side, into a part (explained later) called the accumulator, where it senses low-side pressures. The fact that the pressure and thermostatic switches do their sensing in different locations on the low-pressure side is not significant. They are calibrated to do the job in the locations chosen.

The pressure switch offers the advantage of manufacturing economy, because it also performs the function of an ambient-low pressure switch. To understand how it does this, think of the pressure-temperature relationship and the function of the two switches. The ambient-low pressure switch can be designed to break the circuit to the compressor clutch whenever pressure drops below a certain number, let's say about 46 psi (310 kPa). This protects the system by preventing it from operating if there is a major loss of refrigerant. This pressure control also prevents the system from operating at very low temperature, and if you check the pressure-temperature chart, you will see the switch is open (preventing current flow) at ambient temperatures below 50°F (10°C).

The pressure-type cycling clutch switch also is open at low temperature and pressures to prevent evaporator freeze-up, so it can easily be calibrated to double as an ambient low pressure switch. As it is designed, the pressure-type cycling clutch switch is open at pressures below about 46 psi (310 kPa) when the system is off and system pressures are equalized (the same on both the high and low sides of the system). When the system is turned on, the switch will close at 46 psi (310 kPa) and not open until the low-side pressures are pumped down to about 25 psi (172 kPa).

Normally, it would seem that a switch that operates by sensing pressure in the system would be a problem to replace, that it would be necessary to discharge the system of refrigerant gas when removing the old switch and installing a new one. The pressure switch, however, is threaded onto a fitting that contains a Schrader valve, basically the same as the Schrader valve used in a tire (and, as you will learn, elsewhere in the air conditioning system of most cars). The Schrader valve has a spring-loaded pin that opens when depressed and springs closed when released. As the pressure switch is unthreaded from its fitting, the pin springs close, preventing loss of Refrigerant 12. When the new switch is threaded in, it depresses the valve. Any refrigerant loss during either operation is insignificant.

Orifice Tube

Instead of a thermostatic expansion valve, the CCOT system uses an orifice tube, also called an *expansion tube*. An orifice is an opening, and the orifice tube is nothing more than a tube with a specific size of opening, with a filtering screen (see Fig. 7-3). Because the opening is fixed, that is, it cannot be changed to meet changes in operating conditions, as with the thermostatic expansion valve, it must be sized for maximum refrigerant flow under most conditions.

Normally then, the cycling clutch switch simply turns off the system to stop the flow if it is excessive. As a practical matter, however, under some operating conditions, the orifice can permit more refrigerant to flow than can be completely vaporized. Some of this refrigerant, therefore, leaves the evaporator still as a liquid. If the cycling clutch switch calibration is such that the switch is closed somewhat longer than it should be, under some conditions the amount of liquid refrigerant would increase. Liquids cannot be compressed. The modern compressor will handle a certain amount of liquid without damage, but there is no sense taking a chance. As a result, the receiver-dryer is not used, and instead the system has a similar part called the accumulator (see Figs. 7-1 and 7-4).

Figure 7-3 (*Above*) This plastic filtering screen is the heart of the orifice tube system, in which a fixed opening in the tubing replaces the expansion valve.

Figure 7-4 (*Right*) This look at the accumulator shows how it resembles the receiver-dryer. However, it is located on the low side (suction) of the system, and rather than hold a supply of liquid for high-demand operation, it removes droplets of liquid from the Refrigerant 12 before they could get to the compressor, where they might cause damage.

Accumulator

The accumulator looks like a receiver-dryer; it contains a drying agent (desiccant) and a filtering screen, and it stores excess Refrigerant 12 (the drops that do not vaporize in the evaporator). However, it is located between the evaporator outlet and the compressor, which is the low-pressure side of the system, compared with the high-pressure-side location for the receiver-dryer.

There also is a slight difference in function. Whereas the receiver-dryer holds the extra refrigerant to assure a solid column of fluid for high-demand operation, the accumulator gives up any liquid that will vaporize on the low-pressure side.

The accumulator also has an oil bleed passage, so oil that would otherwise be trapped in the accumulator is allowed to bleed out to the line that carries the vapor to the compressor inlet (see Fig. 7-5). The use of an accumulator also is helpful in recharging a system with Refrigerant 12, a subject covered in Chapter 11.

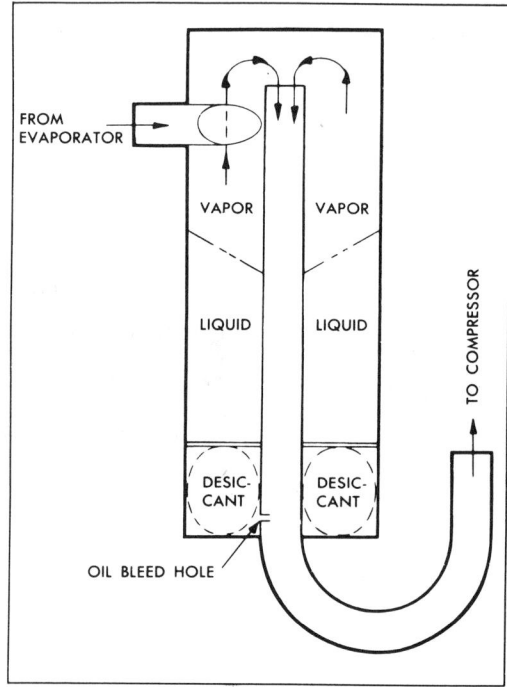

Figure 7-5 This schematic view of the accumulator shows the oil bleed, which permits oil that otherwise could be trapped in the accumulator to flow to the vapor line and be carried with the vapor to the compressor. (Courtesy General Motors Corp.)

Note: Some Ford products with conventional systems (suction throttling valves and receiver-dryers) also have an accumulator. Its purpose is to provide extra protection against liquid getting to the compressor (see Fig 6-4).

Comparison of CCOT and Conventional Systems

A cycling clutch switch that operates within a range of more than 20 psi (138 kPa), with a fixed orifice to meter the Refrigerant 12, cannot be expected to function as precisely as a conventional system with its expansion valve and suction throttling valve. The performance of a CCOT system, therefore, is not quite as good as a conventional system, but on today's smaller cars, it does an acceptable job and helps provide better fuel economy when the air conditioning is on.

Other Cycling Clutch Systems

CCOT is not the only type of cycling clutch system. In fact, the cycling clutch arrangement has been around for many years. It is the only arrangement currently used for add-on air conditioners.

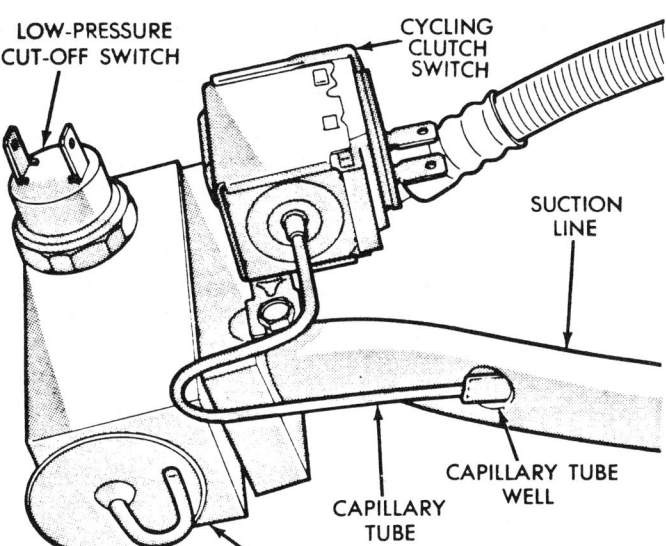

Figure 7-6 The H-type expansion valve in this design is built into a block that also holds the thermostatic-type clutch cycling switch and a low-pressure cutout switch to prevent the system from operating when a lot of Refrigerant 12 has leaked out or ambient temperatures are very low. Note that the capillary tube goes into a well in the low side (suction) line. The well is filled with a special thermal grease. (Courtesy Chrysler Corp.)

In one popular alternative approach, the cycling clutch switch is used on a system with a thermostatic expansion valve and a receiver-dryer on the high-pressure side of the system. This design has the gas-saving advantages of the cycling clutch system and adds some precision by the use of the thermostatic expansion valve. However, the use of the expansion valve means the system is not quite as simple as CCOT.

In one original-equipment variation of the cycling clutch system, both high- and low-pressure lines pass through a junction block just outside the evaporator (see Fig. 7-6). The block contains an H-type expansion valve (the letter H formed by the valve crossing between evaporator inlet and outlet lines). Internal passages in the junction block permit the expansion valve to sense evaporator outlet temperatures, much like the combination valve assembly (expansion valve and suction throttling valve) explained in Chapter 4.

The expansion valve junction block also holds a low-pressure cutoff switch to protect the compressor and a thermostatic-type cycling clutch switch (see Fig. 7-6). Unlike most other cycling clutch switches of this type, the capillary tube is not clamped. Rather it fits into a well (in the evaporator outlet line) filled with a special thermal grease that improves the ability of the capillary tube to sense temperature.

On some systems, particularly add ons, the cycling clutch switch has a control knob that permits the driver to increase or decrease the cycling for reduced or greater cooling effect. This arrangement is popular on add-ons because there is no other way to control outlet air temperature, whereas on factory installations some of the air may be run through the heater core to be warmed, an arrangement called *reheat,* which is explained in Chapter 8.

Also on some installations, the cycling clutch capillary tube end is installed in the evaporator between the tubing and fins for greater sensitivity, rather than clamped to a line just outside the evaporator. In American Motors cars and many add-on systems, the capillary tube passes between the evaporator coils and fins.

QUESTIONS

1. Mechanic A says an advantage of the cycling clutch system over a suction throttling valve type is less power used. Mechanic B says the cycling clutch system is more precise. Who is right?
    a. Mechanic A.
    b. Mechanic B.
    c. Both.
    d. Neither.
2. The major advantage of the pressure-type cycling clutch switch over the thermostatic type is
    a. greater precision.
    b. the pressure type also serves as an ambient-low pressure switch.
    c. the pressure type also serves as a high-pressure cutout switch.
    d. Answers a, b, and c are all correct.
3. The orifice tube
    a. expands and contracts with temperature changes.
    b. is installed at the evaporator outlet.
    c. replaces the expansion valve.
    d. Answers a, b, and c are all correct.
    e. Answers b and c are both correct.
4. The accumulator is used on
    a. all cycling clutch systems.
    b. cycling clutch systems with a thermostatic expansion valve only.
    c. cycling clutch systems with a receiver-dryer.
    d. none of the above.
5. Mechanic A says the accumulator bleed hole is intended to allow oil to pass through to the compressor. Mechanic B says it permits bleeding of excessively superheated vapor back to the evaporator. Who is right?

Questions

      a. Mechanic A.
      b. Mechanic B.
      c. Both.
      d. Neither.
6. An H-type valve is a
      a. thermostatic expansion valve in a junction block at the evaporator.
      b. relief valve in the accumulator.
      c. component of the pressure-type cycling clutch switch.

HANDS ON

1. Locate the part of the liquid line tubing in which the orifice tube is installed.
2. Identify an accumulator.
3. Locate a cycling clutch pressure-type switch on a system so equipped.
4. Locate a cycling clutch thermostatic switch on a system so equipped, and check the tightness of the switch's capillary tube clamp.
5. On a working system, remove the electrical connector from the cycling clutch switch and you should see that the system does not work. Connect a jumper wire across the switch's connector to bypass the switch; now you should see the system work.

8

Moving Cold Air

The components that chill the air surrounding the evaporator are collectively called the *refrigeration system*. They are only half of the system; once the air is chilled, the *distribution system*, the blower (fan) and a duct system with flap doors controlled by cables and engine vacuum, distributes the cold air.

Although each line of cars has a somewhat different duct configuration, the basic principles are the same. It is important that you understand them, for a failure of the distribution system can be just as significant as a failure of the refrigeration system. Consider some common problems with the distribution system:

* The cold air just "oozes" out, thus failing to provide any real cooling to the front seat and none to the rear. Possible reasons: the flap doors are closed or the blower does not work.
* The system blows out only warm air. Possible reason: the cold air is passing through the heater core, which is in the same duct, because a flap that should be closed is not. Or perhaps the flow of water and antifreeze through the heater should have been stopped, but there is a malfunction in the water control valve.

Vacuum and Vacuum Devices

Because so many of the controls in the air distribution system are vacuum controlled, you should understand the source of the vacuum and how it is used to operate the controls. The vacuum comes from the engine. As a piston moves down in a cylinder, it vacates a space in that cylinder, creating a vacuum (see Fig. 8-1). When an intake valve opens, a vacuum also develops in the intake manifold. When the gas pedal is depressed, opening the throttle, a mix of air and fuel rushes in from the carburetor to fill the vacuum. The rapid movement of the pistons and the fact that the throttle is rarely wide open mean that some vacuum almost always exists in the in-

Vacuum Diaphragms

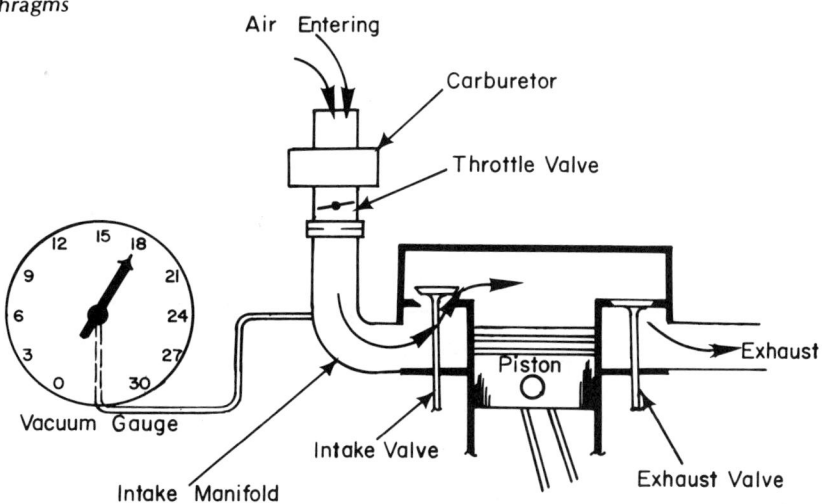

Figure 8-1 The downward movement of the pistons with the intake valves open creates a vacuum in the engine's intake manifold. When the throttle plate is fully closed, the vacuum (as measured on a vacuum gauge) is at its greatest. As the throttle plate is opened, air rushes in and fills some of the manifold, reducing the intensity of the vacuum. At wide open throttle, enough air rushes in to fill the space that there may be little or no vacuum.

take manifold (or on fuel injection systems, in the intake air distributor). For those few occasions when engine vacuum is insufficient (basically wide open throttle), small cannisters serve as reserve tanks to provide vacuum to keep the controls functioning.

The vacuum is usually tapped from the intake manifold, intake air distributor, or the base of the carburetor (which bolts to the intake manifold) by a hose, called a *supply hose*. With specially shaped fittings, many hoses can be connected to a single supply hose.

Vacuum provides power to assist the brakes, to operate many air pollution controls, and, your primary interest, to operate many of the controls in the heating and air conditioning systems.

Note: Diesels operate without a throttle plate and so air fills the vacuum in the intake manifold as soon as it is created. Because there is never any significant amount of engine vacuum, an engine-driven vacuum pump is used to produce the vacuum needed for accessories. On some 1981 General Motors cars made for high fuel economy, engine vacuum is limited and a vacuum pump also may be used with a gasoline engine.

Vacuum Diaphragms

The vacuum diaphragm unit is the most common way engine vacuum is used to operate various devices. It typically consists of a globe-shaped cannister with a flexible fabric (or rubberlike sheet) in the center to divide

102 Moving Cold Air

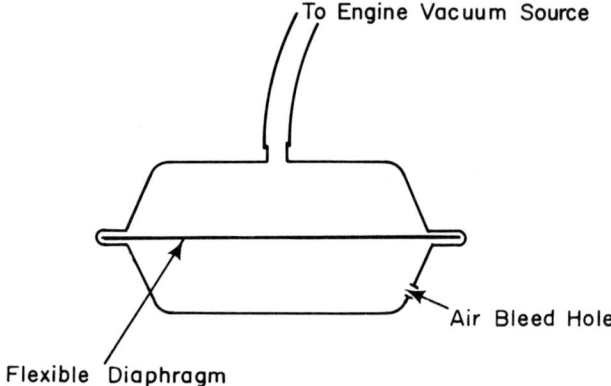

Figure 8-2 Diaphragm divides can into two chambers, one vented to the atmosphere, the other connected to a source of engine vacuum.

the can into two chambers (see Fig. 8-2). One chamber is vented to the atmosphere; the other has a neck for a hose from a source of engine vacuum.

When vacuum is applied to one chamber, the air pressure in that chamber is being lowered to below atmospheric pressure, and the atmospheric pressure on the other side of the chamber is stronger and therefore exerts a push against the diaphragm (see Fig. 8-3). Normally, however, we simply think of vacuum as "sucking" on the diaphragm and drawing it in the direction of the vacuum source. One reason is our familiarity with the drinking straw. When we suck on the end of a straw in a glass of liquid, we lower the pressure inside. As a result, the stronger atmospheric pressure on the liquid forces some of it up the straw.

To convert the vacuum to mechanical work, the diaphragm unit is equipped with a spring and a rod, called a *link*. The link is attached to the

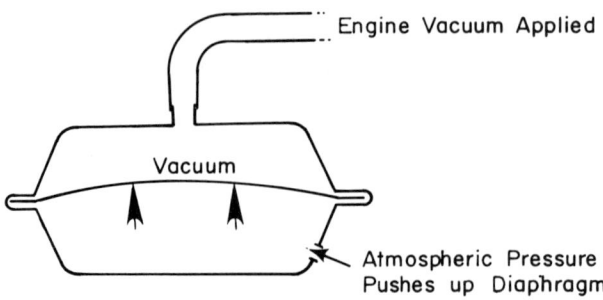

Figure 8-3 When vacuum is applied to one chamber, atmospheric pressure from other side pushes on diaphragm.

Vacuum Diaphragms

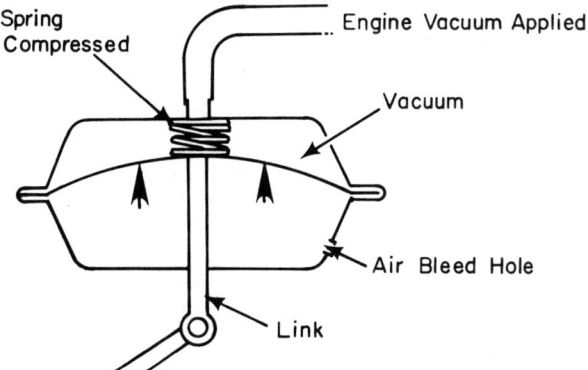

Figure 8-4 Link is attached to diaphragm so the diaphragm movement can be turned into useful work outside the can. Notice spring in vacuum chamber. When vacuum is stopped, spring expands to return diaphragm to center position. Air gradually gets into vacuum chamber, often through tiny opening in chamber.

diaphragm so that, when the diaphragm is drawn by vacuum, the link moves in that direction too. The spring may be placed anywhere, depending on how it is connected. Its function is to return the diaphragm (and the link) to the previous position when the vacuum is shut off. It may be positioned between diaphragm and the end of the vacuum chamber, in which case it will be squeezed when vacuum is applied and then will expand to its normal length (returning the link and diaphragm) when vacuum is released (see Fig. 8-4). Or the spring may be attached to the other side of the diaphragm and the opposite end of the atmospheric pressure chamber. When vacuum is applied, the diaphragm moves and pulls on the spring, extending it. When vacuum is released, the spring contracts to its normal length and pulls back the diaphragm (see Fig. 8-5). Or the spring

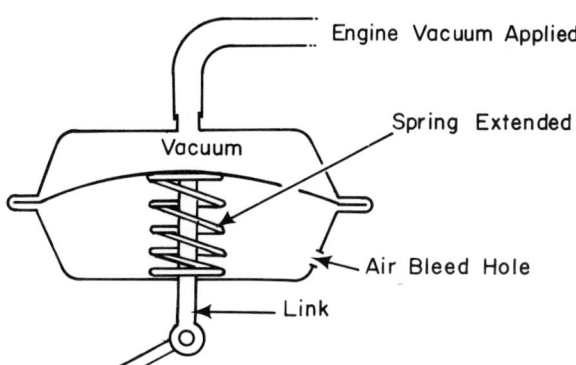

Figure 8-5 In this diaphragm unit, the spring is extended when vacuum is applied. When vacuum is released, the spring contracts and returns the diaphragm to center position.

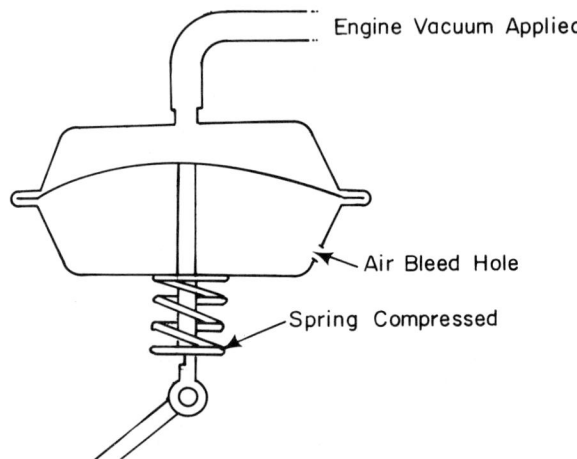

Figure 8-6 The spring in this design is externally mounted and attached to the link, so it contracts when vacuum is applied and expands when vacuum is stopped.

may be installed externally, attached to the end of the link and the diaphragm unit (see Fig. 8-6). In this case it will perform the same way as the spring in the vacuum chamber.

The design of the spring determines how the diaphragm unit performs. If the spring is very strong, it takes a lot of vacuum to flex the diaphragm. If it is very light, just a little vacuum will move it. In many cases, the spring is designed to permit a small amount of diaphragm and link movement when vacuum is light and a greater amount of movement as the amount of vacuum applied is increased. Vacuum diaphragm units also are called vacuum motors and vacuum actuators. The links they operate control flap doors and switches, among other parts.

Vacuum Reservoirs

When the car is being accelerated (open throttle), vacuum in the engine's intake manifold drops. In most cases, acceleration is a relatively brief action, so to maintain the operation of vacuum devices, only a small amount of vacuum is needed. It is supplied by reservoirs, cylindrical can-like or globe-shaped containers (see Fig. 8-7). Included in the lines to these reservoirs is a *check valve*, a little device containing a diaphragm. When engine vacuum drops, the diaphragm valve closes and prevents vacuum in the reservoir from being diluted and lowered by the lower vacuum in the intake manifold. The vacuum in the reservoir then is available to maintain the operation of the air conditioning system's vacuum diaphragm devices.

Figure 8-7 One type of vacuum reservoir.

The Duct System

All automobiles contain a system of ducts under the dashboard to distribute air to the passenger compartment. That air may be from the outside or recirculated from the passenger compartment. The basic structure is a fiberboard or plactic housing from which individual ducts emerge. One duct may go to the top of the engine compartment, just behind the hood, for fresh air. Others go to cooling registers, which are panels with adjustable louvers, much like those in the forced air heating system of the typical house. Still others lead to the front floor of the passenger compartment, where they discharge hot air in winter. Finally, others go to the top of the dashboard, where they release air to defrost the windshield or cause mist to evaporate.

The main housing contains both the evaporator from the air conditioning system and the heater core, which is explained in the following section. The housing also contains flap doors to control air flow. These flaps are moved by vacuum diaphragm units or cables operated by the dashboard controls, which are explained later in this chapter.

The typical duct system has at least four flap doors (see Fig. 8-8). One flap (usually vacuum controlled) determines the source of the air to be conditioned. If it is open, fresh outside air is admitted to the duct system. If it is closed, air is drawn from the passenger compartment. Although outside air is free of smoke and other passenger compartment odors, it may

106 Moving Cold Air

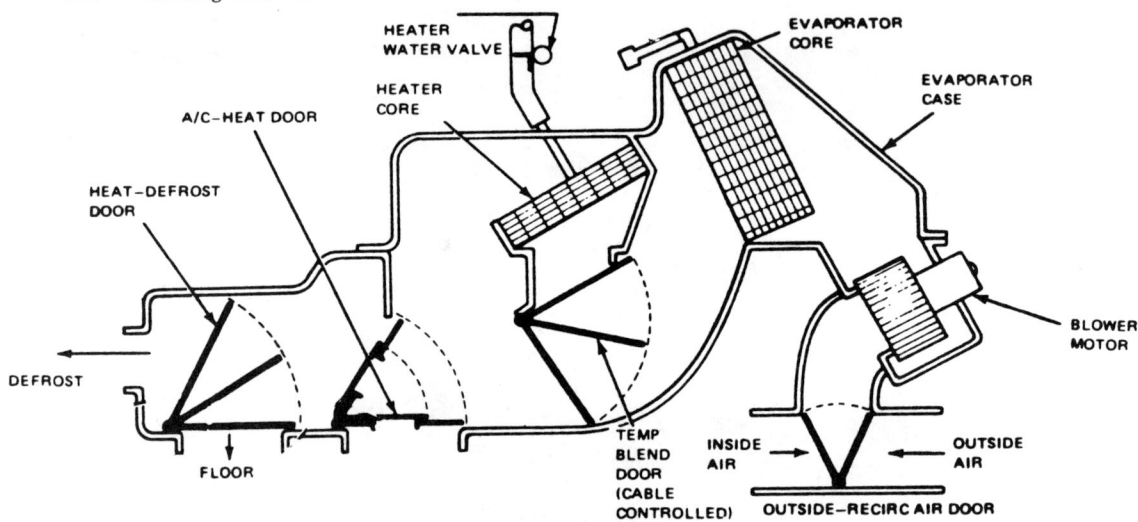

Figure 8-8 This diagram is of a duct housing with three vacuum-diaphragm-controlled flap doors and one door controlled by the dashboard temperature cable. The outside air door position determines if outside air is to be drawn in or if passenger compartment air is to be recirculated. The cable-controlled blend door determines how much of the air will flow through the heater core. The air conditioning and heat door determines if the air goes to the floor or toward the air conditioning registers (in this case it may assume a mid-position so air could go to both). The heat and defrost door determines if the air goes out the floor heater outlets or up through the defrost grilles. (Courtesy Ford Motor Co.)

be warmer in summer than the passenger compartment air. If maximum cooling is desired and the appropriate dashboard control is operated, the air conditioning uses only the passenger compartment air, sending it back through the evaporator for recooling over and over.

Next in the air circuit is a flap called a *blend* door. It is operated by a cable from a dashboard lever that has a range from cold to warm. In the cold position, the door assumes a position that directs the airflow from the evaporator past the heater in such a way that the air will not be warmed. As the lever is moved toward the warm position, the flap forces some of the air to go through the heater core, where it absorbs heat. The closer the door is to the extreme warm position, the more air that is forced through the heater.

Note: You should understand that after a period of operation, particularly when the engine (and therefore the compressor) is running at high speed, the air conditioner could overcool the passenger compartment. It may seem wasteful of the energy spent to cool the air, but the answer is to move the control lever toward warm, to warm up the air as much as desired. This is called *reheat*, and it is considered a desirable feature of factory-installed air conditioners, compared with add-on units. When you turn down the add-on air conditioner by turning the dashboard knob, all you are doing is changing the setting of a thermostatic-type cycling clutch switch, so the switch turns off the compressor clutch more frequently. Most people do not consider this as satisfactory as reheating, which permits very close control of the air temperature.

Next, the air is directed by a third flap (usually vacuum controlled). The flap is moved to a position that directs cold air toward the air conditioning registers. In winter, the heater is on, and the flap is pivoted to direct warm air toward the heater outlets at the floor. This air conditioning and heat flap also may be called a *mode door*, and in some designs may be designed so it can take positions that allow air flow from more than one set of registers. For example, it could permit cool air to flow from the central air conditioning registers and up to the defroster outlets.

Finally, there is a flap (usually vacuum controlled) that determines if air continues to the air conditioning registers, or goes up to the defroster outlets.

The duct system illustrated is just one design, and there are many others.

Engine Cooling System-Heater

The heater in factory air conditioning installations is in the same ductwork as the air conditioning evaporator, and both heater and air conditioning share the same blower motor. Therefore, you cannot ignore the operation of the heating system. In fact, as you will see later in this chapter in the discussion of automatic temperature control, the heater and air conditioning often are combined into a single system.

The heater is an air conditioning in reverse. The duct housing contains the heater core, a component that is basically a small radiator. Connected to the heater core are two hoses, an inlet hose that provides hot coolant from the engine and an outlet to the engine's water pump (see Fig. 8-9).

Hot coolant flows through the heater core where it transfers heat to the air in the duct housing surrounding the core, warming it. The blower forces this warmed air into the passenger compartment. Clearly, this warm air is not desirable at certain times, such as when the weather is warm. For this reason, the heater inlet hose usually contains a valve that can block off the coolant flow to the heater core at this time. Depending on the design of the valve, it may open or close when vacuum is supplied to its diaphragm. The engine is the source of the vacuum, but dashboard controls determine whether or not the vacuum flows to the valve's diaphragm (see Fig. 8-10). *Note:* Cable-controlled valves have occasionally been used. In the extreme cold position, the vacuum flow to the valve is blocked (or allowed to flow depending on design) so the valve is closed. In these cases, the valve is controlled by the dashboard temperature control lever.

It is also a practice to keep the valve open, permitting the circula-

108 Moving Cold Air

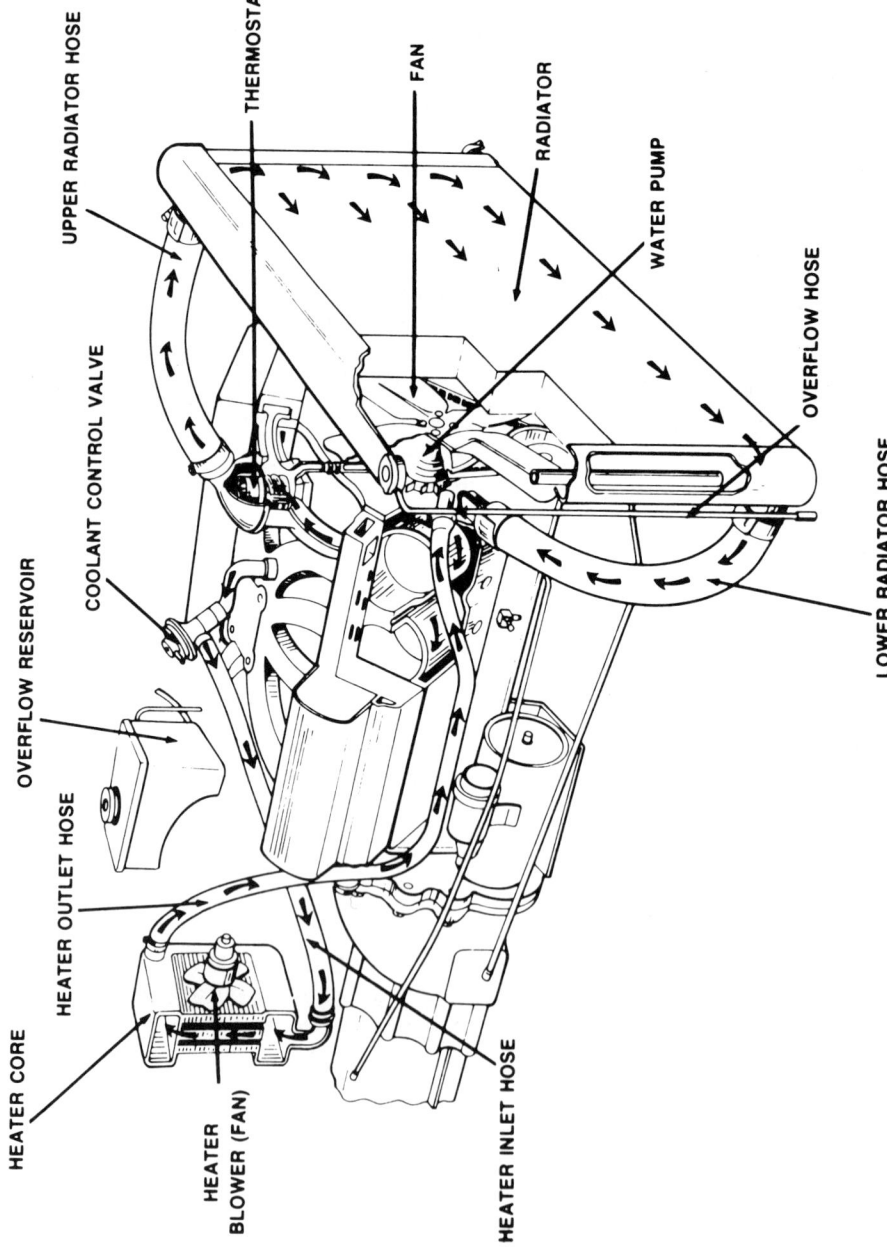

Figure 8-9 This drawing shows how the heating system works. Hot coolant flows through a hose from the engine into the heater core, basically a small radiator. It heats the air in the duct housing and the blower (fan) forces this warm air into the passenger compartment. The coolant continues from the heater core through a second hose into the water pump at the front of the engine. On most systems, a heater coolant control valve is in the hose from the engine, so the flow of hot coolant can be stopped when maximum cooling is desired. (Courtesy DuPont Co.)

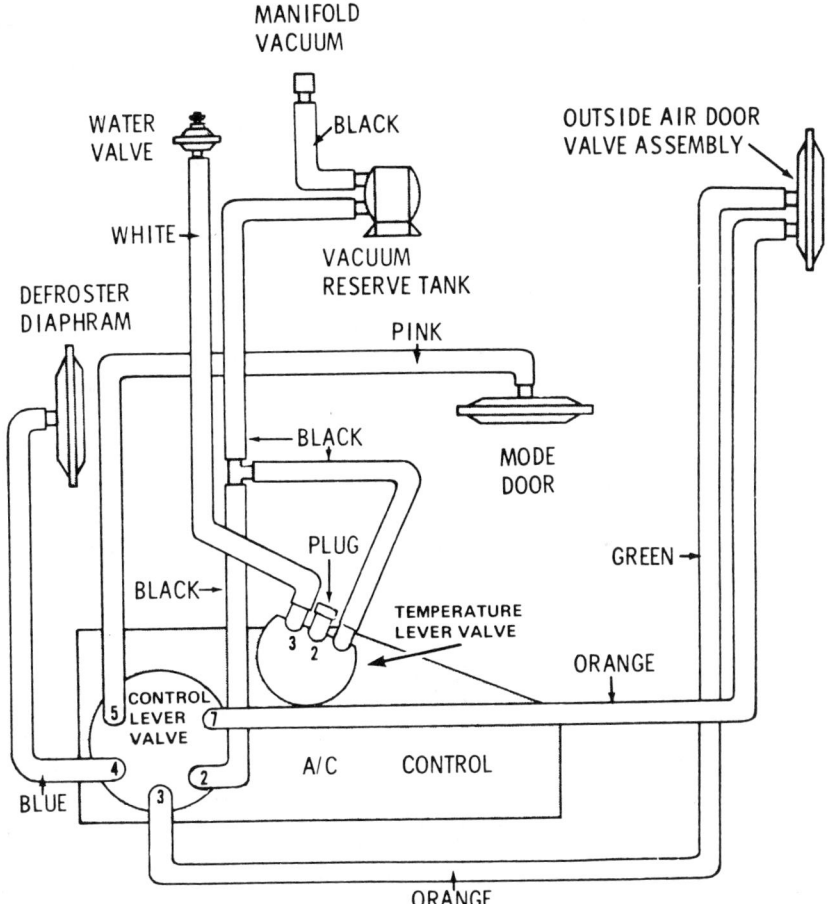

Figure 8-10 This illustration shows how the vacuum system is laid out on one car. Note that there is a valve operated by the temperature lever in the dashboard control, and when the lever is moved, the valve is opened or closed, permitting or denying manifold vacuum to the vacuum-operated water valve (also called heater coolant control valve). This is the same temperature lever that only operates the blend door in other systems. Also notice the control lever valve (also called a vacuum switch). If the vacuum switch is turned so that vacuum can flow from No. 2 (the manifold vacuum source) to No. 4, for example, the diaphragm will operate the defroster door. (Courtesy General Motors Corp.)

tion of hot coolant, any time the air conditioning is on, except (on most systems) when the maximum or high air conditioning position on the dashboard panel is selected by the driver. The ductwork is designed so only an insignificant amount of heat is absorbed from the hot coolant by the cold air. In some newer cars, in fact, there is no heater coolant control valve, and a special flap door is added to the duct housing to minimize heat transfer from the heater core to the air when the air conditioning is on.

Controlling the Flow

The system has a central panel that permits the driver to make basic decisions regarding its operation and the airflow (see Fig. 8-11). This central panel (on the dashboard) not only turns on the refrigeration system, but the blower fan, too, and it decides which flap doors should be in which position in accordance with the driver's selection. On most cars the driver makes the selection and any changes manually at the central panel. On some cars the driver merely picks an interior temperature on a degree wheel and an automatic system turns on the heater and/or air conditioning, mixes hot and cold air if necessary to maintain the selected temperature, and in most cases selects the appropriate blower speeds.

Let's look at each aspect of the control panel's operation. Because each car is somewhat different, the illustrations are based on a representative example. The control panel contains electrical controls, vacuum switches and circuits, and mechanical controls. Although the explanations are simplified, a basic understanding of the electrical circuit and the functions of the switch and the motor are necessary. See Chapter 3.

Electrical Controls

When the driver moves the dashboard control panel lever from OFF to MAX (or HIGH AC) or simply AC (fresh air flap open), many things happen. Let's begin by looking at a common arrangement of the electrical circuits.

One circuit is completed from the ignition switch (a close-by source of current) through a control panel switch to the low-pressure cutoff switch, through that closed switch, assuming refrigeration system pressure is normal, and ambient temperature is above a specified temperature, usually 40°F (4°C). The current flow then continues from that switch to the compressor clutch coil (see Fig. 8-12). It flows through the coil, creating an electromagnetic field that attracts the halves of the clutch. The clutch circuit is now complete and the belt-driven pulley turns the compressor.

On some cars there may be a time-temperature delay relay in the circuit between the ignition switch and the control panel switch. This relay, explained in Chapter 6, either passes or blocks current flow to the control panel (see Fig. 8-13).

If the system is equipped with a thermal limiter and superheat switch, also explained in Chapter 6, these parts are wired into the circuit from the dashboard controls to the clutch coil, just after the ambient switch.

Second Circuit

A second electrical circuit goes from the control panel to the blower motor. It may start in either of two places:

Controlling the Flow

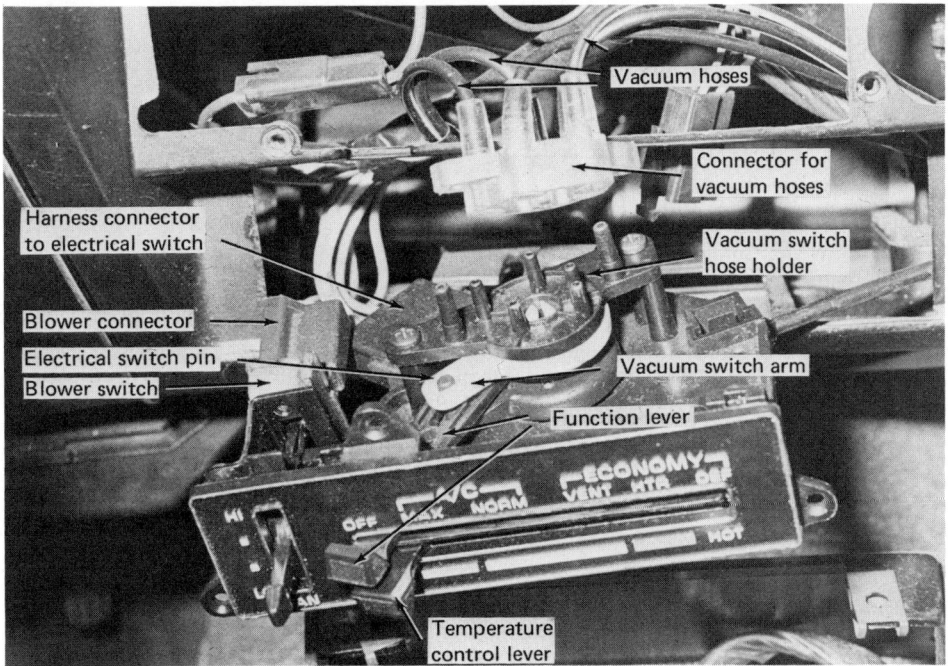

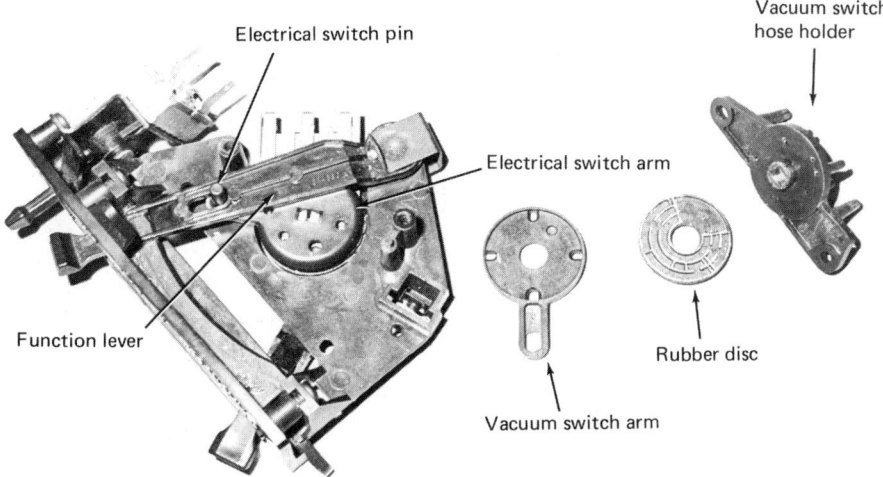

Figure 8-11 Here is a dashboard control switch, shown assembled in the top view, with the vacuum switch removed and disassembled in the lower view. You can see where the vacuum hoses fit on the necks in the top part of the vacuum switch. You also can see how the pin from the electrical switch fits through both the function lever and the vacuum switch arm, so that all electrical and vacuum devices go on or off as the situation dictated by the position of the function lever demands.

112   Moving Cold Air

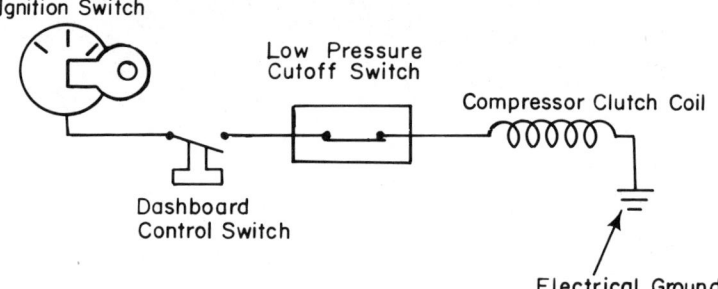

Figure 8-12 Simplified wiring schematic for compressor clutch. With ignition switch on, current can flow to dashboard control switch. If that switch, shown open, is moved to an air-conditioning-on position, current will flow through the switch to the low-pressure cutoff switch, shown closed, and through that to the compressor clutch coil. The coil is electrically grounded to complete the circuit.

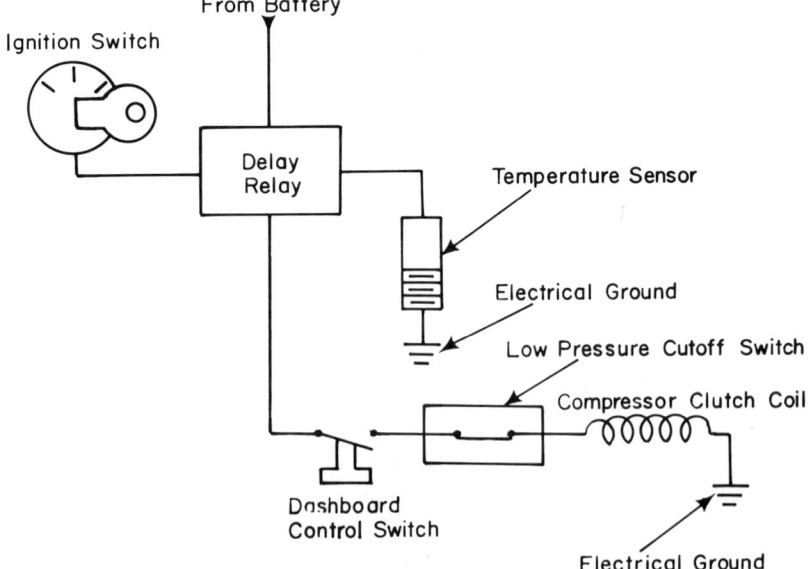

Figure 8-13 This circuit is the same as in Fig. 8-12, except that a time-temperature delay relay is included. The temperature sensor, threaded into the engine coolant jacket, provides an electrical ground for the relay only when coolant temperatures are in the normal range (under 260°F on most cars). If the sensor provides a ground, the relay closes and permits battery current to flow through to the dashboard control switch, and the circuit operation then is the same as in Fig. 8-12. If temperature is too high, the sensor opens and breaks the relay circuit.

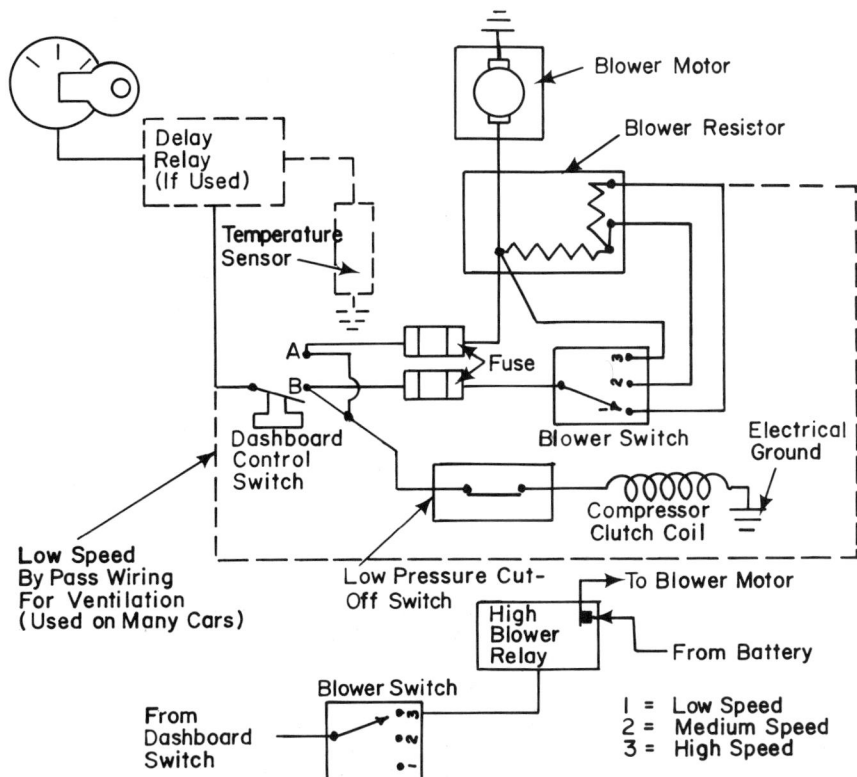

Figure 8-14 This circuit, also simplified, is similar to Figs. 8-12 and 8-13, except that the blower is included. If the dashboard control switch is moved into contact with A (typically MAX AC), note there is a complete circuit that bypasses the blower switch and resistor, and the blower will operate at high speed. Also note the bypass wiring from the ignition key (after the delay relay if used) to the low-speed terminal on the blower resistor. Used on many cars, it keeps the blower operating at low speed for ventilation whenever the ignition is on. If the dashboard control switch is moved to B (typically NORMAL AC), there is current flow through the blower switch. Blower speed therefore, will depend on the position of the blower switch. If it is in No. 1, current must flow through the entire resistor. If it is in No. 2, current must flow through only half the resistor, and so more of it will flow through and the blower will run faster. In No. 3, the circuit bypasses both parts of the resistor. If the current required to operate the blower at high speed is more than the dashboard blower switch can handle, a relay is inserted into the circuit. Current from the blower switch triggers the relay, closing it and permitting current from the battery (acutally from a fuse box circuit connected to the battery through the wiring harness) to flow to the blower motor.

1. When the lever is turned to MAX A/C, the switch on many cars completes a circuit from the ignition switch to a high-speed blower terminal (see Figs. 8-14 and 8-15). The blower is running at high

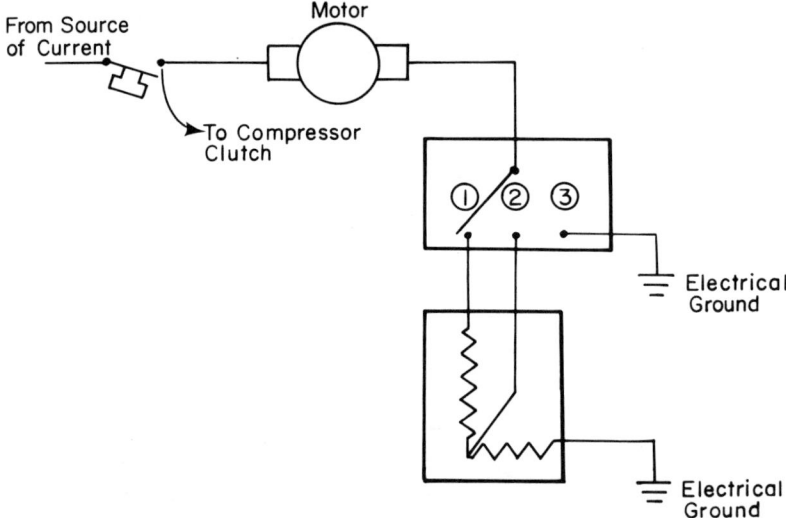

Figure 8-15 Although the conventional way to wire a blower circuit is as shown in Fig. 8-14, what is called ground-side switching also may be used, and it is on some newer Ford products. In this design, as shown, the blower switch on the dashboard completes a circuit to ground, going through a resistor assembly as shown. This prevents damage to the blower switch if there is a short circuit. Note that the resistor is part of the grounding circuit. In No. 1 position, the circuit must be completed through both branches of the resistor before it can go to electrical ground. In No. 2 position, the circuit goes only through one branch (half) of the resistor before it is complete to electrical ground, so more current can flow in the circuit and the blower can spin faster.

speed, regardless of the position of the blower switch lever, for the switch lever has been bypassed.

2. When the lever is turned to A/C, the circuit is completed from ignition current to the blower selector lever terminal. Now the blower speed will be determined by the position of the switch lever. On most cars there is no OFF position for the blower. The blower is always on (even if at low speed), commonly even if the panel's control switch is turned to the OFF position (if the ignition switch is on). Only in some cars is current flow to the blower switch stopped when the dash control is off.

Current flows from the blower switch terminal selected to a part called the *blower resistor*. As its name implies, it resists current flow, and so allows less to reach the blower motor. The less the amount of current, the lower is the blower speed. Therefore, the greatest resistance is posed when the blower speed lever is on LOW. Moving the lever to higher speed positions switches the circuit to resistors that permit a greater current flow, and therefore a higher blower speed.

High Blower Relay

The amount of current required for the highest blower speed may be more than the wiring through the control panel can safely handle. In this case, a relay, called the *high blower relay*, is used. The smaller amount of current through the control panel simply energizes the relay's electromagnet, and a separate higher-current-carrying circuit through the relay is completed to the blower motor (see Fig. 8-14).

Vacuum Switches and Circuits

Moving the control panel lever also operates what is called a *vacuum switch*. A group of vacuum hoses is connected to this switch; one type is shown in Fig. 8-11. One hose is from a source of engine vacuum; the others go to the vacuum diaphragm units that operate the various flap doors in the duct housing and, in some cases, also to the heater coolant control valve.

The vacuum switch, in one common design, is a rotary device with an upper section that is fixed and into which the vacuum hoses are plugged and a lower section that turns when the dashboard control lever is moved. Pegged into this lower section is a rubber disc with grooves that form vacuum flow paths between them (see Fig. 8-11).

Depending on the position to which the lower section and its rubber disc are turned, different vacuum flow paths are defined, and vacuum flows from the source hose, through the switch's flow path, into one or more of the other hoses. The vacuum flow continues through the hose or hoses to the vacuum diaphragm units. When the vacuum switch is in the off position, vacuum is stopped at the switch; it does not flow through.

Mechanical Control

The control panel has one basically manual, mechanical control—the temperature lever, which was explained earlier in this chapter, operates the blend (also called blend air) door.

On cars with a vacuum-operated heater coolant control valve, it is common practice to have a vacuum valve also operated by a cable from the temperature control lever. This valve has two hose connections, one from a vacuum source, the other to the heater coolant control valve. When the temperature lever is in the cold position, there is vacuum flow through the switch to the heater control valve, and the diaphragm shuts the valve. As soon as the lever is moved toward the warm position, the cable movement closes the vacuum valve and vacuum flow to the heater valve is stopped. The heater valve opens and full coolant flow to the heater begins (see Fig. 8-11). Or the coolant valve could operate in the opposite way—vacuum flow off and the coolant valve is closed. In this case, the vacuum valve would work in the opposite way.

Even with the coolant valve closed, a small amount of coolant may flow through the heater valve and heater core to prevent heater core coolant freeze-up. Or the heater coolant control valve may have two diaphragms, one that allows partial flow to prevent heater core coolant freeze-up with the air conditioning on and a second that allows full flow for efficient heater operation in winter. Inasmuch as all modern cars operate with antifreeze in the cooling system the year round, this heater core freeze-up protection may not be found on many cars.

Vacuum Reserve

When you step down hard on the gas pedal, engine vacuum drops. To prevent variations in air conditioning performance during periods of acceleration, the system will commonly have the following:

1. *Vacuum reservoir:* as explained earlier in this chapter, this is a tiny storage tank for vacuum. Some reservoirs resemble food cans; others look like the type of gauges mounted on the dashboard.
2. *Check valves:* these are one-way flow control devices that are drawn open by engine vacuum when that vacuum is stronger than vacuum already in the system. If engine vacuum momentarily drops, perhaps because of heavy acceleration, the valve closes and vacuum is trapped there, permitting the system to continue to operate normally. If the operation at low engine vacuum were to continue for a long period, the operation of the air conditioning would be affected, for some loss of that trapped vacuum would occur. Some air conditioners, however, have switches in series with the wire to the compressor clutch coil, to break the circuit if engine vacuum drops very low, or if the throttle linkage is opened past a certain point (see Chapter 6).

Automatic Temperature Control

The control panel levers (or in some cases knobs or push buttons) permit the driver to make adjustments at will to change the temperature of the air blowing out of the registers. For the motorist who is willing to pay a bit more, there is a system—automatic temperature control—that provides a temperature dial. A degree wheel is set to the desired temperature and an automatic system takes over. In summer it will cool down the passenger compartment as quickly as possible to the desired temperature (or warm it in winter). Then it will force just the right amount of cold air through the heater to provide a discharge of air from the registers that will keep the passenger compartment at the preset temperature.

Several types of automatic temperature control systems are presently in use:

Electropneumatic System

The electropneumatic system uses both electrical and vacuum-operated (pneumatic) components, just as does the manually controlled system. The heart of the system is a device called the *programmer*. It is not a computer, but it does perform similar functions with the aid of electronic devices.

Sensors. In fact, the basic information the programmer receives is from two electronic sensors called *thermistors*, which are temperature-sensitive resistors. That is, if you pass a current through a thermistor, the current flow will vary with changes in the temperature of the surrounding air. The typical thermistor used will pose maximum resistance to current flow at low temperature. As temperature rises, the resistance drops and more current flows through the circuit.

One sensor is at the fresh air inlet of the duct housing to measure the temperature of the outside air coming into the car. The other, called the *in-car* sensor, is in the passenger compartment, generally somewhere in the dashboard. It senses passenger compartment temperature with the aid of an *aspirator* (see Fig. 8-16), a hose that starts at the dashboard and ends in the duct housing, passing the in-car sensor at some point. Air flowing through the duct housing is blown past the bottom of the hose, creating a light vacuum in the hose. This light vacuum is filled by air drawn from the passenger compartment. As the air from the passenger compartment flows through the aspirator hose, it triggers the in-car thermistor.

Degree Wheel. If only the information from the sensors were available, the automatic temperature control would be more automatic than anyone would want. To permit it to respond to the driver's wish, the degree wheel is used. When the driver turns the degree wheel to select a temperature, actually a device called a *variable resistor* is being operated. The higher the temperature selected, the lower the resistance, just as with thermistors. Now, however, we have some input from the driver, for this variable resistor, commonly called a *potentiometer*, is wired into the sensor circuit to an amplifier.

The amplifier raises the strength of the signal from the sensor and potentiometer circuit, but it does not change its basic character. Therefore, this current signal reflects the temperature information that was produced from the original signal to the amplifier. From the amplifier, the strengthened signal goes to the *transducer*, a device that uses one form of energy to operate something else by means of another form of energy. In this case, the transducer uses an electromagnetic field to form a vacuum signal, for the remainder of the system is vacuum controlled.

118 Moving Cold Air

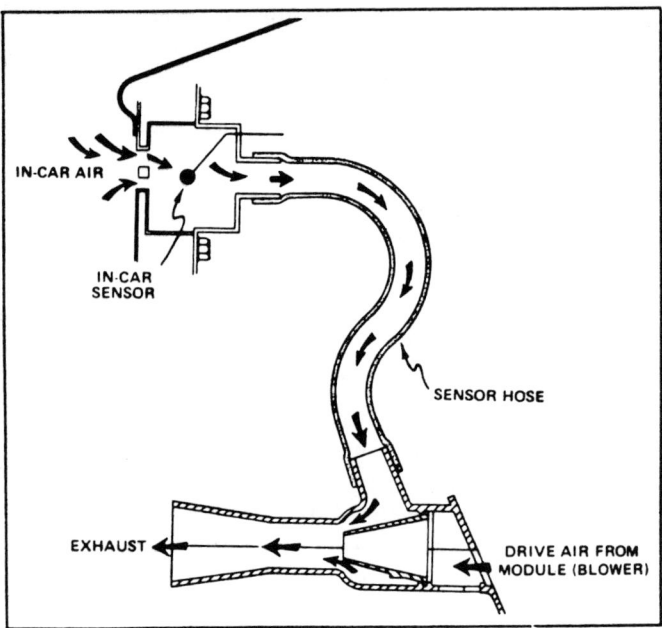

Figure 8-16 In-car sensor for automatic temperature control is located behind dashboard grille. Aspirator hose is under light vacuum from airflow at bottom, and so draws air from passenger compartment past in-car sensor. (Courtesy General Motors Corp.)

Refer to Fig. 8-17, and you will see that engine vacuum is supplied to the transducer, and the amount that can flow out (to a vacuum switch and then to the flap doors) is determined by the opening of a plunger and a needle valve. The stronger the current signal, the stronger is the electromagnetic field it creates, and the more it pulls the plunger (and the needle) down. The farther the needle drops, the greater the amount of outside air that can leak in and dilute the vacuum, reducing its strength. When the current signal from the amplifier drops, a spring pushes up the plunger and needle, closing the valve and allowing full-strength engine vacuum to flow through.

From the transducer, the vacuum flows to a part called a *vacuum checking relay,* and from the vacuum checking relay to the *vacuum motor,* the part that automatically controls the rotary vacuum switch (thus the flap doors in the duct housing), the blower switch, and a shaft to linkage that moves the blend door.

The vacuum checking relay is much like the vacuum check valve described earlier in this chapter. When engine vacuum drops, the relay (see Fig. 8-18) closes to prevent vacuum in the reservoir from being lost through the intake manifold. Its design is more sophisticated for the automatic temperature control system, so it can prevent the vacuum motor from

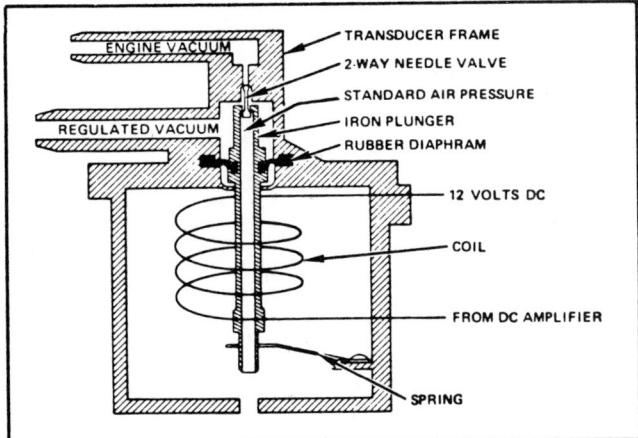

Figure 8-17 This is a schematic drawing of a transducer. Vacuum enters at top, where its flow is controlled by a needle valve attached to a plunger. Plunger position is determined by the strength of a magnetic field created by current from the amplifier flowing through a coil of wire around the plunger. Notice that the plunger is exposed to standard air pressure (from the outside), but that the vacuum is isolated from the air by the sealing effect of the rubber diaphragm. If current flow from the amplifier is high, the magnetic field is strong and it pulls down the plunger, allowing the needle to drop. This permits standard air pressure to flow past the needle and dilute the vacuum, weakening it. If current flow from the amplifier is low, the magnetic field strength is reduced, and a spring pushes the plunger and needle up, closing off the air leak. Then full-strength engine vacuum can flow through, out the transducer. The amplifier, therefore, can convert current into a vacuum flow of opposite strength. More current equals weaker vacuum; less current equals stronger vacuum. (Courtesy General Motors Corp.)

making any mode change, such as from cold to hot air, if the acceleration period is prolonged and the vacuum in the reservoir is exhausted.

The vacuum motor, shown in Fig. 8-19, performs its three functions by simply moving its operating rod an appropriate distance forward or back. It is a vacuum diaphragm device with a spring that pushes the rod all the way to the forward position. When vacuum is applied, the diaphragm is drawn to the rear, pulling the rod with it.

If it moves the rod as far as possible forward (spring action only, no vacuum), the system will deliver the maximum amount of cold air. The rod will turn the vacuum valve rotary switch so the fresh air door will close. The heater coolant valve also will be closed. The rod simultaneously will turn the blower switch lever to high speed and the output shaft so that the blend door will not allow air to flow through the heater core.

If it moves the rod as far as possible to the rearward position (maximum vacuum), the fresh air flap door also will be closed, the rod will turn the blower switch lever to high speed, the heater coolant valve will be open, and the blend flap door will be in a different position for maximum

120   Moving Cold Air

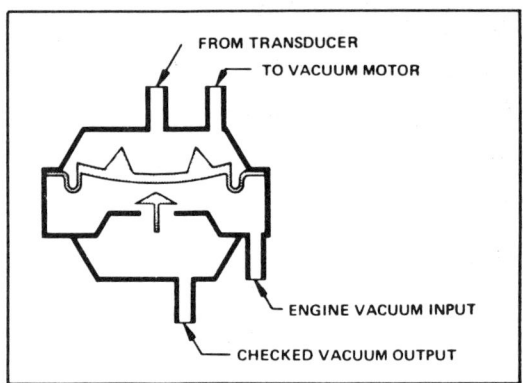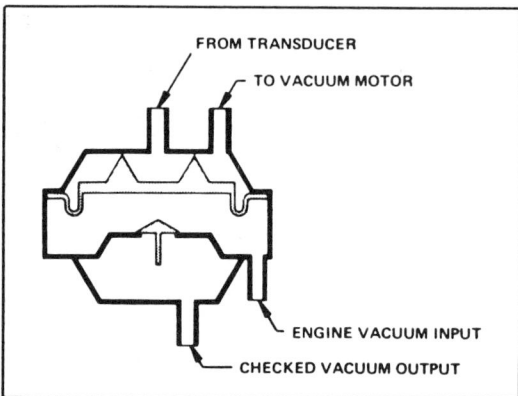

Figure 8-18   The vacuum checking relay uses engine vacuum to control the regulated vacuum from the transducer. When engine vacuum is applied to the relay, it pulls down the diaphragm with the shutoff arrowheads at the top, and pulls open the check valve in the center to complete the vacuum circuit. Regulated vacuum then flows to the vacuum motor (diaphragm unit). When vacuum flow is stopped or slowed, such as during hard acceleration, the diaphragm moves up and the center check valve moves down. This locks the vacuum motor (diaphragm unit), preventing a mode change, such as from cold to heat, for this temporary situation. (Courtesy General Motors Corp. 1973.)

Figure 8-19   (a) A look inside a General Motors Delco programmer for automatic temperature control.

Automatic Temperature Control

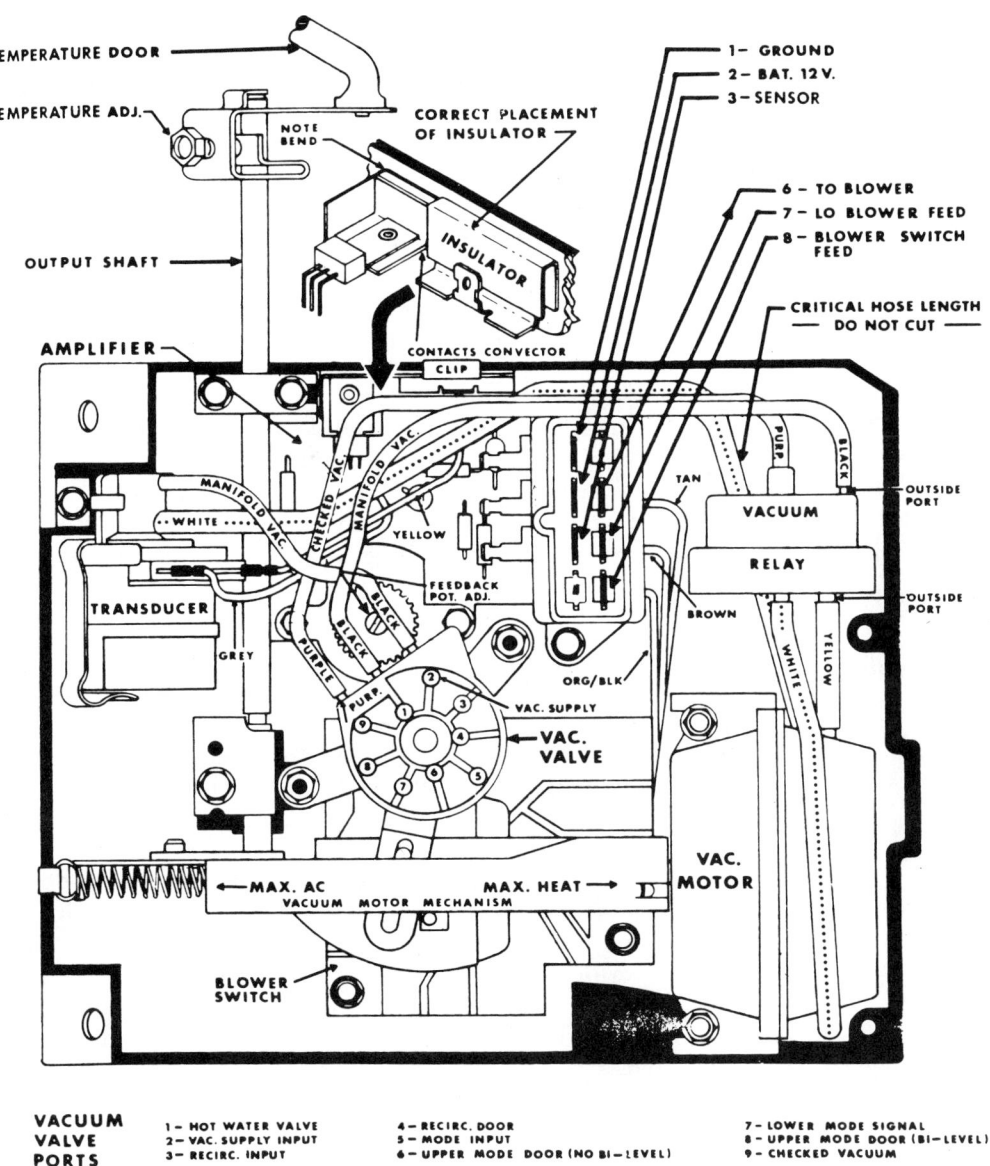

Figure 8-19 *(continued)* (b) Above is drawing with key parts labeled. Notice that when vacuum motor (diaphragm unit) arm pulls in, the system is designed to go into maximum heat, and when it releases, into maximum cooling. Also notice that the movement of the motor arm also operates the rotary vacuum switch, a blower switch, and the linkage to the temperature door in the duct housing. (Courtesy General Motors Corp.)

heat. Some of the same operations can occur for maximum cold and maximum heat because the vacuum switch and blower switch have duplicate functions at both extreme positions.

In the intermediate positions of the vacuum motor rod (modulated vacuum), the fresh air flap door diaphragm will receive vacuum and so will pull open the door. The blower will be at a lower speed, and the blend door will mix hot and cold air in whatever proportion is necessary to maintain the temperature selected.

Feedback Potentiometer. As the system is shown to this point, the vacuum motor rod would swing to extremes as it attempted to provide air at the desired temperature. To provide smooth operation, a variable resistor called a *feedback potentiometer* is used. It is operated by the vacuum motor rod, its resistance changing with the position of the rod. The potentiometer resistance change is transmitted to the amplifier, along with the information from the temperature sensors and degree wheel potentiometer. The signal provided by the feedback potentiometer, in effect, tells the amplifier where the vacuum motor rod is positioned.

The feedback potentiometer may have a screw-type adjustment to permit tailoring the system's performance. Adjustment also may be provided on the degree wheel potentiometer.

Electrically Operated Blend Door

Two automatic temperature control systems operate the blend door with an electric motor. In one (Fig. 8-20), a motor and set of gears receive the electrical signal from the amplifier and operate a link to position the blend door. A feedback potentiometer also is used here to indicate the position of the link.

In a newer, more sophisticated Cadillac design, an electronic control unit operates an electric motor in the programmer that through gears turns a link, somewhat similar to the previous design. However, in this design, the rotary vacuum switch is eliminated in favor of four solenoid vacuum valves. These are electromagnetic components that work somewhat like the magnetic clutch at the compressor. When current is supplied, an electromagnetic field is created that pulls on a rod, opening a valve and, in this case, permitting vacuum to flow through to the vacuum diaphragm at the flap door (see Fig. 8-21).

All-Electric System

The ultimate in electronic-electrical control of air conditioning is the automatic temperature control system introduced on some 1980 Buick Electra models. A minicomputer, called a *microprocessor,* draws informa-

Automatic Temperature Control

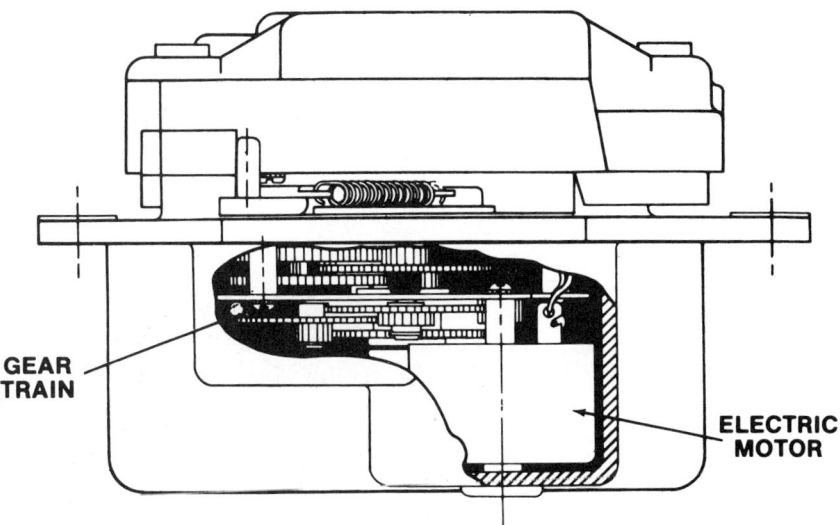

Figure 8-20 In this system, a motor and gears operate the temperature blend door. (Courtesy Chrysler Corp.)

Figure 8-21 This newer Cadillac system uses electric solenoid-operated vacuum valves. The programmer triggers the appropriate solenoids to allow vacuum flow to the diaphragm units.

tion from ambient and in-car temperature sensors and a touch-type temperature control is operated by the driver on the dashboard. The computer then supplies or denies current to electric motors at all the flap doors (see Figs. 8-22 and 8-23).

Use of the microprocessor permits the system to incorporate some built-in diagnostics. If a motor fails, if its wiring connector is defective, or if a flap door does not work, the computer signals the driver by flashing an indicator light on the control panel at the particular mode. If the problem

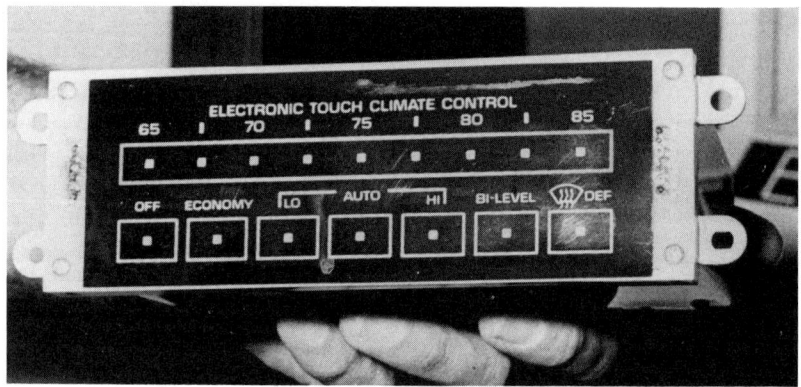

Figure 8-22 Minicomputer is built into dashboard control in this all-electric system, introduced on some Buicks. A touch of the desired temperature triggers a micromovement switch to signal the computer, which operates the temperature control system.

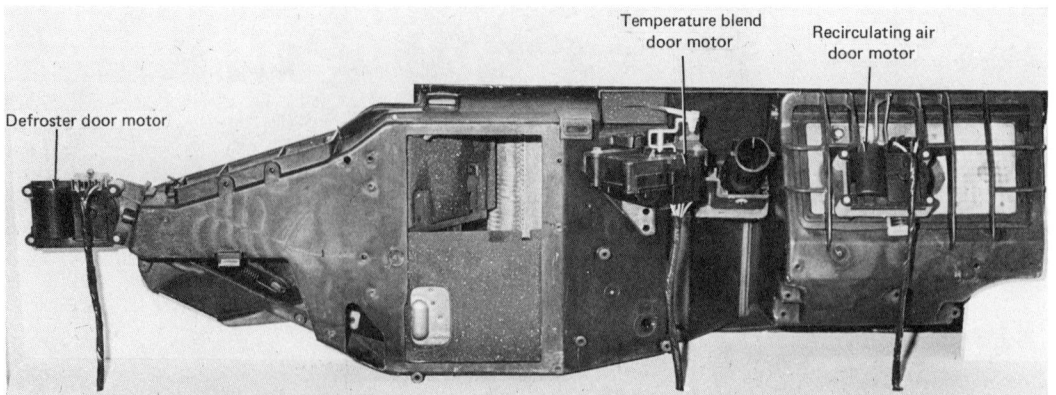

Figure 8-23 This is the duct housing of the computer-controlled all-electric system. Electric motors are used to operate the flap doors instead of vacuum diaphragm units. If a motor or connector fails, the computer triggers a flashing trouble light in the appropriate location on the dashboard control panel.

is in the defrost door motor, for example, the defrost touch button will flash until the problem is corrected. The remainder of the system, however, will continue to function normally. The same is true if the recirculation door motor fails. If the motor fails with the door open, the air conditioner will operate, but will not provide maximum cooling because some outside air is being drawn in.

The electronic-electric system offers these advantages:

* Electronic-electrical systems are more reliable than vacuum.
* When a heavily loaded vehicle is traveling on a long upgrade (such as in a mountainous area), engine vacuum drops sharply as the driver must keep the throttle virtually wide open to maintain cruising speed. Under these conditions, the loss of vacuum may cause the air conditioning system to malfunction, unless, of course, it is one with a vacuum pump to provide help, another approach that is taken on some new cars.

As computers are used more and more on automobiles, computer-controlled air conditioning will obviously become commonplace. The same computer that controls ignition timing, fuel mixture, and exhaust emission control devices could take on this additional task.

In the meantime, the desire for simplicity and lower cost in automatic temperature control systems has led to the wide use of a semi-automatic system that relies entirely on engine vacuum and a new electric system. The semi-automatic differs from the fully-automatic in that all it does is automatically operate the blend-air door to control the temperature selected with the degree lever by the driver. The driver still must select the mode (air conditioning, heat, etc.) and the blower speed.

Semi-Automatic Temperature Control

Most semiautomatic temperature controls are all-vacuum systems; they are much simpler than the fully automatic types with only small sacrifices in convenience and temperature control accuracy. When the driver moves the temperature lever, a cable does two things:

1. In many systems it orients the linkage at a vacuum diaphragm unit that is connected to the blend door, either toward cold or heat (the major movement of the door, however, is automatically controlled).
2. It increases or decreases spring tension on a bimetal spring valve in a part called the *compensator* (see Fig. 8-24). The compensator valve controls vacuum flow to the vacuum motor, as do the electronics and transducer in fully automatic temperature control.

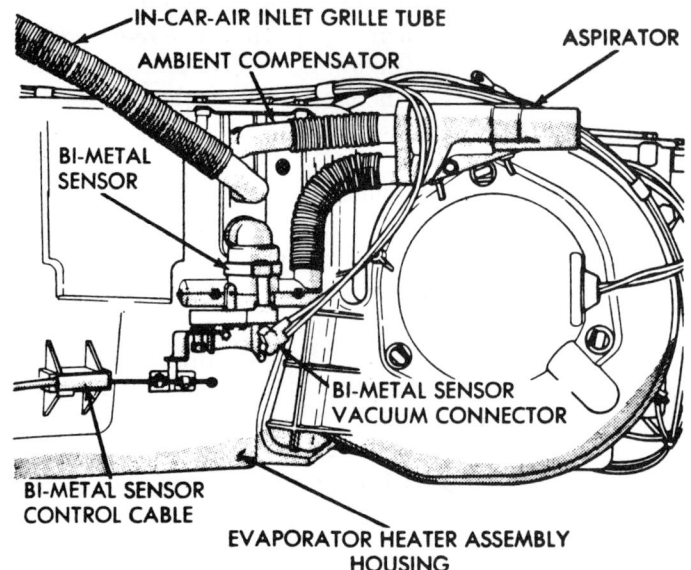

Figure 8-24 This is the semiautomatic temperature control system used on many late-model cars. It is an all-vacuum system that uses a bimetal sensor that is preset by the temperature selection lever on the dashboard control. Then an aspirator hose draws in-car and outside air over the bimetal sensor. The two metals in the bimetal sensor flex a metal strip that controls a valve, which regulates the flow of engine vacuum to a vacuum diaphragm unit. The diaphragm unit then controls the temperature blend flap door. Chrysler, one of the users of this system for several years, in 1980 switched to an all-electric version. The in-car and ambient-air sensors are temperature-sensitive electronic resistors. Also in the circuit is a variable resistor controlled by the dashboard temperature control lever; it converts movement along a temperature scale into a resistance reading that relates to those from the sensors. The electric current that results from the changes imposed by the sensors is transmitted to an electronically controlled electric motor, which moves the temperature blend door. (Courtesy Chrysler Corp.)

Bimetal refers to the fact that the valve is made with two different metals so that it deflects (to open or close a vacuum passage) with changes in temperature. An aspirator tube draws air from the passenger compartment and runs it through a chamber exposed to outside air, called the *ambient compensator*. This chamber heats or cools the outside air slightly to give the system an air "blend" that reflects outside air temperatures, too. The air then flows to the bimetal sensor, which determines if or how much vacuum flows to the diaphragm unit at the blend door. If temperature is high and maximum cooling is required, the bimetal valve closes, stopping vacuum flow and allowing the spring in the diaphragm unit to pull the link (and the blend door) to the cold position. If only a small change in temperature is necessary, the bimetal merely closes enough to restrict vacuum flow, so the link stops short of the full cold position. If heating is called for, the bimetal valve opens and allows vacuum flow. The vacuum pulls on the diaphragm and moves the link to operate the blend door for maximum heating of the air. This system may have a checking relay, as on the fully automatic systems.

The electric semi-automatic has electronic sensors (thermistors) for in-car air and ambient air and a variable resistor on the dashboard temperature lever. They all feed current signals to an electronically-controlled electric motor at the blend door. The electronic controls at the motor assembly determine which way and how far to run the blend door motor.

Testing the Air Control and Handling Systems

Because duct housings, flap door locations, and automatic temperature control systems vary widely among makes of cars and change so from year to year, service details must be obtained from factory service manuals or general manuals that are digests of the factory manuals. These details are outside the scope of this book. You should, however, include at least a basic functional check of dashboard controls and the duct system during troubleshooting, as explained in Chapter 9. You also should check vacuum hose connections and learn to test vacuum diaphragm units with a manual vacuum pump.

QUESTIONS

1. Cold air merely oozes out of the ductwork. Mechanic A says it could be a defective blower. Mechanic B says the problem could be at the flap doors. Who is right?
   a. Mechanic A.
   b. Mechanic B.
   c. Both.
   d. Neither.
2. When vacuum is applied to a diaphragm unit, work is performed by the
   a. vacuum sucking on the diaphragm.
   b. atmospheric pressure pushing on the link.
   c. atmospheric pressure pushing on the diaphragm.

3. The duct housing door operated by a cable to a lever at the dashboard is the
   a. blend door.
   b. heater door.
   c. outside air door.
4. Add-on air conditioning reduces the amount of cooling by
   a. mixing the cold air with warm air from the heater.
   b. drawing in warm outside air.
   c. cycling the compressor clutch more frequently.
5. When the driver turns on the air conditioning
   a. a switch completes the circuit to the compressor clutch.
   b. a vacuum switch applies vacuum to diaphragm unit(s) at the flap door(s).
   c. Both.
6. When the driver turns the degree wheel on a car with automatic temperature control, he or she is
   a. operating a variable resistor.
   b. increasing or reducing spring pressure on a diaphragm on the suction throttling valve.
   c. adjusting the setting of a cycling clutch thermostatic switch.
   d. Answers b and c are both correct.
7. The amplifier in an automatic temperature control system raises the strength of the signal from
   a. temperature sensors in the passenger compartment and outside air inlet.
   b. the degree wheel.
   c. Answers a and b are both correct.
   d. Neither answer a nor b is correct.
8. The transducer in an automatic temperature control system is a device that is supplied with vacuum and regulates that vacuum flow entirely on a
   a. signal from the amplifier.
   b. engine throttle position.
   c. position of the degree wheel.
9. The movement of the automatic temperature control system's vacuum switch is controlled by the
   a. blend door shaft.
   b. vacuum motor rod.
   c. degree wheel.
10. The most common semi-automatic temperature control system is
    a. an all-vacuum system with a bimetal spring valve.

b. a vacuum system with an electric motor to drive the blend door.
c. a vacuum system with solenoid vacuum valves instead of a vacuum switch.

HANDS ON

1. Become familiar with engine vacuum by disconnecting a hose from the base of the carburetor or air intake, or from the intake manifold, and feel the hose neck with the engine running.
2. Locate a diaphragm unit on the duct housing. (Removing the glove box will provide access on some cars. Or you may find one accessible from under the hood or under the dashboard.) Disconnect the vacuum hose and operate the diaphragm unit with a manual vacuum pump. You should see the linkage move. Let the vacuum hold. If the diaphragm unit allows the linkage to retract within less than 2 minutes, it is leaking and should be replaced.
3. Gain access to the electrical and vacuum connectors at the back of the dashboard heater and air conditioning control panel. Consult a factory service manual for the procedure if it is not obvious.
4. On a car with automatic temperature control, locate the in-car sensor grille on the dashboard.

9

Basic System Checkout

As with any electromechanical system, air conditioning requires periodic inspection and preventive maintenance. Many shops advertise this work as a preseason "tuneup." It is a standard part of the shop routine, and it gives you basic familiarity with the tools and test equipment that you must use to do more complex work.

Cooling System, The Place to Start

An air conditioning checkout begins with a cooling system checkout, because the engine cooling system and the air conditioning are closely tied to each other. On virtually all cars, the air that is drawn through the condenser then flows through the radiator (some imported cars have condenser and radiator side by side). The fan that is part of the cooling system therefore is also part of the air conditioning, the imported exception taken. Next, if either the radiator or condenser is restricted externally, so is the airflow through both of them. Or if the internal flow of coolant through the radiator or Refrigerant 12 through the condenser is restricted, the ability of the plugged component to transfer heat to the passing air is reduced. The component becomes quite hot and transfers heat to the other (radiator to condenser or condenser to radiator), and so the performance of both is affected (see Fig. 9-1).

Additionally, the duct housing that uses hot coolant to warm the passenger compartment air in winter is the same that holds the evaporator for summer cooling. The blower that moves the air (hot or cold) into the passenger compartment and the temperature control lever perform functions in both heating and air conditioning. On a car with automatic temperature control, of course, both heating and air conditioning are put under a combination control.

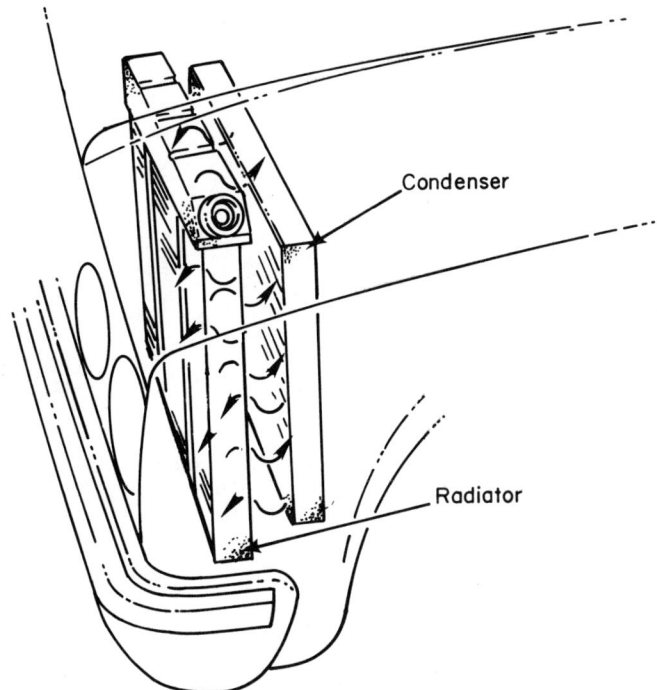

Figure 9-1 Because radiator and condenser are typically in line and so close together, heat transfers from radiator to condenser if cooling system is performing poorly. Condenser also can transfer heat to radiator. Unless both systems are performing properly, the performance of one hurts the performance of the other.

Cooling System Checkout

Although this book does not intend to treat cooling system service in great detail, here are the items you must check as part of a preseason air conditioning tuneup:

1. *Radiator cap.* Check it with a pressure tester (Fig. 9-2); if it fails to hold the specified pressure (within a band of 3 psi or 20 to 21 kPa) for at least 30 seconds, the cap may be defective. Remove it and inspect the inner gasket surface. If this surface has an indentation, remove and reinstall the cap a few times to the tester in an attempt to mate it to the tester. Then repeat the test, and if the cap still fails, replace it.

2. *Front of the condenser.* If it is very dirty and/or covered with bug deposits or leaves, clean it with a soft brush and a detergent and water solution. Wash off detergent residue with a water spray.

Figure 9-2 Test radiator cap with pressure tester as shown. It must hold to within 3 psi (20 to 21 kPa) of specifications for at least 30 seconds to pass.

3. *Condition of the engine coolant.* If it is very dirty or rusty, clean the cooling system with a flushing chemical; then flush with water and refill with a mixture of water and antifreeze (at least 50 percent antifreeze; preferably 70 percent).

4. *Adequate coolant flow through the radiator.* There are two types of radiators, downflow and crossflow. The *downflow radiator* has horizontal tanks at the top and bottom, and the cap is on the same side as the upper radiator hose. To check flow, warm up the engine, remove the radiator cap and run the engine at fast idle. The coolant should not overflow the fill neck. If it does, this indicates that the radiator probably is plugged.

The *crossflow radiator* has vertical tanks at the left and right sides, and the cap is on the same side as the lower radiator hose. To check flow, warm up the engine, remove the radiator cap, and run the engine at fast idle. You should see a speedup in coolant flow. If you are not sure, shut the engine, and to make sure the fan does not run on cars with electric fans, undo the wiring connector. Immediately run your hand over the radiator's finned area. If you feel any significant temperature variation from one part of the radiator to another, plugging is indicated. *Note:* A gradual temperature differential between the inlet and outlet sides, with the radiator cooler as you get to the outlet side, is normal.

The best way to check the radiator is with special equipment that actually measures the coolant flow rate so that you can compare it with specifications (see Fig. 9-3). If the flow rate is substan-

Figure 9-3 This special tester is installed between upper radiator hose and hose neck on radiator. It tests coolant flow rate, cooling system and cap pressure, antifreeze concentration, and for leakage of combustion gases into the cooling system.

tially below specifications, the radiator is plugged and service or replacement is required.

5. **Fan.** The fan should be in good condition and operate properly.
   a. If the fan is a conventional engine-driven type, watch it as it spins. If it wobbles, a loose or cocked belt pulley is likely.
   b. If the fan is an engine-driven clutch type, first check it with the engine off and cold. Give the fan a hard spin. If it makes five revolutions or more, the clutch apparently is defective. Also try to move a fan tip forward and backward (Fig. 9-4). The total movement should be no more than 0.25 inch (6 millimeters). Run the engine, warm it up, and check to see if the clutch engages (engine will roar and fan will obviously be driven). If necessary, block the front of the condenser with cardboard to speed coolant warmup.
   c. If the fan is an electric-motor-driven type, first check for wobble, which would indicate a defective motor shaft. Next warm up the engine and see if the fan turns on, as with the clutch type.

Drive Belts

The condition and tension of cooling system and air conditioning drive belts should be checked simultaneously. Twist over the belts at various

Figure 9-4 To check clutch fan, try to spin it (it should make fewer than five revolutions after a hard spin); then try to move a fan tip forward and backward as shown. Total tip movement should be no more than 0.25-inch (6 millimeters).

Figure 9-5 Only accurate way to check belt tension is with a strand tension gauge as shown. Compare reading on gauge with factory specifications.

points and look for cracks in the underside and splits or glazing on the sidewalls. If you see any, replace the belts. Also check belt tension (Fig. 9-5) and adjust if necessary. Belt tensioning arrangements include:

1. *A bolt through an elongated slot is an accessory bracket.* To remove the belt, slacken the bolt in the elongated slot, plus any other mounting bolts, and push the accessory toward the engine to eliminate tension from the belt. Then work the belt out of the pulley grooves. In most cases, there is a provision on the bracket of one accessory for applying tension to the belt. It may be a hole in the bracket to accommodate a pry bar, an adjusting nut on a stud through a two-piece bracket, or a square hole to accommodate the the drive from a ratchet or breaker bar (see Figs. 9-6 and 9-7).

Figure 9-6 Most common belt adjustment is elongated slot in an accessory bracket. Slacken accessory mounting bolts and use pry bar or strap wrench to pivot accessory to apply tension. Tighten bolt against slot; then tighten other bolt(s).

2. *Adjustable idler pulley.* This pulley has no accessory to drive; it merely serves to guide the belt and provide a tensioning adjustment. To remove the belt, loosen the pulley nut and then push the pulley assembly in the direction that releases tension. If the pulley is located by an adjusting nut on a stud, you may have to turn the adjusting nut to release belt tension. To reapply tension, you must move the idler pulley in the opposite direction. This may be done by turning the adjusting nut on the stud or by applying a wrench

Figure 9-7 Square hole in adjusting bracket permits you to apply tension with ratchet, breaker bar, etc. Just push square drive into the hole.

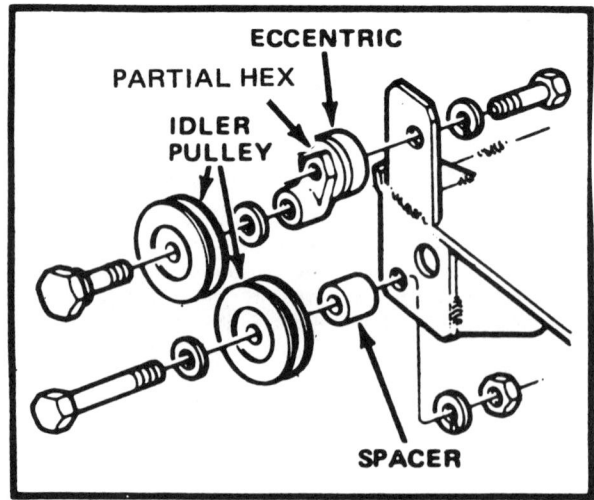

Figure 9-8 Idler pulley may be used to apply tension. In this type you slacken pulley nut; then use open-end wrench on a partial-hex section of the pulley shaft, which is eccentric (camlike). Turning wrench pivots pulley to change tension on belt. (Courtesy American Motors Corp.)

Figure 9-9 This Ford one-belt system controls tension automatically with a spring in a housing that pivots the idler pulley. To release tension for belt removal, insert pry bar in spring tang and yank.

to a section of the pulley shaft which turns a camlike arrangement to pivot the pulley (see Fig. 9-8).

3. *Automatic idler pulley.* This is used on the Ford one-belt system (Fig. 9-9). The idler pulley is attached to a housing containing a large spring. To release tension for belt removal, insert a pry bar in the spring tang and yank. When the pry bar is removed, the spring automatically applies tension through the idler pulley, and the belt never needs further adjustment. The belt is a grooved design on one side and fits into grooved pulleys. The belt also is turned over onto the ungrooved side, which bears against the idler pulley and water pump pulley. *Note:* A few Ford products have a single belt for all accessories but the air conditioning compressor, which has its own belt. In this type, as in some other newer cars with the single belt, there is a manual tensioning arrangement instead of the spring housing.

Once a belt is placed into service, it tends to stretch. Most of the stretch occurs in the first 15 minutes or so of operation, so it is good practice to recheck the tension and readjust if necessary. Most car makers set a higher number for a new belt, so that in most cases even after run-in the belt (now classified as used) is acceptably tensioned.

Note: If the old A/C belt snapped, and so does the new one (and it is the right belt), the problem likely is in the compressor, particularly if poor performance also is reported. Refer to Chapters 12 and 14.

Air Conditioning Drain Tubes

All air conditioning systems have drain hoses from the evaporator to allow moisture that condenses during air conditioning operation to drain to the ground. If the hoses are plugged with road film or damaged, the moisture may not drain properly, and will instead probably leak from the duct housing into the passenger compartment.

Inspect the ends of the hoses (this may have to be done with the car on a lift), and if they are plugged, clean them. If the ends, which are specially shaped on many cars, are cut or otherwise damaged, replace the hoses.

Air Conditioning Basic Performance Check

Ambient temperature must be 70°F (21°C) or higher, such as in the shop, for a basic performance check. The object is to confirm that the system is functioning normally, that the most that the system needs is some additional Refrigerant 12. If the system is not functioning normally, refer to Chapter 12.

Begin the testing of the air conditioning system by turning on the engine and then the air conditioning control on the dashboard. The clutch should lock to the pulley (there will be an audible click if it does), and you should see the pulley and clutch drive plate turn together. If they do not, or if there is any slippage, the clutch is malfunctioning and should be checked (see Chapter 12).

If the clutch engages and the compressor turns, feel for a blast of cold air at the dashboard air conditioning outlets. Insert a thermometer into an air conditioning register and hold it there for a couple of minutes to allow the temperature reading to stabilize (see Fig. 9-10).

The reading should be well below ambient temperature. Some manufacturers provide specifications for temperature differentials (between ambient and the air at the air conditioning registers) for different relative humidities. Still others provide specifications for use of a psychrometer, a special type of hygrometer (humidity measuring instrument) that provides readings that are compared with a chart in the service manual.

Although not as precise as the factory specifications for an individual make, there is a simple, universal approach that generally provides a reliable indication of the condition of the system. Get into the car and close the doors and windows. Start the engine, run it at fast idle, 1500 to

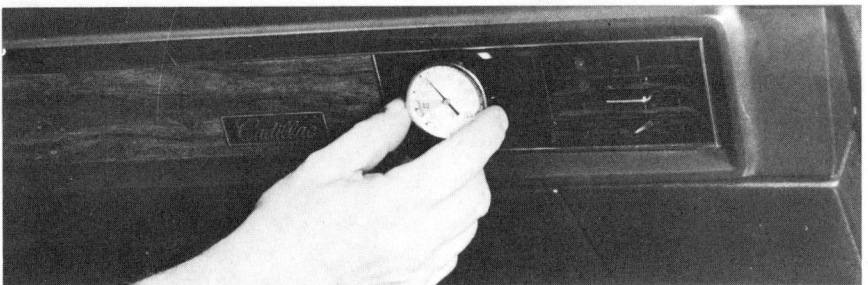

Figure 9-10 Insert thermometer into an air conditioning register with system on about 5 minutes, and hold it there for a couple of minutes to get a stabilized temperature reading, which should be well below ambient.

2000 rpm, turn on the air conditioning (to maximum or high position), and set the blower on high speed (on many cars it will automatically go to high speed). After 5 minutes, take the temperature of the air coming out of the air conditioning registers. If ambient temperatures are about 70°F (21°C), the air coming out of the registers on a normal system should be somewhere between 38° and 52°F (3° to 11°C). For higher ambient temperatures, add 1° to 2°F (0.5° to 1°C) for each 10°F (4° to 5°C).

This procedure almost completely eliminates the humidity factor, because the outside air flap door is closed and the air recirculating from passenger compartment to duct housing is quickly dehumidified. If the weather is unusually humid (90 percent or above), the temperature of the air coming from the air conditioning registers may approach 60°F (16°C).

Note: If the shop is warm, high-side pressures may build up to very large numbers and either open the relief valve or cause the high-pressure switch to open, cutting off the compressor clutch. To prevent this, either park the car far from a wall to allow good air circulation or, even better, place a large floor fan directly in front of the grille.

If the air conditioning system does not pass this test, that is, if the temperature of the air coming out of the air conditioning registers is clearly higher, make the following quick checks to see if the problem is in the refrigeration system or the air distribution system (ductwork and blower).

Refrigeration System

Most older cars and some current models have a sight glass, a tiny window into the refrigeration system. This glass, usually on the receiver-dryer (Fig. 9-11) or in the line close to it, permits you to make a rough check of the refrigeration system. Start the engine, turn on the air conditioning and run the engine at fast idle (1500 to 2000 rpm).

After 5 minutes of operation (this check can immediately follow the preceding test), the sight glass should be clear or at most have an occasional

140 Basic System Checkout

Figure 9-11 Sight glass should be clear or show only an occasional bubble when system is running for 5 minutes or more if it has a full charge of refrigerant. To distinguish between a full charge and none at all (which also will show a clear glass), either turn the system off and on, or wait for the cycling clutch switch on systems so equipped to turn the system off briefly, then on again. At this time, you should see bubbles. If the bubbling continues, the system is apparently low on refrigerant. On cycling clutch systems, the bubbling may be virturally continuous, but should subside noticeably when the compressor is on.

bubble. If there are no bubbles, the system either has a full charge of Refrigerant 12 or none at all. To see if the glass is clear because of a full charge, cycle the system (turn it on and off); as you do, bubbles should appear if the system is full. Have a helper operate the air conditioning controls so you can see the sight glass.

If the bubbling does not stop and the system is operating poorly, a low refrigerant charge is likely. *Note:* On cycling clutch systems, the bubbles will appear whenever the clutch cycles off, and they may not completely disappear (although the bubbling should start to abate somewhat) when the compressor comes on again.

Without Sight Glass (Hand Test). If a system is not equipped with a sight glass, feel the evaporator outlet line (the one from the evaporator to the compressor inlet) and the evaporator inlet line (the one from the condenser or receiver-dryer), as in Fig. 9-12. The evaporator outlet line should be at least slightly cooler than the inlet line. *Note:* Check the inlet line somewhere between the condenser or receiver-dryer and the expansion

141   Air Conditioning Basic Performance Check

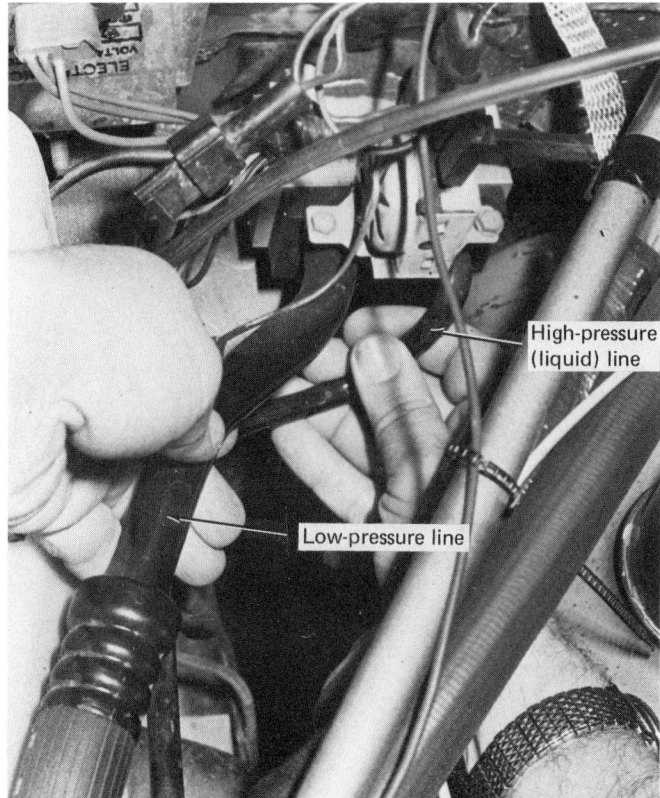

Figure 9-12 Hand test, with one hand at the evaporator outlet, the other just before the expansion valve or tube in the liquid line. The evaporator outlet should be cooler than the liquid line.

valve or orifice tube, not between the valve or tube and the evaporator. If the evaporator outlet line is warmer than the inlet, there is a problem in the refrigeration system. Leak testing and pressure checks, described later in this chapter, are the next steps.

In addition to the hand test, you can check for refrigerant in the system without a sight glass by using a special electronic tester. It clamps to an A/C line and makes a sound if there is a significant amount of refrigerant in the system.

Air Distribution System

Begin a check of the air distribution system by moving the dashboard heater and air conditioning control through all positions to determine if the flap doors are directing airflow properly. If they are not, there is a problem in the duct system, perhaps a poor vacuum hose connection or defective

142   Basic System Checkout

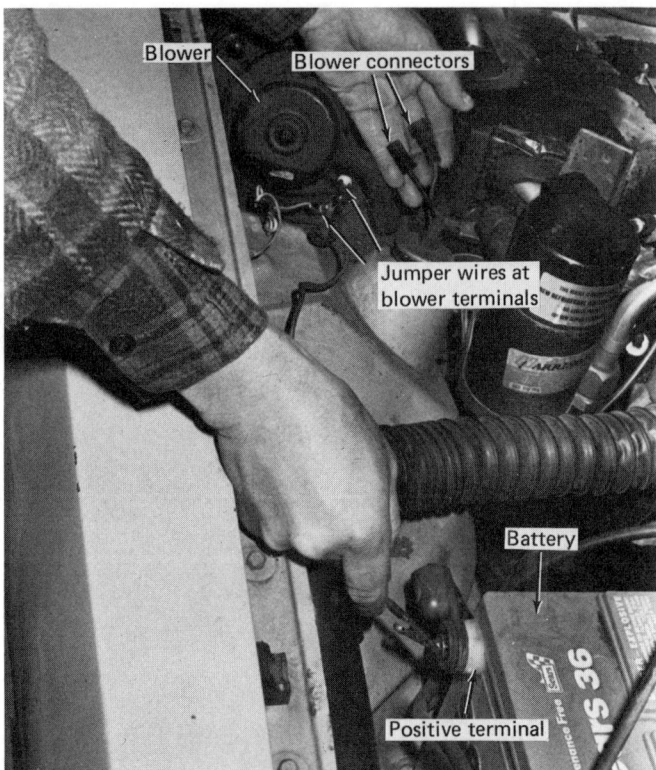

Figure 9-13 To check a blower motor, disconnect the wiring. Connect blower terminal for black or brown wire to electrical ground, other to battery positive terminal, using jumper wires. If the blower now works, any problem is in circuitry to the blower, not the blower itself. On most (but not all) newer cars, blower and wiring are reasonably accessible as shown.

vacuum switch. Or on an electric system a defective flap/door motor or connector is likely (see Chapter 8).

Next, check the blower switch. At maximum or high air conditioning settings, only the high blower or top two blower speeds are often available, whereas at normal air conditioning settings, heater and defrost, you may select the one you wish. If the blower does not work at all, check for a defective fuse. If the fuse is good, disconnect the wiring at the blower (Fig. 9-13), and connect one blower terminal to ground and the other to the battery's positive terminal, using jumper wires. If the blower now works, the problem is in the blower circuit, which includes the switch and perhaps two or more relays. Check the wiring diagram to be sure. *Note:* If the blower motor has just one terminal, disconnect the wire and run a jumper wire from that blower terminal to the battery's positive terminal.

Automatic Temperature Control

To perform a quick check on the automatic temperature control system, locate the in-car sensor's aspirator tube grille, somewhere on the dashboard, usually at or around the top (Fig. 9-14). Turn on the system, set the temperature degree dial to 75°F (24°C), and blow hot air into the grille. The system should go into maximum cooling. Next, blow cold air in, and the system should go into the heating mode. The simplest source of hot air is an electric heat gun or hair dryer. For cold air, spray Refrigerant 12 close to the grille.

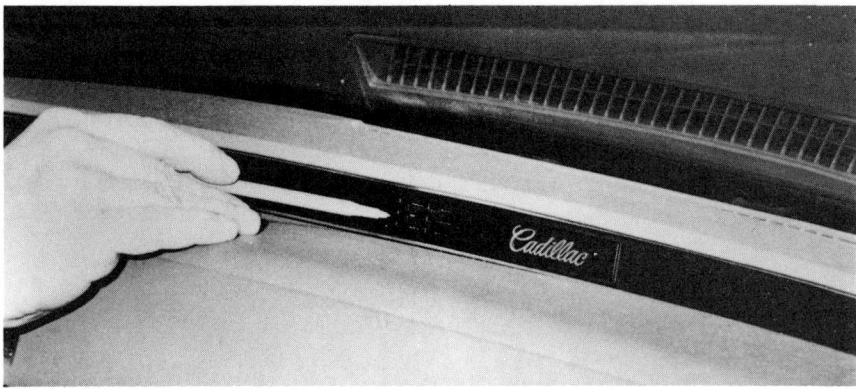

Figure 9-14 In-car sensor on automatic temperature control systems receives air from grille on dashboard, usually at or near the top. Apply heat or cold to grille area to test system reaction.

Refrigeration System Service

If you isolate the problem to the refrigeration system, take this three-step approach:

1. Pressure-test the system. If the system has lost refrigerant, this will be indicated by lower-than-normal pressures, as will be explained.
2. Leak-test the system. If you find minor leaks, you may be able to correct them with simple tightening of fittings.
3. If the loss of refrigerant is minor, you may be able to correct it by a simple addition of refrigerant.

   Note: This chapter covers only pressure testing to find minor loss of refrigerant. If the readings on the pressure test lead you to decide the problem is more than this, more complete troubleshooting is required, as explained in Chapter 12. This chapter,

144 Basic System Checkout

however, will introduce you to pressure test equipment and leak detectors, which are important troubleshooting tools.

Some leakage of refrigerant is perfectly normal, for no system is perfectly sealed. Although some systems will go five to six years and even more without a significant loss, others will require refrigerant additions after two years, even if there are no abnormal indications.

Pressure Testing

Pressure testing is simply measuring the pressure of the Refrigerant 12 in two parts of the air conditioning system: (1) somewhere in the high-pressure side (the portion of the system from the compressor outlet through the condenser and receiver-dryer up to the expansion valve or orifice tube); (2) somewhere on the low-pressure side (the portion of the system from the expansion valve or orifice tube outlet, through the evaporator, the accumulator if used, to the compressor inlet. The purpose of pressure testing is to determine if there is something wrong, which will be indicated by abnormal readings.

Finding Out Where to Check Pressure

You do not have to guess where to check, for the car manufacturer provides test fittings, also called service or test ports, to which you connect hoses from pressure gauges. On some cars the fittings are on or right at the compressor (Fig. 9-15). Or one fitting may be on the compressor and a second one somewhere on the tubing or in a muffler (a cannister in the high-pressure tubing installed to dampen compressor noises), as shown in Fig. 9-16. In other cases, a fitting may be on an accumulator (Fig. 9-17) or on a suction throttling valve (Fig. 9-18).

You must be certain, of course, whether a particular fitting is a high-pressure or a low-pressure fitting. If located on an accumulator or suction throttling valve, it must be a low-pressure fitting because those parts are on the low side of the system. If it is on a muffler, it is a high-side fitting.

If the fittings are at the compressor, follow the hose line from each. If one hose goes to the condenser, the tubing and the fitting are on the high side. If the hose leads back to the evaporator, the fitting is low side. If you find one fitting on the compressor and do not know which it is, check the other fitting; it may be easier to identify.

On some older Chrysler Corporation cars with the V-2 compressor, you may find two test fittings that seem to be on the low side, one on the compressor and a second on the low-pressure line to the compressor inlet (Fig. 9-19). It's true both are low-side fittings, but the pressure readings

Pressure Testing

Figure 9-15 The test fittings for the system may be on the compressor.

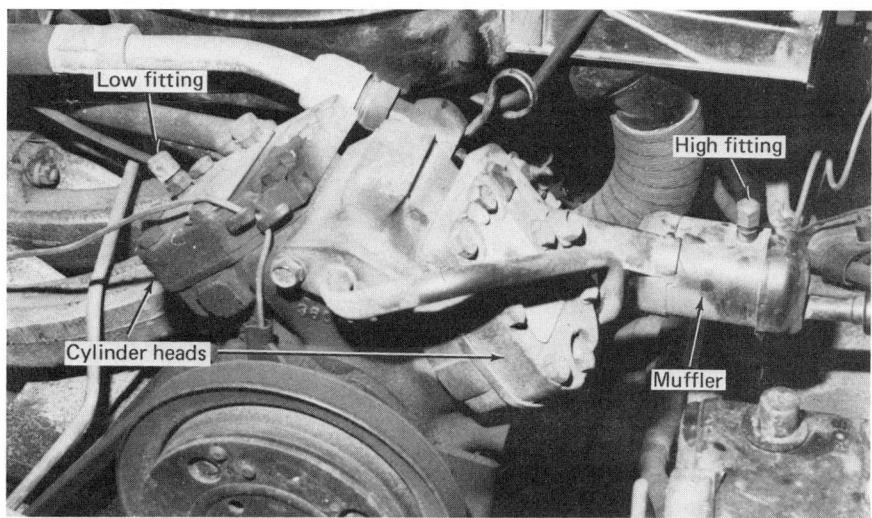

Figure 9-16 On this system, the high-side fitting is on the muffler; the low-side fitting is on the compressor cylinder head.

for each will be different. One fitting is before the evaporator pressure regulator; the second (on the compressor head) is after it. On such cars, you will connect two low-pressure gauges, as explained later.

Basic System Checkout

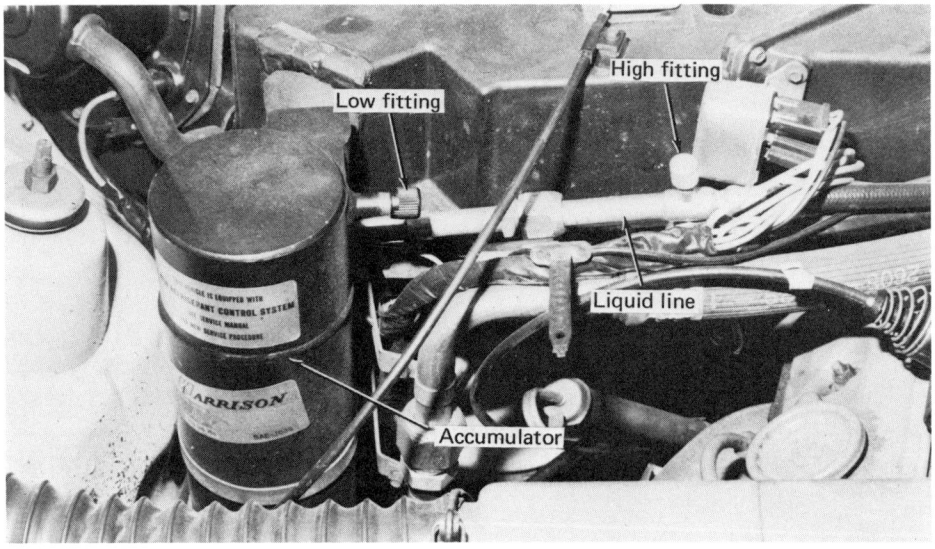

Figure 9-17 In this case, a low fitting is on the accumulator, a high fitting on the liquid line.

Figure 9-18 Note the low-side fitting on this system is on the suction throttling valve. If there are two fittings at or on the compressor, however, one is a low-side fitting and that is the fitting to which the gauge should be connected.

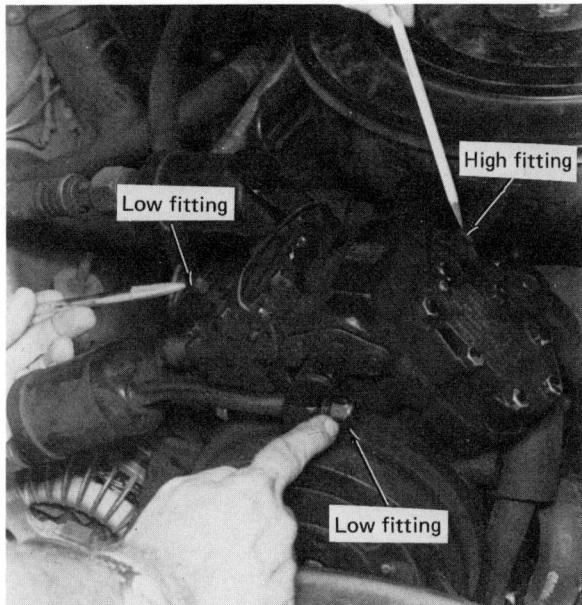

Figure 9-19 This Chrysler system has two low-side fittings, one on the compressor cylinder head and the second on the low-pressure line at the compressor inlet. Connect the manifold's low-side gauge to the fitting at the compressor inlet, another low-side gauge to the fitting at the compressor outlet. Don't confuse this system with the type shown in Fig. 9-16, in which there is only one low-side fitting.

Note: Many Chrysler Corporation cars with the V-2 compressor have only the low-side fitting on the compressor head; on these models, the additional low-side gauge is not used. These cars do not have an evaporator pressure regulator; rather, they are cycling clutch systems.

Many Ford products also have two low-pressure test fittings, one at the compressor and a second on the suction throttling valve (Fig. 9-18). In this case, a second low-side gauge also is used. A similar setup once was used on General Motors cars many years ago, but you are unlikely to encounter it.

On the 1978 through mid-1979 German Audi 5000 (which has a General Motors Valves-in-Receiver system), there is just one test fitting, a low-side fitting on the VIR. This poses some troubleshooting problems, although there also is a sight glass to provide additional assistance. The Audi was the only application of the particular GM system that had a single test fitting (in fact, to date, the only one of any make). There were strong objections from the service industry, and, as a result, the car manufacturer reinstated the high-side fitting in the middle of the 1979 model year.

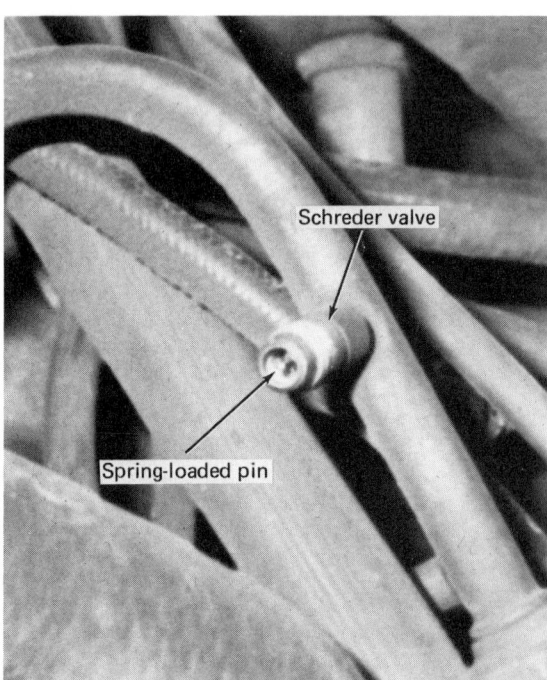

Figure 9-20 Acorn nut is removed to show the Schrader (tire-type) valve in the test fitting.

Note: To help avoid confusion between the low- and high-side test fittings, some systems have different sized fittings (slightly smaller) on the high side. To connect to this smaller size, you must use an adapter between the test fitting and the conventional hose connector.

Schrader Versus Manual Test Fittings

On most cars, the test fittings are Schrader valves covered with threaded caps or acorn nuts (Fig. 9-20). You remove the cap to expose a tire-type valve. When you connect a hose from the gauge, a little bar inside the hose fitting pushes down on the needle, opening the valve and allowing Refrigerant 12 under pressure to flow through to the gauge to provide a reading. The bar is on one side only, so you must connect the hose the correct way (see Fig. 9-21).

Some cars have what are called manual test fittings or manual valves. You also remove a threaded cap, but all you see is a hole, no Schrader valve. Next, take off another threaded cap and you will see a stem that projects from the assembly. This valve stem, which is turned with a special wrench, has three positions (see Fig. 9-22):

1. **Normal,** also called *backseated,* in which the stem is turned fully

149　Pressure Testing

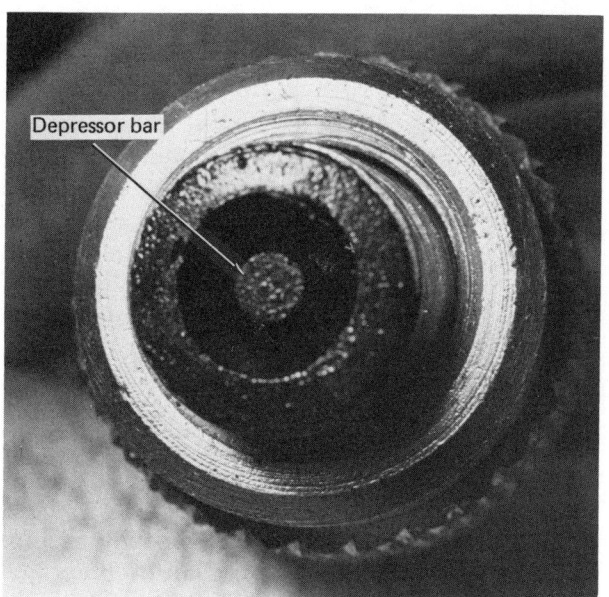

Figure 9-21 Special hose has depressor bar in one end to push open the Schrader valve as you tighten the hose on the test fitting.

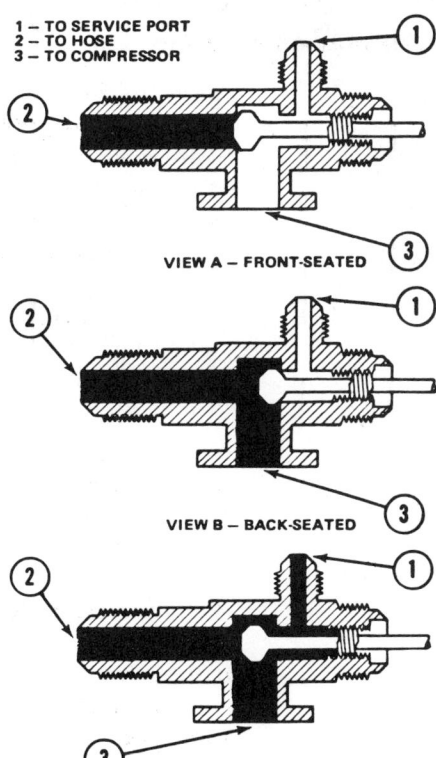

Figure 9-22 Illustration shows three positions of manual valves. Back-seated (fully counterclockwise) is the normal position. Mid-position is for test purposes (refrigerant will flow through the compressor and up the test fitting to produce a reading on the gauge). Front-seated (fully clockwise) blocks refrigerant flow in the lines to the compressor. The compressor now can be unbolted from the valves and replaced without discharging the entire system (see Chapter 14). (Courtesy American Motors Corp.)

counterclockwise. In this position, Refrigerant 12 flows only through the compressor.

2. *Mid-position,* in which Refrigerant 12 flows through the compressor and the hole. If there is a pressure gauge connected to this hole (actually a test fitting of course), it will read system pressure when the valve stem is in mid-position.

3. *Front-seated,* in which the stem is turned fully clockwise. In this position, the valve assembly is closed, and the Refrigerant 12 flow is stopped at the ends of the hoses. The compressor is isolated from the rest of the system, and if you unbolt the manual valves from the compressor, you can install a replacement compressor (or repair that one) without opening the entire system. This saves a considerable amount of work in air conditioning service, as you will see in Chapters 11 and 14.

The gauge hoses for systems with manual valves need not have the depressing bars to open the Schrader valve, so if you are working on both systems, be sure you use the right hose.

Manifold and Gauges

There are two types of gauges: a high-pressure gauge that typically reads 0 to 600 psi (or 4000 kPa) and a combination vacuum-low pressure gauge, called a *compound gauge.* It reads 0 to 30 inches of vacuum (0 to 760 millimeters) and typically 0 to 150 psi (1035 kPa). The two gauges are mounted on a pipe (Fig. 9-23) called a *gauge manifold.*

The manifold has three fittings for hose connections:

1. At the compound gauge for a hose that connects to the low-side test fitting.
2. At the high-pressure gauge for a hose that connects to the high-side fitting.
3. In the center for a hose that connects to the vacuum pump or a container of Refrigerant 12. Or the center fitting may be connected by a hose to a two-way valve, to which hoses from both a vacuum pump and a Refrigerant 12 supply can be connected (see Fig. 11-5).

The manifold also has a hand-operated shutoff valve, called the *manual valve,* at each end. Do not confuse it with the manual valve-type test fitting shown in Fig. 9-22.

Each manual valve on the manifold controls the passage from a gauge to the center fitting of the manifold (see Fig. 9-23). If a manual valve is shut off, Refrigerant 12 can flow up to the gauge, triggering it, but that is all. If a

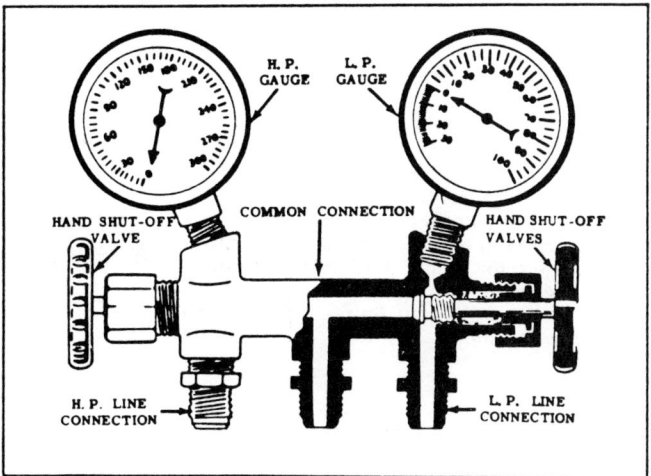

Figure 9-23 Typical gauge manifold has a high- and low-pressure gauge (the low-pressure gauge is called a compound gauge because it also registers vacuum). The handle at each end controls a shutoff valve, which does not affect refrigerant flow to the gauges, but prevents refrigerant from flowing out the center fitting of the manifold when both are closed. Inside view of gauge manifold shows how manual valves control flow out the center fitting. (Courtesy General Motors Corp.)

manual valve is opened, the Refrigerant 12 can continue through the manifold and flow out the center fitting into the atmosphere. Test readings are taken, obviously, with both manifold manual valves closed. To *add* Refrigerant 12 to the system, you attach a hose and refrigerant supply to the center fitting and then open one of the manual valves to allow the Refrigerant 12 to flow through the manifold *into* the system. If you wish to discharge the system, a hose is connected to the center fitting; the other end of the hose is aimed into a collector can (to catch oil, not refrigerant), and the manual valves are opened to allow the system to discharge.

The Third Gauge

On those systems with a second low-side test fitting, you can make special tests of the suction throttling valve or evaporator pressure regulator if you have a second compound gauge. Many gauge manifolds are equipped with a holder for this gauge. Although the third gauge (second compound type) is mounted on the manifold, it is not connected into the manifold passages, and the manual shutoff valves are not involved with it in any way (see Fig. 9-24).

152 Basic System Checkout

Figure 9-24 Third gauge (at left), a second compound type, is used on Chrysler products with two low-side fittings. It also is used for some troubleshooting procedures on older Ford products with two low-side test fittings, as explained in Chapter 12.

Charging Station

Although you can perform all routine discharge, vacuum-pump, and recharge operations with a gauge manifold, vacuum pump, and tank of refrigerant, most shops that do a large volume of air conditioning work have a charging station (see Fig. 9-25). This piece of equipment has the three gauges, a holder for a bulk container of Refrigerant 12, tool storage, a vacuum pump, and a charging cylinder (a cylinder with a calibrated sight glass) so you can measure exactly how much refrigerant has been delivered into the system.

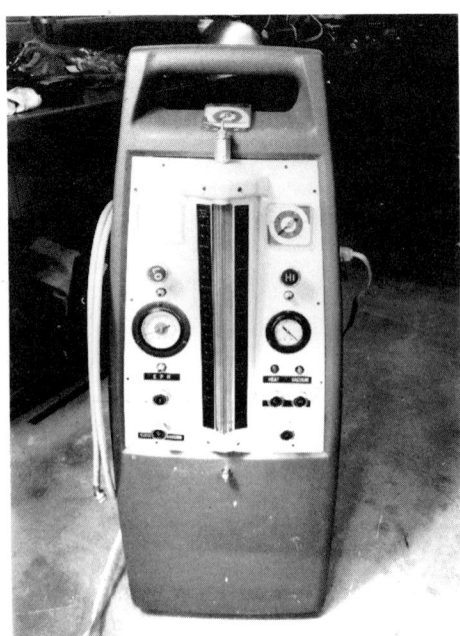

Figure 9-25 Charging station, such as this one, holds all test equipment for troubleshooting, discharging, and recharging the system and for most repairs.

Making the Connections

Whether you are using a gauge manifold or charging station, the low and high manual valves should be completely closed before you make any connections. Next, thread the hoses onto the end ports of the gauge manifold or the gauge ports of the charging station. If the air conditioning has a port for a third gauge, connect a hose from the gauge or charging station to the third port. On a system with Schrader valves, be sure you connect the hose ends without the depressor bars to the gauge manifold or charging station first, and then the depressor bar ends to the test fittings on the system.

Be careful to make the right hose connections—high pressure gauge to high-side fitting, low-pressure gauge to low-side fitting (see Fig. 9-15 to 9-19).

Hand tighten the hose fittings, first at the manifold or charging station end and then at the test fittings on the car. Do not use pliers.

On systems with manual valves at the compressor, crack open these valves (turn clockwise) until you get a reading on the gauges (one to one and a half turns on most systems). (See Fig. 9-26.)

For a stable, accurate reading, you must bleed air from the hoses to the gauges. Crack open one of the manual valves on the manifold, wait a few seconds until you hear Refrigerant 12 hissing out of the center port, and then close the manual valve. Open the other valve and repeat the process. On most charging stations, the procedure is similar, but check the instructions provided by the equipment manufacturer.

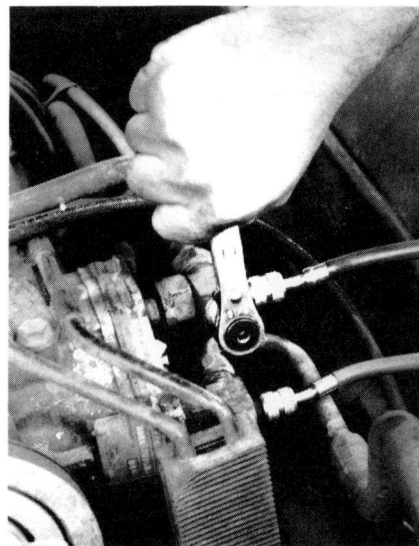

Figure 9-26 Use special ratcheting box wrench to turn stem on manual valves at compressor. Turn stem clockwise until you get reading on the gauge (one to one and a half turns in most cases).

Taking Readings

Start the engine and run it at fast idle (1500 to 2000 rpm). Turn on the system to maximum or high and, if necessary, set the blower at high speed. Allow a few minutes for readings to stabilize. Compare the readings with manufacturer's specifications. Remember that high-side readings vary greatly with ambient temperature, so on a very hot, humid day, the reading may be double the minimum (see Fig. 9-27). In general, if you take a reading within a couple of minutes after turning on the system, you should get numbers that are closer to the low end of specifications. If you wait, obviously, hot weather could raise the pressures to well above the minimums even if there is a problem with the system.

In the absence of specifications, at 70° to 80°F (21° to 27°C) you should get a reading of 140 to 210 psi (965 to 1450 kPa) on the high side and 24 to 35 psi (165 to 240 kPa) on the low side. On some Fords, normal readings may be 20 psi (140 kPa) under the minimums. On Chrysler Corporation cars with the third test fitting, the third gauge (on the compressor cylinder head) should read 1 to 6 psi (7 to 41 kPa) lower than the second gauge.

If both high- and low-pressure readings are clearly low, and the air discharged is not particularly cold, addition of Refrigerant 12 may cure the problem. Chapter 11 describes a complete operation—discharge, vacuum-pump, and recharge the system—but if the readings are only slightly low (perhaps 30 to 50 psi or 207 to 345 kPa under on the high side, and 5 to 10 psi or 35 to 70 kPa on the low side), complete service may not be necessary. Just add Refrigerant 12 (up to two cans) until the pressure readings come up to the normal range, using the recharging procedure only, as described in that chapter. If the pressure readings indicate a more complex problem, proceed to troubleshoot the system as described in Chapter 12.

If the readings are normal on a system with Schrader valves, disconnect the gauge hoses first at the system's test fittings (never from the gauge manifold or charging station first or the system will discharge). On a system with manual valves at the compressor, backseat the valves (turn the stem counterclockwise) and then disconnect the hoses.

No matter what the gauge readings, you also should check the system for minor leaks. You may be able to correct a minor leak before it becomes major and causes a compressor to fail.

Leak Checking

There are five basic ways to check the system for Refrigerant 12 leaks:

1. By looking at the connections for signs of oil. If Refrigerant 12 leaks out, it may carry some oil with it. Unless there is a major loss

PERFORMANCE CHART
CUTLASS WITH V.I.R. SYSTEM
SIX CYLINDER COMPRESSOR

IN FRONT OF CONDENSER		EVAPORATOR PRESSURE AT E.E.V.I.R. GAUGE CONNECTION	ENGINE RPM	DISCHARGE AIR TEMP. R.H. NOZZLE ± 2°F.	PRESSURE HIGH (DISCHARGE) ± 20 PSI
RELATIVE HUMIDITY	AIR TEMP. °F. ± 1 PSI				
20	70 80 90 100	29.5 29.5 30.0 31.0	2000	40 44 48 57	150 190 245 305
30	70 80 90 100	29.5 30.0 31.0 32.0	2000	42 47 51 61	150 205 265 325
40	70 80 90 100	29.5 30.0 32.0 39.0	2000	45 49 55 65	165 215 280 345
50	70 80 90 100	30.0 32.0 34.0 40.0	2000	47 53 59 69	180 235 295 350
60	70 80 90 100	30.0 33.0 36.0 43.0	2000	48 56 63 73	180 240 300 360
70	70 80 90 100	30.0 34.0 38.0 44.0	2000	50 58 65 75	185 245 305 365
80	70 80 90	30.0 34.0 39.0	2000	50 59 67	190 250 310
90	70 80 90	30.0 36.0 42.0	2000	50 62 71	200 265 330

* J-6076 Humidicator can be used to determine Humidity.

Figure 9-27 These Oldsmobile pressure-temperature-humidity charts show why you cannot just use some single chart for all cars, even if you happen to know the relative humidity, or if you are one of the handful of people in the service industry with a device to measure humidity in the shop. And these two charts are for the same car maker, same model year, and basically the same system. You will see even greater differences in temperatures of the discharge air than on these charts, and perhaps even more than the 50 psi (345 kPa) differences in high-side pressure readings. (Courtesy General Motors Corp.)

FOUR CYLINDER COMPRESSOR

PERFORMANCE TEST CONDITIONS

Hood . . . . Raised
Front Doors . . . . Closed
Front Windows . . . . Open
Select Lever . . . . Max. (Recirc.)
Fan Switch . . . . HI
Temperature Lever . . . . Full Cold
Nozzles and Air Outlets . . . . Open
Engine Speed . . . . 2000 RPM

TEST READINGS:

Ambient Air in Degrees F. (In Auxiliary Fan Air Blast Ahead of Condenser)	70°		80°		90°		100°		110°	
Air Quality	Arid	Humid	Arid	Humid	Arid	Humid	Arid	Humid	Arid	Humid
Average Compressor Head Pressure in PSI	145	185	185	225	205	245	240	270	260	310
Average Evaporator Pressure PSI AT SEA LEVEL	28 to 31									
Center Outlet Temperature in Degrees F.	40	42	42	44	44	47	45	48	47	51

PERFORMANCE CHART
TORONADO WITH V.I.R. SYSTEM

IN FRONT OF CONDENSER		EVAPORATOR PRESSURE AT E.E.V.I.R. GAUGE CONNECTION ± 1 PSI	ENGINE RPM	DISCHARGE AIR TEMP. LEFT CENTER OUTLET ± 2°F.	PRESSURE HIGH (DISCHARGE) ± 20 PSI
RELATIVE HUMIDITY	AIR TEMP. °F.				
20	70	29.5	2000	42	195
	80	29.5		44	240
	90	30.0		46	290
	100	32.0		54	335
30	70	29.5	2000	43	200
	80	29.5		47	250
	90	30.0		50	300
	100	35.0		59	355
40	70	29.5	2000	44	210
	80	30.0		47	260
	90	33.0		54	315
	100	39.0		64	375
50	70	29.5	2000	44	210
	80	30.0		49	265
	90	35.0		58	325
	100	42.0		67	380
60	70	29.5	2000	45	215
	80	30.0		51	275
	90	37.0		61	330
	100	45.0		72	400
70	70	29.5	2000	46	225
	80	32.0		53	280
	90	39.0		64	335
80	70	29.5	2000	47	230
	80	34.0		56	295
	90	41.0		67	350
90	70	29.5	2000	48	235
	80	36.0		58	300
	90	43.0		70	365

* J-6076 Humidicator can be used to determine Humidity.

Figure 9-27 (continued)

of Refrigerant 12, however, it should not be necessary to check the compressor oil level or add oil to the system.

2. With a soap-water solution.
3. With a gas-type leak detector, such as a butane or propane type.
4. With an electronic detector.
5. With a leak-tracing dye added to the system. Cans of Refrigerant 12 with dye included are commonly used because they represent a convenient way to get both dye and Refrigerant 12 into the system at the same time (see Fig. 9-28).

Figure 9-28 If you cannot find a leak with external detectors, install a can of refrigerant that contains a dye. Refer to Chapter 11 for installation details, following procedure for liquid-charging into the high side of the system.

Soap-Water Solution

Soap-water solution is the least expensive leak detector. You just brush the soap water wherever the system might leak—at all connections, such as hoses to and from the receiver-dryer or accumulator, at the expansion valve or orifice tube, at the test fittings, at the condenser and over the finned surface of the condenser core, and at the front end of the compressor shaft. If there is a refrigerant leak, the soap water will bubble.

Unfortunately, soap water is not too practical. It is obviously difficult to brush onto an entire condenser without removing the grille, the underside of a tube connection, or the front end of the compressor shaft (where a key seal is located). It usually will indicate only rather large leaks. Your object in an air conditioning tuneup is to find small leaks before they become major, so you should use one of the other testers, all of which have greater sensitivity to leaks and have hoses or probes so that you can check even in relatively inaccessible locations.

Butane

The butane tester (Fig. 9-29) is an inexpensive piece of equipment with a butane gas cartridge (replaceable). Hold the tester upright and turn the cartridge clockwise until you hear gas hissing out at the gas outlet. Light detector and allow a half-minute for the detector to "warm up." There is no flame adjustment.

Then move a search tube over all possible leak points, particularly at the undersides of all joints; if there is a leak, the flame color will change from blue to bright green. The tester sensitivity drops with increasing use; to restore it, a part called the *reaction wire* must be replaced (the tester comes with spare wires).

Figure 9-29 Move search tube of butane-type gas tester over all possible leak points, particularly at the undersides of all joints. If there is a leak, flame color will change from blue to bright green.

Propane

The propane tester, also inexpensive, is operated in a similar manner. Open the gas valve until you just hear the gas hissing out. Light the gas at the chimney opening (see Fig. 9-30). Adjust the flame by operating the manual valve on the tester until it just touches the bottom of the reaction plate, which should turn a dull cherry red. If the flame is too high, the reaction plate may melt.

Now move the search tube over possible leak points. If there is a small leak, the flame color will change from pale blue to yellow. If the leak is major (a rate of significantly more than ½ ounce per year), the flame will change to bright blue-purple. *Note:* Periodically scrape the reaction plate surface gently with a knife to remove a combustion film, which can reduce the sensitivity of the tester.

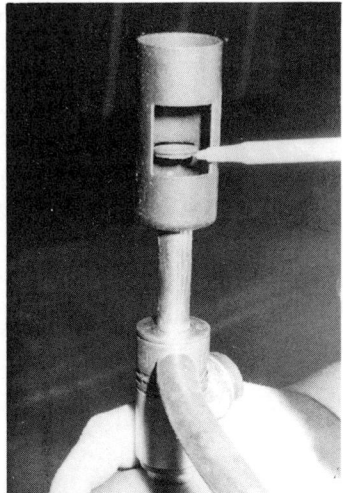

Figure 9-30 Light propane tester at chimney opening. Adjust flame by operating manual valve until flame just touches bottom of reaction plate (to which pen points), which should turn a dull cherry red. Do not set flame too high or reaction plate may melt. Periodically scrape combustion film from reaction plate with knife. Or unbolt reaction plate and install a replacement when it deteriorates badly.

Electronic

The electronic detector is the most expensive and potentially the most sensitive. Some come with a sensitivity adjuster and are calibrated so they will not indicate a leak of less than ½ ounce per year (Fig. 9-31). One tester includes a cartridge of Refrigerant 12 into which you push the probe. This causes a calibrated leak that should trigger the tester if it is working. The typical electronic tester has a buzzer to signal the leak, making it usable (compared with the gas type) for those who are blue-green color-blind. Some have an indicator light, making them suitable for the deaf.

Figure 9-31 Electronic tester is extremely sensitive. Turn sensitivity adjuster in accordance with equipment manufacturer's instructions.

Note: When using an electronic tester, follow the manufacturer's instructions regarding sensitivity settings. On most cars, there is always some leakage of Refrigerant 12 at the front of the compressor. When a system has not been operated for some time, the leakage may show up on an electronic tester (even on some gas testers if severe enough). Therefore, you should run the system for a brief period before checking for leaks, to allow the compressor shaft seal to work itself back into shape. Oil streaks in the area of the compressor shaft seal (leaks that also may hit the hood insulating pad) are usually normal unless a large leak is found.

Correcting Minor Leaks

If you encounter minor leaks at threaded connections, try tightening them with tubing wrenches. The typical connection has an O-ring seal, so it should not require tightening with unusual force. Leaks at Schrader valves may be tightened with a valve tool, which is somewhat similar to the tool used for tire valves.

Major Leaks: When You Can Find Them and When You Can't

When you find a major leak, it normally calls for discharging the system and repair or replacement of a part. If may be a simple matter of changing a gasket or O-ring or installing a new or recored (rebuilt) condenser. See Chapter 13.

If a major leak defies isolation, it is often in the evaporator, which is buried in the duct housing. Corrosion from moisture in the system collects in the bottom of the evaporator on many cars and soon eats its way through. On some cars you can get partial access to the evaporator (without major work), so you can probe it with a leak detector.

In some cases, you can confirm an evaporator leak by examining the moisture drain tubes. If you find oil in the tube ends, it may be refrigeration oil that has leaked from the evaporator.

QUESTIONS

1. Key cooling system checks are
    a. radiator cap and the front of the condenser.
    b. condition of the coolant.
    c. coolant flow through the radiator.
    d. all of the above.

2. Check the clutch-type engine fan by trying to spin the fan with the engine cool.
    a. The fan should spin freely.
    b. It should not move.
    c. It should spin up to five revolutions.
3. A basic performance check of the air conditioning should be made with ambient temperatures of at least
    a. 50°F (10°C).
    b. 60°F (16°C).
    c. 70°F (21°C).
4. If the shop is very warm when you make an air conditioning performance test,
    a. open the car doors to let cold air out.
    b. park the car close to a wall, to avoid having the fan draw in warm air.
    c. Answers a and b are both correct.
    d. Neither answer a nor b is correct.
5. The sight glass on a car so equipped should show bubbling
    a. continuously as long as the bubbling is light.
    b. whenever the system is turned off and on.
    c. at no time.
6. With the air conditioning operating, the evaporator outlet line should feel
    a. warmer than the line between the thermostatic expansion valve and the receiver-dryer or condenser.
    b. colder than the line between the expansion valve and receiver-dryer or condenser.
    c. warmer on a very hot day and colder when ambient temperatures are about 70°F (21°C).
7. When you apply hot air to the in-car sensor grille on a car with automatic temperature control, with the degree wheel set to 75°F (24°C) and ambient temperatures of 70°F (21°C), the system when turned on should
    a. start blowing hot air.
    b. start blowing cold air.
    c. provide a mix of air of about 75°F (24°C).
8. Common locations for pressure test fittings are on the tubing and
    a. condenser.
    b. compressor.
    c. evaporator.
9. If a fitting is on a line that goes to the condenser, it
    a. is a high-side fitting.
    b. is a low-side fitting.

c. could be either high or low side, depending on where the other side of the line goes.
10. If you find two low-side fittings on a car, one of them is for testing the
    a. compressor.
    b. suction throttling valve or evaporator pressure regulator.
    c. thermostatic expansion valve.
    d. Answers b and c are both correct.
11. The manual valve on the air conditioning system is open to the test port when the stem is
    a. front seated.
    b. back seated.
    c. in mid-position.
12. The center fitting on the gauge manifold connects to
    a. the high-side test fitting.
    b. the low-side test fitting.
    c. neither.
13. When opened, the manual valve on the gauge manifold allows Refrigerant 12 to flow
    a. to the gauges.
    b. between high and low sides to stabilize the readings.
    c. out the center fitting.
14. Mechanic A says high-side pressure readings may vary greatly with ambient temperature. Mechanic B says they vary greatly with humidity. Who is right?
    a. Mechanic A.
    b. Mechanic B.
    c. Both.
    d. Neither.
15. Mechanic A says that low pressure readings on both high and low sides may indicate a leak. Mechanic B says that those readings may show the system is low on Refrigerant 12. Who is right?
    a. Mechanic A.
    b. Mechanic B.
    c. Both.
    d. Neither.
16. The most accurate leak detector is
    a. butane.
    b. propane.
    c. electronic.
17. A gas-type leak detector indicates when a leak has been found by
    a. color change of the flame.
    b. the fact the flame suddenly rises.
    c. the fact the flame suddenly goes out.

HANDS ON

1. Pressure test a radiator cap. Then pressure test the cooling system.
2. Check the clutch fan.
3. Check and adjust a drive belt with the curved slot adjuster.
4. Check and adjust a drive belt with an idler pulley arrangement.
5. Locate and check air conditioning drain tubes.
6. Make a temperature check at the air conditioning outlets in the dashboard.
7. Inspect the sight glass on a system so equipped with the system running.
8. Hot wire the blower to the battery to check blower function.
9. Make an automatic temperature control quick check with a hair dryer or heat gun at the in-car sensor grille.
10. Locate the test fittings on Ford, Chrysler, and General Motors systems, including GM Valves-in-Receiver and Ford or GM CCOT.
11. Hook up a gauge manifold set, bleed air from the hoses, and take a pressure test on a system with Schrader valves.
12. Perform item 11 on a system with manual valves at the compressor.
13. Check for leaks at all tubing connectors, control valves, front of the compressor, and along condenser tubes with gas and electronic detectors.
14. Tighten tubing connections with two wrenches, tubing type if available, with tubing-type crowfoots and a torque wrench the best choice.

10

Refrigerant 12

Because so many operations, including test procedures, require the use of Refrigerant 12, you should be familiar with its characteristics and how to handle it in the various containers in which it is supplied.

Containers

Refrigerant 12, which should not be confused with any other number of refrigerants, is the only kind used in automobile systems as a heat transfer fluid. Refrigerant 11, which you also may see in service shops, comes out of its container as a liquid and remains a liquid at normal shop temperature. It is a solvent used for flushing all parts of the automotive air conditioning system except the compressor.

Refrigerant 12 is normally sold in three container sizes:

1. *One-pound cans.* At one time the can held 16 ounces of Refrigerant 12. Today, although it is still called a 1-pound can, it may hold 13, 14, or 15 ounces, depending on the manufacturer. In some cases, the 1-pound can also may contain a leak-tracing dye, a small amount of compressor oil, or a special type of alcohol (to prevent moisture in the system from freezing on systems that do not contain a drying agent in the receiver or accumulator). See Fig. 10-1.
2. *Twelve-pound drum.* This is a popular bulk size.
3. *Thirty-pound cannister.* This is a size most often used in shops that specialize in air conditioning.

Although the 1-pound can is the most expensive way to store Refrigerant 12, even those shops with larger containers keep a supply of the 1-pound cans, for they may be a convenient way to add oil, leak-tracing dye,

Figure 10-1 This 1-pound can contains Refrigerant 12 and a leak detector.

or alcohol to the system. In addition, some shops find them more convenient to use to flush dirt particles (see Chapters 13 and 14) from a new or rebuilt compressor, just prior to installation (see Chapter 14).

Handling Refrigerant 12

Before you even pick up a container of Refrigerant 12, you should know the safe ways to handle it. This begins with an understanding of how Refrigerant 12 behaves. As you learned earlier in this book, Refrigerant 12 has many qualities that are useful in a refrigeration system and contribute to safety. However, under some circumstances it poses dangers from frostbite, explosion, and poison gas.

1. *Frostbite.* As you have learned, Refrigerant 12 vaporizes at -21.7°F (-30°C) at atmospheric pressure, so the instant it leaves the can and goes into the atmosphere it is a vapor. It absorbs heat so quickly that if it comes in contact with the human body it can cause frostbite. The experienced mechanic, therefore, wears goggles to protect the eyes and gloves to protect the skin. Shops that do air conditioning work should have first-aid kits that include instruction procedures for treating frostbite, and all personnel should be familiar with them.

2. *Explosion.* Refrigerant 12 is nonexplosive as a gas in the atmosphere, one of its good qualities. However, in a confined space

under sufficient pressure any gas can explode, and Refrigerant 12 is no exception. As you have learned, Refrigerant 12 pressure and temperature in a confined space always are related in the same way (see Fig. 2-8). The typical Refrigerant 12 can will safely withstand more than 170 psi (1172 kPa) or so, which is developed at about 125°F (52°C); so at normal room and outdoor temperatures there is no problem. If the 1-pound can is exposed to the sun, however, the temperature may exceed the safety limit and produce enough pressure to cause the can to explode. Therefore, keep cans out of direct sunlight, whether stored in the shop or being transported to the shop in a car or truck. Most bulk containers have a pressure relief valve or plug to vent excess pressure to prevent explosion. However, you still should take precautions to prevent explosion of Refrigerant 12.

3. *Poison gas.* Although Refrigerant 12 is not poisonous, when it comes in contact with direct flame, it turns to a poison gas. Direct flame also could cause a can to overheat and explode. Inasmuch as a great deal of air conditioning service is done in cooling system specialty shops, which have torches in regular use, the dual danger is not imaginary.

Tapping into the Refrigerant Container

The methods of tapping into the containers of refrigerant depend on the type, but in any case you must exercise care to prevent the possibility of frostbite.

One-Pound Cans

There are various types of dispensing valves to attach to 1-pound cans. Two of the more common ones are shown in Fig. 10-2. Both lock to the can. With one, you turn down a handle at the top, which punctures the can and closes the valve. With the other, you turn down the valve assembly itself to puncture the can. A separate shutoff valve is built into the valve assembly. It must be closed before you begin to puncture the can.

It is standard practice to include an antiblowback valve in the dispensing valve to prevent the possibility of high system pressure (from an incorrect connection) blowing back into the can. The type with the separate shutoff valve also has a pressure relief valve built into the top as extra protection. Or you can obtain a separate relief valve to use with the type that does not have it.

Once the can is fitted with a dispensing valve, it can be connected to a hose, and the hose connected directly to the air conditioning system,

167 Tapping into the Refrigerant Container

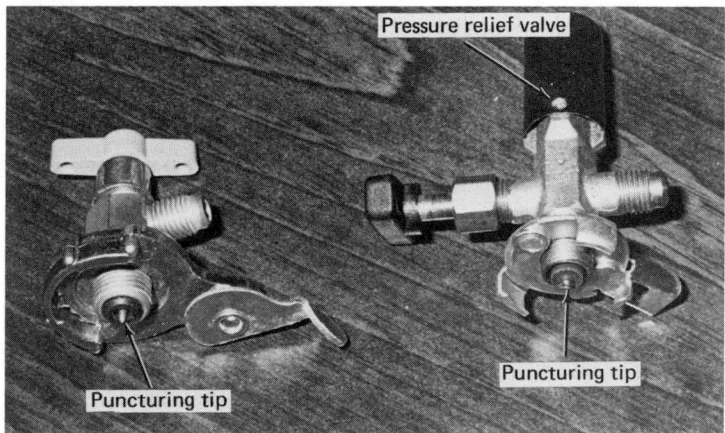

Figure 10-2 These are two types of dispensing valves that attach to 1-pound cans. The one on the left pierces the can when you turn down the handle of the valve. The one on the right pierces when you thread down the dispensing valve assembly.

Figure 10-3 Multican adapters hold as many cans as necessary to recharge the system, in this case up to five. Each connector on the adapter has a built-in check valve, so there is no loss of refrigerant if less than the five cans are used.

through a gauge manifold, or to a multican adapter (see Fig. 10-3). The charging station also will have a fitting for the hose from a 1-pound can if you are using it to inject oil, dye, or alcohol into the system.

Bulk Containers

The bulk container has a shutoff valve similar to that on the 1-pound can dispensing valve. Like the dispensing valve, it has a fitting for a hose, which may be part of a charging station or connected, like the 1-pound can, to a gauge manifold or the air conditioning system itself.

Liquid and Gas

Whatever the type of container, unless it is heavily pressurized it allows the Refrigerant 12 to separate into both liquid and gas. The liquid settles to the bottom; the gas is on top. If you turn the container upside down, the liquid will drain down to the top to the opening of the dispensing valve. This is important to understand, for Refrigerant 12 may be installed in the system either as a liquid or a gas, as you will learn in Chapter 11.

HANDS ON

1. Attach a dispensing valve to a 1-pound can of Refrigerant 12.

2. Demonstrate the pressure-temperature relationship by attaching a pressure gauge to the dispensing valve and taping a thermometer to the can near the bottom. Open the dispensing valve to produce a reading on the gauge. Check gauge and thermometer after a few hours; the readings should align if gauge and thermometer are accurate. *Note:* This procedure also can be used to check a suspect gauge.

11

Discharge and Recharge

To replace such parts as the receiver-dryer, condenser, evaporator, expansion valve, and most compressors, the air conditioning system must be *opened*, that is, the Refrigerant 12 gas must be allowed to discharge from the system into the atmosphere. In addition, all systems absorb moisture, and in time this moisture affects system operation. As a result, the system must be opened to remove it. Also, Refrigerant 12 may leak out, and correcting a significant leak involves opening the system.

Whenever the system is opened, it must be recharged with Refrigerant 12. The overall procedure is called *discharging and recharging* or *evacuating and recharging*. It is the service you undoubtedly will perform most often in a shop. Basically, it is a three-step procedure:

1. ***Discharge:*** to allow the Refrigerant 12 to escape safely from the system. Connect a pressure gauge manifold or charging station and open the valves. You must collect any lubricating oil that escapes with the Refrigerant, so the discharge must be into a container. The amount of oil collected must be measured; if it is more than ½ ounce, it should be replaced with fresh oil. It may be installed during step 2.
2. ***Vacuum pump:*** to place the system under a strong vacuum, to lower the boiling point of any moisture in the system, and allow this moisture to flow out as a vapor. Even relatively small air leaks will weaken the vacuum, so special leak tests must be performed; if there are any leaks, they must be corrected before vacuum pumping can continue.
3. ***Recharge:*** to install a fresh fill of Refrigerant 12, plus any fresh oil and/or alcohol if necessary. There are three basic ways Refrigerant 12 can be installed in the system:
   a. As a gas into the low-pressure side.
   b. As a liquid into the low-pressure side.
   c. As a liquid into the high-pressure side.

Discharging the System

Begin by connecting the hoses from the gauge manifold or charging station to the test fittings on the system, as you learned in Chapter 9. The manual shutoff valves on the manifold or charging station must be closed before this is done.

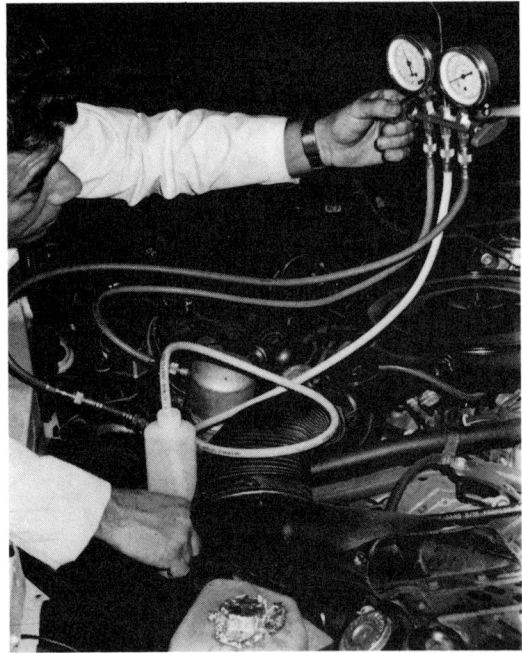

Figure 11-1 Discharge system slowly, first by opening low-side manual valve on gauge manifold. System should be discharged into clean container as shown to collect any oil that may escape.

Gauge Manifold

1. With a gauge manifold, aim the center fitting hose into a clean container.
2. If the air conditioning compressor has manual valves, turn the stems to the mid-position.
3. Finally, slowly open the low-side manual valve on the manifold. Do not open it too much or oil will flow out with the refrigerant. Although you have a container to collect oil, you can save work if you do not allow it to escape in the first place (see Fig. 11-1).
4. When low-side pressure drops to 50 psi (345 kPa), also open the high-side manual valve on the gauge manifold. If you see more than just a faint seepage of oil, you are discharging too quickly. Partly close the manual valves.

5. When pressure readings on the gauges have dropped to zero, discharging is complete. Close the manual valves on the manifold.

Charging Station

The typical charging station has a special valve for discharging. After you open this valve, open the low-side manual valve on the charging station, and when pressure drops to 50 psi (345 kPa), open the high-side manual valve (see Fig. 11-2).

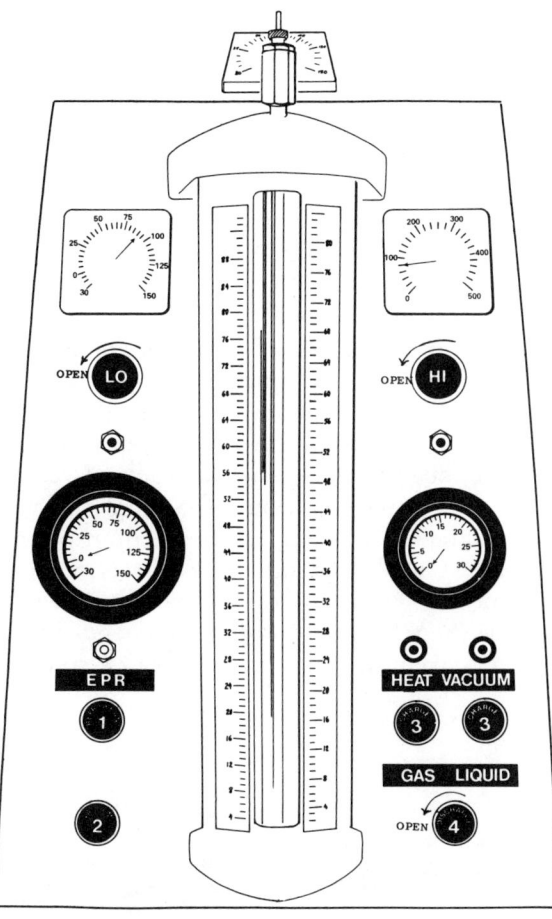

Figure 11-2 If you are using a charging station, discharge by first opening high-side valve as indicated, then low-side valve on charging station. Finally, when pressure on low side has dropped to 50 psi, also open high-side manual valve.

Measuring the Oil

Measure the amount of oil collected and then discard it. If it exceeds ½ ounce, you should add an equal amount of fresh refrigeration oil (the type specified for the system, as explained in Chapter 14). To ensure good oil circulation, do it in either of two ways:

1. With 1-pound cans that contain refrigeration oil during the recharging procedure.
2. With bulk oil poured into an oil injector at the start of the vacuum pumping, as explained later.

Vacuum Pumping the System

Vacuum pumping does not draw water out of the system, but it creates a vacuum that lowers the boiling point of the water, so the water boils and is drawn out as a vapor by the pump. The basic principles of this should sound familiar, for in Chapter 1 you learned that water boils at 32°F (0°C) in a perfect vacuum. Normal ambient temperature when air conditioning service is done is about 70°F (21°C) or higher, so the perfect vacuum (which cannot be obtained anyway) is unnecessary. If a pump can produce a vacuum of 29.3 inches of mercury or better at sea level, the moisture boils at 70°F (21°C), and a quality pump can do even better than that.

At altitudes above sea level, the pump produces less vacuum, but as altitude increases, the boiling point of the moisture drops. For each 1000 feet above sea level, one inch less of vacuum is acceptable.

The refrigeration oil will not boil when the moisture does, so if it is installed at the start of the vacuum pumping, there is no problem. The easiest way to install bulk oil, as previously explained, is with an oil injector (Fig. 11-3), following the procedure shown in Fig. 11-4. Be sure to use the refrigeration oil recommended for the system by the car maker.

Vacuum pumping is a four-step operation.

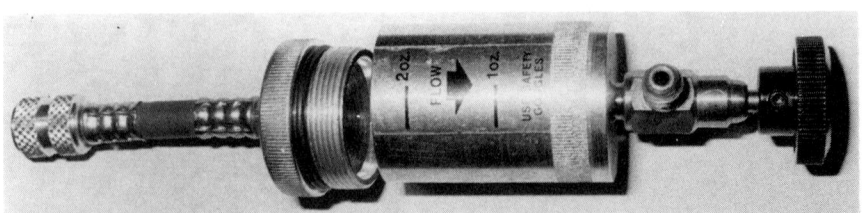

Figure 11-3 Oil injector simplifies installation of bulk refrigeration oil into system.

Vacuum Pumping the System

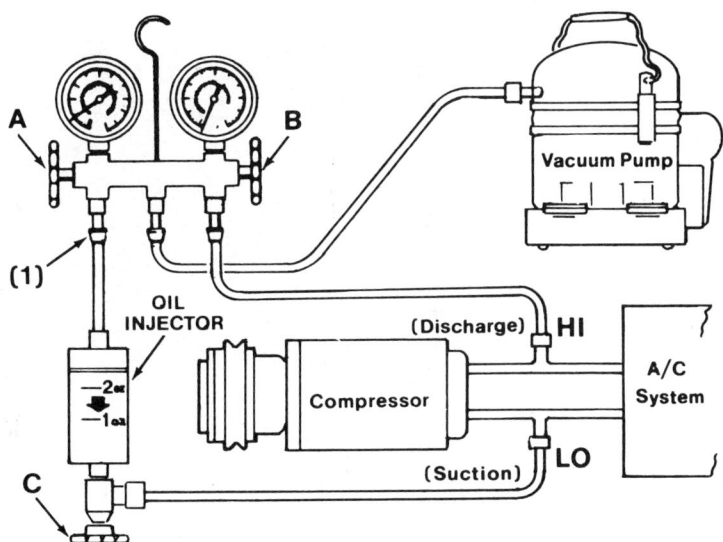

Figure 11-4 To use oil injector, hook it up between low-side gauge on manifold and low-side test fitting as shown. Turn on the vacuum pump and open the high-side manual valve on the gauge manifold. Low-side manual valve on the gauge manifold and valve C on the injector both are closed. Undo the injector cap and add up to 2 ounces of refrigeration oil. Refit the cap. When the vacuum pump is drawing 29 inches of vacuum or more (after several minutes of operation), open the injector manual valve (C). Allow the pump to run for 3 minutes more; then close the high-side manual valve on the manifold. Turn off the vacuum pump and open the low-side manual valve on the gauge manifold. The oil will be drawn into the low side of the system. This procedure can be repeated if necessary to add more oil.

1. Connect the vacuum pump to the hose of the center fitting of the gauge manifold. For best results, connect a two-way valve to the center fitting hose, the vacuum pump to one nipple of the two-way valve, and the Refrigerant 12 supply to the other nipple. This ensures that no air, dirt, or moisture will get into the system from the time vacuum pumping ends and recharging starts (see Fig. 11-5). If you are using a charging station, the connections already are made within the station itself.

2. If you must add oil to the system, this is the time to do it, as shown in Fig. 11-4. When oil addition is complete, or if it is not necessary, you may proceed to vacuum pumping. Turn on the pump, and open both the high- and low-pressure manual valves on the manifold or charging station. *Note:* If for some reason you backseated the manual valves on compressors so equipped after discharging the system, move them to mid-position. Look at the vacuum pump

174   Discharge and Recharge

Figure 11-5 Two-way valve, to which both vacuum pump and refrigerant container can be attached, permits discharging and recharging the system without disconnecting any hoses.

gauge. It should read 29 inches of vacuum or more at sea level within a few minutes. If the pump has been performing properly in previous use, but will not pull down to the necessary vacuum at this time, the odds are there is a leak in the system. Trace and correct the leak before you continue to pump, using the procedures described in the previous chapter. You first will have to install 1 or 2 pounds of Refrigerant 12 to be able to find a leak.

3. Even if the pump pulls down to a satisfactory vacuum, you still must check for leaks. Close the high- and low-pressure manual valves on the gauge manifold or charging station for 5 minutes. If the vacuum drops more than 2 inches in that time, there is a leak you must trace and correct, or air will get into the system and reduce performance. Make this test with the vacuum pump turned off.

4. If the system checks out, let the vacuum pump run for at least 30 minutes. When pumping is complete, close the high- and low-pressure manual valves on the manifold or charging station. If you do not use the two-way valve, disconnect the vacuum pump from the manifold for recharging. If the system is tight, it will hold the vacuum (keeping out harmful air) until you recharge (provided you proceed promptly). However, air will get into the hose from the center fitting and it must be bled out. Otherwise, recharging with refrigerant will push it into the system. Bleeding the hose is part of the step-by-step recharging procedure described later in this chapter.

Recharging the System

Each system has a specified capacity of Refrigerant 12, and recharging is the operation of installing it. The amount you install must be very close to specifications, for too much or too little will result in poor cooling performance.

There are three ways in which Refrigerant 12 can be installed. To use these methods intelligently, you should understand the pros and cons of each.

Gas into the Low-Pressure Side

Dispensing the Refrigerant 12 as a gas into the low-pressure side of the system, with the engine running and the air conditioning on, is the most common procedure, particularly with a gauge manifold. If you hold the refrigerant container upright and open the dispensing valve, the gas under pressure will force its way out through the hose and into the air conditioning system. With the engine running and the system on, the low pressure on the low side of the system will result in the refrigerant being drawn in (see Fig. 11-6).

It sounds good, and it does work. However, as the gas flows out, the pressure in the container gradually drops and the flow starts to slow down. When dealing with a 1-pound can, it is common to have to wait a good number of minutes for the can to empty completely.

Figure 11-6 Gas-charging into the low side is done with the refrigerant container held upright as shown.

The flow of gas can be increased by heating the container to build up pressure, and this often must be done to get the refrigerant installed in a reasonable amount of time. Heating even may be necessary with liquid installation techniques.

Liquid into the Low-Pressure Side

If the Refrigerant 12 container is inverted, the refrigerant will flow rapidly from the container into the system as a liquid, almost as if you were filling a glass with water. The gas remains in the container, so the pressure is virtually unchanged as the liquid flows out. Liquid is the fast way to charge (see Fig. 11-7).

However, on the low-pressure side the refrigerant flow is to the compressor, and that poses a problem. Liquid is not compressible, and if the compressor draws in a slug of liquid, it can be damaged. York two-cylinder compressors were among those very sensitive to liquid, and on Ford products using them, an accumulator was installed in the low side to trap any liquid to protect the compressor.

Figure 11-7 If refrigerant container is inverted as shown, liquid will flow into the system.

One might think that cycling clutch orifice tube systems (CCOT), which have a large accumulator, might be immune to any problems with liquid charging, because when you install liquid into the low side, it is going into the accumulator, a liquid trap. This is true, and it is safe to install 1 or 2 pounds as liquid with the engine off. However, more than that amount will overflow the accumulator and send liquid to the compressor. Therefore, General Motors recommends that on its CCOT you finish the charging with the engine running and the air conditioning on, and charge with gas. It is not that the GM compressors are sensitive to damage from liquid; they are not. However, liquid Refrigerant 12 picks up and "floats away" lubricating oil from the compressor's internal surfaces, and when the compressor is first turned on, the oil floats out of the compressor and the compressor may seize or otherwise fail.

The GM six-cylinder compressor has an internal oil sump, so any oil that floats away is replaced quickly. On the GM radial four-cylinder, however, there is no internal oil supply, and the compressor must wait until it draws in oil from the rest of the system. Thus it is far more likely to be damaged.

If you wish to completely liquid-charge into the low side, there is a liquid charger (Fig. 11-8) device that meters the flow of liquid so that there is no chance of a real slug getting to the compressor. The liquid charger is connected to the low-side fitting on the gauge manifold, although it instead may be connected to the center fitting on the manifold, or the refrigerant container. It may be installed before vacuum pumping and will allow this operation to proceed normally.

With the liquid charger in place, you allow a small amount of refrigerant to flow as a gas into the low side with the engine and air conditioning off; then run the system and air conditioning and liquid-charge the rest of the refrigerant into the low side.

Liquid into the High-Pressure Side

Liquid-charging into the high side with the engine off is the universally accepted procedure for charging stations, and some mechanics do it with

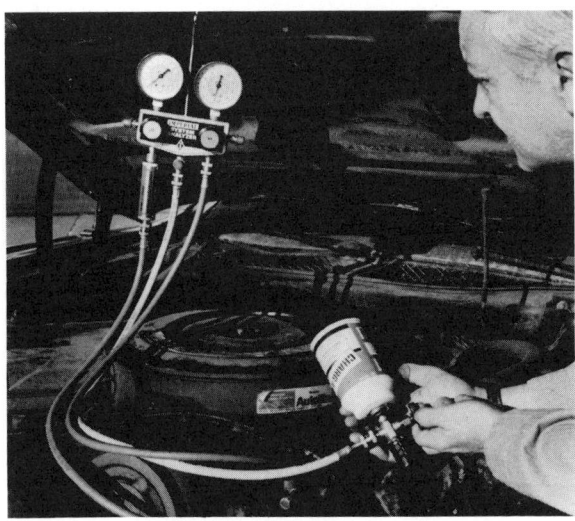

Figure 11-8 Special tool called liquid charger can be used to safely charge liquid into the low side. Liquid charger is the part attached to the low-side fitting on the gauge manifold.

gauge manifolds. With the engine off, under favorable conditions, the pressures will not build up to more than 120 psi (827 kPa), which is under the amount of pressure the 1-pound Refrigerant 12 can will withstand.

A key objection to liquid into the high side with the engine off is that if conditions are not favorable (system restrictions and high ambient air temperatures raising refrigerant pressure, for example), a pressure blowback to the can could occur, and the can might explode. However, as explained in Chapter 10, safety-type dispensing valves with antiblowback protection are readily available. With the charging station, of course, there is built-in antiblowback protection, and the refrigerant container has a built-in relief valve.

A possible problem with liquid into the high side when using a gauge manifold is that at some point the pressures in the refrigerant supply container and in the system equalize at a number that depends on ambient temperature. To get in the remainder of the refrigerant required may call for applying heat to the refrigerant supply container to raise the temperature to above ambient (and therefore increase the pressure of the gas inside the container).

The charging station has a refrigerant electric heater built in, but the 1-pound can or the bulk container does not. There are two approaches you can take if you charge liquid into the high side with a gauge manifold and need additional "push" on the refrigerant inside the supply container:

1. Hook up a charging cylinder between the refrigerant supply container(s) and the gauge manifold before you begin charging. The charging cylinder is available as a separate part, and not only does it have a sight glass to make it easy to see exactly how much refrigerant is going into the system, but it can be obtained with a built-in electric heater.
2. Heat the supply container as you would if you were charging gas into the low side. That is, you can rub the container vigorously with your hands. Or (much more effective) you can immerse it in a pot of water heated to as high as 125°F (52°C). Obviously, even this is not as good as the charging cylinder with an electric heater. Also, it is not as easy to immerse an inverted container in a pot as it is to immerse the upright container when gas is charging into the low side.

Adding Alcohol to the System

A special type of alcohol was used in air conditioning systems on American Motors cars through 1975, for their receivers did not contain a drying agent. The alcohol, which prevents any moisture in the system from freezing, is harmful to any system with a dryer.

When you evacuate a system containing alcohol, you draw out the alcohol and must install a fresh fill. The easiest way is to use 1-pound cans containing alcohol (just as the easiest way to add oil is with 1-pound cans containing oil). Or you can add bulk alcohol during recharging, when indicated in the following instructions. Because so few cars are involved, the actual procedure is explained separately from the recharging operation at the end of this chapter.

Recharging Operation: With a Gauge Manifold into the Low Side, Engine Running and System Turned On

When recharging with a charging station, observe the equipment manufacturer's instructions for low- or high-side charging, as there are variations among different models. The following is low-side charging with a gauge manifold, with the refrigerant as a gas or a liquid (using the liquid charger).

1. The manual valves on the manifold should still be closed from the conclusion of the vacuum-pumping operation. If the refrigerant container or multican adapter was not connected to a two-way valve with the vacuum pump, connect the can or adapter to a hose, and attach the hose very loosely to the center fitting of the gauge manifold. *Note:* If you are using a bulk container of Refrigerant 12, place it on a scale, so you can weigh it and so measure the installation of refrigerant. Or you may install a charging cylinder, a calibrated cylinder with a sight glass, to measure installation of refrigerant. This cylinder, built into the charging station, also is available separately. It can be connected by hoses to the refrigerant bulk container and manifold or two-way valve.
2. If the air conditioning compressor has manual valves, make sure they are set at mid-position.
3. Check manufacturer's specifications to find out how much refrigerant to install. If you are using a multican adapter, attach the appropriate number of cans. *Note:* Because a "1-pound can" does not contain 16 ounces, be sure to take this into consideration when you calculate how many cans you need.
4. Bleed air from the hose that connects the refrigerant container and the center fitting of the gauge manifold. The simplest way to bleed is with a bleed adapter between the hose and the gauge manifold center fitting (see Fig. 11-9). Or you may leave the hose very loosely on the manifold fitting (caught by one thread so it holds in place). Open the Refrigerant 12 dispensing valve and when you hear refrigerant hissing from the manifold center

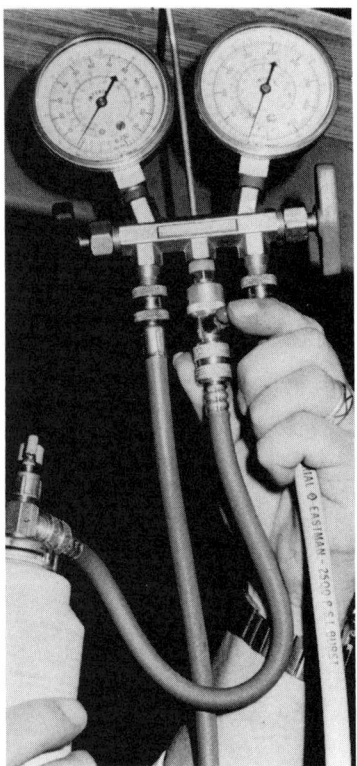 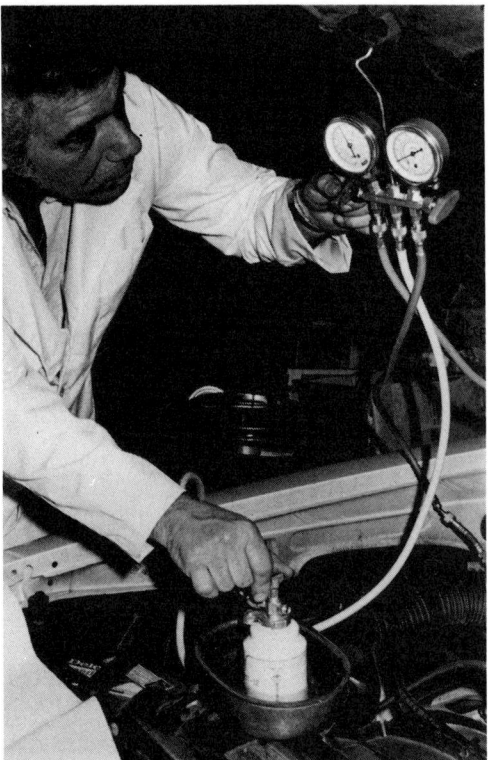

Figure 11-9 (*Left*) Adapter placed between manifold center fitting and hose from refrigerant can permits easy bleeding with hose connections tight. Just press on adapter's flexible cover and you depress Schrader valve, opening it. With dispensing valve on refrigerant container open, refrigerant will flow through and force air out the opened Schrader valve. When you hear hissing for a few seconds, release pressure and Schrader valve on bleed adapter will close.

Figure 11-10 (*Right*) To speed up gas charging into the low side of the system, you can place can in pan of heated water as shown. Water at 125°F (52°C) is at safe maximum temperature.

fitting, close the dispensing valve and hand tighten the hose to the fitting. (Now is the time to add special alcohol to AMC cars through 1975, as explained later in this chapter.)

5. Bypass the cycling clutch switch on cars so equipped, so the compressor will run throughout recharging. A simple way is to undo the wiring connector at the compressor clutch, and with a jumper wire connect directly from the compressor coil side of the connector to the car battery's positive terminal. Bypass the thermal

limiter on General Motors cars so equipped to keep the compressor running during recharging. The limiter is on late-1971 through 1978 models with POA valve systems. Remove the limiter fuse from the connector and hook up a jumper wire from the B to the C terminal of the connector. (On York rotary vane compressors, remove the thermal protector. See Chapter 14.)

6. Close the vacuum-pump side of the two-way valve if used; open the refrigerant container side if it was closed.

7. Run the engine, turn on the air conditioning, and open the low-side manual valve on the manifold. If you are charging gas, hold the refrigerant container upright. If you are charging liquid (with the liquid charger), turn the can upside down and hold it up. Open the container's dispensing valve to allow refrigerant to flow into the system. Watch the pressure gauges. If you see a reading going abnormally high, close the dispensing valve. Look for a restriction in the system and correct it. If refrigerant flow is slow, as is common with gas charging, rub the can with your hands to add heat and increase pressure inside. Or place the can(s) upright in a pan of water heated to 120° to 125°F (49° to 52°C), as in Fig. 11-10.

8. When a 1-pound can is empty, you will feel it is, just as with any other emptied container. If you must disconnect it and install a fresh can, you can do it either of two ways: (1) Close the dispensing valve and carefully remove the dispensing valve assembly (to prevent any gas in the can from getting on you). Attach the dispensing valve to the new can. Although not necessary, shut the manifold manual valves for extra safety. You save bleeding the hose to the manifold center fitting. (2) Close the manifold manual valves and the dispensing valve. Disconnect the hose to the dispensing valve at either end; then open the dispensing valve with the fitting or hose aimed away to vent any refrigerant gas that may be in the can. This method obviously is safer.

9. Attach a fresh can if needed. If you used the second method in step 8, bleed the hose from the can to the manifold center fitting.

10. When charging is done, close the gauge manifold manual valves. Move the compressor manual valves to a backseated position on compressors so equipped. Close the dispensing valve on the Refrigerant 12 container. Disconnect the hoses from the test fittings on the car and then the other hoses. Follow this sequence, for if you leave the hose connections at the test fittings for last, the system will self-discharge if it is fitted with Schraders.

Recharging Operation: With a Gauge Manifold, Liquid into the High Side with the Engine Off

1. Connect the refrigerant container to the center fitting on the manifold using a charging hose and antiblowback protection (such as a safety dispensing valve and/or antiblowback valve in the hose at either end).
2. Make sure the gauge manifold's manual valves both are closed. If the air conditioning has compressor manual valves, set them at mid-position.
3. Check manufacturer's specifications to find out how much Refrigerant 12 to install, as in step 3 for charging into the low side.
4. Bleed air from the hose that connects the refrigerant container and the center fitting of the gauge manifold if necessary, as in step 4 for charging into the low side.
5. Open the manifold's high side manual valve, turn the refrigerant can(s) upside down and hold it up, and then open the dispensing valve on the refrigerant can to allow refrigerant to flow into the system. Watch the pressure gauges, and if you see a reading rising to abnormally high levels, close the dispensing valve. There apparently is a restriction in the system that must be traced and corrected.
6. When a 1-pound can is empty, you will feel it is, and you should replace it with a fresh can, as in steps 8 and 9 of charging into the low side. Complete recharging as in step 10 of charging into the low side.

Use of the Sight Glass

If you are charging an air conditioning system with a sight glass, you may be tempted to use the sight glass as a guide to the amount of refrigerant you should install. Although reference to the sight glass when attempting to correct a poor performance problem was discussed in a previous chapter, it was with regard to it as a general indicator and to give greater importance to pressure gauge readings. In most cases you will substantially overcharge if you add refrigerant until the sight glass goes clear with the system running. If you are charging liquid into the high side, you also face the danger of a pressure blowback, for once you start the engine and turn on the system, the high side pressures will build up, perhaps to several hundred pounds per square inch.

Adding Alcohol to AMC Cars

Before adding special alcohol to an AMC car through 1975, make sure the receiver has not been replaced with one containing a drying agent. If the receiver is an original equipment or factory replacement part, it will not have the dryer.

To install bulk alcohol, use the AMC procedure, which follows and includes gas charging into the low-pressure side with a gauge manifold, or use the charging station method.

1. Check American Motors specifications for the amount, which should be on a decal on the compressor. If not, add 2 milliliters (1/15 ounce) for each pound of Refrigerant 12 that goes into the system. The alcohol used is anhydrous alcohol and is available from automotive refrigeration parts sources.
2. Hook up the manifold gauge set and your Refrigerant 12 container, and proceed as you would with any other system, up to and including the point where you bleed air from the hose that connects the Refrigerant 12 container and the center fitting of the gauge manifold (step 4 in the recharging operation into the low side). Both manual valves on the gauge manifold should be closed.
3. Hand tighten the hose connection at the manifold center fitting when bleeding is done, and close the dispensing valve on the Refrigerant 12 container. With the dispensing valve closed, the Refrigerant 12 push is stopped.
4. Disconnect the hose from the gauge manifold center fitting and keep the hose end above the level of the Refrigerant 12 container. Refrigerant 12 is heavier than air, and if you are careful, it will remain in the hose. Quickly pour the alcohol into the hose and reconnect the hose to the manifold.
5. Most AMC compressors have manual valves at the compressor, so turn the low-side valve to mid-position and reopen both the Refrigerant 12 dispensing valve and the low-side manual valve on the gauge manifold. The refrigerant will flow into the system and carry the alcohol with it.

Adding Alcohol with a Charging Station

1. Proceed as you would for any other system, up to and including the filling of the 5-pound charging cylinder with Refrigerant 12.
2. If the air bleed was opened to assist filling the charging cylinder, close it.

3. Close the valve from the bulk container. The station's high and low manual valves should be closed at this time, but if for some reason they are not, close them now.
4. Disconnect the low-side hose at the station's fitting, pour the alcohol into the hose, and then reconnect the hose to the station's fitting.
5. Turn the compressor's low-side manual valve to the mid-position and proceed to charge the system through the low-pressure side in accordance with the equipment manufacturer's recommendations.

QUESTIONS

1. When using Refrigerant 12, you should
   a. wear safety goggles.
   b. keep the container away from direct flame or high heat.
   c. Answers a and b are both correct.
2. Mechanic A says the air conditioning system must be discharged carefully to prevent a lot of oil from getting out of the system. Mechanic B says it should be discharged carefully to prevent moisture from getting in. Who is right?
   a. Mechanic A.
   b. Mechanic B.
   c. Both.
   d. Neither.
3. For moisture in the air conditioning system to boil at 70°F (21°C), the vacuum pump at sea level must produce at least
   a. 27.4 inches of mercury (696 mm).
   b. 28.9 inches of mercury (734 mm).
   c. 29.3 inches of mercury (744 mm).
   d. 29.8 inches of mercury (757 mm).
4. For each 1000 feet (305 meters) above sea level,
   a. add 2 inches of mercury (51 mm) to the vacuum specification the pump must draw.
   b. deduct 1 inch of mercury (25.4 mm) from the vacuum specification.
   c. deduct 2 inches of mercury (51 mm) from the vacuum specification.
5. The vacuum pump will not pull down to the specified vacuum. Mechanic A says to connect two pumps in parallel to remove moisture. Mechanic B says let the pump run longer to compensate. Who is right?
   a. Mechanic A.
   b. Mechanic B.

c. Both.
d. Neither.

6. If a can of Refrigerant 12 is inverted, the Refrigerant 12 flows out
   a. as a gas under low pressure.
   b. as a gas under pressure that depends on ambient temperature.
   c. as a liquid under low pressure.
   d. as a liquid under pressure that depends on ambient temperature.

7. Liquid charging with a charging station is approved by all car makers if you
   a. charge only into the low side.
   b. charge only into the high side.
   c. simultaneously charge into both high and low sides.

8. On a cycling clutch orifice tube system with its suction side accumulator, you may safely charge
   a. all the liquid through a test fitting on the accumulator, with the engine off.
   b. one to two pound cans of liquid into the accumulator with the engine running and air conditioning on and the remainder as a gas with the air conditioning and engine off.
   c. one to two pound cans of liquid into the accumulator with the engine off, the remainder as a gas with the engine and air conditioning on.

9. A major advantage of a charging station over a gauge manifold is
   a. a charging cylinder with a sight glass to measure Refrigerant 12 flow.
   b. the ability to automatically meter alcohol into the system.
   c. both of the above.

10. Bleeding the gauge manifold or charging station hoses is necessary to purge
    a. air.
    b. moisture.
    c. contaminated oil.

11. To be able to run the compressor if desired during recharging on a system with a thermal limiter,
    a. remove the limiter fuse from the connector.
    b. remove the limiter and ground the B terminal of the connector.
    c. remove the limiter and jump across the B and C terminals.

12. Alcohol may be added with Refrigerant 12 to a system
    a. with an accumulator.
    b. without a drying agent in the receiver.
    c. Answers a and b are both correct.

HANDS ON

1. Connect a gauge manifold, vacuum pump, and Refrigerant 12 supply. Discharge, vacuum pump (and check for leaks), and recharge the system properly.
2. Repeat item 1 using an oil injector, and add any necessary clean refrigeration oil to the system.

12

Air Conditioning Troubleshooting

Air conditioning refrigeration problems generally fall into three categories: (1) little or no cooling, (2) intermittent operation, and (3) excessive noise. The cooling problem is the most common and also the most complex, so it takes up most of this chapter. Cooling problems often have overlapping possibilities, which adds to the complexity.

This chapter breaks troubleshooting down into two segments: a preliminary checkout and detailed troubleshooting. You learned the basics of the preliminary checkout in Chapter 9, so they will be mentioned with minimum explanation.

Preliminary Checkout

1. Begin by making a basic check of those things outside the refrigeration system that also could cause little or no cooling, as explained in Chapter 9:
    a. Dashboard controls and duct housing flap doors operating properly.
    b. Normal blower operation.
    c. On a car with automatic temperature control, use the quick check procedure of Chapter 9 to indicate basically proper function.
    d. Check the cooling system.
2. Follow with a general underhood checkout. Have someone turn on the dashboard control and see that the clutch engages and smoothly operates the compressor. Feel the tubing at the evaporator inlet (between condenser and expansion valve or orifice tube) and the evaporator outlet tubing (or accumulator). The inlet should be clearly warmer than the outlet, which should be cool to cold (see Chapter 9). If not, a refrigeration problem is apparent and further testing is appropriate.

3. Finish up the preliminary checkout with a visual inspection. Look at the sight glass on cars so equipped for clues to the refrigerant charge. Check for obvious physical damage or deterioration, such as the following:
   a. Is the front of the condenser exterior plugged with leaves, road film and the like?
   b. Is there a frost mark somewhere, which indicates an internal restriction? It may be on tubing, receiver-dryer, condenser, expansion valve, or orifice tube. Confirm on the high side of the system by feeling the line on each side of the frost mark. One side will be warmer.
   c. If there is an expansion valve or cycling clutch switch with an external capillary tube, make sure the tube is not kinked, is properly clamped, and is covered with insulation (or correctly inserted in a well in the refrigeration line).
   d. Compressor oil loss. Light seepage stains at the front seal area, perhaps an oil streak on the hood's insulating pad, are normal, but anything more probably indicates a real leak that must be checked.

Detailed Troubleshooting

Detailed troubleshooting can be performed in many ways. In this book, it is organized into a three-step process:

1. Pressure testing and comparison of test results with a troubleshooting chart (see Figs. 12-1 and 12-2).
2. If the results of pressure tests are not clear-cut (along with the results of the preliminary checkout), use the specific troubleshooting guides, which are based on those of the car makers. Each guide is a step-by-step type, with a step determined by the results of the immediately previous one.
3. Tests of individual components are special tests used when the results of pressure testing and the troubleshooting guides still are not positive, or when you wish to double-check yourself. Some of the tests are made on the car; others are done with the component removed and taken to the work bench.

Covered in this section are the following:

1. Moisture (internal and external freeze-ups). This is part of the component section because freeze-ups can affect and be affected by some of these components.
2. Compressor clutch.

189 Detailed Troubleshooting

Figure 12-1 Pressure-test system with gauge manifold, as shown, or charging station. After system has been on several minutes, take gauge readings.

High Side	Low Side	Possible Cause of Poor or No Cooling
Normal to Low	Low	1. Suction throttling valve or evaporator pressure regulator stuck open. 2. Restriction in system. 3. Thermostatic expansion valve stuck closed, or orifice tube plugged. 4. Low refrigerant level (check for leaks). 5. Moisture in system. 6. Defect in compressor (perhaps reed valves or head gaskets).
Low	High	1. Suction throttling valve or evaporator pressure regulator stuck closed (third gauge will go to zero or vacuum). 2. Plugged compressor inlet screen. 3. Defect in compressor (perhaps reed valves or head gaskets). 4. Cycling clutch switch staying open too long.
High	High	1. Cooling system defect (poor airflow through condenser, engine running too hot, defective fan, clogged radiator). 2. Heater water control valve on when it should be off. 3. Overcharge of refrigerant. 4. Thermostatic expansion valve stuck open.
Normal to High	High	1. Suction throttling valve defective—holding to high pressure
High	Low	1. High-side restriction at compressor 2. Moisture in system.
Normal to High	Normal to High	1. Air in system. 2. Too much oil in system 3. Cooling system defect (poor airflow through condenser, engine running too hot, defective fan, clogged radiator).
Normal to Low	Normal to Low	1. Plugged evaporator 2. Restricted condenser 3. Moisture in system
Erratic	Erratic	1. Malfunctioning cycling clutch switch 2. Thermostatic expansion valve capillary tube kinked 3. Malfunctioning suction throttling valve or evaporator pressure regulator.

Figure 12-2 Troubleshooting chart.

3. Compressor.
4. Thermostatic expansion valve or orifice tube.
5. Suction throttling valve (POA type) and evaporator pressure regulator.
6. Cycling clutch switch.

Step One: Pressure Testing

Connect the pressure gauges as explained in Chapter 9. If there is a second low-side fitting, as on older Chrysler and Ford products, connect a second compound (vacuum-low pressure) gauge to the suction throttling valve fitting of Ford products or to the cylinder head of Chrysler products.

Run the engine with the air conditioning on for 5 minutes and take pressure readings; then refer to the chart (Fig. 12-2). In most cases, the pressure readings will indicate the likely problem area, particularly when you combine the results with those from the preliminary checkout.

As you can see from the chart, however, there may be more than one cause for a particular set of pressure readings. You also must always be aware that pressure readings themselves vary greatly with ambient temperature and performance of the cooling system.

For this reason, you must understand that what may be a normal reading on a moderate day (70°F, 21°C), for example, 140 psi (965 kPa), may be a low pressure reading for a hot day (100°F, 38°C). This is particularly true if the cooling system is in poor condition. When the cooling system is working poorly, it runs hotter, and some of this heat is transferred from radiator to condenser (because they are so close to each other). Adding heat at this point is the opposite of what should be happening—cooling to reduce pressure—so the pressure remains somewhat higher than normal.

Another factor in troubleshooting is that pressure readings may vary according to the precise location of a problem. For example, a restriction normally produces lower pressure readings in the system. If there is a restriction at the compressor outlet, however, the pressure will build up temporarily and then drop if the pressure relief valve is forced open.

Step Two: Troubleshooting Guides

The chapter contains troubleshooting guides for the following systems:

1. Cycling clutch and orifice tube (see Fig. 12-3).
2. Cycling clutch and expansion valve (see Fig. 12-4).
3. Suction throttling valve and expansion valve (also covering thermal limiter) (see Fig. 12-5).

191 Step Two: Troubleshooting Guides

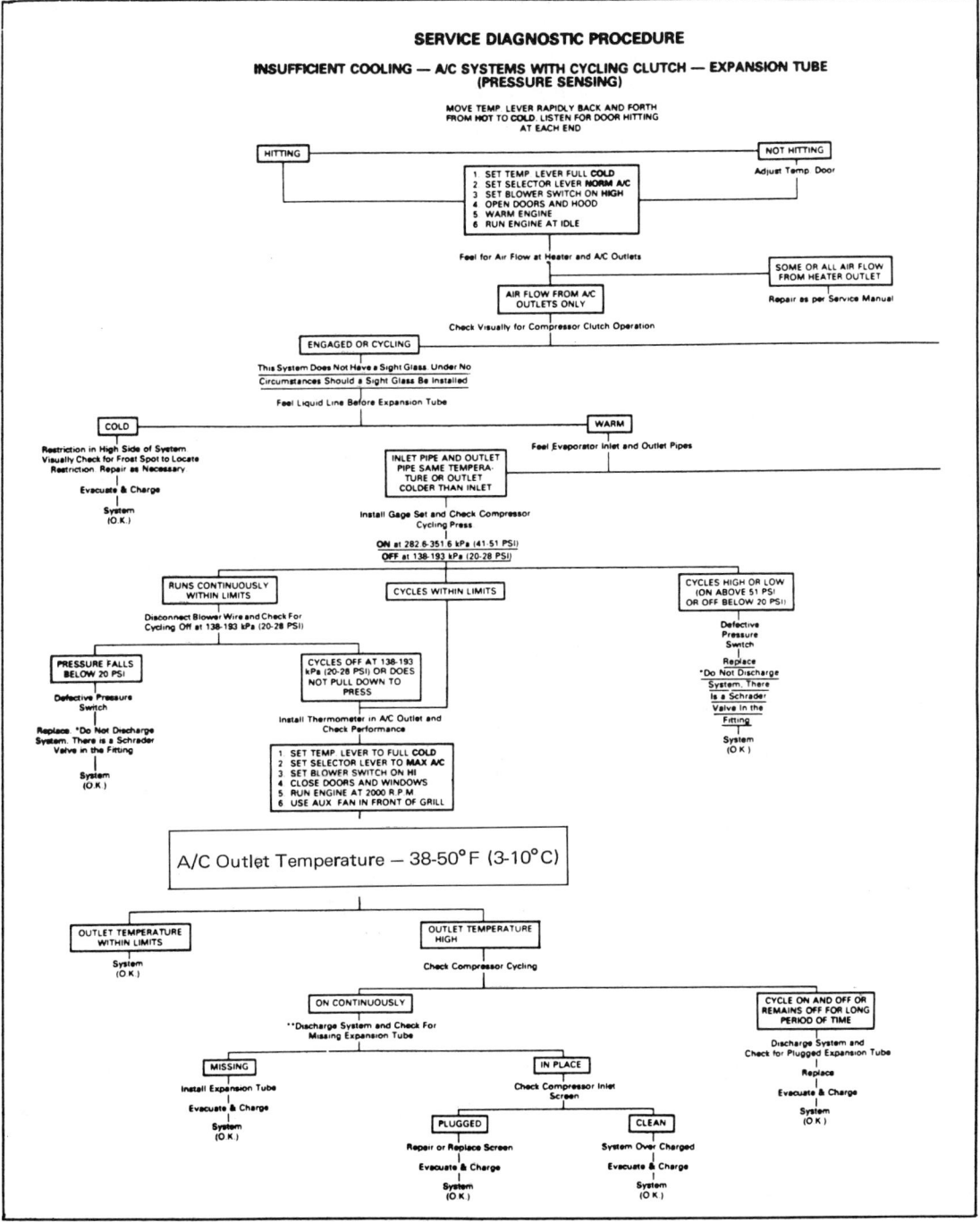

Figure 12-3 Diagnostic procedure for cycling clutch orifice tube system. (Courtesy General Motors Corp.)

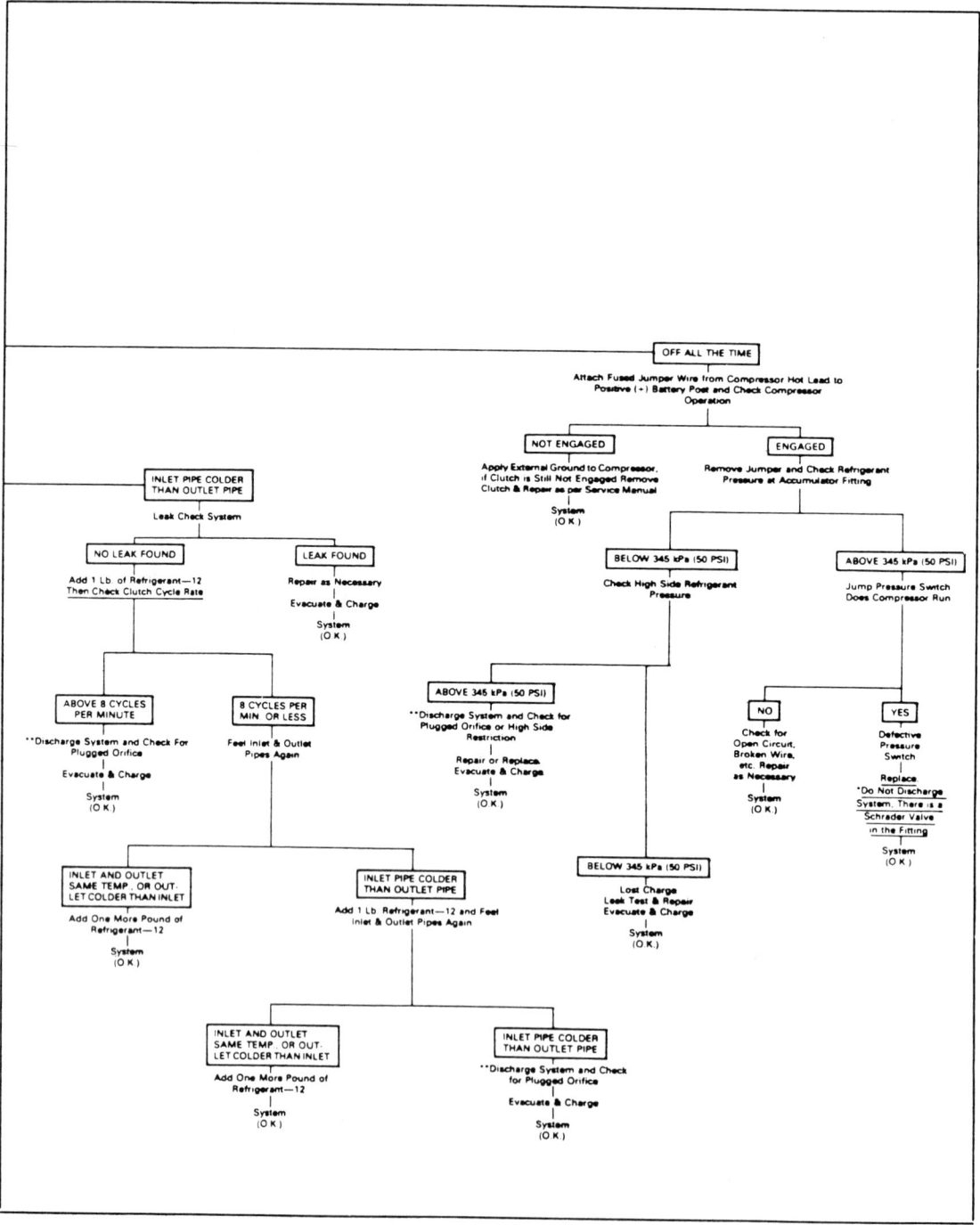

Figure 12-3 (continued)

193 Step Two: Troubleshooting Guides

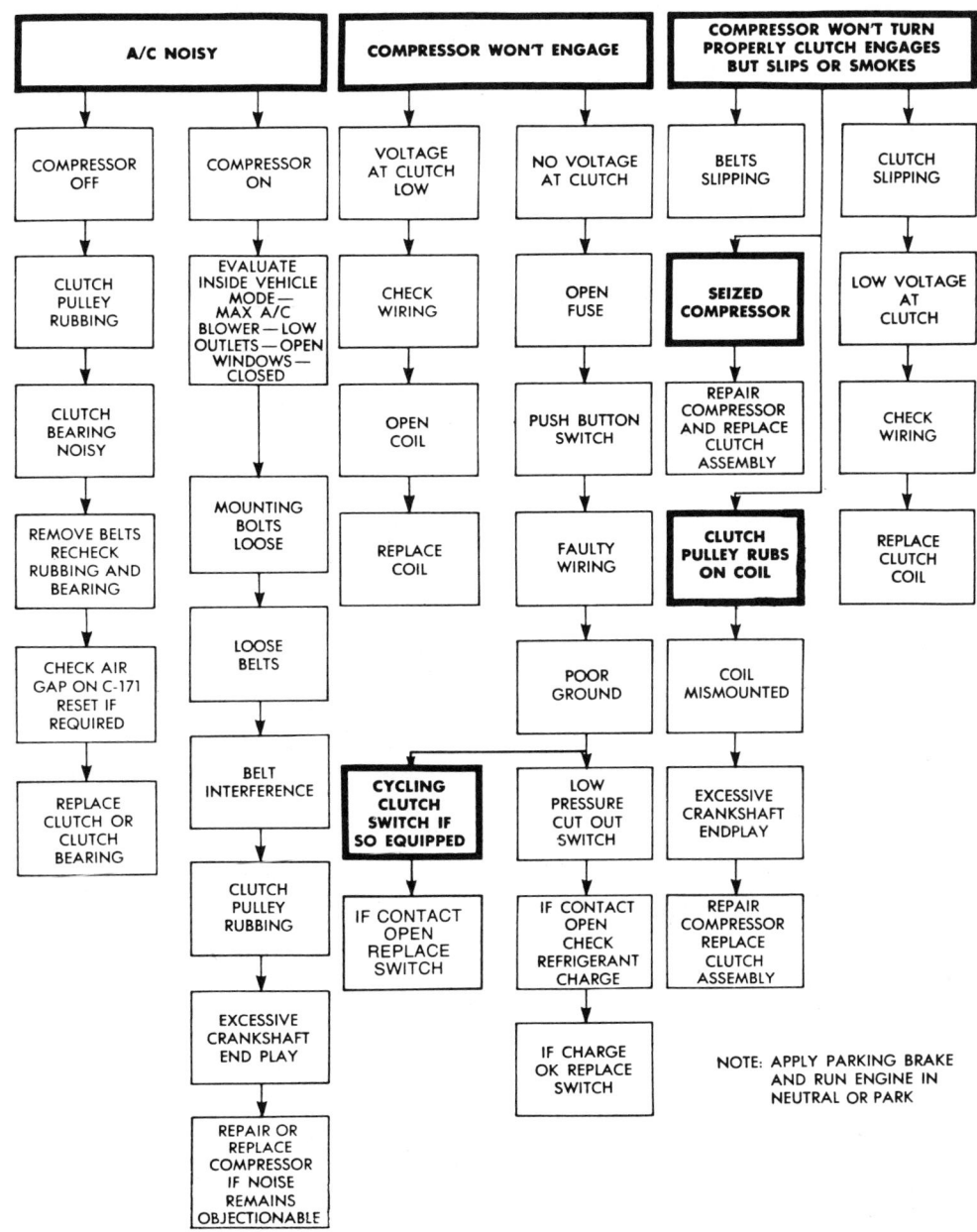

Figure 12-4 Diagnostic procedure for cycling clutch with expansion valve system. (Courtesy Chrysler Corp.)

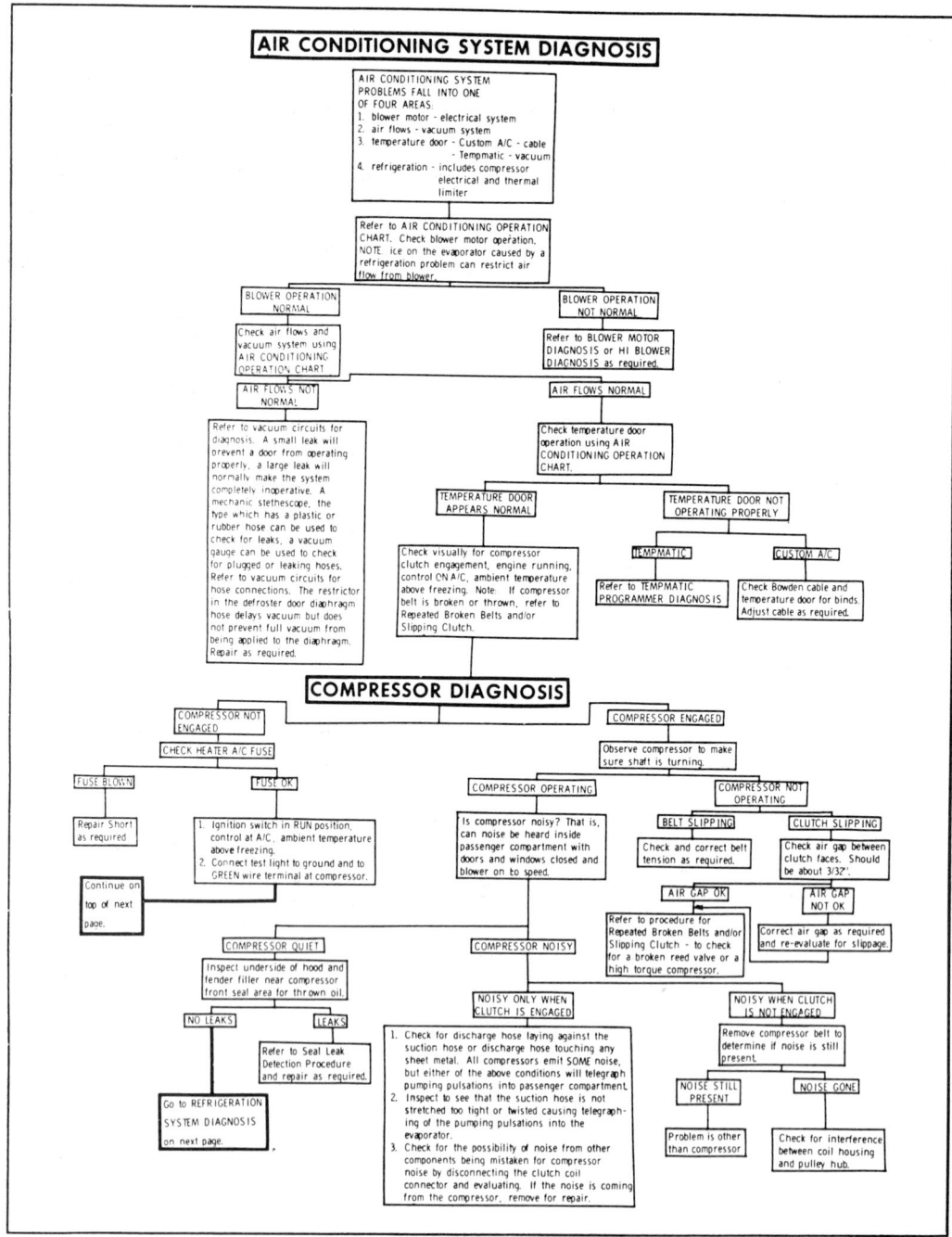

Figure 12-5 Diagnostic procedure for system with POA-type suction throttling valve and expansion valve (also includes thermal limiters). (Courtesy General Motors Corp.)

Step Two: Troubleshooting Guides

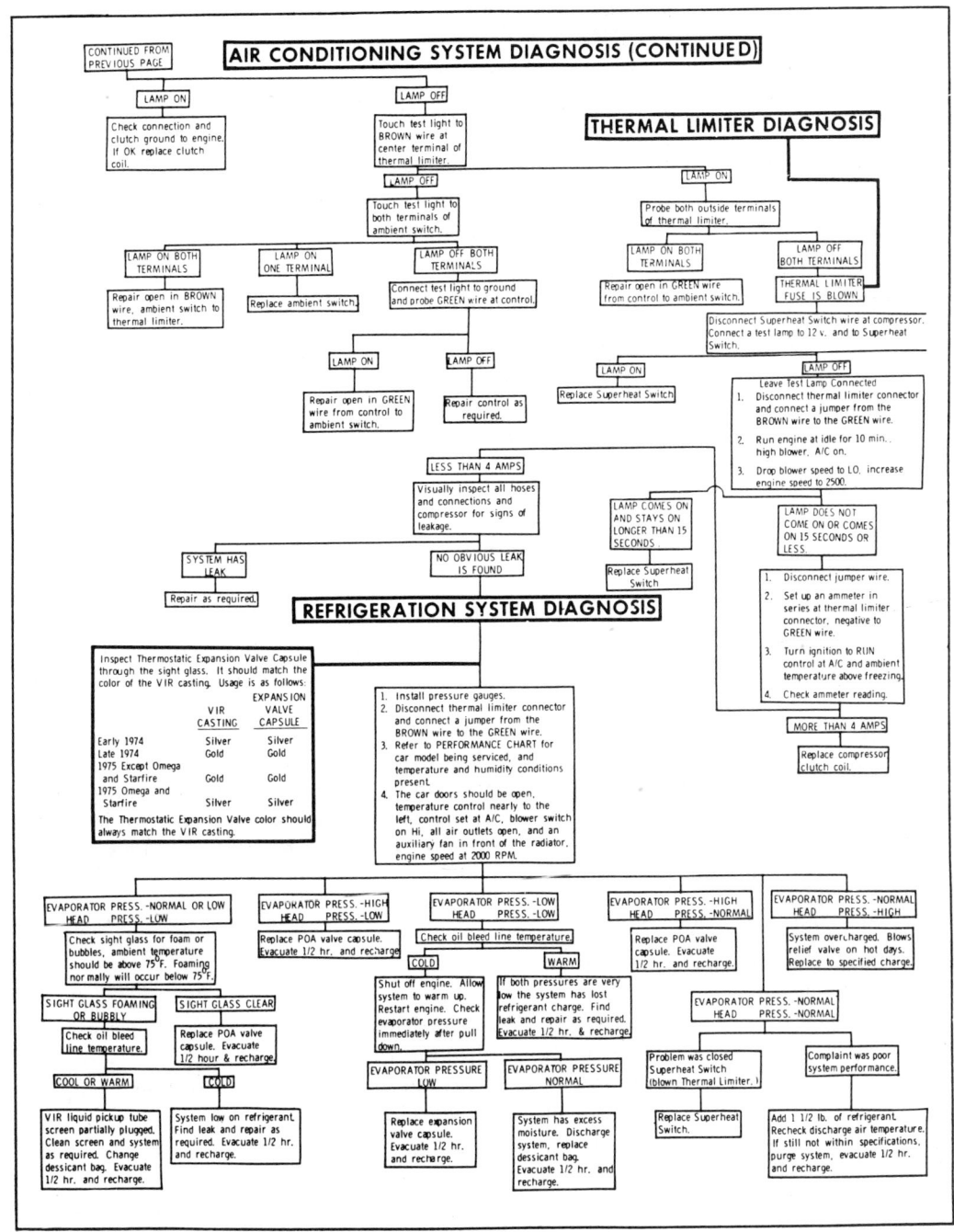

Figure 12-5 (continued)

4. Evaporator pressure or temperature regulator and expansion valve (see Fig. 12-6).

Step Three: Moisture and Component Testing

Some of the test procedures in this section involve the use of special testers. The testers, however, are relatively inexpensive and readily available from sources other than the car manufacturer.

Moisture Problems

Moisture-caused freeze-ups are such common problems that they deserve attention special and thought. If the motorist complains that the system produces cool air for a brief period after it is turned on and then the air turns warm, moisture freezing into ice is the prime suspect. There are, however, two forms of moisture freeze-up, and they have completely different causes and, to some extent, different cures.

Moisture in the System

If there is moisture inside the system, it freezes in the expansion valve or orifice tube, blocking refrigerant flow. Or if there is a restriction (even an otherwise minor one), the moisture may freeze at the restriction, further limiting refrigerant flow.

Or there could be a defective suction throttling valve (or evaporator pressure or temperature regulator) or cycling clutch switch. If any one fails in the open position, the air conditioning overcools. Moisture in the air surrounding the evaporator not only condenses as it should, but it freezes on the evaporator coils and fins, blocking the airflow. The signs of each problem are as follows:

Internal Moisture

1. If the car is a 1977-1978 Oldsmobile Toronado, it has a valves-in-receiver with a sight glass that has a moisture indicator (see Fig. 12-7). Low moisture is indicated by a blue color, moderate by pink, and heavy moisture by white.
2. If the problem occurs when ambient humidity is very low, moisture already in the system is indicated.
3. If during a pressure test the low-side gauge reading goes to a vacuum at the time the cool air from the dashboard outlets turns warm, it indicates moisture in the system (freezing at the expansion valve

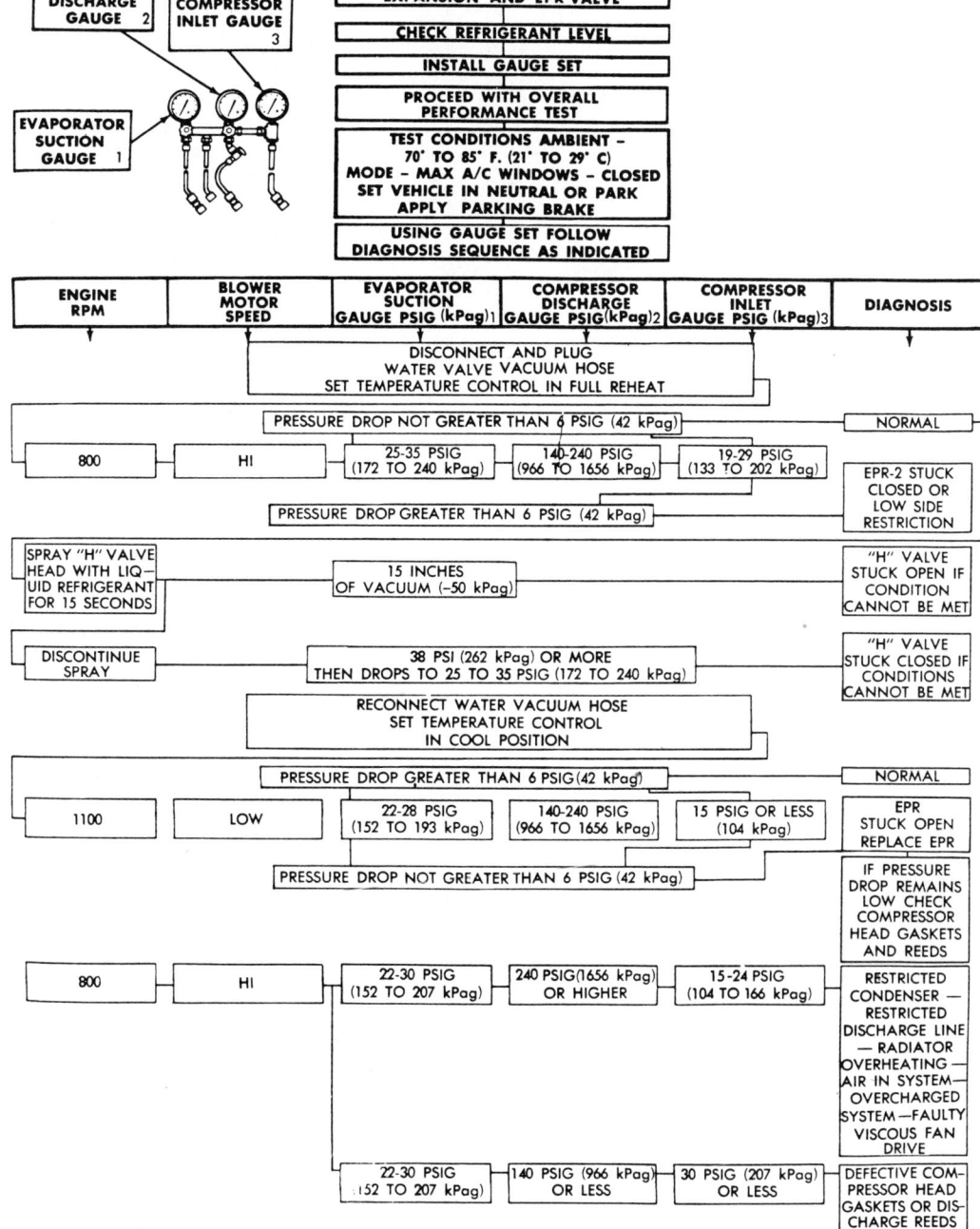

Figure 12-6 Diagnostic procedure for system with expansion valve and evaporator pressure or temperature regulator. (Courtesy Chrysler Corp.)

Figure 12-7 Expansion valve capsule on General Motors Valves-in-Receiver had moisture indicator visible through sight glass on all 1977–1978 Oldsmobile Toronados. You also may find it on some 1976 General Motors cars of all makes.

or orifice tube, blocking refrigerant flow and allowing the compressor to draw the low-side pressure down to a vacuum).

4. Soak a rag in hot water, wrap it around the expansion valve or orifice tube, and if the system starts to function again, you have another indication of moisture in the system (see Fig. 12-8).

External Freeze-up on the Evaporator

1. Park the car after the system just stops working, wait a while, and try it again. If it now works, and there is a puddle of water on the ground (at the location of the drain tubes), there apparently was ice that melted from the evaporator coils and fins and drained out. Freeze-up caused by a defective suction throttling valve (or evaporator pressure regulator) or cycling clutch switch is apparent.

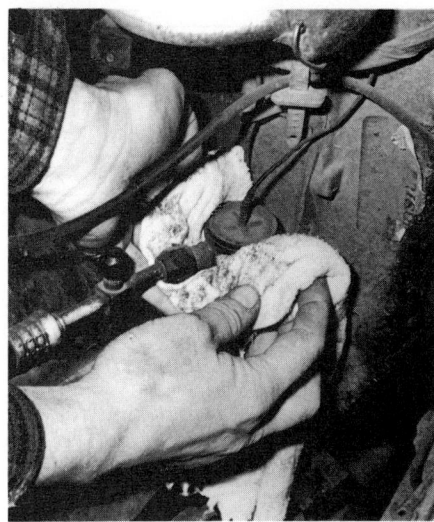

Figure 12-8 Hot rag on expansion valve can give troubleshooting clue to moisture in system. If system begins to function again, moisture is indicated.

2. Reduction in airflow from dashboard outlets.
3. Problem occurs most rapidly on humid days.
4. On cycling clutch systems, a cycling clutch switch test indicates switch is on excessively long (see test procedure in this chapter).
5. Evaporator outlet pipe (and accumulator on cycling clutch orifice tube systems) may show frost.
6. If there is easy access to any part of the evaporator, you may be able to touch the coils and fins with a probe from an electronic thermometer to sense temperatures of 32°F (0°C) or below, which tell you that the evaporator is iced up.
7. Pressure test readings may indicate a defective suction throttling valve or evaporator (pressure or temperature) regulator (see chart).

Curing the Problem

The cure for moisture in the system is to discharge, vacuum pump, and recharge (see Chapter 11); also replace the receiver-dryer or desiccant bag in the accumulator for future protection. To correct a freeze-up on the evaporator coils and fins, you must change a defective part.

1. If it is a suction throttling valve or evaporator (pressure or temperature) regulator, you must discharge the system to get it off. Therefore, you must vacuum pump and recharge, too.
2. If it is a cycling clutch switch sticking closed, it can be replaced without discharging the system.

Parts replacements are covered in Chapter 13.

Compressor Clutch

Although it is possible for a compressor clutch drive plate to stick to the rotor-pulley assembly, this is a rare problem resulting from a short in the wiring harness. Generally, the problems are clutch slippage or total failure to engage.

Slippage

If the clutch slips (you may see smoking from the friction), check for the following:

1. Excessive gap between drive plate and rotor-pulley mating surfaces. Measure with a feeler gauge and compare with specifications as explained in Chapter 14, which also covers clutch service.
2. Improper current draw. Disconnect the current feed wire at the clutch; it is the wire that will turn on a test lamp when the ignition and air conditioning controls are on (see Fig. 12-9). Connect one lead of an ammeter to the current feed wire and the other to the terminal from which the feed wire was disconnected. The ammeter should read to specifications, usually in the 2.5- to 4.0-ampere range. If the reading is outside specifications, the clutch coil is defective or poorly grounded. Most coils have an electrical ground provided by a wire screwed into the compressor body (see Fig. 12-10); a few coils use an ambient switch. Others ground the coil by whatever method is used to retain it to the compressor (bolts, snap rings, etc.). The external wire and screw, of course, can be checked without disassembly.

   Note: On older clutches with brushes, a low reading may be caused by worn brushes or poor brush contact with the slip ring. Remove for inspection.
3. Binding in compressor. Try to turn the drive plate by hand. Some resistance is normal, but if you cannot turn it, proceed to a compressor checkout. Also check the compressor if the drive belt snaps and pressure readings point to a compressor problem.

Total Failure to Engage: Current to Clutch Coil

If the clutch will not pull in at all, begin with a check for current to the clutch coil. Disconnect the current feed wire, attach a test lamp to it and to ground, and turn on the ignition and air conditioning controls. If the test lamp lights, there is current to the clutch coil and the problem is in the clutch assembly. Check for a secure ground connection if it is an external

Compressor Clutch

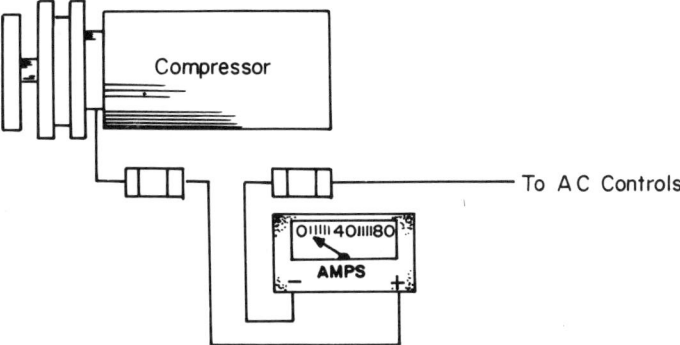

Figure 12-9 Connect ammeter between current feed wire and clutch coil in series, as shown. If there are two terminals at the clutch coil instead of one, connect the other terminal to an electrical ground. Ammeter should read to specifications.

Figure 12-10 If there is a ground for the compressor coil at the compressor as shown, you can check it for tightness, as shown.

wire, or (if it provides the ground) bypass the ambient switch, then proceed as follows:

1. Make a current draw test. If the coil fails, disassemble the clutch and replace.
2. If the coil passes the test, a mechanical problem in the clutch assembly is apparent, such as a cocked rotor-pulley or coil in contact with the rotor-pulley. Disassemble the clutch to pinpoint the cause.

Total Failure to Engage: No Current to Clutch Coil

The wiring harnesses of different cars vary so greatly, and changes occur from year to year; it is impossible to provide a single wiring schematic or even a few. If there is no current to the clutch coil, you should check the air conditioning wiring diagrams in the manufacturer's shop manual to see what components are in the circuit, such as switches, fuses, and relays.

In the common designs, however, you may spare yourself the time required to trace the compressor clutch circuit by checking the following items, which (after a fuse) are the most likely to be responsible.

1. On cars with a cycling clutch system, the cycling clutch switch (thermostatic or pressure type) is always in the circuit and it is easy to test for failure to close. Remove the wiring connector and connect a jumper wire across its two terminals (Fig. 12-11). If there now is current to the clutch, the switch is apparently defective and should be replaced.

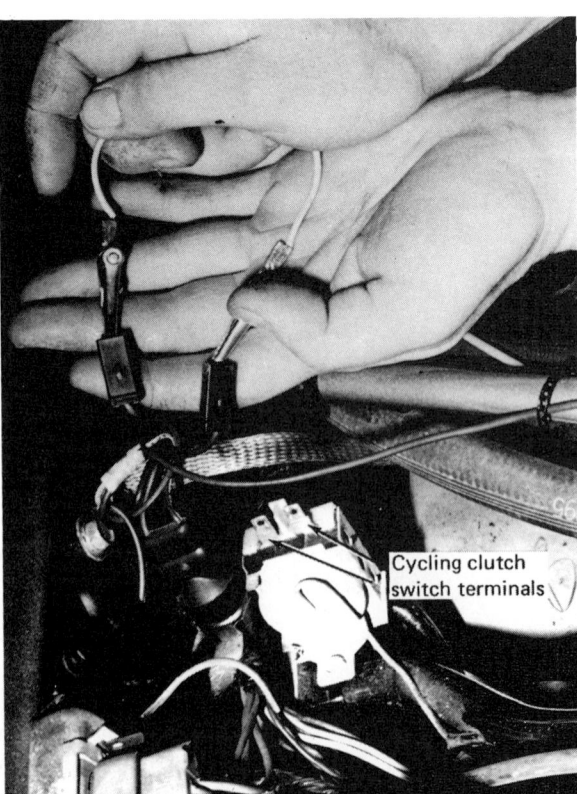

Figure 12-11 To bypass cycling clutch switch, removing wiring connector (in this case two individual connectors) and hook up a jumper wire across them as shown.

2. Whatever the low-pressure protection, it should be tested. On most cars there is a single switch that is designed to open if ambient temperatures are low or if Refrigerant 12 pressures are low (as a result of a leak). Remove the switch connector, hook up a jumper wire across the two terminals (see Fig. 12-12), and if there now is current to the clutch, either the switch is defective or the system pressures are too low. *Note:* The pressure-type cycling clutch switch also performs this function, but you will find the switch on systems with the thermostatic-type cycling clutch switch.

3. On General Motors cars with a thermal limiter and superheat switch, check for a blown thermal fuse by removing the fuse's electrical connector and hooking up a jumper wire across its B and C terminals. If the compressor now operates, the thermal fuse is blown. Do not just replace the thermal fuse, or it may blow again almost immediately. First, make sure Refrigerant 12 pressure is adequate. Then check the superheat switch, which with correct pressure should be open (so as not to provide an electrical ground for the fuse heater). Proceed as follows:

   a. Run the engine at fast idle; then turn on the air conditioning and allow several minutes for system pressures to stabilize.

   b. Connect one lead of a test lamp to the battery positive terminal, the other to the switch terminal. If the test lamp does not light, the switch is open as it should be. If it lights and stays on for more than 15 seconds (and Refrigerant 12 pressure is normal), replace the superheat switch. It is possible for the superheat switch to close for

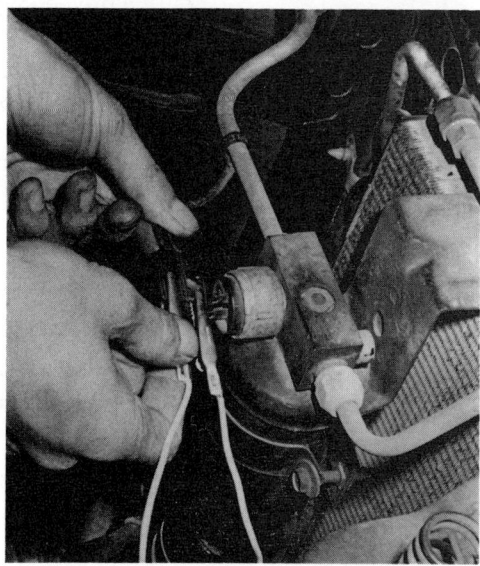

Figure 12-12 If any switch is to be bypassed, the procedure is basically as shown in Fig. 12-11. In this case, there is one connector and the jumper can be hooked across it easily.

a brief period under normal conditions (the thermal limiter has a time delay to allow for this), but not for more than 15 seconds. *Note:* Do not confuse the superheat switch with the ambient low pressure switch used on later models without thermal limiters, for both look similar and are threaded into the compressor. The thermal limiter was used on late-1971 through 1976 models, except Chevrolet Corvette, Vega and Chevette, and on 1977–1978 Toronado and Eldorado.

Caution: If you replace a compressor with either a superheat switch or pressure switch, make sure the compressor has the same switch as the car. If a superheat switch compressor is installed on a car with a pressure switch the clutch coil circuit will be complete only part of the time. The part-time completion could result in clutch slippage and premature failure.

4. On cars with a compressor clutch cutout switch, check for a defective switch. This switch has been standard equipment on many smaller engines to break the air conditioning circuit at full throttle when the power is needed for acceleration. In addition, a cutout switch has been a common add-on device for fuel economy, so it may be found on any car. The original equipment switch most often is a mechanical device on the throttle linkage, usually at the carburetor. The add-on is spliced into a vacuum hose, so it opens when engine vacuum drops. Both switches are wired into the compressor clutch current feed wire. If the switch fails in the open position, the clutch will not engage. To check, connect a jumper wire across the switch's wiring connector terminals, and if the clutch now engages, the switch is defective. *Note:* With the vacuum switch, you can also check the switch directly by connecting a battery-powered test lamp or ohmmeter to the switch terminals and applying a strong vacuum (such as with a hand pump if you are working with the engine off). The typical switch should show a complete circuit (test lamp on or zero resistance) at 8 inches of vacuum or more.

Compressor

The compressor is subject to four general problems: (1) seizure (it will not turn); (2) it leaks refrigerant and oil; (3) it is not compressing the refrigerant; and (4) it is noisy (this subject is covered later in the chapter).

Seizure

When a mechanical device such as a compressor seizes, the usual cause is inadequate or no lubrication. If your preliminary check discloses ap-

Figure 12-13 Check oil bleed lines for kinks, connections for looseness.

parently significant oil loss from the front of the compressor, don't be surprised if the compressor is seized.

Compressor seizure also may occur if there is plugging or a sticking valve in any of the oil bleeds, or if used, an external line that is kinked. The bleeds in the suction throttling valve, evaporator pressure regulator, expansion valve and accumulator allow oil to bypass these parts when they are closed, so compressor lubrication is not interrupted.

If seizure is not caused by an obvious leak, the bleeds are suspect (see Fig. 12-13). You can look for a kinked bleed line on an external suction throttling valve or change the bleed valve as a separate part on the General Motors Valves-in-Receiver. If there is nothing you can service separately in this situation, however, replacement of the valve is advisable when changing a seized compressor.

Caution: False Seizure. When first started after a month or more without use, General Motors' two most popular compressors, the radial four cylinder and the six cylinder (also used on many Ford and Audi cars) are subject to a mild form of seizure called *false seizure*. If attended to early, it is harmless and can easily be corrected if you know what to do.

What happens is that with the system off, changes in ambient temperature cause expansion and contraction of the Refrigerant 12, which results in oil flowing from the very smooth surfaces in the compressor. The surfaces resist movement without the oil film, and the compressor behaves as if seized, which in a sense it is. If, however, you can turn the compressor shaft, some lubricant will again reach these surfaces. Using a clutch drive plate holder (see Chapter 14), try to turn the drive plate counterclockwise to break the shaft loose. Once it is loose, turn it clockwise several times. Then start the engine and turn on the air conditioning; the compressor should turn by itself smoothly. This technique works only if the problem is truly a false seizure, and it may save an unnecessary replacement or overhaul. It has no effect on a compressor that really is seized.

Caution: External Seizure. Although it is rare, a compressor may seize only externally at the rotor-pulley bearing. It is rare because the bearing normally would become unacceptably noisy long before seizure. Further, the drive belt would slip obviously long before complete seizure. If a car has been out of use for a long time and left in an adverse setting, it is possible. Under these conditions, you should keep the rotor-pulley bearing in mind.

Leakage

Some slight leakage is normal, but when severe, the loss will be at a rate of ½ pound per year or more and performance will suffer. See Chapter 9.

Poor or No Compression

When the compressor inlet and outlet pressures are virtually the same, with the low side high, the usual cause is in the compressor, such as a leaking head gasket or weak or broken reed valves. If the drive belt snaps in hot weather at high speed or the clutch slips badly under those conditions, the outlet (high-side) reed valve is suspect. Turn the drive plate clockwise by hand; then release after one full revolution. If the compressor seems to want to go backward, that is a confirming clue. Gaskets and reed valves are replaceable on many compressors, as explained in Chapter 14.

Caution: Do not condemn the compressor, however, for on some systems the same pressure readings might also occur if the expansion valve had a wide operating range, was stuck open, and the system had a minimum-adequate refrigerant supply. Make the compressor checks previously described, and make sure the system has a normal charge of Refrigerant 12. Carefully feel the compressor, and if it is abnormally hot (enough to singe your skin), the compressor apparently is at fault. You may double-check, however, by testing the expansion valve on cars so equipped.

Expansion Valve and Orifice Tube

Valve Stuck Closed or Orifice Tube Blocked

When pressure readings indicate the expansion valve is stuck closed or the orifice tube is blocked, make these additional checks on the car:

1. As explained under moisture problems, check for the possibility of an internal freeze-up. Apply a rag soaked in very hot water to the valve, and if pressure readings drift toward normal and the system starts to discharge cold air, melting has occurred. Correct the problem by discharging, vacuum pumping, and recharging as explained in Chapter 11.
2. If the thermostatic expansion valve has an external capillary tube, this test procedure can be effective: run the engine at fast idle, turn on the air conditioning, set it to maximum or high, and close the windows. Allow the system to run for about 10 minutes. Then unclamp the capillary tube bulb from the evaporator outlet tube (or remove it from a well in the outlet tube) and hold the bulb in your hand (see Fig. 12-14). The warmth from your hand will simulate superheated Refrigerant 12 at the evaporator outlet, and if the expansion valve is okay, it should open wide. The low-side pressure reading should go up as a result of increased Refrigerant 12 flow. If this does not happen, the expansion valve apparently is stuck closed.

Expansion Valve Stuck Open

The possibility of an expansion valve stuck open may be indicated by pressure test readings and the fact that the system does not perform in less than really hot weather. This may not sound as if it is pinpointing

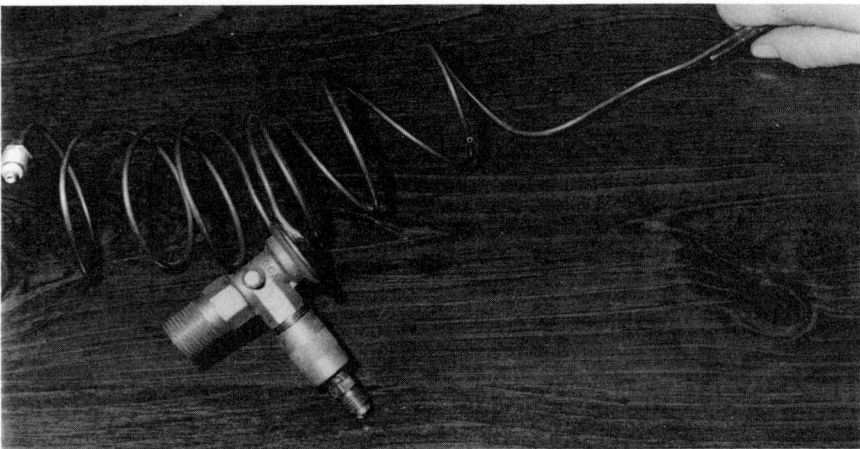

Figure 12-14 Hold expansion valve capillary tube bulb in your hand to warm it (expansion valve shown removed from car for illustrative purposes). Expansion valve should open wide, and low-side reading should rise as a result of increased refrigerant flow.

anything, but remember that all that happens if the expansion valve sticks open is that the maximum amount of Refrigerant 12 will flow into the evaporator at all times. If it is a really hot day, performance may seem close to normal. If it is not, however, the evaporator does not need all the Refrigerant 12, and when it gets more than it needs, the Refrigerant 12 will not vaporize completely; thus it will absorb little heat. Here are two additional on-car test procedures, one for the expansion valve that has an external capillary tube and another for the expansion valve built into a combination assembly at the evaporator tubing connections:

1. *On-car test, expansion valve with capillary tube.* Connect pressure gauges. Run the engine at fast idle with the air conditioning control on maximum or high. Close the car windows. After 10 minutes, unclamp the capillary tube from the evaporator outlet or remove it from its well in the outlet. Spray the bulb end for 15 seconds with liquid Refrigerant 12 and the low-side pressure reading should drop. Stop spraying and the reading should rise, in some cases briefly above a normal reading.
2. *On-car test, combination valve.* Repeat the previous test for this type, except spray the valve assembly head at the location of the expansion valve with Refrigerant 12 for 15 seconds. The results should be the same.

Note: In either case, you may see sweating (moisture droplets) on the low-side hose between evaporator and compressor. This is a sign of an expansion valve stuck open and may confirm the diagnosis.

Suction Throttling Valve

It is sometimes difficult to isolate a problem to the expansion valve or suction throttling valve. If, for example, you get a high reading on the low-pressure side, and what might be considered a high reading on the high pressure side, you may wonder which valve is defective.

If the system has two low-side test fittings (as on older Chrysler and Ford products), you can confirm the performance of the suction throttling valve or evaporator pressure regulator. If after visual inspection of the cooling system, another key possibility, you still are not sure, perhaps the expansion valve tests will answer your questions. If they do not, you can bench-test the suction throttling valve (the evaporator pressure regulator, too). The system must be discharged for replacement of either the thermostatic expansion valve or suction throttling valve, so there is really no extra work except to remove and bench-test. For details on removal of these components, see Chapter 13.

Bench Testing Suction Throttling Valve and Evaporator Pressure Regulator

To bench-test, you need a special tool and a supply of Refrigerant 12. Run refrigerant through the valve and measure the pressure at which it controls to see if it is within specifications (about 28 to 31 psi or 193 to 214 kPa on most systems). If the pressure reading is right, you know the valve will maintain refrigerant flow so the moisture on the evaporator coils does not freeze. If you see refrigerant flow from the valve (the test is done with liquid Refrigerant 12), you will know that the part is not stuck closed. There are two tool setups you can use:

1. Bench test with adapter and gauge manifold. If the system has an externally mounted suction throttling valve with a Schrader test valve, adapter permits you to attach the valve inlet to the center hose on the gauge manifold (see Figs. 12-15 and 12-16). The high-side gauge hose goes to the Refrigerant 12 can, the low-side hose to the suction throttling valve's Schrader. Invert the Refrigerant 12 can so liquid refrigerant will flow; then very gradually open the manual valve at the high-pressure gauge of the manifold. Refrigerant 12 will flow through the suction throttling valve and come out from the outlet if the valve is not stuck closed. *Caution:* Aim

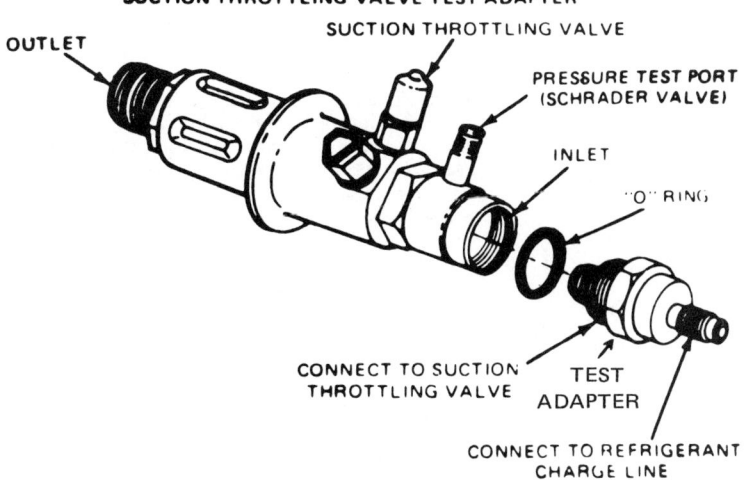

Figure 12-15 Special test adapter is used to check suction throttling valve. Install adapter in valve inlet and connect hose to both adapter and center fitting on gauge manifold. Connect low-pressure gauge hose to the test port with the Schrader valve. Connect high-pressure gauge hose to a can of refrigerant and invert the can so liquid will flow.

210 Air Conditioning Troubleshooting

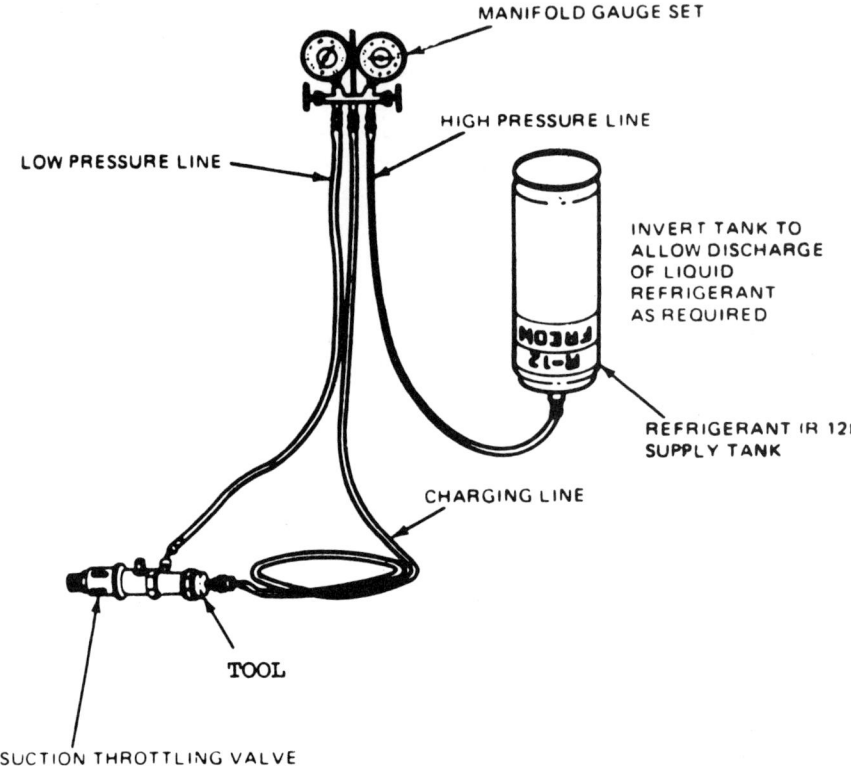

Figure 12-16 With all connections made as illustrated, open the high-side manual valve on the manifold very gradually. As the valve is opened, refrigerant will flow through the manifold into the suction throttling valve. When the refrigerant pressure in the suction throtting valve reaches a control point, you will hear a popping noise as the valve opens and closes. Open and close the gauge manifold's manual valve a few times to repeat the popping, and so double-check. Compare the reading on the low-side gauge with specifications, typically 28.5 psi (196 kPa) at sea level, increasing 0.5 psi (3.5 kPa) for each 1000 feet above sea level. Suction throttling valve should hold to very close to specifications; if it is off by even a few pounds per square inch or kilopascals, it should be discarded. You also should see a gradual increase in pressure to the control point if you operate the gauge manifold manual valve carefully and the suction throttling valve is working smoothly.

the outlet away from you to avoid contact with refrigerant. The flow rate will gradually increase until the control pressure is reached, as indicated on the low-pressure valve of the gauge manifold. Then the valve will close and open (there may be a popping noise when this occurs). Compare the pressure gauge reading with factory specifications. If the reading is below specifications, it means that the valve is open too much and not providing the back pressure to the evaporator, and the temperature on the evaporator coils has dropped so low that moisture condensing on the coils is freezing and blocking airflow. If the reading is above specifications, there is too much back pressure, which causes poor cooling performance.

2. With all other suction throttling valves, a special tester can be used for bench-testing (Fig. 12-17). This tester also can be used for the Chrysler evaporator pressure regulator. Insert the valve assembly in the tester, thread on the cap, and connect a can of Refrigerant 12. Invert the can and open the can's dispensing valve so liquid Refrigerant 12 will flow through. As with the other type of suction throttling valve and the manifold gauge, the pressure will build up, in this case on the gauge in the tester, until the control point is reached. *Caution:* As with the other arrangement, aim the outlet (in the tester cap) away from you to avoid contact with the Refrigerant 12.

Cycling Clutch Switch

The most common problem with a cycling clutch switch is a complete failure—it does not close and the compressor clutch fails to engage. Or the switch may stay closed too long, fail to open, or be open too long. Troubleshooting is simple.

Switch Does Not Close

Remove the switch wiring connector, hook up a jumper wire across its two terminals, and turn on the ignition and air conditioning; if the compressor clutch now engages, the switch is obviously defective.

Switch Stays Closed Too Long

If the switch stays closed too long, moisture may freeze up on the evaporator coils and fins, as explained earlier in this chapter under moisture problems. In the most severe case, when the switch never opens, this problem surely will occur.

Refer to Fig. 12-18, which shows typical clutch cycling times for Ford products, which are reasonable for most original equipment systems. If you do not want to watch the clutch to see when it disengages, hook up a test lamp (or audible tester) to the compressor clutch current feed wire and an

Air Conditioning Troubleshooting

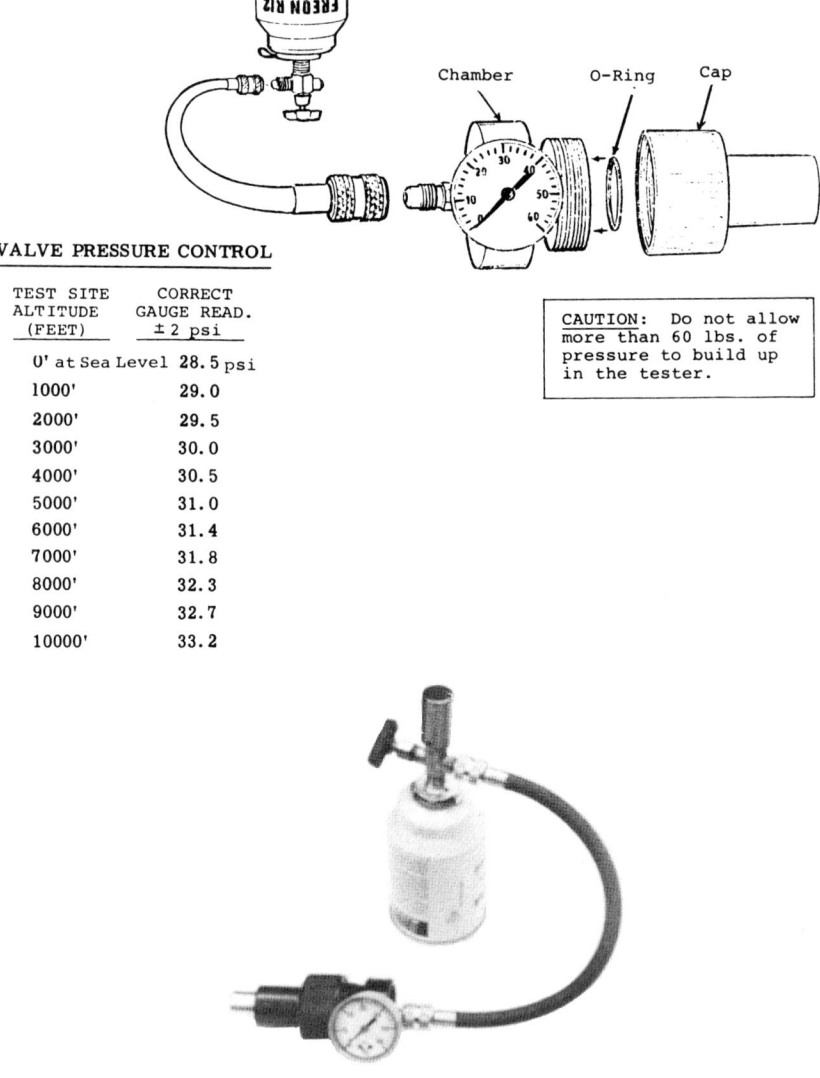

VALVE PRESSURE CONTROL

TEST SITE ALTITUDE (FEET)	CORRECT GAUGE READ. ±2 psi
0' at Sea Level	28.5 psi
1000'	29.0
2000'	29.5
3000'	30.0
4000'	30.5
5000'	31.0
6000'	31.4
7000'	31.8
8000'	32.3
9000'	32.7
10000'	33.2

CAUTION: Do not allow more than 60 lbs. of pressure to build up in the tester.

Figure 12-17 Many suction throttling valves do not have a Schrader valve, and to test them easily, you can use a special tool with built-in gauge. Remove cap, insert valve, refit cap, and gradually open dispensing valve on refrigerant can (inverted so liquid will flow). A gradual increase in pressure will be displayed on the gauge until the control point is reached.

Cycling Clutch Switch

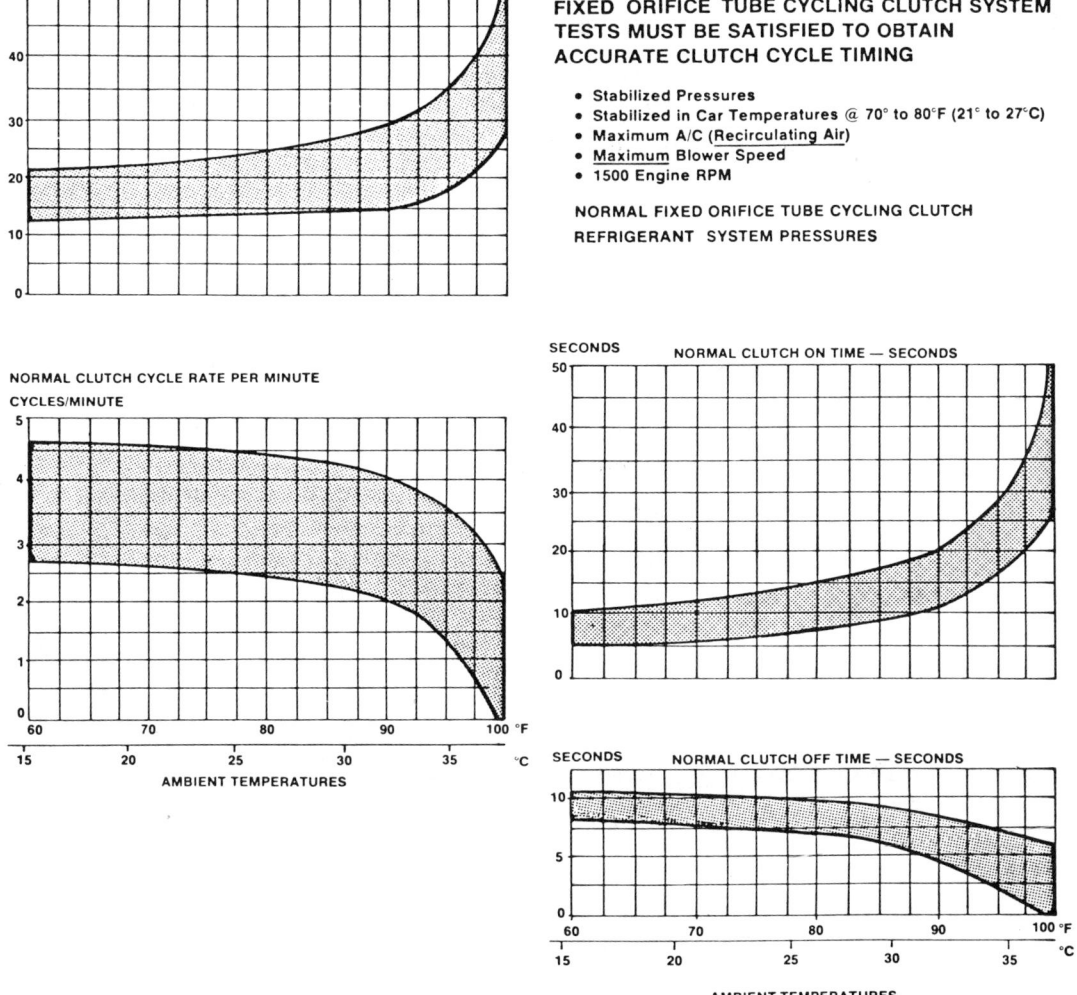

NORMAL CLUTCH CYCLE TIMING RATES — FIXED ORIFICE TUBE SYSTEMS

Figure 12-18 Chart shows typical clutch cycling times for Ford products. On a very humid day, however, the clutch may go several minutes between cycles (on-and-off operations of the clutch).

electrical ground. When the lamp goes off (or the audible tester makes no sound), the cycling clutch switch has opened.

Switch Stays Open Too Long: Thermostatic Type

Turn on the system, and if the switch goes off (disengaging the clutch) long enough for the air from the dashboard outlets to turn warm, the switch is open too long. You can make a more precise test of the switch to determine if it opens at freezing temperatures and closes at warm temperatures without removing the switch from the system.

1. Peel back insulation (if used) and unclamp the thermostatic switch capillary bulb from the liquid line.
2. Unplug the wiring connector from the cycling clutch switch and connect a battery-powered test lamp or ohmmeter across the switch terminals.
3. If ambient temperatures are above 50°F (10°C), the lamp should light or the ohmmeter should indicate no resistance, which means the switch is closed. If it is colder, apply heat to the end of the capillary tube.
4. Spray Refrigerant 12 on the capillary tube end and the test lamp should go out or the ohmmeter should register infinite resistance, indicating the switch is open.

If the switch fails to close in step 3 or open in step 4, replace it.

Switch Stays Open Too Long: Pressure Type

The same basic test (does the switch go off so long that the air from the air conditioning outlets turns warm) can also be made. For greater precision, connect a pressure gauge to the low side and see if the clutch disengages at 20 to 28 psi (138 to 193 kPa) and engages at 41 to 51 psi (282 to 353 kPa). If the switch cannot be tested on the car, it can be checked with a special bench tester (Figs. 12-19 and 12-20) into which the switch threads. Remove the switch from the accumulator (the switch is threaded onto a Schrader valve, so the Schrader closes as the switch is unthreaded, and no refrigerant is lost during removal or reinstallation).

With the switch threaded into the tester, connect a can of refrigerant to the tester and a battery-powered test lamp or ohmmeter across the switch terminals. The test lamp should be off, the ohmmeter should indicate maximum resistance (infinity, ∞).

Open the dispensing valve on the refrigerant can and allow pressure to build up. The test lamp should go on, the ohmmeter needle should

Figure 12-19 Pressure switch is threaded into bench tester with gauge as shown. Can of refrigerant is connected to tester, and ohmmeter probes are held to pressure switch terminals. Dispensing valve on refrigerant can is opened to allow pressure to build up gradually. When it reaches control point (41 to 51 psi or 282 to 353 kPa), the switch should close and ohmmeter needle should swing to zero resistance position.

swing to zero resistance when tester gauge pressure is somewhere in the range of 41 to 51 psi (282 to 353 kPa).

Press the bleed valve on the tester; refrigerant will escape and pressure on the tester gauge will begin dropping. When it drops to somewhere in the range of 20 to 28 psi (138 to 193 kPa), the test lamp should go out and the ohmmeter needle should swing to maximum resistance.

If the pressure switch fails either at low or high pressure, it should be replaced. Use the bench tester on a new switch before installation.

Intermittent Operation

The refrigeration aspects of intermittent operation actually were covered in the previous section of this chapter, but in the sense of a failure that would be considered lack of cooling rather than intermittent operation. If, for example, the cycling clutch switch on systems so equipped were to stay off until the air from the ducts turned warm, that would be a *cooling* performance problem. If the switch were to stay off and cause warm air to

216 Air Conditioning Troubleshooting

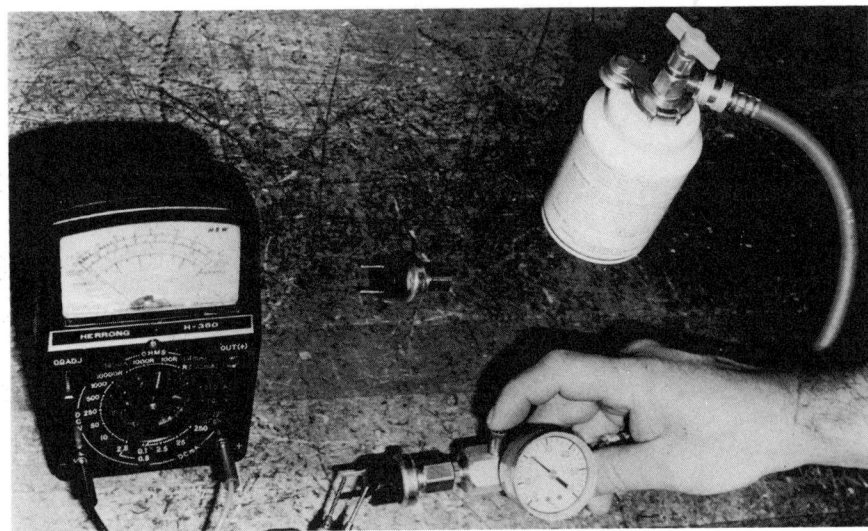

Figure 12-20 Press pressure bleed on tester and allow pressure to bleed off gradually. When pressure drops to 20 to 28 psi (138 to 193 kPa), the switch should open and ohmmeter reading should swing all the way over to infinite resistance.

blow out only for a brief period, then turn on and produce good cooling for a period, then stay off, then turn on, and so on, that would be an *intermittent* operation problem.

With any complaint of intermittent operation, you must get the most detailed information possible from the customer. For example, does the system cool briefly, stop briefly, then cool again? In this case, a defective cycling clutch switch (staying off too long) is a likely cause on cars so equipped. Or the problem might be a poor capillary tube attachment for the expansion valve. There are other refrigeration system possibilities, but they are remote. A vacuum system problem, described next, is a strong possibility.

Or does the system always cool properly after it is first turned on, and then stop cooling altogether for long enough to convince the motorist the system is not working, so he or she shuts it off. After a while, the driver tries it again, and it works for a while. This is a moisture problem, also covered earlier.

Vacuum System Problems

If the system cuts out when the car is accelerating or climbing in mountainous areas, vacuum leakage is indicated, assuming the car is not equipped with a vacuum-operated compressor cutout for fuel economy.

Figure 12-21 Try to flex plastic neck; if it moves, it is cracked and the part must be replaced.

Check for poor vacuum hose connections at the dashboard control panel, the diaphragm units on the duct housing, the heater water control valve, the vacuum reservoirs, and the check valves. If a hose neck is plastic, flex it with a finger. If it actually moves, it is cracked (see Fig. 12-21).

Also test the check valves, which should temporarily hold vacuum even when the throttle is opened. Connect a vacuum gauge to the outlet side of a check valve, run the engine, and then blip the throttle. If the vacuum gauge reading drops instantly, the check valve is leaking and should be replaced.

Note: If the car is going up a long upgrade, the length of time with inadequate vacuum from the engine may cause the air conditioning to stop performing normally. If the problem occurs only at this time, it is something the customer should be told to accept.

Electrical Causes of Intermittent Failure

The only time you can pinpoint an electrical cause for an intermittent failure is when the system is malfunctioning as a result. If you wish to try, you can feel terminals for looseness and inspect for corrosion when the system is operating, but that is really hit or miss. Further, defective relays are a frequent problem on some systems. If the intermittent operation occurs constantly, you can try to eliminate some possibilities by bypassing one switch at a time with a jumper wire and then operating the air conditioning to see if the problem has disappeared.

Excessive Noise

All air conditioning compressors make some noise, but if it is clearly excessive, here are the primary causes:

Squeals. Check the drive belt for looseness or for glazed sidewalls. If the system has just been turned on after a long period, allow some time for the compressor seal to reshape itself to conform to the compressor shaft. Only if the noise remains should the seal be replaced. If you are not certain if the noise is from the compressor shaft seal, check with a mechanic's stethoscope. *Note:* After a new seal is installed, allow up to an hour for it to work itself in.

Vibration. Loose compressor mountings are the first things to check. Also look for cracks in the mountings. The compressor itself may become noisy if low on oil, so if you see oil streaks from the compressor shaft seal, check for leaks (some oil streaking is normal). If you catch a seal leak in time, you may be able to save the compressor.

Growling. If the system growls when turned on, the compressor is the source of the noise. If there is a growling noise when the system is off, but it goes away when the system is turned on, it is probably in the bearing on which the pulley is spinning. For once the system is on, the pulley is locked to the compressor drive plate and shaft, and the pulley bearing is effectively out of the picture. You can double-check the pulley bearing as follows: (1) with the system on, the pulley should turn without any signs of "wobble"; (2) with the system off, turn the pulley by hand (drive belt removed), and you may feel bearing roughness if the bearing is defective. On most compressors, the pulley bearing is replaceable as an individual part. Refer to Chapter 14.

QUESTIONS

1. One of the following is *not* likely to produce low pressure readings on both the high- and low-side gauges with the system running.
   a. Defective compressor
   b. Thermostatic expansion valve stuck open.
   c. Low refrigerant level.
2. The high- and low-side pressure readings (system running) both are high. Mechanic A says this could be caused by a thermostatic expansion valve stuck open or an overcharge of refrigerant. Mechanic B says it could be caused by the cooling system. Who is right?

a. Mechanic A.
b. Mechanic B.
c. Both.
d. Neither.

3. When the high-side pressure reading is high and the low-side pressure reading is low (system running), the problem is more likely to be at the
   a. expansion valve or orifice tube.
   b. condenser.
   c. compressor outlet.

4. The high- and low-side readings are normal (system running), but cooling performance is poor. Mechanic A says the problem could be air in the system. Mechanic B says a plugged orifice tube is likely. Who is right?
   a. Mechanic A.
   b. Mechanic B.
   c. Both.
   d. Neither.

5. A frost mark on a refrigerant line or the receiver-dryer (system running) indicates
   a. a restriction in the system.
   b. the suction throttling valve may be stuck open.
   c. a normal condition on a humid day.
   d. the receiver-dryer desiccant bag is loaded with moisture.
   e. all the above.

6. There is normal current to the magnetic clutch terminal, but the clutch does not engage. Mechanic A says the problem could be a defective time-temperature delay relay. Mechanic B says it could be a defective clutch coil. Who is right?
   a. Mechanic A.
   b. Mechanic B.
   c. Both.
   d. Neither.

7. The clutch slips and the drive belt snaps in hot weather. The high-side pressure readings are low and the low-side readings are high with the air conditioning running. Mechanic A says the problem could be a defective compressor outlet reed valve. Mechanic B says it might be a seized compressor pulley bearing. Who is right?
   a. Mechanic A.
   b. Mechanic B.
   c. Both.
   d. Neither.

8. The high- and low-side pressure readings are very close to each other with the air conditioning running. Mechanic A says the problem could be a defective compressor. Mechanic B says it might be a suction throttling valve stuck open. Who is right?
   a. Mechanic A.
   b. Mechanic B.
   c. Both.
   d. Neither.
9. If pressure tests (system running) and other tests indicate blockage at the thermostatic expansion valve or orifice tube, you may confirm the problem by
   a. heating the thermostatic expansion valve with a hot rag.
   b. checking for liquid discharge from the low-side fitting with the system off.
   c. Answers a and b are both correct.
10. The pressure-type cycling clutch switch stays open until 80 psi (550 kPa) instead of the specified 46 psi (317 kPa). The result of this will be
    a. no cooling under 78°F (26°C).
    b. freeze-up on the evaporator coils in moderately humid weather.
    c. loss of the low-pressure protection function.
11. The compressor growls when the air conditioning is off. The growl virtually disappears when the system is turned on. Mechanic A says the problem could be a defective compresser shaft bearing. Mechanic B says it could be a defective compressor pulley bearing. Who is right?
    a. Mechanic A.
    b. Mechanic B.
    c. Both.
    d. Neither.
12. The air conditioning works well for a brief period only, on a very humid day. In other weather, it functions normally. Mechanic A says the problem could be moisture in the system. Mechanic B says it could be a defective suction throttling valve or evaporator pressure regulator, on systems so equipped, or a defective cycling clutch switch. Who is right?
    a. Mechanic A.
    b. Mechanic B.
    c. Both.
    d. Neither.

HANDS ON

1. Connect a gauge manifold and pressure test an air conditioning system.
2. Make a current draw test of a compressor clutch coil with an ammeter.
3. Bench test a pressure-type cycling clutch switch.
4. Bench test a POA-type suction throttling valve or evaporator pressure regulator.

13

Replacing Parts

The nuts-and-bolts, turning wrenches procedures used to replace the different components in the air conditioning system are outside the scope of this book. Each system is different, and there are wide differences also in the way the same system may be installed in different cars. Further, in most cases the major part of the job may involve gaining access by removing parts from systems other than air conditioning. You therefore need general tool assortments and some experience in routine underhood wrench-slinging. This chapter, therefore, is restricted to those techniques with which you should be familiar when replacing air conditioning components.

Components That Can Be Replaced Without Discharging the System

Not all component replacements require discharging the Refrigerant 12 in the system. You may change the following without discharging:

* *Compressor drive belt.* Drive belt inspection and service is covered in Chapter 9.
* *Compressor clutch.* The service of compressor clutches is covered in Chapter 14.
* *Compressors with manual valves.* The service of this compressor is covered in Chapter 14.
* *Dashboard air conditioning controls and other electrical and vacuum system parts.* Work on vacuum and electrical components varies greatly from car to car. Aside from the basic checkout explained in Chapter 9, you should refer to the car maker's service manual for details.

* ***Cycling clutch switch*** (thermostatic or pressure type). Changing a cycling clutch switch is a straightforward procedure, although access to the switch may be difficult on American Motors cars and on add-on units, where it may be partly installed in the ductwork. Tips on cycling clutch switch replacement and specific details on late-model AMC cars are given later in this chapter.

Components That Can Be Replaced Only after the System Is Discharged

Most components can be replaced only after the system has been discharged. You should never attempt to remove a part that involves discharging the system unless the system is completely discharged, as explained in Chapter 11. Even then, loosen any connection very slowly so that any Refrigerant 12 gas trapped inside may bleed out harmlessly.

General Guidelines to Parts Replacement

Although the physical removal and replacement of defective parts may be a straightforward job, when working on air conditioning there are certain things you should keep in mind:

1. Whenever you take apart a connection, you must replace the old gasket or O-ring seal. First clean any dirt or metal burrs from the fitting, coat the new gasket or O-ring with clean refrigeration oil, and then slip it into place.
2. If a connection is to be open for more than a couple of minutes, plug it to keep out moisture. This step is important even if you will be vacuum pumping the system later.
3. When you tighten an O-ring-type hose connection, always use two open-end wrenches to avoid twisting the O ring inside (see Fig. 13-1). Where available, tubing-type open-end wrenches or crowfoot should be used. For best results, one should be a torque wrench with a crowfoot adapter to permit tightening to factory specifications.
4. When you are replacing a major component, large or small, flush the new part with a special cleaning agent, such as dry nitrogen or Refrigerant 11 (don't confuse with Refrigerant 12). Run at least 1 pound, preferably 2, through a large component such as a condenser or evaporator. Also flush a compressor, but never with Refrigerant 11, only with Refrigerant 12. It is not as good a cleaning agent as Refrigerant 11, but Refrigerant 11 can harm a

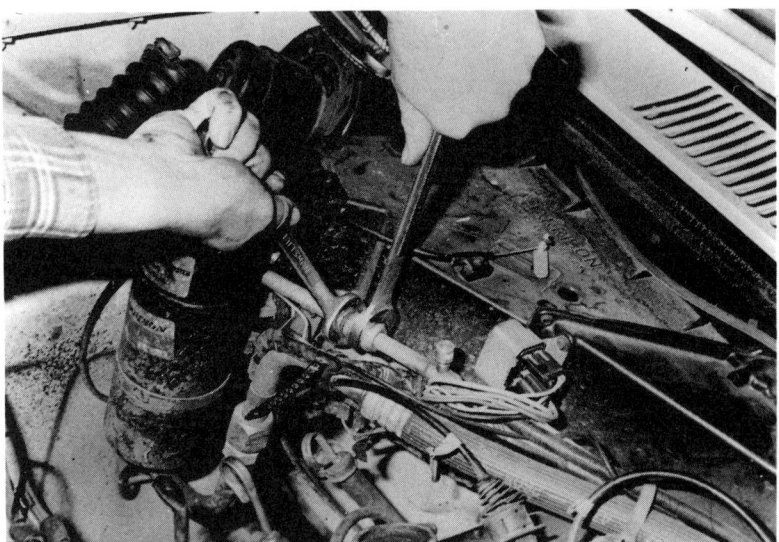

Figure 13-1 When you tighten an O-ring-type hose connection, use two wrenches as shown to avoid twisting the O-ring inside. If available, use torque wrench with crowfoot bits.

compressor. Commercial flushing guns are readily available; follow the gun manufacturer's usage instructions.

5. Before you replace what you think is a defective part, check for a plugged screen, particularly at a thermostatic expansion valve, suction throttling valve, or compressor inlet port. If you find a plugged screen, and the part itself can be reused, flush the system and install a new receiver-dryer or accumulator (on the Valves-in-Receiver, install a new desiccant bag).

6. If a system has been opened by collision or other physical damage or has been left open for more than a few minutes, install a new receiver-dryer or accumulator, and on the Valves-in-Receiver, a new desiccant bag.

7. Whenever you are replacing a major part (condenser, evaporator, receiver-dryer, or as covered in Chapter 14, the compressor), collect and measure the amount of oil in the component and install an equal amount of fresh refrigerant oil in the replacement part. If the part being replaced has been leaking, check manufacturer's specifications for the amount of oil that should be poured in before the part is installed.

Now let's look at some of the things to which you should pay special attention during replacement of particular components.

Expansion Valve with Capillary Tube

Always note exactly where the capillary tube is clamped (mark the location before you remove it, if necessary), so you can install the new part in the same spot.

If the bulb is covered with insulating material, be careful not to damage it when you remove it, but if you do, be sure to replace it. The insulation isolates the bulb from ambient air in the engine compartment, which would cause incorrect temperature sensing.

If there is any corrosion at the capillary tube clamp location, clean it off with a suitable solvent or a wire brush.

Cycling Clutch Switch: Thermostatic or Pressure Type, Except AMC

The replacement procedure for cycling clutch switches of the thermostatic type is very similar to that for expansion valves, except that it is not necessary to discharge the refrigeration system. The procedures regarding capillary tubes apply to the cycling clutch switch too. If the capillary tube goes into a well in the line (Chrysler products), the well should be filled with a special thermal grease. If the well is empty or nearly so, repack it with grease before inserting the end of the capillary tube.

If the system is equipped with a pressure-type cycling clutch switch, unthread it from the Schrader valve on which it is installed and thread on the replacement.

Cycling Clutch Switch: American Motors Cars

Most AMC cars have a cycling clutch system with a thermostatic-type cycling clutch switch that is preset by the position of the dashboard temperature control lever, which also operates the duct housing blend air flap door (see Fig. 13-2).

When replacing the cycling clutch switch, you also should adjust the switch and cable; the whole operation is as follows:

1. Disconnect the battery cable (for safety). Gain access to the cycling clutch switch by removing the package tray outlet and the instrument panel center housing.
2. Remove the screw and clip that hold the cycling clutch switch capillary tube to the evaporator housing; then remove the capillary tube from its guide.
3. Take out the radio and remove the control panel attaching screws and the center duct.

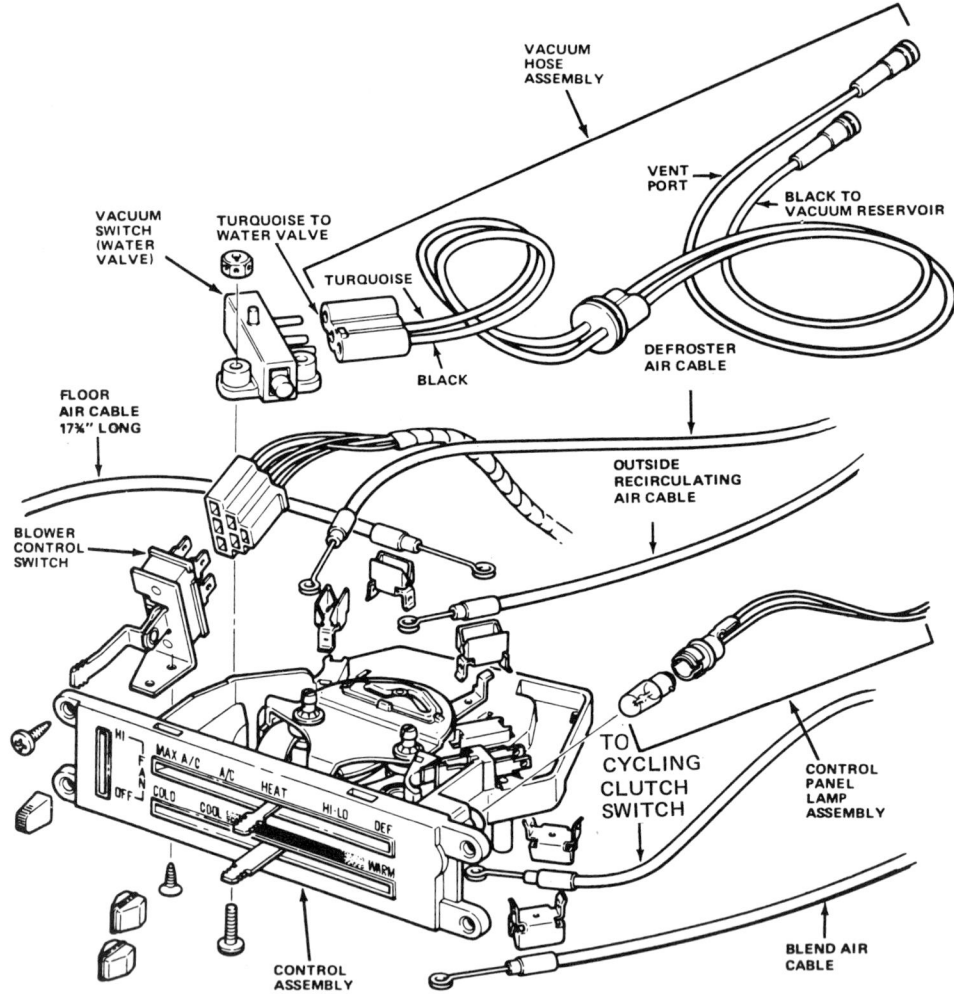

Figure 13-2 This exploded view of dashboard air conditioning controls of American Motors cars shows that it includes a cable to the cycling clutch switch to preset it. (Courtesy American Motors Corp.)

4. Lower the control panel and disconnect the wiring to the cycling clutch switch. Remove the screws that hold the switch to its bracket and disconnect the control panel temperature control cable from the switch.
5. Install a new switch on the bracket, and connect the wiring and the temperature control cable.

6. Adjust the cable, which has a self-adjusting clip, beginning by holding the temperature control lever in mid-position and pushing the self-adjusting clip about a half-inch toward the end of the cable.
7. Move the cycling clutch switch's crank arm to the cold detent position; then move the temperature control lever from mid-position to the cold setting. This will cause the cable to slip through the self-adjusting clip to the proper position.
8. Reinstall the center duct, control panel and screws, and the radio.
9. Run the capillary tube to the evaporator housing. Make a 90-degree bend at the line marked by the colored tape on the tube, and insert the end into the tube guide (on the front of the evaporator housing, between the evaporator core fins).
10. Attach the tube with clip and screw to the evaporator housing; then reinstall the dashboard center panel and the package tray outlet. Reconnect the battery ground cable.

Orifice Tube

The orifice (expansion) tube on most cars so equipped is a plastic part with a filtering screen built in (Fig. 13-3). Once you undo the connection at the evaporator inlet, the end of the tube is exposed for removal.

Although some factory shop manuals have recommended using needle-nose pliers to extract the old tube, the likely result of this approach is to break apart the tube and to be unable to get the remainder out. You should only attempt removal with a special tool that you slip over the

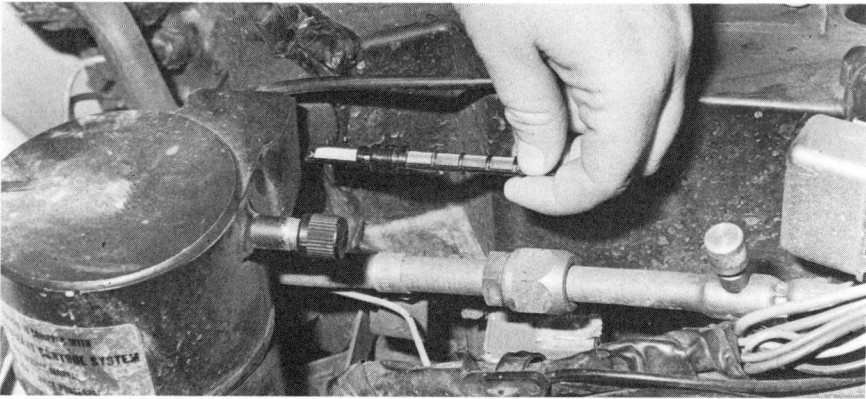

Figure 13-3 Orifice tube is a plastic part with a filtering screen and a brass tube. It is shown removed from the liquid line tubing into which it fits.

228   Replacing Parts

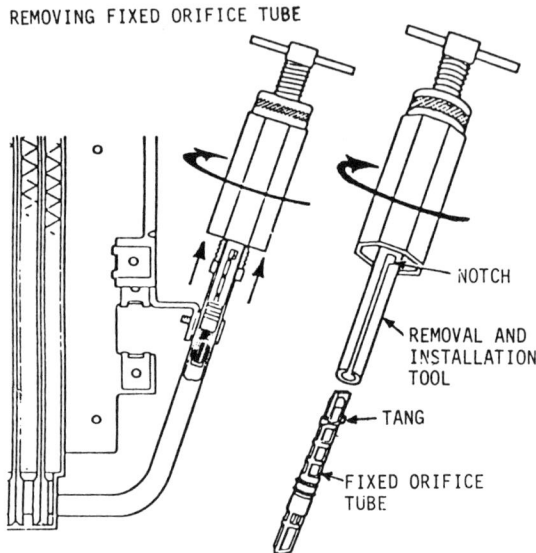

Figure 13-4 This is one of the several tools available for removing an orifice tube. To use, disconnect line and pour some refrigeration oil into tube to lubricate seals. Insert the tool and turn the T-handle only enough to engage the tabs on the orifice tube. Hold the T-handle and turn down (clockwise) the exterior threaded sleeve. The orifice tube will be pulled out. To install a replacement orifice tube, just push it in until it stops against dimples in the liquid line.

orifice tube and turn to lock onto projecting tabs (see Fig. 13-4). Even with this tool, a deteriorated orifice tube may break apart. If this happens, the safest approach is to remove it with another special tool (Fig. 13-5). If that also fails to do the job, cut off the evaporator inlet line just after the section that holds the orifice tube and splice in a repair kit available from air conditioning parts suppliers.

Evaporator Pressure Regulator

This Chrysler version of the suction throttling valve is in the compressor inlet. For details on replacement, see Chapter 14.

Receiver-Dryer and Accumulator (except Valves-in-Receiver Design)

Receiver-dryers and accumulators are often unnecessarily replaced because of minor dents. They should only be changed if there is moisture in the system (resulting in icing of the expansion valve or a similar fault), if there

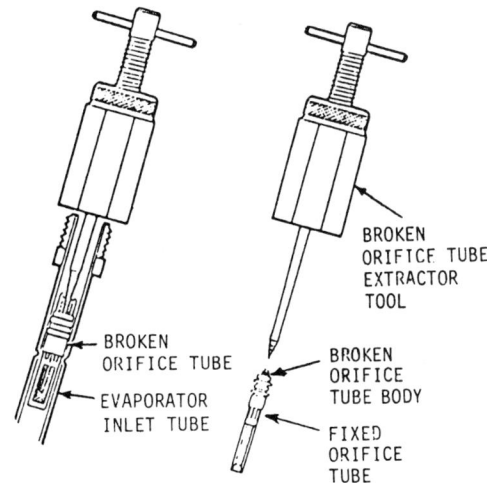

Figure 13-5 If orifice tube breaks, use an extractor tool as shown. Turn down the T-handle until the threaded, pointed tip goes into the brass tube and is secure in it. Then pull on the tool and the broken piece should come out. If the brass tube pulls out of the plastic body, remove it from the end of the extractor, thread it in again, this time into the plastic, and it should pull the plastic part out easily.

has been a major leak (in which case a lot of moisture probably is in the system), if a filtering screen anywhere in the system is plugged, or if the system has been left open for more than a few minutes. The new receiver-dryer should be left capped until you are ready to install it, or the desiccant inside will absorb moisture from the air.

Servicing the Valves-in-Receiver

Five replacements can be made on the General Motors Valves-in-Receiver (VIR):

1. Desiccant bag
2. Expansion valve
3. POA-type suction throttling valve
4. Liquid bleed valve
5. Main body

It is possible to do some service work on the VIR without removing it from the car. However, you have to discharge the system anyway, so to

230 Replacing Parts

prevent dirt from getting in, remove it and service it on the bench, beginning the job (after the system is discharged) at the car as follows:

1. Clean all surface dirt from the VIR and all lines that connect to the component.
2. Disconnect the compressor inlet line, the oil bleed line, and the condenser outlet line. Discard the old O-rings; then plug the ends of all the lines and the VIR line fittings.
3. Loosen the evaporator inlet and outlet lines at the VIR; then take out any screws or bolts that hold the VIR in place in the car.
4. Slide the VIR off the evaporator outlet line and then off the evaporator inlet line. Discard the O-rings and plug the ends of the lines.
5. For access to the desiccant bag (Fig. 13-6), begin by loosening the capscrews that hold the cylindrical shell to the VIR body. Push on the shell to break its seal to the VIR body; then remove the screws and lower the shell. The desiccant bag is inside.

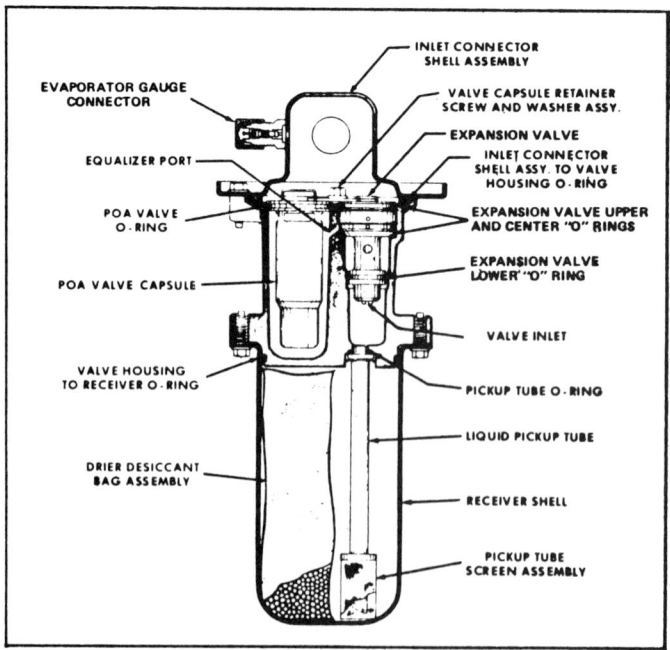

Figure 13-6 Desiccant bag is in bottom of Valves-in-Receiver as shown. To gain access for removal, take off bottom shell from the receiver body. (Courtesy General Motors Corp.)

6. Replace the VIR body-to-shell O-rings and lubricate with refrigeration oil. Collect the oil inside the shell. Wash the pickup tube filter screen and the interior of the shell with solvent and blow dry.
7. If only the desiccant bag is to be replaced, install it and an amount of fresh oil equal to what was collected (or 1 ounce, whichever is greater). Then quickly reassemble the shell to the VIR body, install the capscrews, and tighten. Refit the VIR to the system immediately, using new O-rings well lubricated with refrigeration oil at all fittings.
8. If any other parts are to be changed, leave the desiccant bag replacement for last.

Replacing the Expansion Valve in the Valves-in-Receiver

1. Mark the VIR body and the top cover for correct reinstallation.
2. Remove the capscrews that hold the top cover to the VIR body; then lift off the cover. Remove the old O-ring and discard (See Fig. 13-7).
3. Remove one of the new capscrews (with washer) that hold the expansion valve and suction throttling valve capsules. Loosen the other screw three turns.

Figure 13-7 After capscrews are out, lift off cover from Valves-in-Receiver as shown. Replace O-ring before reassembly.

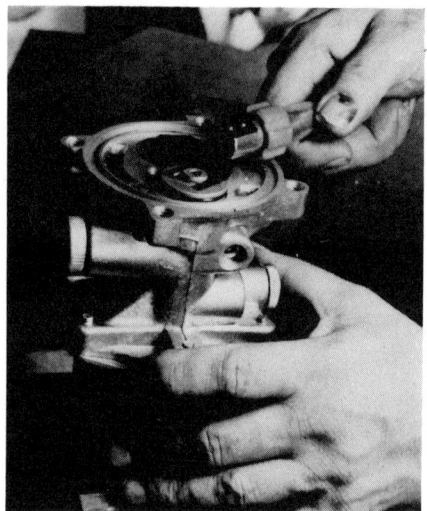

Figure 13-8 Removal tool easily pries up expansion valve.

4. Attach the removal tool to the expansion valve top flange and move the handle of the tool over the remaining (loosened screw). Press down on the handle of the tool and the expansion valve capsule should break loose; some trapped refrigerant may escape (see Fig. 13-8).
5. When the expansion valve is free, disengage the tool, take out the remaining screw, and lift out the expansion valve.
6. Lubricate and install new O-rings on the replacement expansion valve. Early VIRs, with a silver expansion valve, take three O-rings (upper, center, and lower). Late models (with a gold expansion valve) have three grooves, but install only the center and lower O-rings. Also replace the O-ring in the expansion valve cavity. Lubricate all O-rings and the cavity with refrigeration oil.
7. Lubricate the expansion valve capsule with refrigeration oil and push it into place.
8. Reinstall the capsules' retaining screws and tighten them.
9. Inspect the top cover's O-ring surface to make sure it is not scored or burred, which would damage the O-ring seal. If it is not, install a new O-ring, well lubricated with refrigeration oil, and refit the top cover.
10. Replace the desiccant bag as explained previously. When refitting the VIR, use new O-rings, well lubricated with refrigeration oil, at all line fittings.

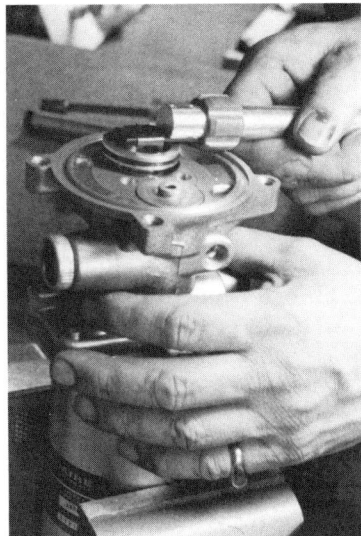 

Figure 13-9 (*Left*) Removal tool also lifts up POA-type suction throttling valve.

Figure 13-10 (*Right*) To remove liquid (oil) bleed fitting, insert special tool shown into cavity, engage fitting, unthread, and remove. Tool is similar to that used to remove tire valves. Thread in replacement valve finger tight, then one half-turn more. Mark the knob end of the tool before final tightening so you know when you have made a half-turn.

Replacing the Suction Throttling Valve

Replacing the POA-type suction throttling valve capsule is similar to changing an expansion valve capsule, with the following differences:

1. To make sure that all pockets of Refrigerant 12 have been allowed to escape, remove the cylindrical bottom shell and loosen the expansion valve first.
2. Insert the other end of the removal tool into the baffle of the POA capsule; then press down on the handle of the tool to break it loose (see Fig. 13-9).
3. There is only one O-ring to replace on the POA body. As with the expansion valve, however, install the capsule, well lubricated with refrigeration oil, by hand.
4. For extra protection of a new POA, install a filtering screen assembly on top of the valve before refitting the capscrews. This filter is not original equipment, but is readily available from air conditioning service parts outlets.

Replacing the Liquid Bleed Valve

This little Schrader valve is designed to allow oil to bypass the POA-type suction throttling valve when it is closed for compressor lubrication. It should open at about 10 psi (70 kPa). If it does not, the compressor life will be shortened. If it sticks open, system performance could be reduced.

You could check the valve with a manual air pump or by hand, but it is cutomary to replace this inexpensive part whenever a valve capsule is replaced (see Fig. 13-10). Insert a special tool into the valve cavity, and turn and unscrew the valve. Thread in the replacement valve finger tight, and then turn 180 degrees more (one half-turn).

If Valves-in-Receiver Body Is to Be Replaced

If you are replacing the entire VIR body for any reason (damaged threads in fittings, the parts you need are not available, etc.), you must change over the liquid refrigerant pickup tube from the old assembly. The tube is held by a special retaining ring, which has several locking tangs. To remove the retaining ring, insert a thin, small screwdriver and pry up, working around the complete circumference of the ring. When the ring is free, you can pull out the pickup tube.

To install the pickup tube in the new VIR body, place a new O-ring and new retaining ring on the pickup tube (see Fig. 13-11); then push the end of the tube into its hole. Place the special tool over the tube (Fig. 13-12) and push down, which forces the retaining ring into position, where it locks. Then reinstall the pickup tube screen.

Refrigerant Hose

You have two choices when a refrigerant hose leaks: service or replace. If possible, the service option is the easiest, for in the typical engine

Figure 13-11 To install pickup tube, place new O-ring and retaining ring on it as shown; then push end into hole in receiver body.

Figure 13-12 Use installing tool as shown. Place it over the tube and push down, which will force the retaining ring (the O-ring as well) into position and lock it.

compartment installing a new hose under, over, and around everything else takes care, patience, and lots of time. In addition, it is much more costly.

Hose Service

If a hose is in good condition except at the point where it leaks, it normally can be serviced. The type of service depends on the location of the leak and the cause.

Leak at a Fitting. If a fitting leaks, you normally can reseal it with a new O-ring (or gasket) as explained earlier in this chapter. If the fitting cannot be so simply serviced, you can replace it. Cut the hose just behind the fitting, or if it is a crimped-on fitting, cut just after the crimped-on part ends.

If there is enough free play in the hose, lubricate and install a repair fitting and secure it with a worm-drive hose clamp (Fig. 13-13). If the repair fitting will not reach the connection now, use a tubing connector, then a short section of bulk refrigerant hose (never ordinary hose), and then a replacement fitting. Install worm-drive clamps on each side of the tubing connector and a third clamp to hold the replacement fitting.

If the damage is to the hose at the fitting rather than the fitting itself, and there is some slack in the hose, you may be able to reuse the fitting and need nothing more than a worm-drive clamp to replace the crimp clamp used in production.

With a hacksaw, cut through the crimp clamp and the first layer of hose. Peel off the crimp clamp, trim the hose end square, lubricate and reinstall the fitting (use a new O-ring of course), and secure with a worm-drive hose clamp (see Fig. 13-14). *Caution:* It is important that you not cut

236 Replacing Parts

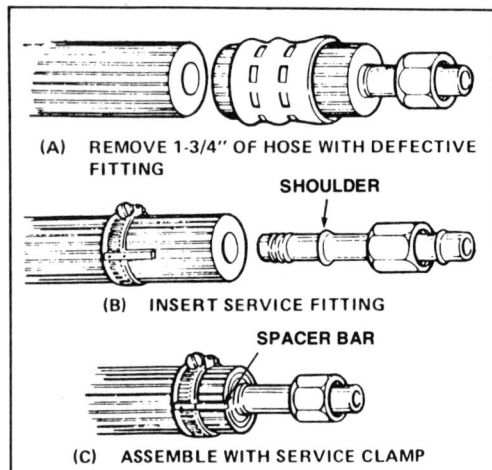
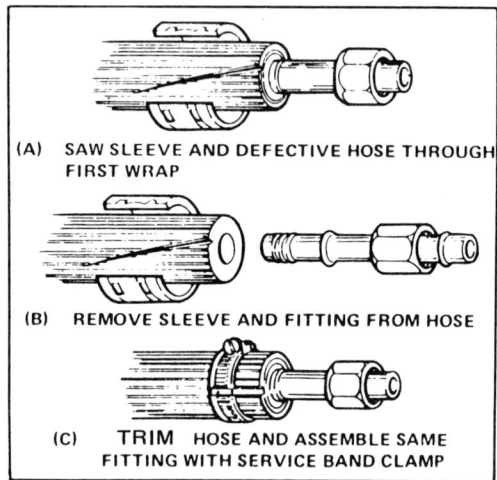

Figure 13-13 (*Left*) To replace defective fitting, follow procedure shown in illustration. Note spacer bar, which properly positions clamp. (Courtesy General Motors Corp.)

Figure 13-14 (*Right*) To get rid of a defective section of hose at a fitting, follow procedure shown in illustration. If you are careful, the old fitting can be reused if in good condition. (Courtesy General Motors Corp.)

completely through the hose (just the first layer as explained), or you could damage the sealing beads on the fitting. You may have to struggle a bit to get the fitting out of the remainder of the hose, but this is what you must do.

Leak away from a Fitting. If a hose leaks somewhere away from a fitting, the cure is to cut away the damage and install a connector, as follows:

1. Cut the hose in two where it is leaking.
2. Trim the cut ends square.
3. Lubricate a piece of connector tubing with refrigeration oil and insert it into the cut ends. The connector has locating beads (so you know how far in to push it) and sealing beads, on which the clamp is positioned.
4. Secure the hose ends with worm-drive clamps over the sealing beads. Tighten the clamps with a torque wrench to 40 pound-inches (23 newton-meters).

New Hose Installation

If a refrigerant hose is generally deteriorated, or if there is an actual leak at more than one point, you should install a replacement hose. The new hose may not be an exact duplicate of the original (it will probably be somewhat longer), so careful routing is critical. Keep it at least 3 inches (or about 0.1 meter) away from the exhaust manifold and make sure it does not touch the engine at any hot spot either. If necessary, use rubber blocks as a cushion wherever in the line rigid tubing is used.

Make sure the hose is curved very gently. A rule of thumb is that the radius of the curve should be four to five times the diameter of the hose, to prevent restriction to the flow of Refrigerant 12.

QUESTIONS

1. If you open the system for replacement of such parts as condenser, receiver-dryer, and compressor, you should
   a. replace any O-ring or gasket.
   b. plug the system to keep out moisture.
   c. flush the replacement part.
   d. All of the above.
2. If the orifice tube on a CCOT system is stuck in place,
   a. pull it out with needle-nose pliers.
   b. pull it with a tool that locks on its projecting tabs.
   c. Answers a and b are both correct.
3. When servicing a Valves-in-Receiver,
   a. replace it if the shell has any dents.
   b. the work should be done on the bench.
   c. the desiccant bag can be changed as a separate part.
   d. Answers a, b, and c are all correct.
   e. Answers a and b are both correct.
   f. Answers b and c are both correct.
4. Mechanic A says a new hose should be installed if cutting off a bad fitting does not permit the hose, with a new fitting, to reach the connection. Mechanic B says the new hose should be installed if there is leakage and/or deterioration at several points. Who is right?
   a. Mechanic A.
   b. Mechanic B.
   c. Both.
   d. Neither.
5. When installing a new hose, route it so
   a. any curves are four to five times the hose diameter.
   b. the hose is at least 3 inches (0.1 meter) from hot spots in the engine compartment.
   c. Answers a and b are both correct.

HANDS ON

1. Replace an orifice tube. Discharge, vacuum pump, and recharge the system properly, performing the steps at the appropriate times.
2. Replace a receiver-dryer or accumulator. Discharge, vacuum pump, and recharge the system properly.
3. Remove and reinstall the Valves-in-Receiver expansion valve, POA valve capsules, and the desiccant bag. Discharge, vacuum pump, and recharge the system properly.
4. Remove and reinstall a pressure-type cycling clutch switch.
5. Remove and reinstall a thermostatic-type cycling clutch switch.

14

Compressor Service

The compressor has the most moving parts of the air conditioning system and, therefore, is the component that usually requires the most work. Although it is possible to rebuild most compressors completely, increasing numbers of designs are not rebuildable in the shop. The trend is to limit shop repairs to clutch work, test fittings, the shaft seal, and perhaps the head gaskets and reed valve plates. If a compressor needs more, it is probably seized and impractical to rebuild in the shop. Even if the compressor is not seized, you may not be able to get the detail parts you need, even if the manufacturer allows in-shop overhaul. When the compressor needs more than covered in this chapter, get a new or factory rebuilt compressor.

This chapter, therefore, covers oil level checks, and clutch, shaft seal, and head gasket and reed valve service. The compressors in this chapter represent virtually everything used on American cars and many Japanese models. They are General Motors radial four cylinder and six cylinder, Chrysler C-171 and Nippondenso six-cylinder models, Sankyo (formerly called Abacus) five-cylinder, Tecumseh and York two-cylinder, Chrysler V-2 two-cylinder, and York rotary vane.

Compressor Service Notes

The following procedures apply to all compressors:

1. Whenever you replace a compressor with a new or rebuilt component, flush the entire system with Refrigerant 11 and the compressor with Refrigerant 12. Never flush the compressor with Refrigerant 11.

2. If a compressor, or the inlet fitting, has a screen, clean it in solvent when performing any compressor service that requires discharge of the system.
3. All seals, O-rings, gaskets, and valve plates should be lubricated with refrigeration oil immediately prior to assembly. However, do not soak gaskets in refrigeration oil.
4. After you mount a compressor, whether new, factory rebuilt, or overhauled in your shop, turn the drive plate by hand several times to clear oil that may have accumulated in the head(s), and which as a result could damage the reed valves when the compressor is activated.

General Motors Radial Four Compressor

This compressor (see Fig. 14-1) described earlier in Chapter 4, is the Scotch yoke type. Like other compressors, the clutch can be serviced without removing the compressor from the car or even discharging the system. All clutch parts are available for replacement individually. For illustrative

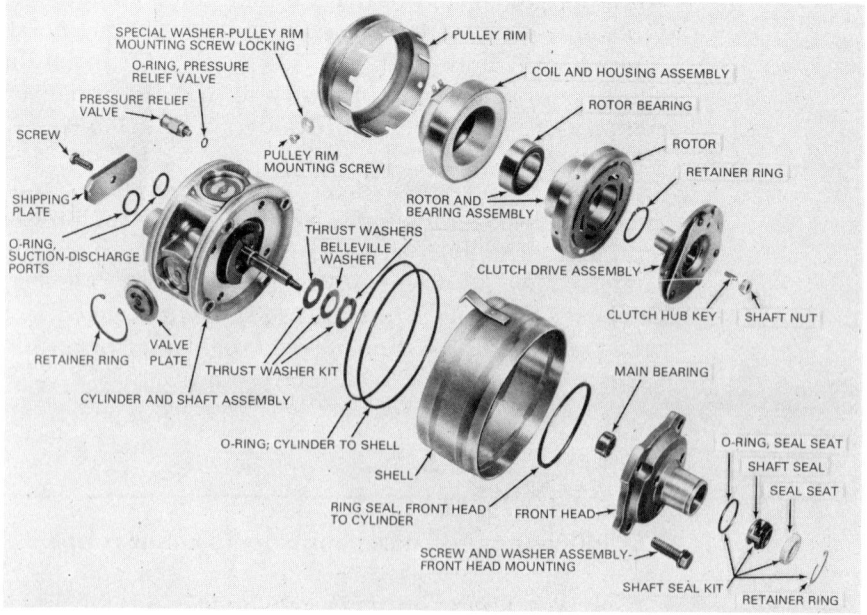

Figure 14-1 Disassembled view of General Motors radial four compressor. Note that cylinder and shaft assembly are not taken apart, as they are available for service only in the assembled form shown. (Courtesy General Motors Corp.)

purposes, however, the clutch work is shown being performed on a work bench.

Internal parts of the four-cylinder compressor that may be replaced during bench service include the reed valve plates, the main bearing and thrust washers, and the seals. You also could replace the cylinder block and shaft assembly (it is serviced only as an assembly), but if that component is defective, obtaining a complete compressor, new or rebuilt, is a more common step.

Leak Testing

Before you disassemble a radial four-cylinder compressor, you should check it for internal leakage, assuming that you did not find external leakage with the leak detector. Make sure the compressor contains a reasonable amount of oil (2 ounces is enough). Install a GM compressor test plate on the rear head of the compressor (this test plate also is used on the GM six cylinder as shown in Fig. 14-2). Turn the entire compressor several times very slowly to circulate oil throughout (not just the crankshaft or drive plate).

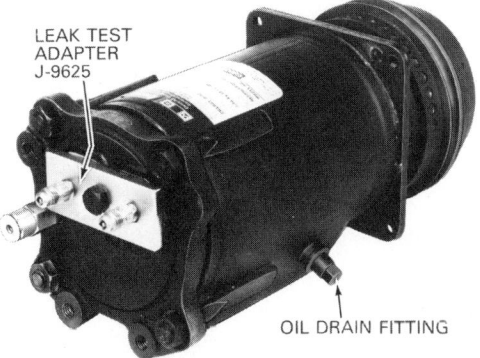

Figure 14-2 Leak-test adapter attaches to back of radial four or six-cylinder General Motors compressor as shown. (Courtesy General Motors Corp.)

Attach a holding fixture to the compressor and put it in a bench vise. Next, connect a manifold gauge set (using hose adapters if necessary) to the test plate. Make sure the compressor is mounted in the bench vise so the inlet port does not aim downward (or the oil will drain out). Close the gauge manifold manual valves.

With a wrench on the shaft nut, turn the compressor crankshaft at a speed of about one revolution per second, for a total of 10 revolutions. Use a watch to check your speed (10 revolutions in 10 seconds). The compressor should build up an air pressure of 50 psi or more on the high-side gauge. If the reading is under 45 psi, there is an internal leak, probably a defective valve. The compressor must be disassembled.

242 Compressor Service

Drain the oil from the compressor and proceed to service the compressor as required. The complete procedure is shown in Figs. 14-3 to 14-44.

Figure 14-3 Although clutch and seal work can be done with compressor on the car, it is usually easier to do it on the bench. If the bench work is your choice, install holder to back of compressor and insert holder in a vise.

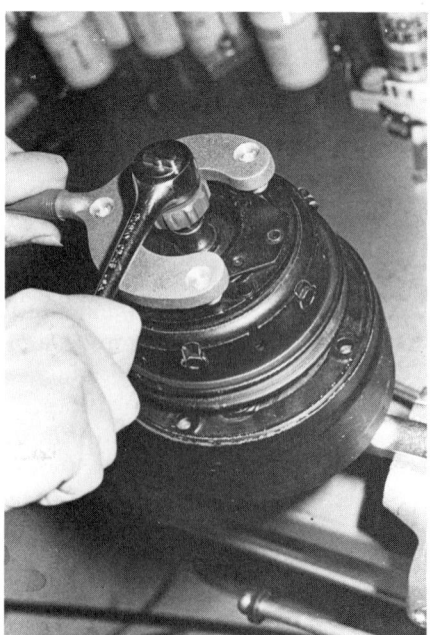

Figure 14-4 Disassembly begins with removal of shaft nut. Y-shaped holder tool has dowels that project and fit into holes in clutch plate, so the plate can be kept from turning while socket wrench is used to loosen pulley nut.

Figure 14-5 This pulling tool is used to remove the clutch drive plate.

Figure 14-6 Exterior of tool is threaded into clutch drive plate, then is held with open-end wrench as shown. Socket wrench is used to turn down center screw of tool against compressor shaft. This forces drive plate up and off. The drive plate is located by a key, as shown in Fig. 14-1. If this key does not come out with drive plate, remove it from recess in compressor shaft with needle-nose pliers.

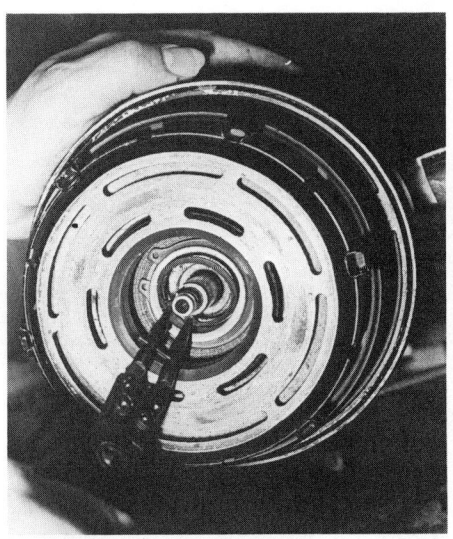

Figure 14-7 (Left) If the job to be done is replacement of the compressor shaft seal, proceed to remove the inner snap ring as shown. This snap ring holds the seal assembly in place.

Figure 14-8 (Right) Split-collet tool is inserted and goes into the seal's seat. Turn the T-handle on the tool as shown and the outer section is forced against the inner circumference of the seat, locking it to the seat.

244 Compressor Service

Figure 14-9 (*Left*) Lift up and the seal seat comes out easily as shown.
Figure 14-10 (*Right*) This is a special tool used to remove the seal itself. Tool is pushed down against the seal, then twisted until its tangs lock on the seal.

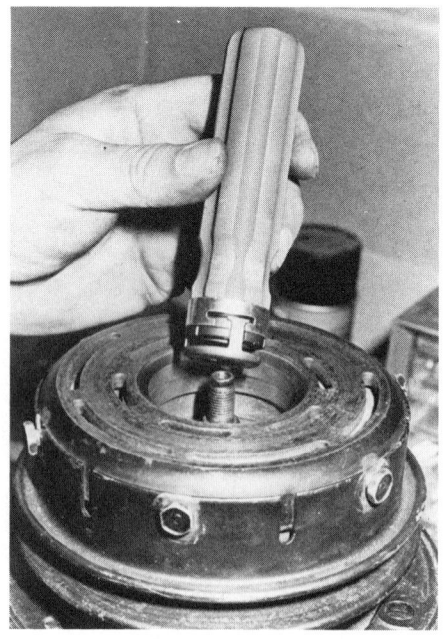 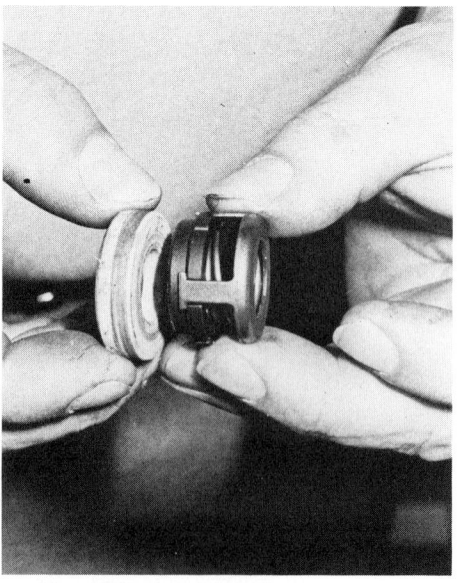

Figure 14-11 (*Left*) Tool is pulled up and seal is extracted as shown.
Figure 14-12 (*Right*) Closeup look at the ceramic seat, at left, and the spring-loaded seal. Iron seats were used through 1968.

General Motors Radial Four Compressor

Figure 14-13 (*Left*) Seal assembly removal is completed by extracting the ceramic seat's rubber O-ring with hook.

Figure 14-14 (*Right*) Seal area is cleaned; then new seal is installed, in reverse of removal shown in Fig. 14-10. Next, a limiter is dropped in, as shown, to help installation of a new ceramic seat O-ring.

Figure 14-15 (*Left*) New O-ring, well lubricated with refrigeration oil, is placed in the opening as shown.

Figure 14-16 (*Right*) Special pusher tool is inserted to move O-ring down. Limiter previously installed ensures that O-ring goes only down to its groove, where it seats itself.

Figure 14-17 (*Left*) Limiter has served its purpose and is removed with special tongs. Ceramic seat next is installed with split-collet tool, in reverse of removal as in Fig. 14-8. Shaft protector is available to place over compressor shaft to protect seat from being chipped. Seal assembly is secured with snap ring, installed as in reverse of Fig. 14-7.

Figure 14-18 (*Right*) Clutch drive plate is installed next. Key is inserted into the slot to which the pen points, so it projects down about 3/16 inch (5 millimeters). Key is curved, so it stays in place. Clutch contact surfaces are cleaned if necessary before drive plate is installed.

Figure 14-19 Clutch drive plate installation tool looks similar to removal tool, but inner part threads onto compressor shaft.

Figure 14-20 (*Left*) Drive plate installation tool is in place, threaded onto compressor shaft. Unlike removal tool, socket is held firm with ratchet, so inner part of tool does not move. Outer part is turned with open-end wrench to force clutch drive plate down. Notice feeler gauge in place between clutch contact surfaces. Clutch plate is forced down until clearance between surfaces is within specifications, as measured with feeler gauge.

Figure 14-21 (*Right*) If removal of the clutch assembly is the job to be performed, it begins with removal of the clutch drive plate as in Figs. 14-4 to 14-6. Next remove the outer (clutch) snap ring, to which the arrow points.

Figure 14-22 Snap ring is removed with special pliers as shown.

248 Compressor Service

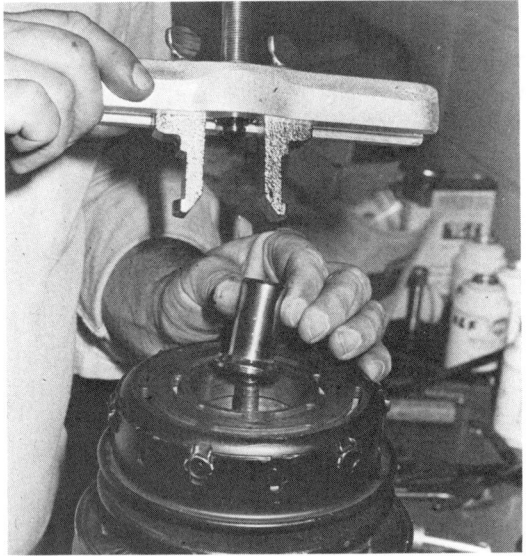

Figure 14-23 (Left) The clutch rotor-pulley assembly is removed with a puller. The type shown has jaws that grip on the inside. To protect the end of the compressor shaft, a pilot is placed over the end as shown.

Figure 14-24 (Right) The forcing screw of the puller is turned down against the pilot, so the jaws draw up on the rotor-pulley assembly.

Figure 14-25 (Left) Complete rotor-pulley assembly is drawn up, then lifted off as shown.

Figure 14-26 (Right) Rotor-pulley assembly can be disassembled. If bolts that hold it together, have locktabs, they must be straightened with a chisel and hammer as shown, so the bolts can be loosened and removed with a wrench.

Figure 14-27 This is the rotor-pulley assembly taken apart. At left is the bearing housing, in the center is the coil, at right is the pulley.

Figure 14-28 (Left) If the clutch surface is in good condition and the only problem is a defective bearing, the old bearing can be driven out, using a driver and hammer. The housing is supported between two blocks of wood as shown.

Figure 14-29 (Right) New bearing is driven in from the opposite side, using the driver and an installation adapter into which it fits.

Figure 14-30 (*Left*) New bearing is hammered in, as shown, until it seats in the assembly.
Figure 14-31 (*Right*) Once bearing is in place, hub is punch-staked in a few places to positively secure it. New stake holes are made; the old ones are not reused.

Figure 14-32 (*Left*) When rotor-pulley assembly is put together again, it is ready for installation. The coil has three projecting dowels (pen points to one) that go into holes in the front head of the compressor to hold the coil.
Figure 14-33 (*Right*) Rotor-pully assembly is installed. If necessary, hammer is used to tap it into place, making sure dowels in coil go into holes in front head. Job is completed by installing clutch drive plate as in Figs. 14-18 to 14-20; then install pulley nut.

General Motors Radial Four Compressor

Figure 14-34 If major compressor work is necessary, clutch is not installed. Instead, front head of compressor is removed, beginning with bolt removal as shown.

Figure 14-35 Front head then can be lifted off as shown.

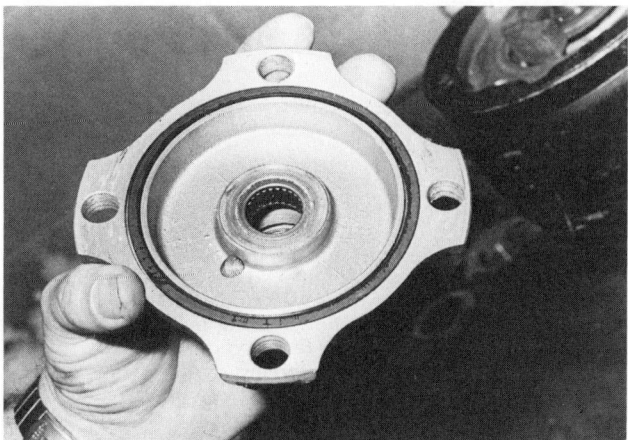

Figure 14-36 Compressor front bearing is in front head. If bearing has been noisy, it should be replaced.

252 Compressor Service

Figure 14-37 (*Left*) Front bearing is removed by supporting front head on blocks of wood, then driving out bearing with special driver and hammer as shown.

Figure 14-38 (*Right*) New bearing is driven into front head from opposite side as shown.

Figure 14-39 If there is apparent problem with valves, shell is removed for access. This job can be done with clutch and heads in place, as shown, using puller with special jaws. Note that clip is inserted to lock puller's forcing screw to the holder bolted to back of compressor. The result is that when forcing screw is unthreaded it will pull up on back of compressor. Steps in puller jaws will butt against shell and hold it from moving.

Figure 14-40 So that shell can slide down, locktab is bent up and away from compressor rear head as shown.

Figure 14-41 (*Left*) Forcing screw is unthreaded, pulling up on rear head while shell is restrained by jaws. Cylinder and shaft assembly is being exposed. Note O-ring seal that shows; there is a second O-ring at front end too.

Figure 14-42 (*Right*) Shell is free and can be lowered away, exposing both O-rings and the valve assembly in one cylinder.

Figure 14-43 (*Left*) Snap ring that retains valve is removed as shown.
Figure 14-44 (*Right*) Valve can be pulled out for replacement. For reassembly, two O-rings are replaced. Shell is drawn on with puller, in reverse of Fig. 14-41. Bottom lips on puller jaws force shell up into position.

Bench Testing for External Leakage

You also can use the test plate to check for external leakage. You may use the procedure as being more helpful than on-the-car testing, as a double-check of on-car tests, or as a precheck before recharging a system on which the compressor seal has been replaced or other major work has been done.

Note: You also may follow this test with the internal leak check, provided there is no external leakage, when compressor service has been completed.

The external leak test is made as follows: Install the test plate on the rear head of the compressor; then connect a manifold gauge set (and adapters if necessary) to the test plate. Attach a refrigerant drum or an adapter with four or five cans of refrigerant to the gauge manifold.

Open the gauge manifold manual valves to allow refrigerant to flow into the compressor. With a leak detector, check for leakage at the pressure relief valve, the pressure switch (if it is on the compressor) or the superheat switch (on older systems with thermal limiters), at the compressor shell-to-cylinder joints, compressor front head seal, and compressor shaft seal.

Service Notes

When replacing the Belleville (spring-type) washer and thrust washers on the compressor crankshaft, install the first thrust washer with the tang pointing out of the compressor, the Belleville washer with the high center pointing out, and the remaining thrust washer with the tang pointing into the compressor.

As with all O-rings, bearings, and seals, lubricate the washers with clean refrigeration oil (525 viscosity is recommended for GM compressors).

There is no oil level check hole or dipstick for the radial four compressor. Drain the old oil out the inlet and outlet ports before you begin service and measure. If more than ½ ounce, add the amount measured, using fresh oil. If less, drain the compressor and add 3 ounces if you have overhauled it or 4 ounces if you are installing a new or factory-rebuilt compressor. If you flush the system, fill with 6 ounces of new oil.

General Motors Six-Cylinder Compressor

The service procedures for the six-cylinder GM compressor (Fig. 14-45) are very similar to those for the radial four, including external and internal leak testing and replacement of the shaft seal with the ceramic seat. The six-cylinder has had other types of seal assemblies, but the ceramic seat type has been used since the late-1960s, so you are unlikely to service any other type. *Note:* Most GM six-cylinders have an oil-absorbent sleeve over the seal area. Replace this sleeve when changing a seal (see Figs. 14-45 and 14-87).

Like the radial four, there is no dipstick arrangement for checking oil level. Drain from the ports to measure the amount of oil remaining in the compressor. If you collect more than 4 ounces, refill an overhauled compressor with that amount of fresh oil; on a new or factory-rebuilt compressor, use that amount plus 1 ounce. If you collect less than 4 ounces, drain the compressor and install 6 ounces of fresh oil in an overhauled compressor and 7 ounces in a new or factory-rebuilt compressor. If you flush the system, fill with 10.5 ounces of fresh oil (525 viscosity refrigeration oil is recommended for GM compressors).

CAUTION: If you install a rebuilt six-cylinder compressor, be sure it has the same type of low-pressure protection as the original. If you install a compressor with a superheat switch on a car with a pressure switch, the clutch coil circuit will be complete only part of the time. The part-time completion could result in clutch slippage and premature failure.

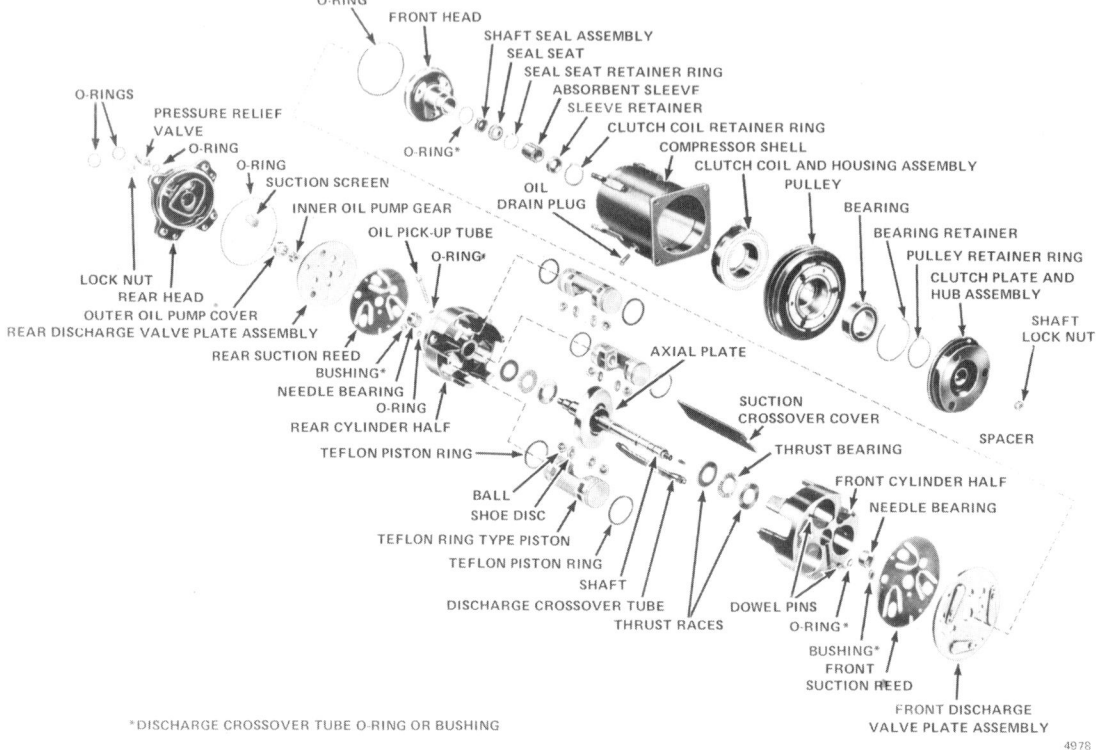

Figure 14-45 Exploded view of General Motors six-cylinder compressor. Although shaft lock nut is removed as in Fig. 14-4, there also is a retainer (snap) ring that must be removed with special pliers before clutch drive plate can come off. Also note absorbent sleeve used on most GM six-cylinder compressors. Replace it as part of seal service (also see Fig. 14-87).

Compressor Overhaul

If you are merely servicing the clutch, proceed as follows:

1. Remove the shaft nut (see Fig. 14-4 on the radial four).
2. With special snap ring pliers, remove the drive plate retaining ring.
3. Using a puller that threads into the drive plate, remove the drive plate (see Fig. 14-46). Take out the key that locates the pulley on the shaft.
4. With special snap ring pliers, remove the pulley bearing-to-head retaining ring.
5. Place a protective pilot on the hub of the front head, and remove the pulley assembly with a two-jaw puller whose jaws are external

257 General Motors Six-Cylinder Compressor

Figure 14-46 Once snap ring is out, drive plate on six cylinder is removed with puller tool in manner similar to that on radial-four compressor, as shown.

and fit into the pulley belt groove and whose forcing screw bears down on the protective pilot.

6. If you wish to replace the pulley bearing, pry out the bearing-to-pulley retaining ring with a small, thin screwdriver; then drive out the pulley bearing with a driver inserted from the inboard end and a hammer.

7. To install a new bearing, drive it in from the outboard side of the pulley with a suitable driver and hammer. The driver should ride on the outer race of the bearing to prevent damage.

8. Install the bearing retaining ring to lock it to the pulley. If this is all you are doing, tap the pulley into place on the hub; then position the key on the drive plate, put the plate into position on the shaft, and push it into place with a special tool (see Fig. 14-20 on the radial four). Press the plate down and measure the clearance with a feeler gauge between the drive plate and the pulley's clutch surface. The clearance should be about 0.090 inch (2.3 millimeters). Stop pressing when clearance is correct.

Coil Replacement

If the clutch coil is to be replaced, delay steps 6 to 8 (pulley remains off); note the coil position in relation to the shell of the compressor and then take out the retaining ring that holds it to the compressor. Lift the coil off, install a replacement, and refit the retaining ring.

Shaft Seal and Reed Valve Plates Service

Before you replace the shaft seal or do any other significant work on the six-cylinder compressor, you should check for the possibility that the compressor has been mishandled during a previous overhaul or damaged in a collision or shipping. Any of these can cause the piston drive plate ("sausage slice") to shift and move many things out of position as a result. If this happens, the shaft seal will leak, for example. The only cure is to replace the compressor.

To test for this possibility, remove the drive plate and place a flat bar (a special tool) across the pulley hub. Thread down the pulley nut until it is finger tight against the flat bar (see Fig. 14-47). Now hook a special wire feeler gauge around the shaft at the inboard end of the threads, and try to work the wire feeler gauge into the tiny gap under the flat bar. One feeler gauge is 0.026 inch thick and it should go in with no difficulty. A second feeler gauge (0.075 inch thick) should not go in, or should go only if forced. If the second feeler gauge fits in without difficulty, discard the compressor. If it does not, you can proceed to seal replacement, which is basically the same as for the radial four compressor (see Figs. 14-7 to 14-17), or to reed valve plate replacement (Figs. 14-48 to 14-53).

Figure 14-47 (Left) Flat bar is held in place by pulley nut on six-cylinder compressor. Hook-type feeler gauge is worked into gap under flat bar. There are two feeler gauges used. The smaller one (0.026-inch-thick wire) should fit in with no difficulty. The second gauge (0.75 inch thick) should not go or go in only if forced. If second gauge fits in easily, discard compressor. If not, it can be serviced.

Figure 14-48 (Right) Replacement of reed valve plates on six-cylinder begins with removal of four nuts on rear head of compressor, as shown.

General Motors Six-Cylinder Compressor

Figure 14-49 (*Left*) Next, rear head is lifted off, exposing oil pump in center. Remove the oil pump.

Figure 14-50 (*Right*) Lift off reed valve plates (both outlet and inlet plates commonly stick together as shown). If the plates stick in the compressor, pry up on the outlet reeds to free up the plates.

Figure 14-51 Use special tool to remove oil pickup tube and replace O-ring on tube.

260 Compressor Service

Figure 14-52 *(Left)* To replace front reeds, turn compressor over and push out compressor from its shell. Then lift off front head as shown.
Figure 14-53 *(Right)* Remove front reeds. You can pry up with putty knife if necessary to free the plates.

Nippondenso and Chrysler C-171 Compressors

The Nippondenso and Chrysler C-171 compressors both are six-cylinder designs with sausage-slice drive plates (see Chapter 4), as on the General Motors six cylinder. However, service of these compressors is different from the GM type.

The C-171 has an internal shaft seal that can be serviced with a special kit. Also serviceable are reed valve plates, O-rings and gaskets, and the clutch.

The C-171 clutch, however, can be serviced without removing the compressor from the car, as follows: (For other services, see Appendix.)

1. Remove drive plate nut, holding the plate with a holder and removing the nut with a socket.
2. Using a special puller of the type that threads into the drive plate, pull the drive plate. Take out the plate locating key from the shaft and any shims.
3. Inspect the friction contact surfaces of the drive plate and the pulley for scores and substantial wear. If the clutch has been slipping, this is what you are likely to find. The plate and pulley surfaces are mated at the factory by a special operation, so you must replace

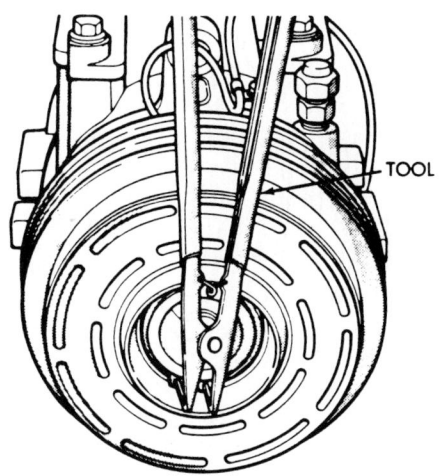 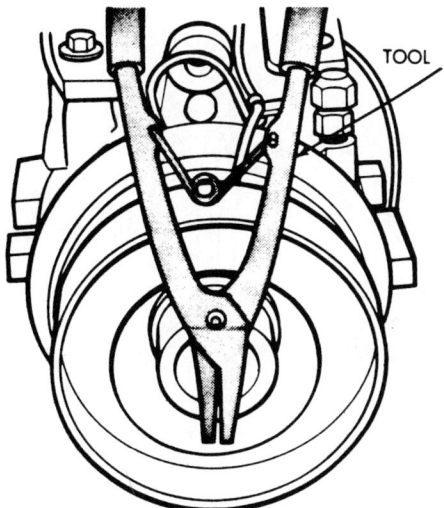

Figure 14-54 *(Left)* After drive plate is out on Chrysler C-171, remove pulley snap ring with snap ring pliers as shown. (Courtesy Chrysler Corp.)

Figure 14-55 *(Right)* Use special pliers to remove the snap ring that holds the clutch coil, as shown. Then remove the screw that holds the ground wire to the compressor, undo the wire clip, and take the coil off the compressor. (Courtesy Chrysler Corp.)

both or slippage between parts would result. The pulley bearing is not replaceable, so if it is defective, change both pulley and drive plate (see Fig. 14-54).

4. Remove the retaining ring that holds the clutch coil; then slide the coil off the compressor. When you install a replacement coil, make sure the pin projecting from the compressor aligns properly with the hole in the coil. Also check the distance the pin projects from the compressor. It should be just under ⅛-inch (2.5 to 3 mm). If it is greater, the pin could come out of the housing, allowing the coil to turn. This would result in failure of the coil wires. If the pin extends out too far, gently tap it down to the recommended depth. Make sure the retaining ring bevel side faces outward. After the ring is installed with special snap ring pliers, seat the ring by pressing all around with a screwdriver. (See Figs. 14-55 and 14-56).

5. Install the pulley (by tapping on the oil slinger with a block of wood if necessary, as in Fig. 14-57) and its retaining ring (bevel side outward) with special snap ring pliers. After the ring is installed, seat it by pressing all around with a screwdriver.

6. If the original drive plate and pulley are being reused, you can try the same stack of shims, whatever their thickness. If not, place a test

262 Compressor Service

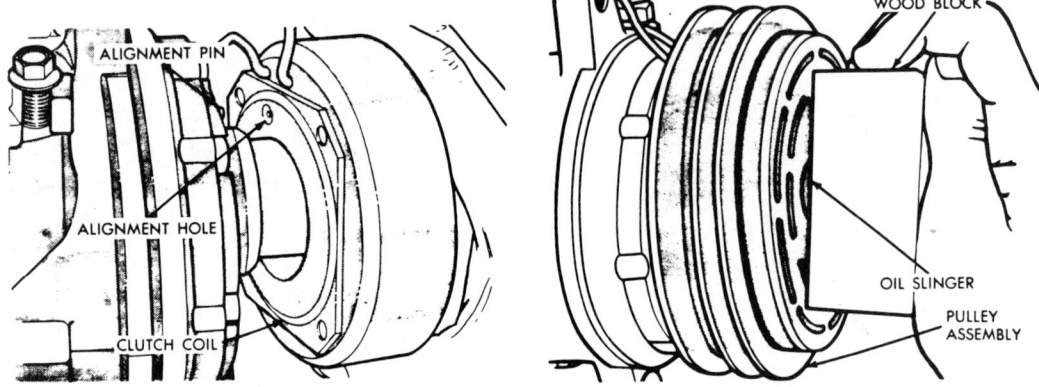

Figure 14-56 (*Left*) When you install a clutch coil on the Chrysler C-171, make sure the holes in the coil align with the pins on the compressor, as shown. (Courtesy Chrysler Corp.)

Figure 14-57 (*Right*) Use block of wood as shown, and tap on oil slinger to seat pulley assembly on Chrysler C-171. Then install snap ring. (Courtesy Chrysler Corp.)

stack 0.100 inch thick (25.4 millimeters) on the shaft; then install the key on the shaft.

7. Install the drive plate, making sure the key engages the slot in the drive plate. Push down on the plate until it is hand tight against the shims. Measure the clearance between the pulley and drive plate contact surfaces with a feeler gauge (Fig. 14-58). It should be 0.020 to 0.035 inch (0.5 to 0.9 millimeters). If it is less than the minimum, remove the plate and add shims. If it is greater than the maximum, remove the plate and take away shims.

8. When the gap is right, install the lockwasher and pulley nut, and tighten the pulley nut to specifications (12 to 14 pound-feet or 16 to

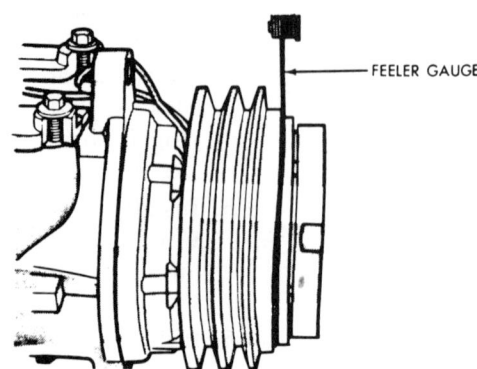

Figure 14-58 Measure gap between friction surfaces of clutch with feeler gauge. Adjust gap if necessary by installing or removing shims. (Courtesy Chrysler Corp.)

C-171 Oil Level

19 newton-meters). Recheck the clearance between drive plate and pulley contact surfaces with a feeler gauge to make sure it is still correct. Spin the pulley a few times and recheck. It is good practice to check clearance at four or more places around the circumference to be sure.

The entire system with a C-171 has a capacity of 9 to 10 ounces of a special wax-free refrigeration oil recommended for this compressor. Five ounces should remain in the compressor (if you find less, adjust the level, through the oil drain plug hole; see Fig. 14-59). If you install a new compressor, it may come with the full charge of 9 to 10 ounces. In this case, either flush the entire system or drain oil from the compressor to reduce the amount to the specified 5 ounces. *Note:* If the drain plug is damaged, a replacement is available as a detail part.

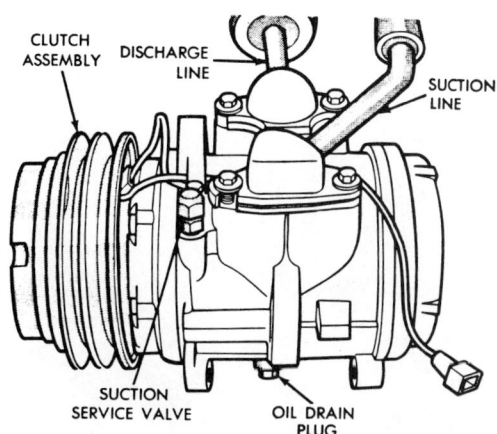

Figure 14-59 Chrysler C-171 compressor has an oil drain plug as shown. (Courtesy Chrysler Corp.)

Nippondenso Service

As with the Chrysler C-171, the Nippondenso shaft seal, and reed valve plates (and pulley bearing) can be replaced. The Nippondenso shaft actually has two seals, an outer seal accessible in a manner similar to the GM radial four, an inner seal serviced as shown in Fig. 14-69 to 14-73. The complete service procedure is covered in Figs. 14-60 to 14-74.

264 Compressor Service

Figure 14-60 (Left) Nippondenso service begins with removal of pulley nut with socket wrench. Use oil filter wrench as shown to hold the clutch drive plate.

Figure 14-61 (Right) On the Nippondenso, you must take off the clutch for all service work, so begin by threading the special pulling tool shown into the drive plate-hub assembly.

 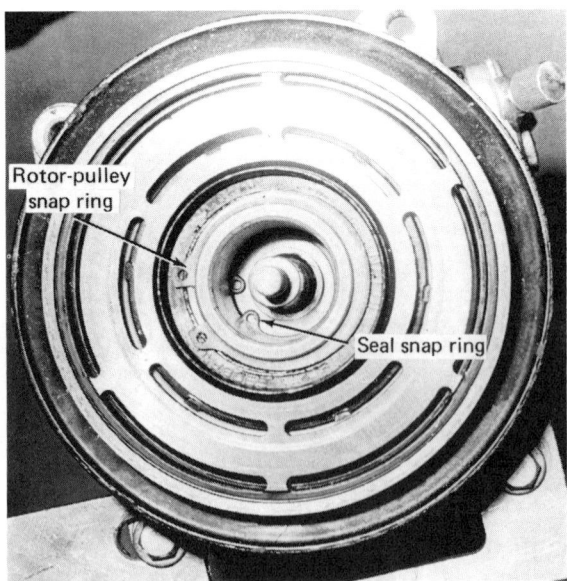

Figure 14-62 (Left) Hold the outer part of the special pulling tool while you turn down the inner part of the tool (the forcing screw), and the drive plate-hub will come up. Collect the shims underneath the drive plate-hub.

Figure 14-63 (Right) As on many American compressors, the Nippondenso seal is held by a snap ring (the smaller snap ring, recessed into the hub).

Figure 14-64 (*Left*) Remove the Nippondenso seal snap ring with special pliers as shown.
Figure 14-65 (*Right*) A split collet tool, as shown, is the type used to remove the seal on the Nippondenso compressor.

Figure 14-66 Hold the split collet part of the tool with a wrench, turn the knurled outer cylinder, as shown, and the collet will expand and lock against the inner circumference of the Nippondenso compressor seal.

Figure 14-67 (*Left*) Lift out the split-collet tool and there is the seal, trapped on the lower end of the collet.

Figure 14-68 (*Right*) Unlock the tool and lift off the seal. Installation of a new seal is the reverse of removal. Use a tool similar to that shown in Figs. 14-18 to 14-20 to install the drive plate-hub assembly. When you install the hub, be sure to refit the shims you collected and measure the gap between the clutch contact surfaces. It should be 0.021 to 0.036 inch (0.5 to 0.9 millimeter) measured at three points around the circumference. *Note:* As long as you are working on the compressor to this extent, it is good practice to replace a second seal under the compressor cylinder head. If you are planning to do so, or if you are working for access to the reed valves, do not install the outer seal or clutch at this time.

Figure 14-69 For access to the second Nippondenso seal, begin by removing the rotor-pulley assembly. Start by taking out the snap ring as shown.

267 Nippondenso and Chrysler C-171 Compressors

Figure 14-70 (Left) Next, remove the rotor-pulley assembly, using an external jaw puller if necessary (with the one shown, the jaws go into the pulley groove). In many cases, however, you can remove and reinstall it by hand.

Figure 14-71 (Right) The Nippondenso coil also is held by a snap ring. Remove it as shown, lift off the coil, and remove the cylinder head bolts.

Figure 14-72 (Left) Lift the cylinder heads up and off as shown.

Figure 14-73 (Right) Lift off the inner seal as shown and install a replacement. If seal replacement is the job, refit the heads, using new O-ring seals, and then install the outer seal. You can pressure-test the Nippondenso compressor with a test plate, as used on the General Motors compressors shown in Fig. 14-2. Install the clutch assembly to complete the job.

268 Compressor Service

Figure 14-74 If you wish to replace the reed valves, lift off the reed valve plate as shown.

Nippondenso Oil Level

The Nippondenso compressor has an oil capacity of 13 ounces (390 milliliters). In normal operation, much of the oil is distributed through the system, so before discharging the system, run it for 10 minutes at fast idle (air conditioning on maximum and blower on high). Then discharge the system, remove the compressor, and take out the drain plug.

Drain the oil into a measuring container. If it is used oil, discard it after measurement. If the compressor is new or rebuilt, and the oil is fresh, drain it into a clean container so it can be used.

If the amount of oil drained from a compressor that was on the car is less than 3 ounces (90 milliliters), pour 6 ounces (180 milliliters) of new oil into it after the compressor has been serviced. If the amount drained is 6 ounces (180 milliliters) or more, install an equal amount of new oil. If you are installing a new or rebuilt compressor, measure 6 ounces (180 milliliters) of the new oil that was drained, and pour it back into the compressor. A 500 viscosity refrigeration oil is recommended for the Nippondenso compressor.

Sankyo SD-5 Compressor

The Sankyo SD-5 compressor, a five-cylinder design (see Chapter 4), actually is basically the same in overall design to a General Motors compressor discontinued some 20 years ago. In many of the specifics, however, it is both different and similar. The details are not significant, for the GM compressor is so long out of production you will probably never see it.

You can replace all clutch parts, including the bearing, change a shaft seal, and replace the reed valve plates on the Sankyo SD-5. The service procedures are shown in Figs. 14-75 to 14-97.

Figure 14-75 (*Left*) Sankyo SD-5 compressor service begins, as on other compressors, with removal of the pulley nut, using a socket wrench and a special holder, as shown, to restrain the drive plate.

Figure 14-76 (*Right*) Unlike other compressors, a puller that threads into the exterior of the drive plate is used as shown. When the forcing screw is turned down, the drive plate is pulled up. The plate is located by a key that fits into the plate and shaft, as on other compressors. The key, not shown, must be reinstalled in the drive plate when it is refitted. When the key is removed, also remove and collect any shims between the drive plate and rotor-pulley. Also see Fig. 14-86. *Note:* For seal service, proceed directly to Figs. 14-86 and 14-87.

Figure 14-77 (*Left*) Remove the clutch external snap ring as shown.
Figure 14-78 (*Right*) Next, take out the clutch internal snap ring as shown.

270 Compressor Service

Figure 14-79 You can remove the rotor-pulley with this external jaw puller as shown. Observe the protector over the shaft to provide a surface for the puller's forcing screw.

Figure 14-80 Sankyo rotor-pulley also can be removed with this puller, which has internal jaws that lock against the inner circumference of the part. A shaft protector also is used for the forcing screw.

Figure 14-81 (*Left*) To replace a Sankyo clutch coil, begin by removing the snap ring as shown.

Figure 14-82 (*Right*) Then lift off the Sankyo clutch coil as shown and install the replacement.

Sankyo SD-5 Compressor

Figure 14-83 *(Left)* If the Sankyo rotor-pulley bearing is defective, begin removal by taking out snap ring with special pliers as shown.
Figure 14-84 *(Right)* Then drive out bearing as shown, with rotor-pulley supported on blocks of wood.

Figure 14-85 *(Left)* Drive in new bearing from opposite side as shown. Then reinstall snap ring.
Figure 14-86 *(Right)* If necessary, remove compressor shaft shims as shown. Shim pack can be changed if necessary to ensure that clearance between clutch contact surfaces is 0.016 to 0.030 inch (0.4 to 0.78 millimeter). Special drivers are used with a soft hammer to tap rotor-pulley and drive plate into position.

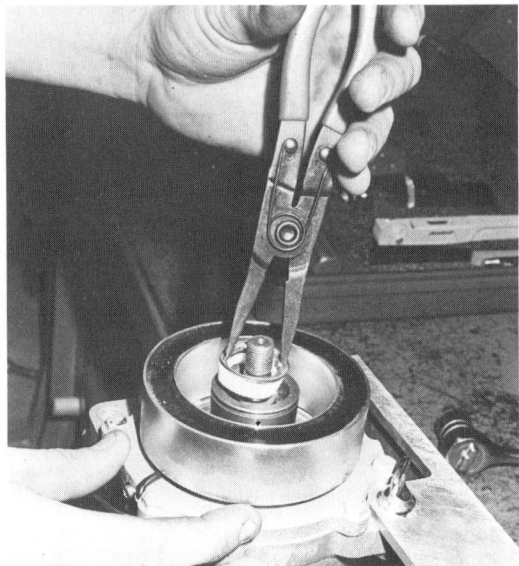 

Figure 14-87 (Left) If seal assembly on Sankyo SD-5 is defective, do not reinstall clutch. Instead, begin by pulling out felt sleeve as shown. This is similar to the sleeve you will find on the typical General Motors six-cylinder compressor.

Figure 14-88 (Right) Next step in Sankyo SD-5 seal replacement is the snap ring. Remove it as shown.

 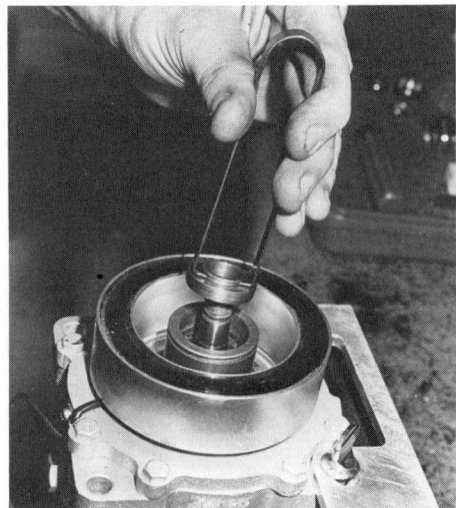

Figure 14-89 (Left) Insert tweezerlike tool as shown. Squeeze it and jaws will lock on seal seat.

Figure 14-90 (Right) Pull and seal seat comes out as shown.

Sankyo SD-5 Compressor

Figure 14-91 *(Left)* Use hook tool to work O-ring out of groove in hub of Sankyo SD-5 compressor.
Figure 14-92 *(Right)* Lift O-ring out as shown.

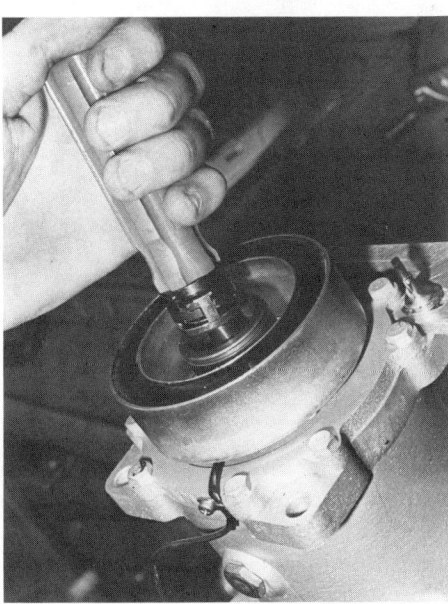

Figure 14-93 *(Left)* Use puller, similar to General Motors arrangement, to grip old seal and remove. Also see Figs. 14-10 and 14-11.
Figure 14-94 *(Right)* When you are ready to install new seal, place protector over end of shaft as shown. Then fit the new seal. Reassembly is the reverse of disassembly, paying particular attention to properly seating the O-ring (well lubricated with refrigeration oil) in its groove.

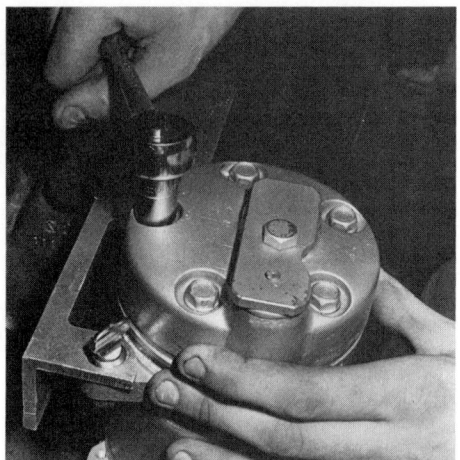

Figure 14-95 For access to the reed valve plates, remove the bolts from the cylinder head on the opposite side of the compressor, as shown.

Figure 14-96 Pry off the reed valve plates with a putty knife as shown.

Sankyo Oil Level

The Sankyo SD-5 is designed to be mounted in the car in any number of angles. Therefore, you must determine the in-car mounting angle by positioning the angle gauge (Fig. 13-98) across the flat surfaces of the two front mounting ears. Center the bubble on the angle gauge and read the mounting angle to the closest degree. *Note:* For illustrative purposes, Fig. 14-98 shows the compressor on the bench.

Once you have determined the mounting angle, proceed as follows:

1. Remove the oil fill plug.
2. To be able to insert the dipstick, you must turn the clutch drive

275 Sankyo SD-5 Compressor

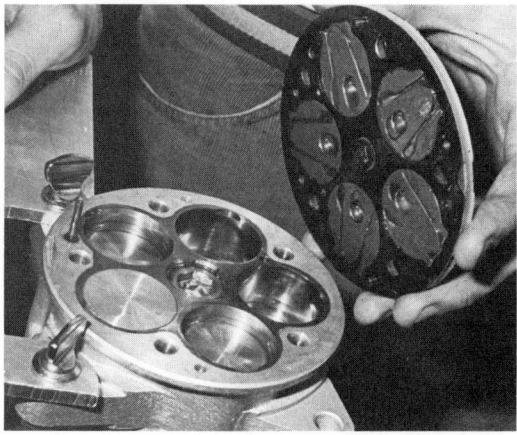 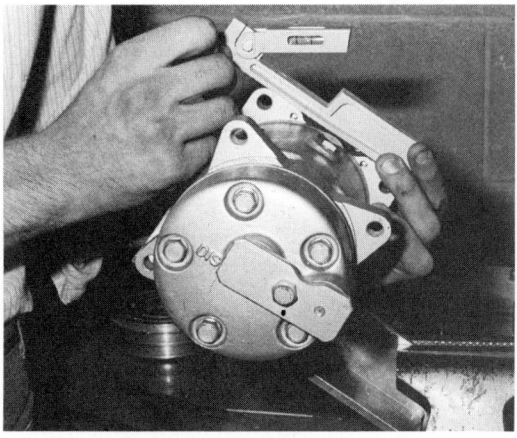

Figure 14-97 (*Left*) With reeds off, you also can inspect the cylinders.
Figure 14-98 (*Right*) Although the beginning of the oil level check is shown with the Sankyo SD-5 compressor in a vise, this merely simulates the job in the car, using the angle gauge as shown. Measure the angle of the compressor as mounted, with the bubble level centered and the gauge across the mounting ears as shown.

plate so the internal parts are properly positioned. Otherwise the dipstick will not go in all the way. As you face the clutch, note if the mounting angle is to the right or left (see Fig. 14-99).

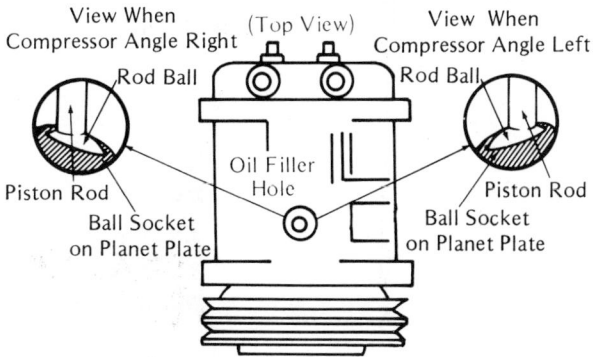

Figure 14-99 Run the compressor for 10 minutes with the engine operating at fast idle. Remove the oil filler plug at the top of the compressor and, while looking through the hole, turn the clutch drive plate. If, as you face the compressor, the left ear is higher than the right, you should see the piston rod as for the "compressor angle right." If, as you face it, the right ear is higher than the left, you should see the piston rod as for the "compressor angle left." In this position, you can insert the oil dipstick to check the oil level.

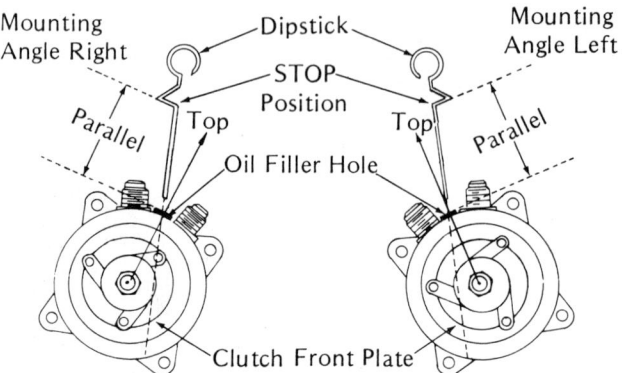

Figure 14-100 This is how the dipstick is inserted.

3. If it is to the right, center the parts as shown in Fig. 14-99 as they are moving toward the rear of the compressor on the discharge stroke. If it is to the left, center them as they are moving toward the front of the compressor on the intake (suction) stroke.
4. Insert the dipstick as shown in Fig. 14-100. Note that the bottom surface of the dipstick bend is flush with the surface of the oil fill plug hole.
5. Compare the dipstick reading with the chart (see Figs. 14-101 and 14-102). The numbers in the chart refer to slot lines on the dipstick, and the correct oil level varies both according to the mounting angle in degrees and the model of the compressor (SD-508 or SD-507).

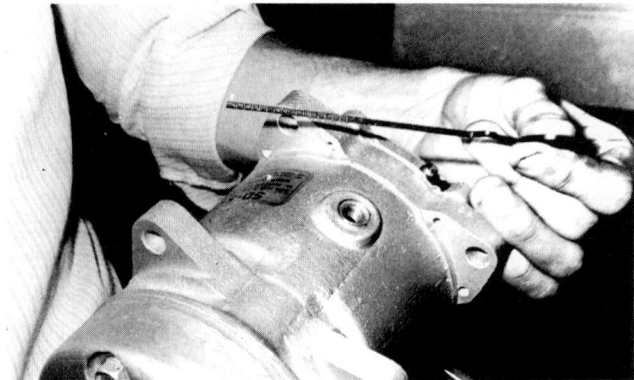

Figure 14-101 Remove dipstick and note how many notched lines up the dipstick is the oil level. Then refer to Fig. 14-102.

Mounting Angle In Degrees	Acceptable Oil Level In Increments	
	SD-508	SD-507
0	4-6	6-10
10	6-8	7-11
20	7-9	8-12
30	8-10	9-13
40	9-11	10-14
50	9-11	11-16
60	9-12	12-17

Figure 14-102 This chart shows the acceptable oil level in increments (notched lines on the dipstick) for different mounting angles and the two popular Sankyo SD-5 models, the 508 and 507. If the oil level is low, add clean oil; if it is high, take out oil. Then refit the oil filler plug, taking care to keep it clean and not to twist it. Correct oil capacity for a Sankyo SD-5 compressor is 5 ounces (150 cubic centimeters) of Suniso 5GS or equivalent.

Tecumseh and York Two-Cylinder Compressors

The Tecumseh and York compressors are two-cylinder designs (see Figs. 14-103 and 14-104), very similar in physical layout. The Tecumseh is cast iron; the York is aluminum. These compressors may be installed with Schrader valves either in the lines or at the compressor, but the typical setup is with manual valves bolted to the cylinder head (see Fig. 14-105). The manual valve most commonly used is a type called the Rotalok.® The manual valves have three positions:

1. *Fully counterclockwise* or back-seated. The Refrigerant 12 can flow through the compressor for normal system operation, but the gauge test port is closed.
2. *Mid-position.* Refrigerant 12 can flow through the compressor for normal system operation, and the gauge test port is open, so gauge readings can be taken.
3. *Fully-clockwise* or front-seated. No Refrigerant 12 can flow through the compressor.

This final position means that the Refrigerant 12 is stopped at the ends of the inlet and outlet lines at the compressor. If you wish to replace a York or Tecumseh compressor with manual valves, without evacuating and recharging the entire system, all you must do is isolate the compressor from the rest of the system.

278   Compressor Service

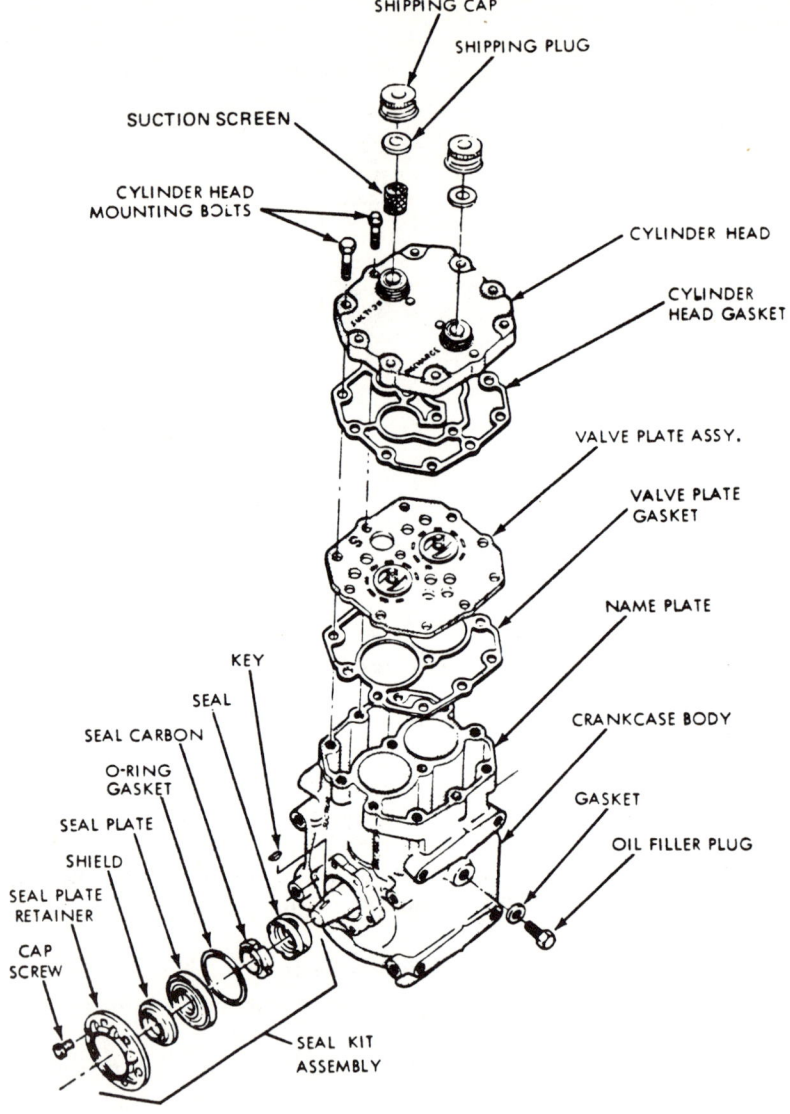

Figure 14-103 Exploded views of the Tecumseh compressor. (Courtesy Ford Motor Co.)

Isolating the Compressor

1. Hook up a gauge manifold set to the test ports. Close both manual valves on the gauge manifold.
2. With a special wrench, turn the compressor's manual valves to the mid-position. The gauges will show system pressures.

Tecumseh and York Two-Cylinder Compressors

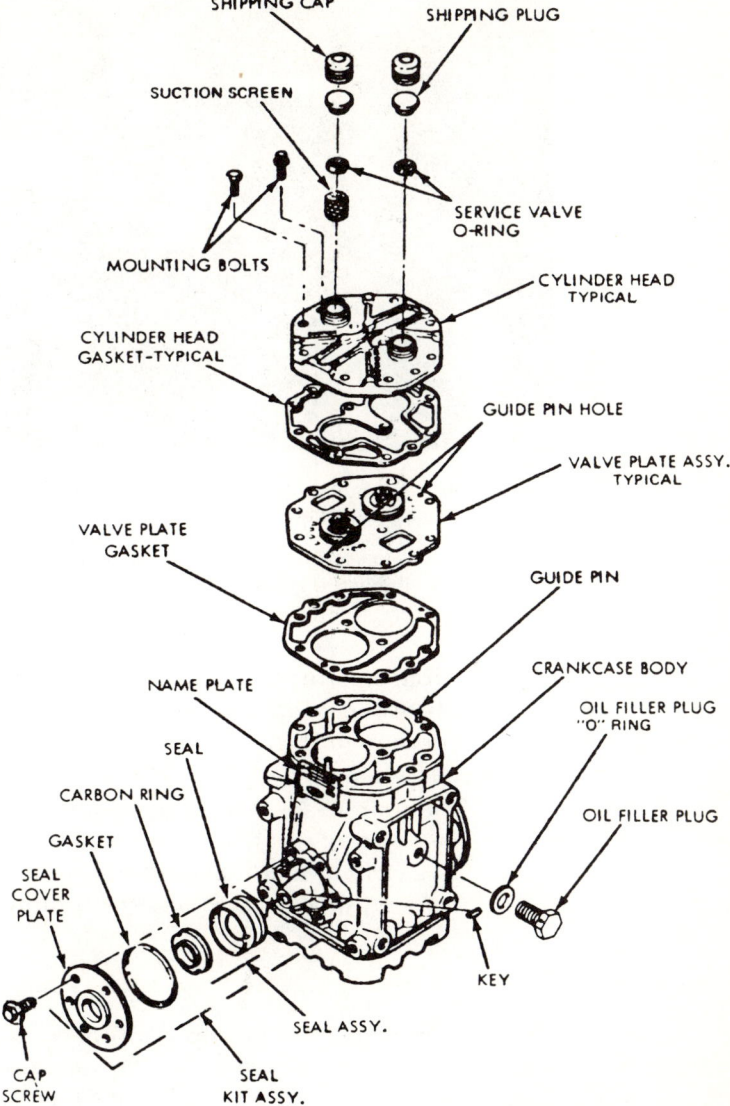

Figure 14-104 Exploded view of the York compressor. (Courtesy Ford Motor Co.)

3. Start the engine and turn on the air conditioning.
4. Turn the low-pressure manual valve on the compressor very slowly clockwise to the front-seated position. When low-side gauge pressure drops to zero (or less); immediately stop the engine and turn off the air conditioning; quickly complete the front-seating of the low-side manual valve on the compressor.

Figure 14-105 Although some applications of the Tecumseh and York two-cylinder compressors have Schrader valves, the manual valve arrangement (shown with thread-on caps removed from valve stems) is the most common. It permits replacing the compressor or removing it for service without discharging the entire system.

5. Front-seat the high-pressure manual valve on the compressor. Slowly crack open the oil level plug to release any Refrigerant 12 pressure in the compressor.
6. The compressor is now isolated. Unbolt the manual valves from the compressor. You may perform any compressor service work necessary at this time or install a replacement compressor. Before an overhauled or replacement compressor can be installed, the oil level must be checked and the compressor purged of air.

Tecumseh and York Oil Level

The Tecumseh and York compressors have an oil reservoir (sump), so the level is commonly checked with a dipstick through an oil fill plug hole. You can buy suitable dipsticks or make them from ⅛-inch-diameter rod to the dimensions shown in Fig. 14-106. The compressors may be mounted vertically or horizontally. If horizontally mounted, the oil check hole is on the side of the crankcase that faces up. For a vertical mounting (cylinder head on top as in Figs. 14-103 and 14-104), the oil check hole is on the side at the top, 90 degrees counterclockwise from the front seal (and clutch).

Total capacity is 10 ounces on the York and 11 ounces on the Tecumseh. With a vertical compressor mounting, the oil level should be ⅞ to 1⅛ inches up the dipstick on a York or ⅞ to 1⅜ inches on a Tecumseh. With a horizontal mounting, it should be 13/16 to 1 3/16 inches up the stick on a York or ⅞ to 1⅜ inches on a Tecumseh.

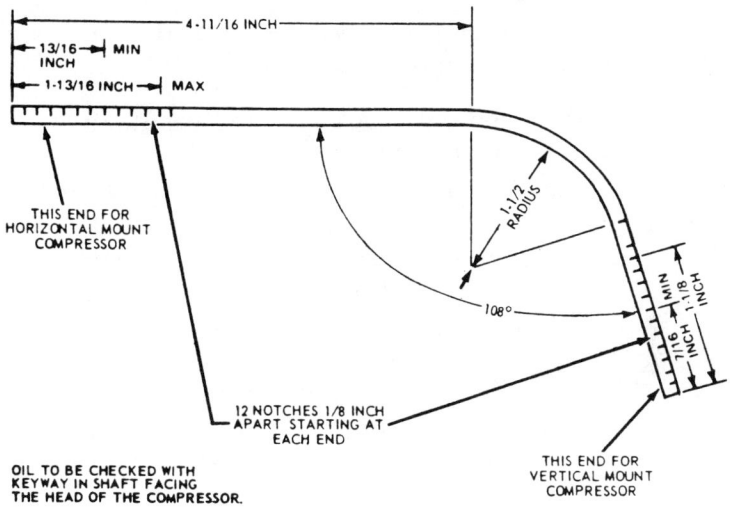

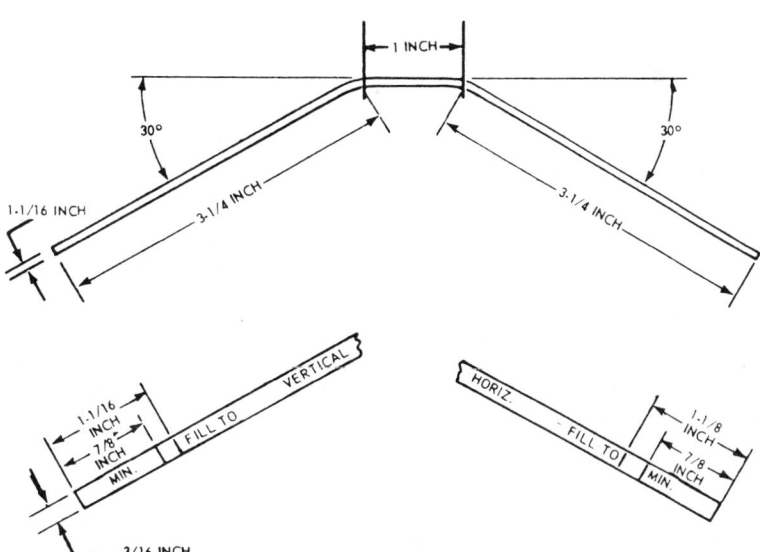

Figure 14-106 Dimensions and markings for dipsticks you can make for York (top) and Tecumseh compressors, from flattened ⅛-inch-diameter rod (or you can buy the dipsticks from a tool supplier). Insert dipstick into oil filler hole until it bottoms. On horizontally mounted compressors, the oil check hole is on the side of the crankcase that faces up. On the opposite side is an alternate oil check hole for a different mounting. Whichever you use, angle the dipstick as you insert, so it bottoms against the lower side of the crankcase, not against the boss. (Courtesy Ford Motor Co.)

Returning the Compressor to Service

Before returning the Tecumseh or York compressor to service, it must be purged of air, as follows:

1. Thread the caps onto the manual valves' test ports and mount the compressor in the car.
2. Reconnect the manual valves to the compressor, using new gaskets.
3. Back-seat (turn fully counterclockwise) the low-side manual valve to allow Refrigerant 12 to flow into the compressor.
4. Turn the compressor outlet (high-pressure side) manual valve to the mid-position; then loosen the test port cap, and refrigerant gas will force any air out of the compressor.
5. Once the refrigerant flows (hissing) from the compressor, back-seat (turn counterclockwise) the outlet manual valve and tighten the test port cap. The compressor now is ready. The small amount of Refrigerant 12 lost when isolating a compressor and purging it of air during reinstallation should have no effect on system performance If performance is affected, however, check system pressures and add Refrigerant 12 if necessary.

Tecumseh and York Service

Clutch. The clutches used on Tecumseh and York compressors are similar to those used on other compressors, such as the Nippondenso. Refer to the illustrations for clutch work. *Caution:* Tecumseh and York clutches have pulley bearings that pose replacement dangers (to the pulley) unless you have tools approved by the car maker for the job. Therefore, if a pulley bearing fails and you do not have the precise tools specified, replace the pulley assembly.

Shaft Seal. The shaft seal can be replaced on many cars without removing the compressor and, in any case, without discharging the system (only isolating the compressor), as follows:

1. Remove the clutch and the screws that hold the seal plate to the compressor.
2. Remove the seal plate. On late-model Tecumsehs, the seal plate assembly is a three-piece design, including a shield and retainer. See Fig. 14-107.
3. Using a special puller, remove the old shaft seal as shown in Figs. 14-108 and 14-109. The tool locks onto the seal behind the spring holder, that part of the seal assembly farthest back on the shaft.

Figure 14-107 (*Left*) Seal service begins with removal of the plate assembly as shown. Alignment tool is being used in center to keep out dirt.
Figure 14-108 (*Right*) Lock special puller onto seal behind the spring holder.

Figure 14-109 Pull out seal as shown.

Figure 14-110 (*Left*) Insert new seal assembly and press it into place with special tool as shown. If seal must be assembled from detail parts, make sure raised rim of carbon ring faces outward and seal end that fits carbon ring is facing it.

Figure 14-111 (*Right*) Install new O-ring in groove as shown.

4. Install the new seal assembly on the special tool and push it into place on the shaft.
5. Replace the O-ring gasket on the seal plate; then position the seal plate on the shaft (see Figs. 14-110 and 14-111). Use the other end of the special tool to center the seal plate on the shaft, as shown in Fig. 14-112.

Valve Plate and Head Gasket. Replacement of the valve plate and/or head gasket also can be done on the car, and with the compressor isolated, rather than discharging the system. Proceed as follows:

1. Unscrew the manual valves from the compressor head.
2. Remove the compressor cylinder head screws; then tap under the valve plate ears (which project from the compressor) to free up the cylinder head and valve plate. Note where all cylinder head screws came from, for they are not all the same size. Observe cylinder head and valve plate positions so you can reinstall or install the replacement part correctly. There may be alignment letters or dowels or, if you wish, you can dab paint on the exterior of the cylinder head and compressor for alignment (see Figs. 14-113 to 14-115).
3. Carefully clean any gasket residue from parts to be reused.
4. Apply a thin coat of fresh refrigeration oil to each side of the valve plate and cylinder head gaskets; then place them down, install all head screws and thread them in finger tight.

285   Tecumseh and York Two-Cylinder Compressors

Figure 14-112   (*Left*) Use alignment tool as shown to center the seal plate versus the shaft; then install and tighten screws to secure the plate.

Figure 14-113   (*Right*) Remove screws that hold cylinder head to Tecumseh or York compressor as shown.

Figure 14-114   With head off, you can see the reed valve plate.

286 Compressor Service

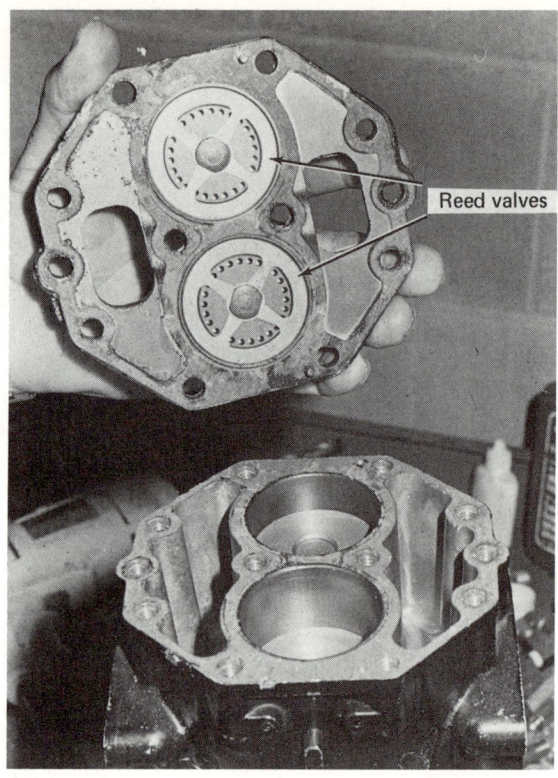

Figure 14-115 Lift off valve plate for replacement and to inspect cylinders. Installation is basically the reverse of removal.

5. Tighten all the screws in two stages to specifications (15 to 23 pound-feet or 20 to 31 newton-meters for the York and 20 to 24 pound-feet or 27 to 31 newton-meters for the Tecumseh). This means if you are tightening to 20 pound-feet (27 newton-meters), tighten first to 10 pound-feet (13 to 14 newton-meters), then to the final torque. Use a criss-cross pattern; that is, after tightening one screw, tighten the one directly opposite, then one next to the one directly opposite that, then the one directly opposite the third screw, and so on.

Chrysler V-2 Compressor

The Chrysler V-2 compressor, like the Tecumseh and York, has bolt-on cylinder heads that can be removed without taking off other parts first. Unlike other designs, it has the suction throttling control, in this case called an evaporator pressure regulator (or in some cases an evaporator temperature regulator), in the compressor itself. Not all V-2 compressors have the control (because they are cycling clutch systems). If a compressor

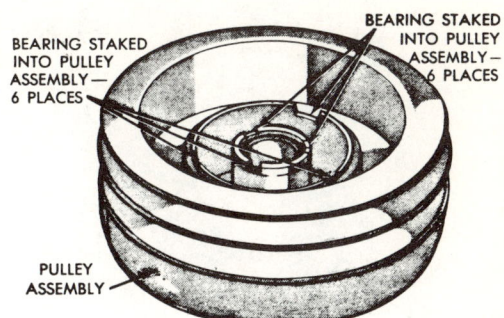

Figure 14-116 When new Chrysler V-2 bearing is installed, stake it onto pulley in six places as shown. (Courtesy Chrysler Corp.)

has it, however, it can be replaced without major compressor work, only disconnecting the compressor inlet line. The compressor clutch is serviced in basically the same way as the Sankyo and other compressors. The pulley bearing is replaceable with a suitable pulley driver. After installing the replacement, stake it onto the pulley in six places (see Fig. 14-116).

Seal Replacement

1. Remove the clutch and coil.
2. Remove the crankshaft seal and bearing housing bolts and pry the housing off with two screwdrivers inserted in the slots provided (see Fig. 14-117).
3. Drive the stationary seal seat out of the housing with a suitable driver from the outboard to inboard side (see Fig. 14-118). Tap the replacement seal seat in with a suitable driver from inboard to outboard side.
4. Remove the old seal from the crankshaft, using a tongs-type puller against the inboard edge of the seal.
5. Two types of replacement seals are available (see Fig. 14-119). If you have the cartridge type (which has a wave spring around the outer circumference), make sure the tangs of the two pieces index

Figure 14-117 Begin Chrysler V-2 seal removal by prying housing off with two screwdrivers as shown.

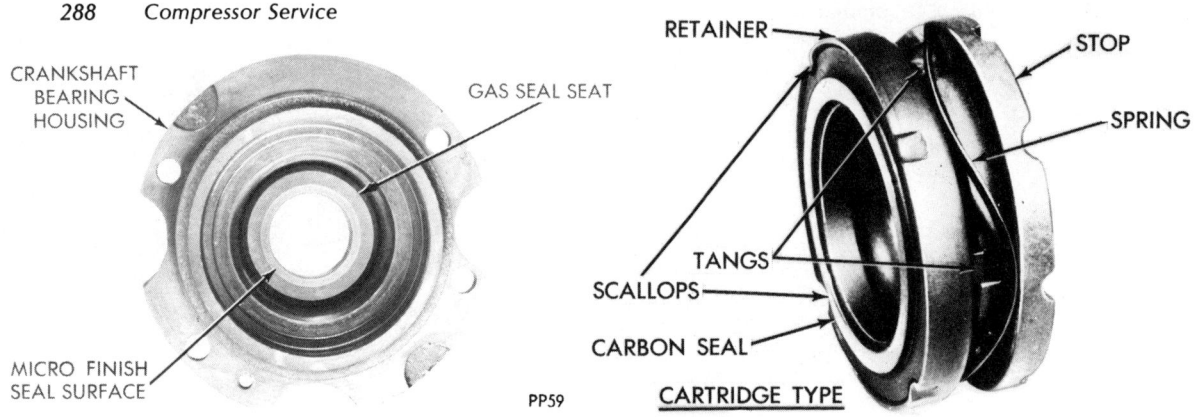

Figure 14-118 (*Left*) Drive the seal seat out of the housing. The seat has a very fine (micro) finish, so be sure to use a driver that will not touch the finish area.

Figure 14-119 (*Right*) This is the cartridge-type seal used on Chrysler V-2 compressors. Make sure the tangs (as shown) index properly. Other seals are a unitized design and the question does not apply. Do not touch the face of the carbon seal at any time. Installation of the seal is with a push-on tool, similar to that used for the Tecumseh and York (see Fig. 14-110).

properly. On the seal with the coil spring in the outer circumference, called the unitized seal, you do not have to worry about this. In either case, do not touch the face of the carbon surface of the seal at any time.

6. Install the new seal on the crankshaft (carbon surface outboard), using a suitable push-on tool. Both the seal and the crankshaft should be generously lubricated with refrigeration oil before this step.

7. Install the seal and bearing housing on the compressor, making sure the bolt holes are aligned. Install the bolts, turn down finger tight, and then tighten in two stages (first to 6 pound-feet or 8 newton-meters and then to 12 to 13 pound-feet or 16 to 17 newton-meters), using a criss-cross pattern as explained for the Tecumseh and York compressor.

Valve Plate and Head Gasket Service

The Chrysler V-2 compressor has two cylinder heads and two reed valve plates (see Figs. 14-120 to 14-122), but otherwise the jobs of head gasket and valve plate service are the same as on the Tecumseh and York compressor. You may, however, obtain pilots to position the cylinder heads during installation. Tighten the head bolts to 23 to 27 pound-feet (31 to 38 newton-meters).

Figure 14-120 Lip on each bank of Chrysler V-2 compressor helps remove stuck head and valve plate. Do not pry on either, but instead tap on removing lip with plastic hammer to free up head and valve plate.

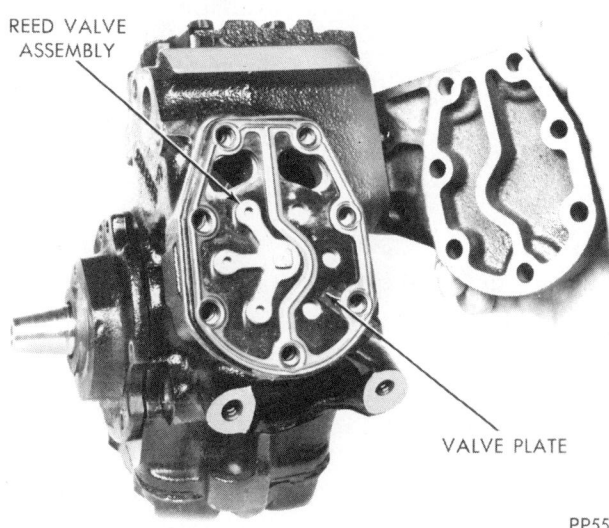

Figure 14-121 With head off, reed valve plate is accessible.

Evaporator Pressure Regulator Service

The evaporator pressure regulator (or the evaporator temperature regulator used on older Chrysler products with automatic temperature control) can be replaced on the car, after disconnecting the compressor inlet (suction) line, as follows:

290 Compressor Service

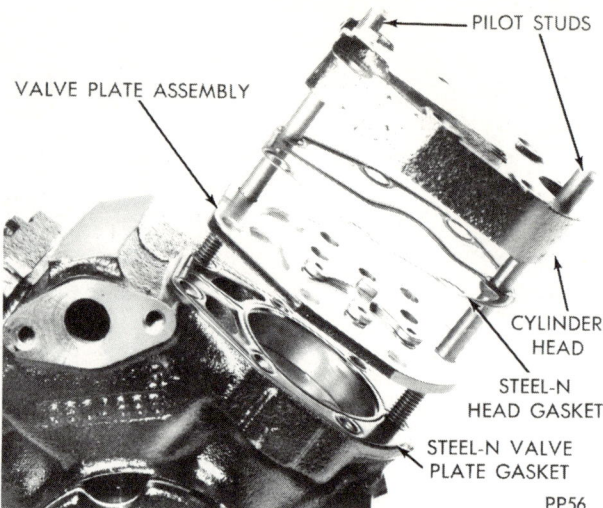

Figure 14-122 When installing replacement parts, use pilot studs for proper alignment. Note two special steel gaskets.

1. With a thin screwdriver, pry out the retaining ring (Fig. 14-123).
2. Remove the valve itself with a pulling tool designed for the job. If not available, you may be able to reach in with your fingers and pull it out. If it sticks, try prying with a small, thin screwdriver, placing the blade in the groove of the valve post.
3. Remove the screen from the end of the inlet line fitting. Clean if possible or replace.
4. Push in the new regulator until it seats below the surface of the compressor port.
5. Place the retaining ring over the valve (tabs facing outboard) and push the clip into place with a ¾-inch socket (see Fig. 14-124). *Note:*

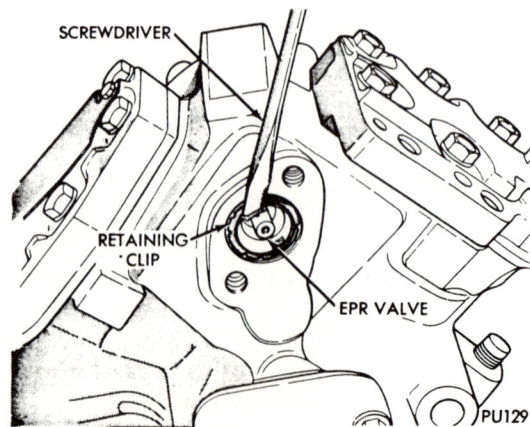

Figure 14-123 Pry out retaining ring from compressor inlet with thin screwdriver. (Courtesy Chrysler Corp.)

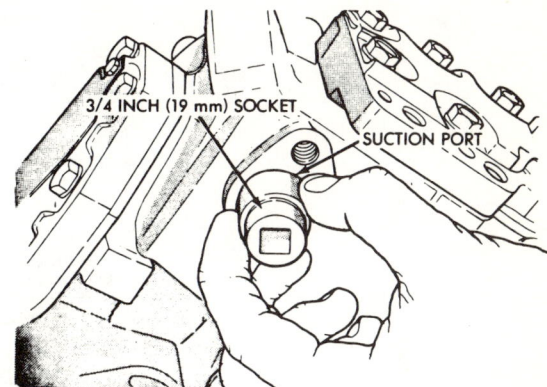

Figure 14-124 Install new evaporator pressure regulator; then push retaining ring into place with ¾-inch socket as shown. (Courtesy Chrysler Corp.)

On older V-2 compressors, there is no retaining ring and the regulator can only be removed with a special puller. Once the puller engages the valve, turn slightly counterclockwise to free it and its O-ring seal (see Fig. 14-125). Use the pulling tool to install the new regulator, also turning the part (well lubricated with refrigeration oil) slightly counterclockwise, this time to install it.

6. Reinstall the compressor inlet line, using a new gasket. Tighten the screws that hold the line to 8 to 14 pound-feet (10 to 19 newton-meters) on older compressors without the retaining ring and to 14 to 19 pound-feet (19 to 26 newton-meters) on newer compressors with the retaining ring.

Figure 14-125 Special tool to pull and install evaporator pressure regulator is necessary on many Chrysler V-2 compressors without the retaining ring.

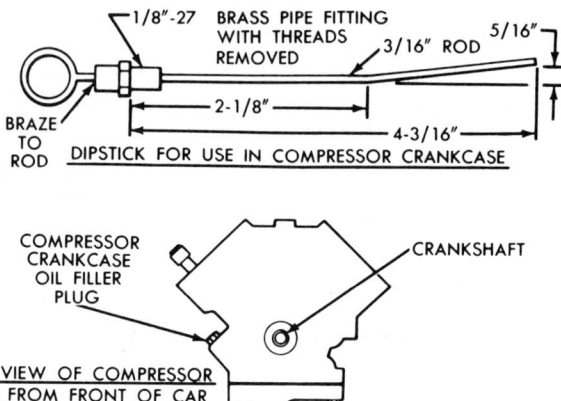

Figure 14-126 Illustration shows how to make up dipstick from ³⁄₁₆-inch rod and location of oil filler plug. New compressor should contain 10 to 12 ounces of oil, and a level of 3 to 3.4 inches (76 to 87 millimeters) up from end of dipstick. For system in operation (MAX AC, blower on high, temperature lever on warm for 15 minutes, then discharge system completely), a lower dipstick level is normal, corresponding to 6 to 8 ounces of oil. The level should be between 1¾ to 2⅜ (45 to 60 millimeters) on a six-cylinder engine, 1⅝ to 2⅜ inches (41 to 60 millimeters) on a V-8 or any Chrysler V-2 compressor set vertically on the bench.

Oil Level

The V-2 compressor has an oil reservoir. To check the oil level, remove the oil fill plug, and insert a dipstick (purchased or made in your shop as shown in Fig. 14-126). The level should be between 3¾ inches (76 to 87 millimeters) up from the end of the dipstick, which is equal to 10 to 12 ounces of oil. If below, add fresh oil to bring the level up to specifications.

York Rotary Vane Compressor

Although the housing, shaft, rotor, and vanes on the York rotary vane compressor are not serviceable, you can replace the parts that are customarily changed on most other compressors. They include the clutch and clutch bearing, the shaft seal, the compressor outlet (discharge) reed valve, the oil reservoir gasket, and the thermal protector, a heat-sensitive device that breaks the compressor clutch circuit if compressor outlet temperature exceeds 295°F (146°C).

The oil reservoir gasket replacement is an obvious procedure: unbolt the oil pan, remove the gasket, install the new gasket, and refit the reservoir. Torque the screws to 8 to 12 pound-feet (11 to 16 newton-meters) and the nuts to 15 to 22 pound-feet (20 to 30 newton-meters).

York Rotary Vane Compressor

Figure 14-127 (*Left*) Removal of York rotary vane compressor clutch begins with taking out a screw that holds the drive plate to the shaft. Once the screw is out, thread the long, thin screw from the puller into its hole. Then install the puller as shown in the illustration, threading its three bolts into holes in the drive plate. Turn the forcing screw down against the head of the long, thin screw to pull the plate up and off.

Figure 14-128 (*Right*) To remove the rotor-pulley assembly, begin by removing its snap ring as shown, using special pliers that expand when squeezed together.

Other service procedures are shown as follows:

1. Clutch service (Figs. 14-127 to 14-134).
2. Seal replacement (Figs. 14-135 to 14-137).
3. Reed valve replacement (Figs. 14-138 to 14-142). The compressor has only a discharge (outlet) reed valve. There is no valve on the inlet side, only a port.
4. Thermal protector replacement (Figs. 14-143 and 14-144).

Oil Level

The rotary vane compressor system has an oil capacity of 6 ounces (180 milliliters) when the system takes 2 pounds of Refrigerant 12. For each additional pound of refrigerant, an additional ounce (30 milliliters) of oil is installed in the system.

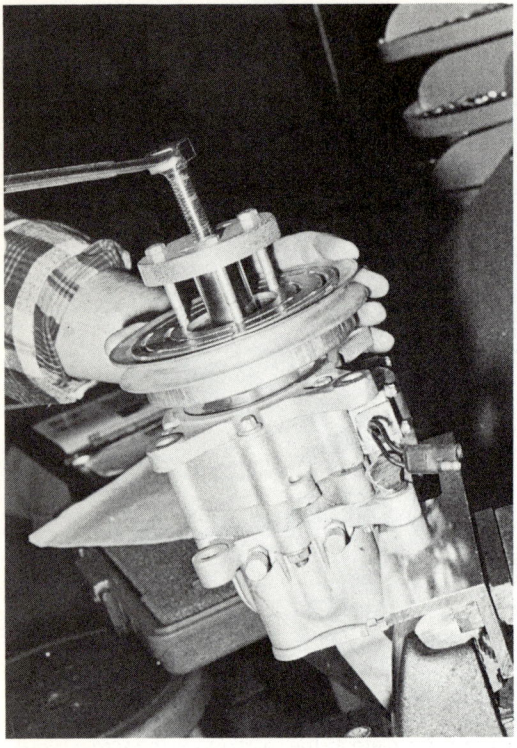
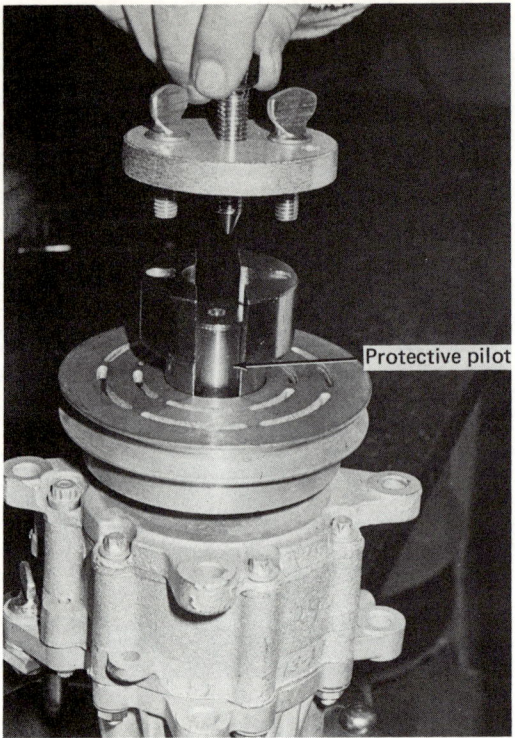

Figure 14-129 *(Left)* If the rotor-pulley has tapped holes, place protective pilot over end of the compressor shaft and use puller with screws that thread into them, as shown.

Figure 14-130 *(Right)* If the rotor-pulley does not have tapped holes, use puller that locks against internal grooves in it. As you install the internal fingers, also insert protective pilot over end of compressor shaft. Then thread wing-screws into internal fingers.

Figure 14-131 Forcing screw of internal fingers puller is turned down against pilot on shaft, and rotor-pulley is drawn up.

York Rotary Vane Compressor

Figure 14-132 (Left) Remove three screws that hold clutch coil; then twist coil and lift it up and out. Installation of new clutch parts is the reverse of removal.

Figure 14-133 (Right) To replace rotor-pulley bearing on some clutches, begin by taking out snap ring as shown. On others, pry out the snap ring with a screwdriver.

Figure 14-134 (Left) Bearing is driven out with driver and hammer from drive plate contact surface side. It is driven in, as illustrated, using an adapter under the removal driver.

Figure 14-135 (Right) Shaft seal assembly can be changed with clutch coil and rotor-pulley in place. Reach in with special pliers that contract when you squeeze the handles to remove the seal snap ring as illustrated.

Figure 14-136 (*Left*) Insert special seal seat puller, twist to lock in the seat, then pull straight out to remove seat as illustrated.

Figure 14-137 (*Right*) Insert seal removal tool, twist to lock, and pull seal straight up and out. As you can see, this tool locks in the seal in much the same way as most other compressors. New seal and seat installation is the reverse of removal.

Figure 14-138 (*Left*) Begin removal of reed valve cover by taking out four screws in the cover as illustrated. Although not shown, thermal protector comes off when screws are removed.

Figure 14-139 (*Right*) Next, remove two screws that thread through compressor body into the reed valve cover, as illustrated.

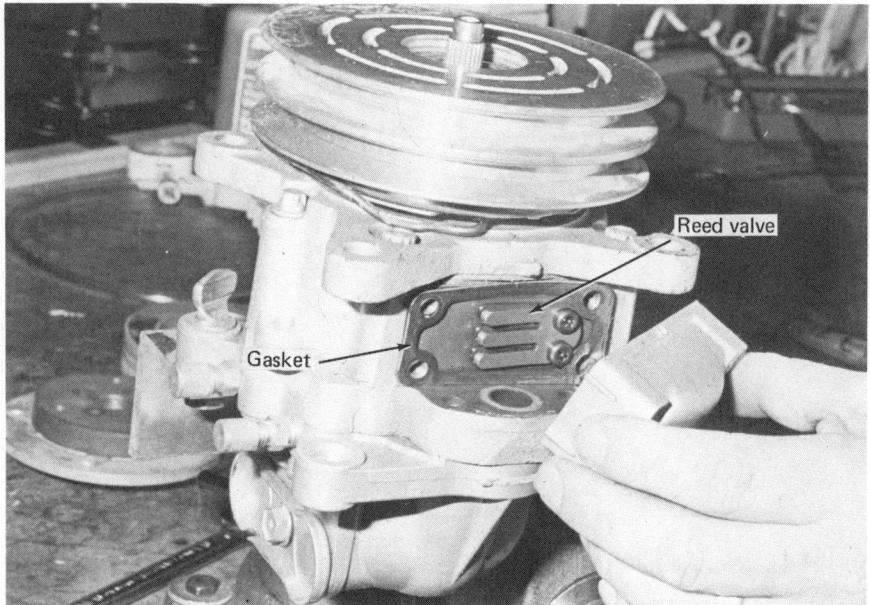

Figure 14-140 Reed valve cover pulls straight off as shown in most cases. If stuck, tap it with a soft hammer. Replace the cover gasket.

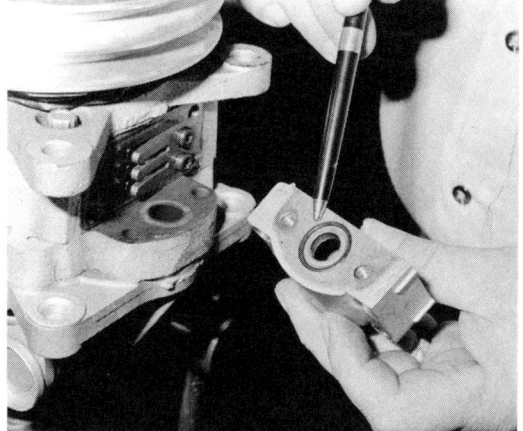

Figure 14-141 (Left) Remove screws that hold the reed valve, as shown.
Figure 14-142 (Right) When completing the job of reed valve replacement, be sure to install new O-ring in valve cover, as indicated. Torque screws to 8 to 12 pound-feet (11 to 16 newton-meters).

298 Compressor Service

Figure 14-143 *(Left)* Thermal protector (to which wiring connects) is held to reed valve cover by bracket and two cover screws.

Figure 14-144 *(Right)* Loosen two screws, lift up bracket, and thermal protector can be removed as shown. After replacement, torque screws to 8 to 12 pound-feet (11 to 16 newton-meters).

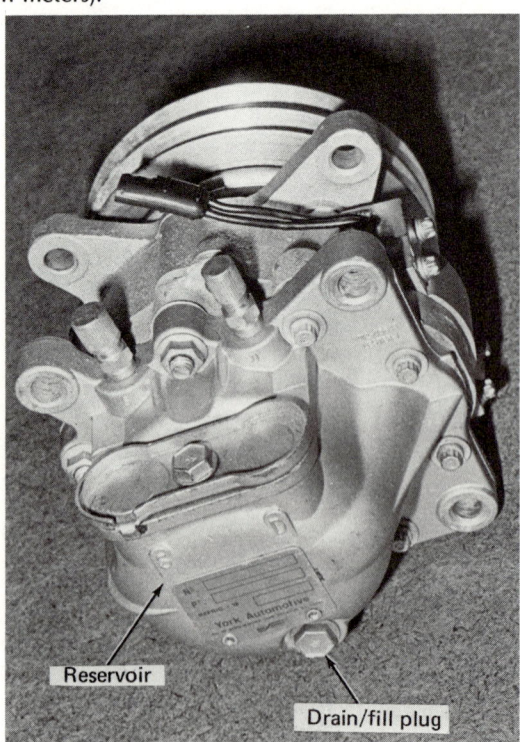

Figure 14-145 Rear view of York rotary vane compressor shows oil reservoir and oil drain and fill plug.

Drain the oil from the compressor and measure; there is a drain plug (Fig. 14-145) in the reservoir. If less than 2 ounces (60 milliliters), add 2 ounces of fresh oil (Suniso No. 5 or Texaco Capella E grade 500). If more, add fresh oil equal to what was drained through the oil plug hole or into the compressor outlet (discharge) port. When adding a full fill of oil to a rebuilt compressor, drain the oil, then pour back the indicated amount. If the system has leaked an apparently significant amount of oil, flush it completely and add a full charge.

QUESTIONS

1. Before turning on the air conditioning, after installation of a rebuilt or shop-overhauled compressor, turn the drive plate by hand several times to
    a. lubricate the pulley bearing.
    b. clear oil from the head(s).
    c. build up some Refrigerant 12 pressure in the cylinders.
2. Two compressors that are very similar in layout are
    a. Tecumseh and York
    b. General Motors six cylinder and Chrysler C-171.
    c. Sankyo and Chrysler V-2.
    d. Answers a, b, and c are all correct.
    e. Answers a and b are both correct.
    f. Answers a and c are both correct.
3. The complete clutch assembly must be removed to replace shaft seals on
    a. General Motors four- and six-cylinder compressors.
    b. Chrysler V-2 and Tecumseh compressors.
    c. Answers a and b are both correct.
4. A test plate bolts to the back of this compressor so that you can check shaft seal leakage on the bench.
    a. General Motors four- and six-cylinder compressors.
    b. Sankyo.
    c. Chrysler V-2 and C-171.
    d. All of the above.
5. The compressor clutch coil generally is held by
    a. two half-moon collars bolted together.
    b. a retaining key.
    c. a retaining ring.
    d. lockplate and bolts.

HANDS ON

1. On a General Motors axial six-cylinder compressor, remove and reinstall the clutch and check the shaft's axial plate position with a flat bar or straight edge and wire-type feeler gauges.
2. On a General Motors axial six-cylinder or radial four-cylinder compressor, replace the shaft seal and seat.
3. With a commercially available flushing gun, flush a compressor with Refrigerant 12, following the gun manufacturer's instructions.
4. With a commercially available flushing gun, flush a condenser with Refrigerant 11, following the gun manufacturer's instructions.
5. Service other compressors if available, following the procedures in Chapter 14.

15

Rotary Vane Air Cycle

As explained in Chapter 2, Refrigerant 12 has come under scrutiny as a possible health hazard. It is a chlorinated fluorocarbon, a type of fluid that has been banned in other applications, including aerosol containers. It remains in use for air conditioning, and thus far no attempt to ban it has been made, because there is no suitable substitute that is not similar. This is not to imply that fluorocarbon air conditioning is the only possible type. However, other systems suffer from other deficiencies, making them impractical for automotive and most household use. One of these hitherto impractical systems, air cycle refrigeration, is being developed in a novel new form, rotary vane air cycle (ROVAC), which may make it suitable in the not-too-distant future.

The principle of air cycle refrigeration is very similar to that of refrigerant gas. A compressor compresses the air, which raises pressure above atmospheric and temperature to well above ambient. The hot, pressurized gas flows into a heat exchanger, much like the condenser, where it gives up most of the heat to the atmosphere. It is still under pressure, but at very close to ambient temperature.

If we now let that pressurized air go back to atmospheric pressure by simple expansion, its temperature will drop. This basic principle of heat was explained in Chapter 1. When heat is concentrated, in this case by compressing the air, the temperature rises. When the air expands, the heat is spread out over a larger area, and although the Btu content of the air is the same, the temperature drops.

Many aircraft use this principle for air conditioning the passenger compartment, for the jet engine has available a surplus of compressed air that would otherwise be wasted. The power required to operate an air cycle refrigeration system is normally greater than for Refrigerant 12, which is used in what is called a vapor cycle. For this reason, air cycle refrigeration has been limited to jet aircraft, where the compressed air is already available.

302 Rotary Vane Air Cycle

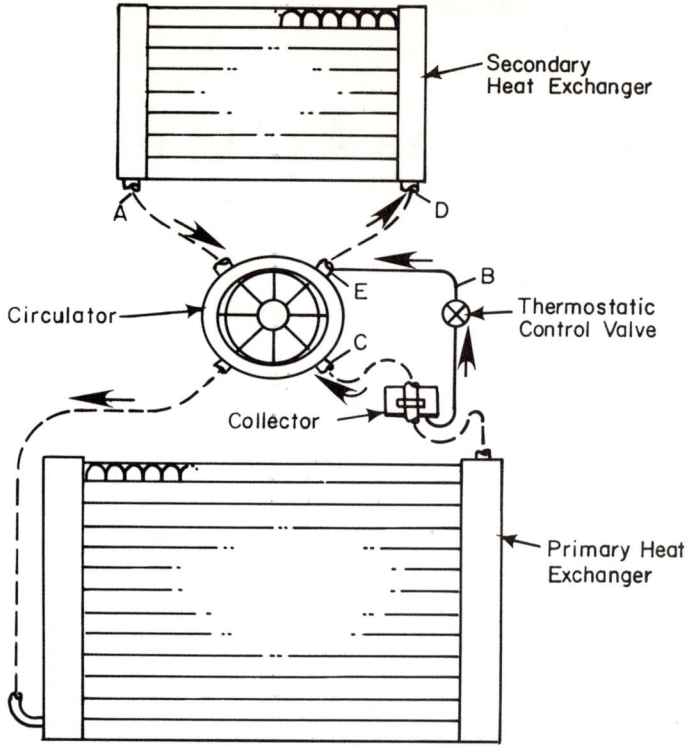

Figure 15-1 This is a schematic of the air-vapor cycle of the ROVAC system. The circulator (equivalent of compressor in the ROVAC design) draws air and vapor from the secondary heat exchanger (equivalent of evaporator). The circulator compresses the air-vapor, raising its temperature and sending it to the primary heat exchanger (equivalent of condenser). Here is gives up heat to the atmosphere, and its temperature drops to nearly ambient. However, it remains under pressure. The vapor, a chemical that is not a fluorocarbon, starts to liquify as the air-vapor flows out. The liquid collects in the collector while the flow of pressurized air (C in the drawing) continues into the expansion side of the circulator. In the circulator it expands and its temperature drops. The work performed during the expansion is used to help turn the circulator rotor. If extra cooling is needed, a thermostatic control valve (much like a thermostatic expansion valve in a conventional system) allows liquid to flow through. The liquid is sprayed through a fixed orifice at E into the chilled air leaving the circulator. The air-vapor flows (at D) into the secondary heat exchanger, where it absorbs heat from the passenger compartment. When it leaves the secondary heat exchanger at A, the vapor is saturated. There is a small amount of liquid, which holds some oil to lubricate the circulator.

Rotary vane air cycle has created interest because it is an air cycle refrigeration system that compresses the air in one side of a compressor and then lets it expand on the other side (see Figs. 15-1 and 15-2). Compressed air performs work as it expands (and its temperature drops), and by allowing the expansion in the compressor, some energy of compression can be recovered. That is, the expanding air helps turn the compressor. The two-chamber compressor is called a *circulator*.

Air does not hold as much heat as vapor, so the air cycle must move more air in order to get the same cooling effect. The size of the heat exchangers (condenser and evaporator) must be larger than for a vapor system, but because ROVAC works at very low pressure (about 40 psi or 275 kPA), the components need not have great strength.

The present ROVAC design is not a purely air system, but air and vapor (see Fig. 15-1). The vapor has greater heat-carrying ability than air, and so to increase the cooling capacity of the system, a liquid is added. Alcohols and hydrocarbons in various forms are being tried in the development of the system. These liquids turn to vapor when they absorb heat in the evaporator.

The liquid is sprayed into the circulator outlet (where the air has expanded and its temperature has dropped). The cold air chills the spray, which along with the cold air flows into the evaporator. Air and vapor absorb heat, then flow into the compression side of the circulator, and from there into the condenser, where the vapor condenses back to a liquid. The air, with the liquid droplets, then flows into a liquid collector, which separates the liquid from the air. The air continues into the expansion side of the circulator; the liquid bypasses to the circulator outlet.

The entire ROVAC system is presently so far from an optimum stage that it has not yet been proved that it can produce energy efficiencies that equal or exceed that of the Refrigerant 12 vapor system. The inventor,

Figure 15-2 This is one of the early ROVAC circulators. Notice the vanes in the rotor.

Figure 15-3 Although ROVAC is far from the production stage for automobiles at this time, there have been experimental installations, such as the one shown. The wrap around the circulator was an insulating pad to reduce noise. Notice that the hoses are of larger diameter than those in conventional air conditioning, as the volume of air ROVAC must handle is greater than the volume of vapor in a conventional system.

Thomas Edwards, believes that it can, particularly inasmuch as its output is relatively independent of engine speed (cooling is increased by allowing increased spray of liquid).

The circulator shown in this chapter (see Fig. 15-2) is a massive pump, an obvious case of overdesign with no thought of cost. The low pressure the system requires should not need anything this substantial, and, indeed, Edwards has recently completed a much more compact, lighter, cheaper circulator.

Government agencies have supported the ROVAC effort on the theory that if an alternative to fluorocarbon refrigerant is available, a ban on its use would not cause major problems for the automobile and other industries.

If ROVAC does make the grade (see Fig. 15-3), many of the skills you have learned in servicing Refrigerant 12 vapor cycle systems will be useful. Pressure testing, checking a thermostatic valve, replacing hoses, and overhauling compressors will be among the services the system will require. Although one of the refrigerants is air, the contribution of the liquid also will be important, so even leak testing could be a part of the picture.

Glossary

A/C Abbreviation for air conditioning.

Acceleration cutout switch. Also called **compressor clutch cutout switch.** A switch that automatically opens, chopping the current to the compressor clutch and thereby stopping compressor operation. The switch opens at full throttle on some cars but at moderate throttle positions on others, depending on the type of switch.

Accumulator. A liquid refrigerant trap used in a cycling clutch orifice tube (CCOT) system. It may be used to trap liquid, preventing it from reaching the compressor, on other systems.

Air handling system. Also called **air distribution system.** The housing, ducts, flap doors, and blower fan that distribute air in the passenger compartment to the appropriate outlets.

Ambient-low pressure switch. See ambient switch.

Ambient sensor. A temperature sensor that provides an outside air temperature signal for an automatic temperature control type of air conditioning system.

Ambient switch. A switch that opens and closes in response to changes in ambient temperature. It is wired into the compressor clutch circuit, so that the compressor cannot come on at very low ambient temperatures. The switch usually serves as a low-pressure protective device too.

Ambient temperature. The temperature of the surrounding air, typically the outside air.

Ammeter. A meter that measures current flow in amperes.

Anhydrous alcohol. A special alcohol that is put in some automobile air conditioning systems that do not have a receiver-dryer in order to prevent moisture in the system from freezing and blocking refrigerant flow.

Antifreeze. A chemical, typically ethylene glycol, that mixes with water in the engine's cooling system to form a liquid that freezes at much lower temperatures and boils at much higher temperatures than water alone does.

Aspirator. A hose that draws passenger car air over a sensor in order to provide an in-car temperature signal for an automatic temperature control type of air conditioning system.

Atmospheric pressure. The pressure exerted by the atmosphere by virtue of its weight. It is greatest at sea level, typically being 14.7 pounds per square inch or 101 kilopascals.

Automatic temperature control. A system that uses automatic or semi-automatic controls to operate both the air conditioning and heater in order to provide automatically the air temperature selected by the driver.

Axial compressor. A piston-compressor in which the cylinders are arranged in a circle around the center line of the compressor shaft and parallel to the center line.

Barometer. An instrument that measures atmospheric pressure.

Bearing. A part that supports and reduces the friction of a rotating part. Bearings may be plain but smoothly finished metal shells, a circular cage of steel rollers or balls.

Belleville washer. A saucer-shaped spring-type washer.

Bench test. A test procedure performed on a part that has been removed from the car.

Bimetal valve. A valve that is made of two different metals that cause the part to bend in two different directions, depending on whether the valve is heated or cooled. The bending in reaction to the temperature changes permits the bimetal to be useful in an air conditioning control.

Bleed. Also see oil bleed. To remove an impurity or to allow a liquid to bypass a main circuit. Liquid bleeds are commonly used in air conditioning systems to permit oil to flow even when certain control valves are closed.

Blend door. See temperature control door.

Blower. An electric motor-driven fan that forces air through under-dashboard ducts to outlets in the passenger compartment.

Blower resistor. A part that resists the flow or current to the blower motor, thereby reducing its speed. The greater the size of the resistor through which the current must flow, the lower is the motor speed. The blower switch position determines whether the current must pass through the complete resistor (low speed), only part of the resistor (medium speed), or bypass the resistor completely (high speed).

Boil. To turn a liquid into a vapor by heating.

Boiling point. The temperature at which a liquid turns to a vapor.

British Thermal Unit (BTU). The amount of heat that is needed to raise the temperature of one pound of water 1°F.

Capillary tube. A narrow-diameter bendable tube filled with a gas. It often has a bulge at one end, this end clamped against a refrigerant-carrying tube. Temperature changes in the refrigerant-carrying tube cause the gas in the capillary tube to expand and exert pressure or to contract and relieve pressure on a flexible diaphragm. The diaphragm movement controls a valve or switch in the air conditioning system.

CCOT. See cycling clutch orifice tube.

Celsius. Also called **centigrade.** A temperature scale in which water boils at 100° and freezes at 0°. It is abbreviated C.

Charge. To add refrigerant to an air conditioning system.

Charging cylinder. A cylindrical container for refrigerant that has a calibrated sight glass so that the mechanic can measure the flow of refrigerant into the air conditioning system.

Charging station. A piece of service equipment that combines all the tools that are needed to discharge and recharge an air conditioning system with refrigerant.

Checking relay. Also called **vacuum checking relay**. A vacuum-flow device that blocks the loss of vacuum in an automatic temperature control type of air conditioning system when the engine's vacuum drops during acceleration or other high-load operations.

Check valve. A one-way air or liquid control valve. It closes to prevent reverse flow.

Chlorinated fluorocarbon. The chemical family into which air conditioning refrigerants such as Refrigerant 12 fall. It is believed that chlorinated fluorocarbons have an adverse effect on the atmosphere, and that the chlorine content is an important factor.

Circuit. Wiring that permits current to flow from and eventually back to a source, such as a battery.

Circuit breaker. A device that is designed to open automatically an electrical circuit when current flow exceeds a predetermined level. It may reset itself automatically when the current flow is below the limit.

Circulator. An air compressor that is used in the rotary vane air cycle system (ROVAC) of air conditioning. Air is compressed in one half and allowed to expand in the other half, helping to turn the circulator's rotor.

Clutch. A device that locks two parts together, including when one is in motion and the other still or when the two are turning at different speeds. A magnetic clutch is used on the compressor of an automobile air conditioning system.

Clutch brushes. Electrical contacts that are used in older clutch designs.

Clutch coil. The coil of wire that creates the magnetic field that energizes the compressor clutch, locking the compressor shaft to the belt-driven pulley.

Clutch current draw. The amount of current measured in amperes that flows to the clutch coil when the air conditioning is turned on.

Clutch fan. A radiator fan controlled by a fluid-filled device that allows the fan to freewheel, so that it does not draw engine power, until the coolant has reached operating temperature.

Clutch slippage. When the two contact surfaces of the magnetic clutch do not lock together securely so that power is not smoothly transferred; or, when the power transfer cannot occur, such as when the compressor shaft will not turn. In these cases, one clutch contact surface turns faster than the other (if the other turns at all).

Combination valve. A valve assembly that contains more than one part, such as an expansion and a suction-throttling valve.

Compound gauge. A typical low-pressure test gauge, which has a scale that indicates both pressure and vacuum.

Compressor. A pump that is driven by a belt from the engine crankshaft in order to circulate refrigerant through the air conditioning system.

Compressor clutch. The magnetic clutch that locks the compressor shaft to a belt-driven pulley. The belt also wraps around the engine crankshaft pulley so that power from the crankshaft turns the compressor.

Compressor shaft. The shaft that moves the pistons or rotor to operate the compressor of an air conditioning system.

Condensation. Conversion of vapor to liquid.

Condenser. A heat exchanger that cools compressed vapor from the compressor down to near the ambient temperature in an air conditioning system.

Condenser comb. A comb-shaped tool used to straighten fins on the condenser.

Conductor. Something that can transmit electricity, such as a metal wire.

Control pressure. In a suction throttling valve, evaporator pressure or temperature regulator, it is the back pressure that the part is designed to hold in order to prevent moisture from freezing on the exterior of the evaporator coils.

Coolant. Water, or more typically a mixture of water and antifreeze, circulated through an engine to cool it.

Coolant control valve. Also called **heater water control valve.** A valve spliced into the heater inlet hose to regulate the flow of coolant from the engine to the heater. It may be controlled by a cable or vacuum switch at the dashboard.

Corrosion. A deterioration of metal, which may impede the flow of electricity in a circuit or the transfer of heat in a cooling system; if the corrosion passes through the metal, a leak may occur. Rust is a type of corrosion.

Crossflow radiator. A radiator in which the coolant flow tubes are positioned horizontally.

Cycling clutch. An air conditioning system in which a temperature-sensitive switch turns the compressor clutch on and off as necessary to maintain system operation without permitting evaporator temperatures to drop so low that moisture freezes on the evaporator coils.

Cycling clutch orifice tube. A cycling clutch air conditioning system in which a tube with a calibrated opening (the orifice) is used instead of an expansion valve.

Degree wheel. Temperature selector on the dashboard of a car with an automatic temperature control type of air conditioning system.

Dehumidify. To remove moisture from the air. An air conditioner performs this function in addition to lowering air temperature.

De-ice switch. A temperature-sensitive switch at the evaporator, that shuts off current to the compressor clutch when the moisture on the evaporator coils is about to freeze. The control switch in a cycling clutch system performs this function.

Desiccant. See drying agent.

Diaphragm. See vacuum diaphragm unit. A flexible sheet that divides a container into two chambers. In typical automotive use, a vacuum is applied to one chamber, lowering the pressure inside, and the diaphragm flexes in that direction.

Digital display. An electronic panel in which digits are displayed. It may be used to display the temperature selected by the driver in an automatic temperature control system.

Discharge. To allow refrigerant to flow out of the system into the atmosphere or a holding tank.

Discharge line. The tubing from the compressor outlet to the condenser inlet. In this line, the refrigerant is a high-temperature, high-pressure vapor.

Discharge pressure. Also called **high pressure** and **head pressure**. The pressure of the refrigerant at the outlet side of the compressor.

Discharge reed. Also called **outlet valve** and **high side valve**. The reed valve at the outlet side of the compressor.

Discharge side. Also called **high pressure side**. The part of the system from the compressor outlet to the expansion valve or orifice tube.

Dispensing valve. Also called **tap valve**. The part that attaches to a can of refrigerant to permit dispensing refrigerant into the system.

Downflow radiator. A radiator in which coolant flows from a tank at the top through vertical tubes into a tank at the bottom.

Drain tube. A tube in the duct housing that allows moisture that condenses during air conditioning operation to flow out and to the ground.

Drive belt. A belt, V-shaped in the cross section, that is used to transfer power between pulleys, around which it is wrapped and tightened.

Drying agent. Also called a **desiccant**. The material used in the receiver-dryer to absorb moisture from the refrigerant flowing in the air conditioning system.

Duct housing. The plastic or fiber board component in which the heater, evaporator, and blower are installed and to which are attached ducts that carry air to the center and bottom of the dashboard and to the windshield for defrosting.

Electromagnet. A magnet developed by passing current through a coil of wire.

Electropneumatic. A system that uses electricity and air pressure or vacuum to control moving parts. Many automatic temperature control type of air conditioning systems are of this type.

Energize. To activate a power-using device.

Equalizer line. Tubing connected from expansion valve to suction throttling valve in order to provide a low-pressure side pressure signal for the proper operation of the expansion valve. On many systems, a drilled passage is used instead of the external tubing.

Evacuate. To discharge refrigerant from the air conditioning system into the atmosphere or a holding tank and then to vacuum-pump the system in order to boil away moisture.

Evaporation. Change of a liquid to a vapor.

Evaporator. A heat exchanger through which low-temperature refrigerant flows, absorbing heat from the surrounding air. It is installed in the duct housing.

Evaporator pressure regulator. A valve used in some systems to create enough back pressure on the low-pressure side of the system to prevent the evaporator pressure and therefore the temperature from dropping so low that a condensing moisture would freeze on the exterior of the evaporator. It is similar in operation to a suction throttling valve.

Evaporator temperature regulator. A valve that performs the same function as the evaporator pressure regulator but that is controlled by a temperature sensitive switch that is mounted to sense evaporator temperature.

Expansion tube. See orifice tube.

Expansion valve. See thermostatic expansion valve.

Fahrenheit. A temperature scale in which water boils at 212° and freezes at 32°. Abbreviated F.

False seizure. An apparent seizure of some General Motors compressors. What actually occurs is that some of the internal parts lock together because lubricant has floated away during an extended period without compression operation. The compressor can be restored to normal operation without disassembly.

Fan. See blower.

Fast idle. An engine idling speed considerably above the minimum necessary for the engine to sustain operation with no load. It is typically 1000 to 1500 revolutions per minute above the minimum.

Feedback potentiometer. An electronic device that produces a resistance signal in accordance with the position of the diaphragm motor link in an automatic temperature control programmer. The signal is used to help smooth out vacuum motor link movement.

Filtering screens. Screens inserted in various parts of the air conditioning system to remove foreign particles. Typical locations are at the expansion valve, receiver-dryer, and compressor inlet.

Flap door. An air control device in the duct housing controlled by a cable or vacuum used to direct air flow according to the dashboard control position selected.

Flooding an evaporator. Allowing too much refrigerant to flow into the evaporator. Because all of it does not vaporize, poor performance results.

Fluorocarbon. See chlorinated fluorocarbon.

Flush. To purge foreign particles from air conditioning components. Except for compressors, flushing is commonly done with Refrigerant 11, which has solvent qualities, not Refrigerant 12.

Freezing point. The temperature at which water turns to ice. It is 32°F (0°) at sea level.

Freon. A trade name for air conditioning refrigerant, such as Freon 12.

Fuse. An electric safety device spliced into a circuit. Typically, it is designed to melt, opening the circuit to stop current flow, if the current flow in the circuit has become excessive.

Fusion. Melting, such as the change of ice into water.

Gas. See vapor.

Gas charge. Also called **vapor charge.** To add refrigerant to the air conditioning system in vapor form.

Gauge manifold. A pipe-like part to which pressure gauges are attached to measure pressures in the air conditioning system. It has fittings for hoses that connect to the system and manual valves that can be opened or closed to regulate refrigerant flow into or out of the system.

Ground. An electrical term that in automotive usage refers to the utilization of the metal parts of the car, such as the body and engine, to complete a circuit back to the battery. Both the battery and the circuits are connected to the metal, a procedure called grounding.

Head gasket. A seal between the cylinder head and the main body of the compressor.

Head pressure. Also called **high side pressure.** Refrigerant pressure in the system from the compressor outlet to the expansion valve or orifice tube.

Heat. A form of energy. It comes from the transformation of other types of energy, such as burning fuel or operating a mechanical device.

Heat exchanger. A part through which a fluid is circulated in order to give up heat to the cooler surrounding area or to absorb heat from a warmer surrounding area.

Heat transfer. The movement of heat from a warmer to a cooler area.

Heater water control valve. Also called heater coolant control valve.

Heater core. A radiator-like part through which hot engine coolant is circulated to warm air in the duct housing and thus to heat the passenger compartment.

High blower relay. A relay used to carry the greater amount of current necessary to operate the blower at high speed.

High-pressure cutout switch. A switch in the high side of the air conditioning system designed to open and thereby to stop current flow to the compressor clutch if pressures exceed a safe limit. It is rarely used if the system has a high-pressure relief valve.

High-pressure relief valve. A valve in the high side of the air conditioning system designed to open if pressures exceed a safe limit.

High side. Also called **high-pressure side.** The high-pressure side of the air conditioning system from the compressor outlet to the inlet of the expansion valve or orifice tube.

Hot gas bypass valve. A valve used in the past in air conditioning systems to meter hot refrigerant gas into the evaporator to prevent moisture from freezing on the evaporator exterior.

Humidity. Moisture in the air.

H-valve. A type of expansion valve.

Hydrochloric acid. A harmful acid that can form in the air conditioning if there is moisture in the system.

Idler pulley. A pulley, a key purpose of which is to be movable, to provide tension adjustment if necessary for a drive belt. Many air conditioning compressor belts are adjusted by moving an idler pulley.

Inches of mercury. A common measurement for the intensity of a vacuum.

In-car sensor. A sensor in the dashboard that produces a signal indicative of passenger compartment temperature to an automatic temperature control type of air conditioning system.

Infinity. Without a limit. On the ohmmeter scale, it refers to a circuit in which current cannot flow because an opening exits somewhere in the circuit. The digit 8 written sideways is the symbol for infinity.

Insulation. A covering designed to slow heat transfer or leakage of electricity. Examples include the wrap around the low-side line from evaporator to compressor, and the wrap on the capillary tube where clamped to refrigerant tubing. Also, it is the covering on a wire to prevent leakage of electricity.

Jumper wire. A wire with clips at each end. It is used to bypass parts of an electrical circuit for test purposes.

Key. Also called **Woodruff key.** A piece of metal that fits into slots in a shaft and a part that fits on the shaft to prevent the part from turning relative to the shaft. The drive plate of a compressor clutch is typically held in position on the compressor shaft by a key.

Kilopascals. Measurement of pressure in the metric system. One kilopascal is approximately equal to 6.895 pounds per square inch. Abbreviated kPa.

kPa. Abbreviation for kilopascals.

Latent heat. Hidden heat. It is heat that causes a change of state, such as solid to liquid and liquid to vapor, without changing the temperature.

Latent heat of fusion. Heat required to turn a solid to a liquid without changing the temperature. In air conditioning, the term also may be used to refer to the amount of heat that must be removed from a liquid to change it to a solid without changing the temperature.

Latent heat of vaporization. Also called **latent heat of evaporation.** Heat required to turn a liquid to a vapor.

Leak detector. A tool used to find places in the air conditioning system where refrigerant is leaking into the atmosphere.

Liquid bleed. See oil bleed.

Liquid charge. To add refrigerant to the air conditioning system in liquid form.

Liquid charger. A device that breaks liquid refrigerant into a very fine spray so that it can safely be installed in the low side of the system without endangering the compressor.

Liquid line. The tubing in the high side of the system in which the high-pressure refrigerant is in liquid form. This runs from the condenser outlet to the expansion valve or orifice tube inlet. In some usage, however, only the line from the receiver-dryer to the expansion valve or orifice tube inlet is called the liquid line.

Low side. Also called **low-pressure side** and **suction side.** The low-pressure side of the air conditioning system, which runs from the evaporator inlet to the compressor inlet.

Magnetic clutch. The type of clutch used to lock the compressor to the belt-driven pulley and thus to turn on the air conditioning system.

Manifold gauge set. See gauge manifold.

Manual valves. Test fittings installed on some air conditioning compressors. They must be turned with a wrench in order to permit pressure-testing and other system services. The term also may be used to refer to the manually controlled shutoff valves on gauge manifolds and charging stations.

Millimeters of mercury. Metric system measurement for the intensity of a vacuum.

Mode door. A flap door in the duct housing the position of which determines whether air will flow to the heater outlets at the floor or to the air conditioning outlets at the center of the dashboard.

Moisture indicator. Moisture-sensitive sleeve installed behind the sight glass of some air conditioning systems. It changes color when there is moisture in the system.

Muffler. Container with sound-reducing baffles installed in an air conditioning line. It is commonly installed on the high side to reduce compressor noises. On some systems, it also may be installed on the low side.

Multican adapter. A part that holds several small cans of refrigerant in order to make it more convenient to fill an empty air conditioning system.

Motor. Any device designed to produce motion or to perform work. Although electricity is the source of energy in most cases, air also may be used either pressurized or in a vacuum.

Ohm. The unit of resistance measurements. It is the amount of resistance encountered by one ampere flowing at a pressure of one volt.

Ohmmeter. A meter that measures resistance to current flow in an electrical circuit.

Oil bleed. A tube or passage that permits oil to flow to the compressor for lubrication under adverse conditions, such as when an air conditioning control valve is plugged or closed.

Oil injector. A tool used to simplify the injection of refrigeration oil into the air conditioning system.

Oil plug. A threaded plug in the body of an air conditioning compressor that can be removed to measure oil level and/or to drain and refill the compressor with oil.

Open circuit. A circuit that, at the time of a test, is incomplete. This may be because of a wiring break or intentional, because a switch is in the off position.

Opening the system. Term used to describe discharge of refrigerant from the system either as an individual service or in conjunction with replacement of a defective part.

Orifice tube. Also called **expansion tube.** A tube with a carefully sized fixed opening, instead of a variable-opening expansion valve.

O-ring. An O-shaped sealing ring that is used extensively throughout the air conditioning system.

Overcharge. Adding too much refrigerant to the system. It can cause harmful buildup of high-side pressures.

Pilot-operated-absolute and suction throttling valve. See POA.

Pilot valve. A small arrowhead-tip valve that controls the action of a larger valve in the same part. Also see POA.

POA. Abbreviation for pilot-operated-absolute. A type of suction throttling valve that uses a small pilot valve to operate a main valve.

Pounds per square inch. Measurement of pressure. Abbreviated P.S.I. Also see P.S.I.G.

Power draw. The amount of current used by an electrically operated component.

Programmer. The assembly that controls the heating and air conditioning systems to maintain a selected temperature in many automatic temperature control type of air conditioning systems.

Pressure cap. See radiator pressure cap.

Pressure relief valve. See high-pressure relief valve.

Pressure switch. Also called **discharge pressure switch.** An electric switch that opens to stop current flow to the air conditioning compressor clutch, thus stopping the system when high side pressure drops too low, because of either low ambient temperatures or low refrigerant supply.

Pressure-temperature relationship. Refers to the fact that, whatever level refrigerant pressure is at, refrigerant temperature is at a related level, except in a superheat situation.

Pressure test. To measure the pressures in the high and low sides of the air conditioning system.

P.S.I.G. Abbreviation for pounds per square inch, gauge. The pressure as indicated on a gauge in pounds per square inch, not including atmospheric pressure.

Puller. A tool used to remove a part that fits tightly, typically from a shaft. In air conditioning work, pullers are used to remove compressor clutch parts.

Pulley. A circular part with a perimeter groove into which a belt fits. The pulley is attached to a shaft; when the belt turns, it powers the shaft through the pulley.

Pump. A device that raises, compresses, and/or transfers fluids. The air conditioning compressor is a type of pump.

Purge. To rid a system of foreign particles and moisture.

Radial compressor. A compressor with the pistons arranged in a circle around the cross section of the shaft.

Radiator pressure cap. A sealing cap on the fill neck of the radiator. It contains a spring-loaded pressure valve that allows system pressure to build up to a safe value (raising the boiling point of the coolant) and then opens to vent excessive pressure, if necessary.

Receiver. Similar to a receiver-dryer, but it does not contain a drying agent. It was used until the mid-1970s on American Motors cars. Alcohol in the system prevented any moisture from freezing.

Receiver-dryer. Also called **receiver-dehydrator.** Cylindrical container that holds a small amount of extra refrigerant that it releases to the system to compensate for periods of high demand and for minor seepage of refrigerant into the atmosphere. The dryer is a moisture-absorbing material in the container.

Recharge. To refill a system with refrigerant after it has been discharged and vacuum-pumped.

Recirculation door. The flap door that pivots to allow passenger compartment air to recirculate through the evaporator for additional cooling. This book uses the terms "outside air door" or "fresh air door."

Reed valve. A spring-metal flap that covers an opening. It can be pushed away by fluid under pressure, permitting fluid flow through the valve opening. When pressure is released, it will spring closed. It can be drawn open by vacuum and will spring back when the vacuum is released.

Refrigerant 11. A chlorinated fluorocarbon that has solvent qualities and is often used to flush foreign particles from all parts of the air conditioning system except the compressor.

Refrigerant 12. The heat transfer fluid used in automobile air conditioning systems. It is a chlorinated fluorocarbon.

Refrigerant 22. A heat transfer fluid used in many household air conditioning systems. It is a chlorinated fluorocarbon that contains less chlorine than Refrigerant 12.

Refrigeration oil. A special oil for refrigeration and air conditioning systems.

Refrigeration system. The part of the air conditioning system that includes compressor, condenser, evaporator, control valves and switches, and tubing. It absorbs the heat from air in the duct housing and transfers it to the outdoors.

Reheat. Warming air that has been chilled by the evaporator by passing it through the heater core. This is accomplished either by moving the temperature control door by operating a dashboard lever or automatically by an automatic temperature control system. Reheat permits tailoring temperature of the passenger compartment to suit individual preference. It is a feature available only on original equipment air conditioning systems.

Relative humidity. The percentage of moisture in the air compared with the maximum amount that the air can hold.

Relay. An electromagnetic switch. A small amount of current is applied to form an electromagnet that pulls closed a second switch through which a great deal of current can flow. Also a device that uses a small amount of vacuum to control a larger vacuum flow. Also see checking relay.

Resistance. That which prevents the free flow of electricity. It is measured in ohms (the greater the number of ohms, the higher the resistance).

Resistor. A part designed to pose a more precise, usually greater resistance to the flow of electricity than ordinary wire would.

Restriction. A partial blockage. In the air conditioning system, it restricts refrigerant flow. It may be caused by foreign particles, ice formation, or a pinch in tubing.

Retaining ring. A C-shaped ring that fits in a groove to hold a part to a shaft. A popular type is called a snap ring. See **snap ring pliers**.

Rotalok valve. A brand of manual valves used as a test fitting on many air conditioning compressors.

Rotary vane compressor. A compressor that uses a part called a rotor with sliding vanes (blades) that move in and out of slots in the rotor to form compartments of varying sizes in the compressor housing. Fluid is drawn into large compartments, squeezed as the compartments become smaller, and then forced out of the compressor.

Rotor-pulley. The part of the compressor clutch that is mounted on a bearing and is belt-driven. It has a surface that magnetically adheres to the compressor shaft drive plate so that the belt drives the compressor when current is supplied to create a magnetic field in a coil of wire underneath it.

ROVAC. Name for an air conditioning system (rotary vane air cycle) that uses air as the principle heat transfer fluid.

Saddlebag. Extension of the duct housing in the left and right front corners of the car between the padding and the exterior of the car. Some custom-designed air conditioning systems have the evaporator in the right saddlebag.

Safety-type dispensing valve. A dispensing valve for a refrigerant can. It is made with a relief valve and/or valve that prevents pressure blowback into the can.

Saturated vapor. When the space holds as much vapor as it can. In this situation, the vapor remains in contact with the liquid.

Schrader valve. A spring-loaded valve of the type used in tires. When the pin is depressed, the valve opens; when the pin is released, the valve closes. The Schrader is used as a test fitting so that hoses from pressure gauges can be connected to the system. Refrigerant also is added throught the Schrader. Most systems today use Schrader valves; those that do not have manual valves.

Scotch yoke. A substitute for connecting rods in the General Motors radial four-cylinder compressor. The yoke assembly combines two rods and two pistons into a single unit.

Seizure. When a rotating part, such as an engine or compressor, cannot be turned as a result of mechanical failure.

Semi-automatic temperature control. A simplified version of an automatic temperature control system. It merely controls the position of the temperature control door. It does not choose between heat and cold nor does it select blower speeds. These choices must be preselected by the driver.

Sensible heat. Heat that causes a change in temperature but not a change in state that is, a solid remains a solid, a liquid remains a liquid, and a vapor remains a vapor.

Sensor. A part that senses something, such as temperature or pressure, converts it into an electrical signal, and transmits that signal to another electrical device, such as an amplifier or a computer. Temperature sensors are commonly used in automatic temperature control type of air conditioning systems.

Series circuit. A circuit in which all the parts that use electricity are in a line so that they all operate simultaneously. If one part fails, the circuit breaks and none works.

Shaft seal. The seal assembly at the front of the compressor that minimizes leakage past the compressor shaft.

Short circuit. A defect in a circuit. The circuit is completed short of reaching the part that it is supposed to operate. Defective insulation, which allows the current to leak out to an electrical ground, is a common cause of a short circuit. Or a short may be between wires in a harness, allowing a circuit to be completed even if a control switch is off.

Sight glass. A window built into the high side of the refrigeration system so that liquid refrigerant flow and whether there are any air bubbles in it can be seen. The sight glass usually is on the liquid line at the receiver-dryer. A sight glass also may be used in a charging cylinder.

Sling psychrometer. A device for measuring relative humidity. Although the tool has been prescribed for air conditioning tests for some cars, it is rarely found in service shops.

Slugging. When liquid refrigerant gets to the compressor. It may cause noise and in some cases compressor damage.

Solenoid. An electromagnetic switch. Current is supplied to form an electromagnetic field, that pulls on a metal rod, thus performing mechanical work, such as moving a valve. The pulling on the rod by the magnetic field also may operate an electric switch through which current flows to complete a circuit separate from that which formed the electromagnet. In this case, it also performs the job of a relay.

Solenoid vacuum valve. A valve that opens or closes to pass engine vacuum to a vacuum-operated device. The valve is moved by a solenoid and is returned to the original position by a spring.

Solvent. A chemical that dissolves corrosion and dirt: a cleaning agent.

Snap ring pliers. Pointed-tip pliers made for the removal and installation of a type of retaining ring called a snap ring. Two types of snap ring pliers are customarily used, one for rings that must be expanded to remove and another for rings that must be contracted to remove. There also are pliers that handle both types of rings.

Specification. A number that represents a clearance, tightness, or other important dimension for a component. The specification is provided by the manufacturer for accuracy in servicing or adjusting the component.

Spring-loaded. Use of a spring to hold a moving part in one position so that, when the part is moved another way by a force, it will return to the original position when the force is released.

Squirrel cage blower. A fan that is shaped like a paddle wheel. The design is commonly used in automobile duct housings instead of the simple multiblade fan.

Starving an evaporator. A condition when too little refrigerant is flowing into the evaporator perhaps because of a restriction or a defective expansion valve.

Suction accumulator. See accumulator.

Suction line. Also called **tailpipe**. The low side tubing. It runs from the evaporator outlet to the compressor inlet.

Suction side. The low side of the air conditioning system.

Suction throttling valve. A valve designed to hold some back pressure in the suction line in order to keep pressures and temperatures in the evaporator high enough so that moisture condensing on the outside of the evaporator does not freeze.

Superheat. Addition of heat to a fluid after it has completely vaporized. In this situation, temperature increases but pressure does not.

Superheat spring. A spring that is part of the controlling mechanism in an expansion valve.

Superheat switch. A temperature sensing switch in the compressor of some General Motors cars. It is used with a thermal limiter.

Switch. A part that has movable electrical contacts so that the circuit in which it is inserted can be opened or closed as desired.

Tailpipe. See suction line.

Tap valve. See dispensing valve.

Temperature. A measurement of heat intensity. Farenheit and Celsius are two of the commonly used temperature scales.

Temperature control door. Also called **blend door** and **blend-air door**. The flap door in the duct housing that regulates the flow of air through the heater core. The door is positioned by moving the temperature lever on the dashboard of manual air conditioning systems; it is controlled automatically by automatic temperature control systems.

Temperature differential. The difference in temperature between two adjacent areas. In automobile air conditioning, it may refer to the difference between the outdoors and the passenger compartment with the air conditioning operating.

Test fitting. A threaded fitting that accepts a hose from the gauge manifold, charging station, or refrigerant container dispensing valve. One test fitting is on the high side, and another is on the low side; some systems have a second low side fitting. Most test fittings are the Schrader valve type, but some are fitted with manual valves.

Test lamp. A lamp with two wires attached for checking current flow in a circuit. If the lamp lights when properly attached, there is current flowing.

Test plate. A plate that bolts to the rear of some compressors and to which hoses can be attached for bench-testing the compressor.

Thermal limiter. A fuse-like device that melts when refrigerant pressure in the system is dangerously low. It is triggered by a superheat switch.

Thermal protector. A temperature sensor attached to the exterior of a compressor. If compressor temperature rises too high, the protector opens up internally, breaking the circuit to the compressor clutch and thereby stopping the air conditioner.

Thermistor. A temperature sensor that develops a signal based on varying resistance according to changes in temperature.

Thermometer. Instrument that measures heat intensity in Fahrenheit, Celsius, or other scales.

Thermostatic expansion valve. Also called **expansion valve.** Temperature regulated valve that meters refrigerant flow into the evaporator.

Throttle linkage. Linkage from the pedal to the throttle plate in the carburetor or air intake of a fuel injection-equipped car.

Time-temperature delay relay. A relay that opens to block current flow to the compressor clutch, turning off the air conditioning, whenever coolant temperatures are very high and for about the first half minute after the engine starts in order to allow engine operation to stabilize.

Ton of refrigeration. A measurement equal to 12,000 British thermal units.

Transducer. A device that uses one form of energy to supply power in another form.

Tubing wrench. A specially shaped wrench that grips the hexagonal sections of tubing fittings better than a conventional open-end wrench.

Vacuum. Air pressure below atmospheric pressure.

Vacuum diaphragm unit. A vacuum-operated device. When vacuum is applied, the unit assumes one particular position. Also may be called vacuum motor or vacuum actuator.

Vacuum pump. A pump that produces a vacuum.

Vacuum reservoir. A storage container for vacuum, which is discharged during heavy engine loading when engine vacuum drops.

Valve. A movable lid over an opening. The valve may be shifted to allow vapor or liquid flow through the opening. The valve movement may be controlled automatically or manually.

Valves-in-Receiver. Also called **V-I-R.** A receiver-dryer that includes the expansion valve and suction throttling valve in a combination assembly.

Vapor. Also called **gas.** A fluid in a form in which there are no solid or liquid particles.

Vapor charge. See gas charge.

Variable resistor. A resistor whose resistance changes for a specific reason, such as change in temperature or because of the movement of a manual or automatic control.

Volt. Measurement of electrical pressure. It takes one volt to push one ampere of current through a wire with one ohm resistance.

Voltmeter. Test instrument that measures volts in a circuit.

V-type compressor. A compressor shaped somewhat like the letter V. It is similar in layout to a V-type engine.

Appendix

Servicing the Chrysler C-171 Compressor

This is in addition to clutch service, which is covered in Chapter 14.

If only the crankshaft seal is to be replaced, follow A-1 through A-6 and A-13 through A-17.

If reed valves are to be replaced, change the crankshaft seal too. Follow all steps except A-8 through A-11. Even if there is only a leak at the compressor body O-ring, covered in A-8 through A-11, you will have to remove the compressor through bolts to change the O-ring. So, you should also remove front and rear covers and replace their O-rings, and you should change the crankshaft seal too. Therefore, perform A-1 through A-17.

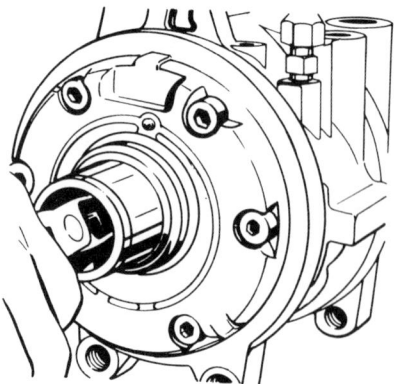

Figure A-1 Compressor shaft seal is an internal assembly, so front cover must come off. After removing clutch assembly as described in Chapter 14, begin front cover removal by taking out the crankshaft key, using side-cutter pliers as shown.

Servicing the Chrysler C-171 Compressor

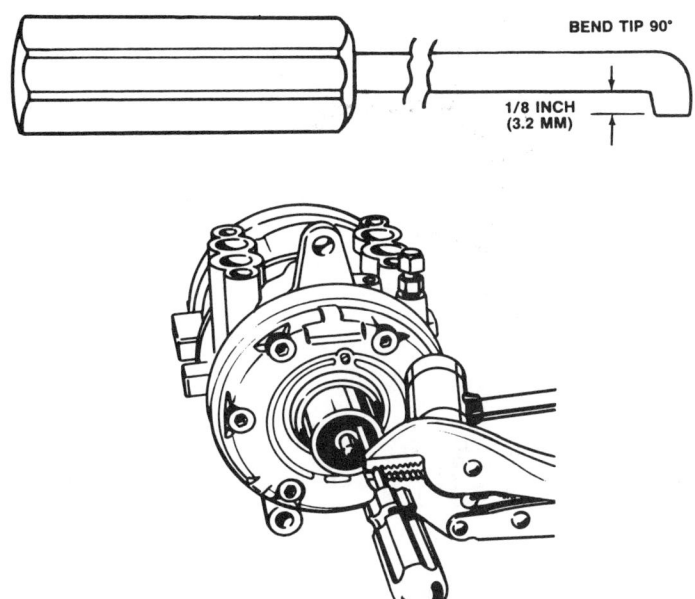

Figure A-2 If the key can't be removed with the pliers, make a special tool from screwdriver as shown, then hold screwdriver shank with locking pliers and reach in with screwdriver tool to dig out key, as you tap on cover with soft head hammer, as shown.

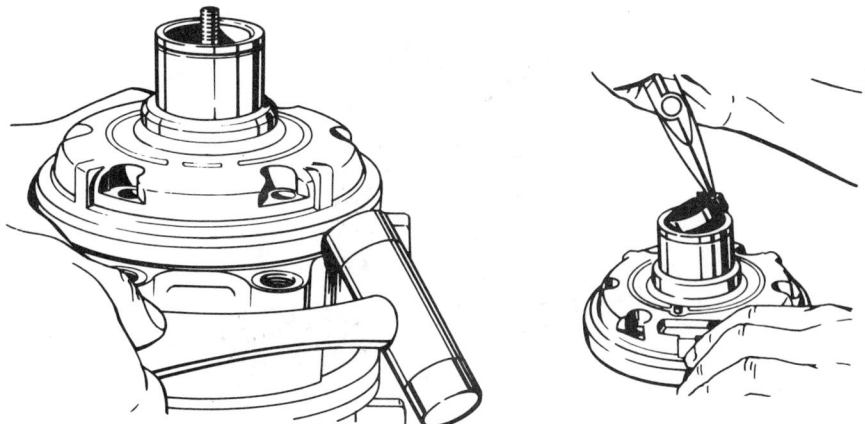

Figure A-3 (*Left*) Remove the six compressor through bolts with a 6 mm Allen wrench, then dislodge the front cover by tapping on the outside diameter as shown. Remove the O-ring seal from the front cover and discard. During reassembly, install a new one.

Figure A-4 (*Right*) With needle-nose pliers, remove the felt and its retainer from the front cover as shown.

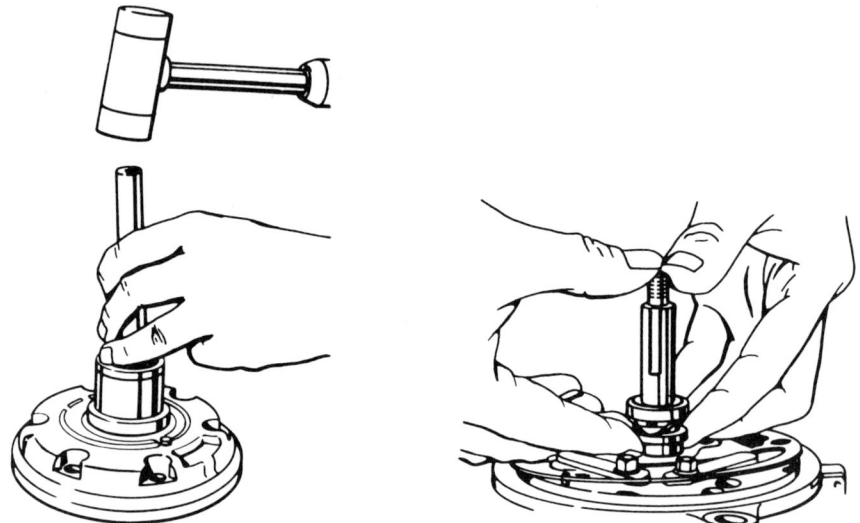

Figure A-5 *(Left)* Put front cover on flat surface with neck up, and with a soft drift (such as brass) tap out the seal plate as shown.

Figure A-6 *(Right)* Lift the shaft seal cartridge from the crankshaft as shown.

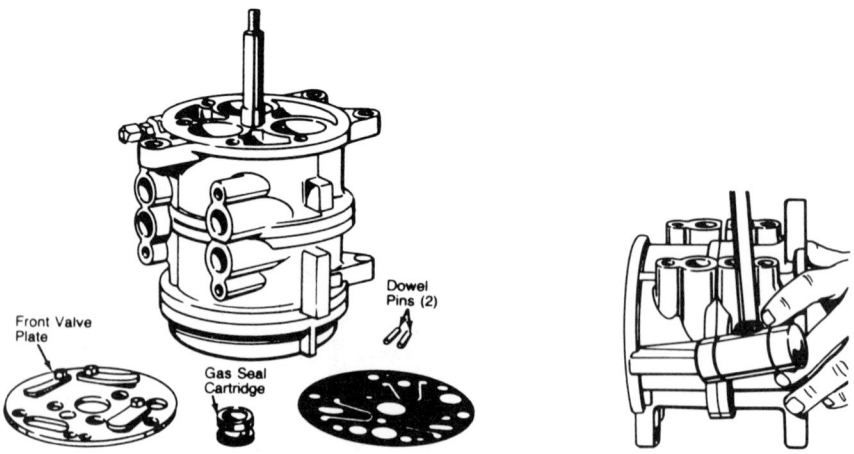

Figure A-7 *(Left)* Remove dowel pins, valve plate, suction reed valve (the plate at lower right), and steel-n-gasket (discard the gasket). Repeat this procedure at the rear cover.

Figure A-8 *(Right)* If leak-testing uncovered a leak at the compressor body O-ring, the O-ring can be replaced. Begin by tapping on the compressor body lugs with a plastic hammer as illustrated, to start separation of the front and rear sections of the body.

Servicing the Chrysler C-171 Compressor

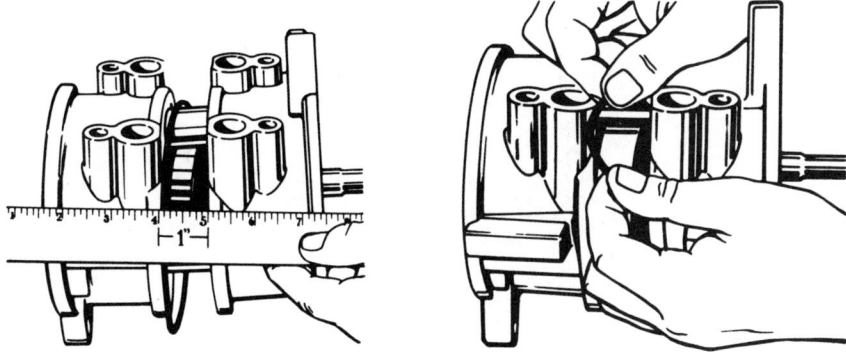

Figure A-9 *(Left)* Do not separate the body sections more than one inch, as illustrated, or internal parts may be dislodged.

Figure A-10 *(Right)* Inspect the O-ring for nicks, cuts, burrs, etc., as shown. Then cut the O-ring and discard it. Also inspect the O-ring sealing groove for scratches, porosity and dirt. Clean out dirt, but replace compressor if you find scratches or porosity.

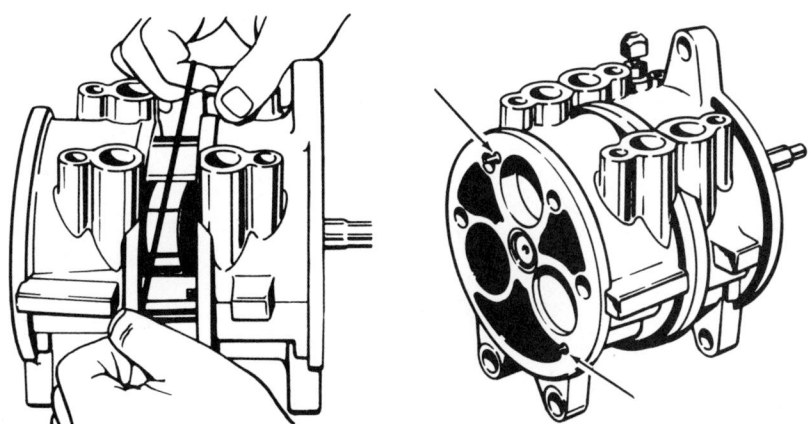

Figure A-11 *(Left)* Install a new O-ring by carefully stretching and passing it over the rear housing to the center of the compressor as illustrated. The O-ring should be dry during this procedure. Then lubricate it with refrigeration oil and position it in its groove. Push the front and rear sections of the compressor together carefully.

Figure A-12 *(Right)* Begin compressor reassembly by installing the dowel pins in the rear housing as shown, then install the suction reed valve. It is possible to install the suction reed valve backwards by mistake, but if this happens, all the compressor through bolts will not go in, tipping you off to the error. Install the rear valve plate assembly over it, then install a new steel-n-gasket. Lubricate a new O-ring and carefully install it in its rear cover groove, then install the rear cover on the rear compressor section. Hold compressor and rear cover together, and place on bench so compressor is resting on rear cover with crankshaft facing upward. Install dowel pins in front compressor section, then suction reed valve, next front valve plate assembly.

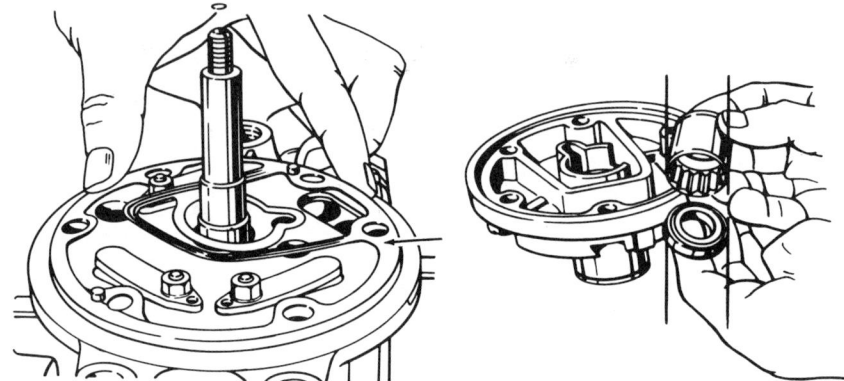

Figure A-13 (Left) Install steel-n-gasket as shown. Then clean crankshaft, coat lightly with refrigeration oil. Lubricate crankshaft seal cartridge with refrigeration oil and install it on the crankshaft, being careful to position it correctly at the slotted section of the crankshaft.

Figure A-14 (Right) Lubricate crankshaft seal's seat and the O-ring for that seat with refrigeration oil. Install the O-ring on the seat. Match up the seat with a socket wrench of a size that makes contact with the outer diameter of the seal seat plate.

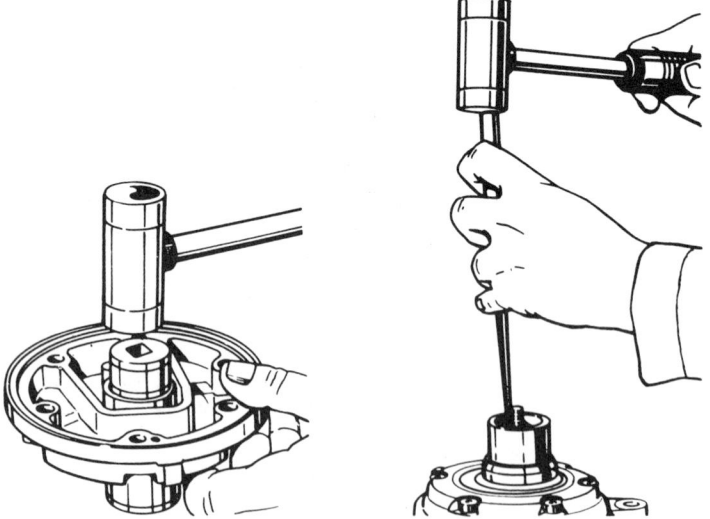

Figure A-15 (Left) Place the seat on the front cover so the sealing surface of the seat faces toward the inside of the compressor (toward the seal on the crankshaft). Then use the socket as a driver and tap the seat into position as illustrated, using a hammer.

Figure A-16 (Right) Install the six compressor through bolts finger tight, then torque to 22 lbs. ft. (29 Newton-meters), then tap the key into position on the crankshaft with a punch and hammer as shown.

Servicing the Chrysler C-171 Compressor

Figure A-17 Install the felt and felt retainer in the front cover and locate it at the base of the cover neck by pushing down all around its circumference with a punch or drift as shown. Install nine ounces (266 milliliters) of refrigeration oil in the compressor through the suction port. Check the compressor for smoothness by hand-turning it with a wrench on the pulley nut (temporarily reinstalled for the check), about a half-dozen revolutions. Remove the pulley nut and reinstall the clutch assembly as explained in Chapter 14. Place caps over the refrigerant line ports unless the compressor is being reinstalled immediately.

Index

A

Acceleration cutout switch, 88
Accumulator, as anti-liquid protection, 87
   in cycling clutch system, 94-96
Air distribution system, 100
   basic check, 141
Ambient-low pressure switch, 84, 112
Ambient switch, 83
   bypassing, 203
Ammeter, hookup of, 41
Ammonia, 21
Amperes, 39-40
Anti-blowback valve, for Refrigerant 12, 166
Aspirator, in automatic temperature control, 117
Atmospheric pressure, 8, 13
Audi 5000, 147
Automatic temperature control, 116
   basic system check, 143
   electro-pneumatic type, 117
   mini-computer (microprocessor) type, 122

B

Barometric pressure, 8
Basic air conditioning system, 27
Bellows, in POA suction throttling valve, 71
   in POA-type evaporator pressure regulator, 78
Belts, drive; inspect and adjust, 133-137
Bi-metal, sensor in semi-automatic temperature control, 126
Bleeding air from refrigerant hoses, 153
Blend door, in air distribution system, 106
   electrically-operated type, 122, 126
   operation of door, 115
Blower (fan), 100
   basic check, 142
   in circuit, 113
   relay, 115
   resistor, 113-114
Boiling point, of Refrigerant 12, 21
Boiling water, 6
Btu (British Thermal Unit), 2
Bulk containers, of Refrigerant 12, 168
Butane, as leak detector, 158

C

Capillary tube, 59
CCOT, 91
Celsius, degrees, 3
Charging cylinder, 152

Charging station, 152, 171
Charts
    pressure-temperature-humidity, 155
    pressure-temperature relationship, 28
    troubleshooting, 189, 191-195, 197
Circuit, electrical, 33
    failures, 38
    short, 38
    types, 37
Circulator, in ROVAC air conditioning system, 303
Collision damage to system, 224
Combination valve, in junction block, 62
Compensator, in semi-automatic temperature control, 125
Compressor, basic, 22
    axial five-cylinder, 48
    axial six-cylinder, 49
        service GM type, 255-260
    Chrysler C-171 service, 260-263, Appendix
    general service procedures, 239-240
    in-line two-cylinder, 45
    isolating, 278
    leak-testing GM, 241, 254
    Nippondenso, 260
        service, 263-268
    noises, 218
    oil collection, 170, 224
    oil measuring, 172, 224
    radial-four cylinder, 51
        service, 240-255
    return to service, 282
    Sankyo service, 268-277
    seizure, 204-205
    Tecumseh service, 277-286
    troubleshooting, 204-206
    valves, 45
    vane-type rotary, 51
        service of York type, 292-299
    V-2 type, 47
        service, 287-292
        with two low-side fittings, 147
    York in-line two-cylinder service, 277-286

Compressor clutch, 52-54
    basic check, 138
    circuit, 112
    troubleshooting, 200-204
Condensation, 7
    to remove humidity, 14
Condenser, 25-26
    cleaning front of, 131
Control panel switch for air distribution system, 110-114
Coolant control valve—see Valves, water control
Coolant, inspection and flow tests, 132
Cooling system checkout, 130-137
Cycling clutch orifice tube system, 91
Cycling clutch switch, 92
    bypassing, 202
    service, 225-227
    testing, 211, 213-216

D

Dashboard control panel (switch) for air distribution system, 110-114
Degree wheel, in automatic temperature control, 117
Dehumidification, 20
Delay relay, time-temperature type, 88
    application, 110, 112
Desiccant, in receiver dryer, 54
    replacement in Valves-in-Receiver, 224
Diaphragm, in switch, 33, 88
    in expansion valve, 58
    vacuum unit for air distribution system, 101
Discharge, system of Refrigerant 12, 169-172
Dispensing valves for Refrigerant 12, 167
Distribution system, for air, 100-127
Drain tubes (hoses) from evaporator, 138
Drive belts, inspect and adjust, 133-137
Duct system for air distribution, 100
    operation, 105-109

E

Electronic leak detector, 159
Electro-pneumatic, type of automatic temperature control, 117
Expansion tube, in cycling clutch system, 94-95
   replacement, 227-228
   troubleshooting, 206-208
Expansion valve—see Thermostatic expansion valve
External freezeup, on evaporator coils, 198
Evaporation, 6
   from boiling, 13
   from skin, 18
Evaporator, 24
   flooding and starving, 59
Evaporator pressure regulator, 76-78
   service, 289-291
   testing, 211
Evaporator temperature regulator, 78-79

F

Fahrenheit, temperature scale, 3
False seizure, on GM compressors, 205-206
Fan, 18
   air conditioning type, see Blower
   cooling system type, test, 133
Feedback potentiometer, 122
Flooding the evaporator, 59
Flushing new parts to clean, 223
Freon, brand of Refrigerant 12, 22
Fresh air flap door, 106, 110
Frostbite, danger from Refrigerant 12, 166
Fuse, 37
Fusion, 8

G

Gas, 6
Gas charging of Refrigerant 12, 176

Gauges and manifold, 150
   testing accuracy, 168
Ground, electrical, 37
   application, 112

H

H-type expansion valve, 62, 97
Hand-test, as basic system performance check, 140
Heat, 4
   effect on liquids and gas, 6
   exchangers, 22
Heater, 107
Heater water control valve—see Valves, water control
Heat transfer, 4
   between radiator and condenser, 131
   blocked by insulation, 5
   in air conditioning, 20
High-blower relay, 115
High-pressure relief valve, 86
High-pressure side, of air conditioning system, 28, 63
Hoses, Refrigerant 12, service, 235-236
   replacement, 236-237
Humidity, 14
   effects of removal, 13-14
   relative, 14

I

Ice box, 18
Inches of mercury, as a measure of vacuum, 13

J

Jumper wire, use of, 42
Junction block, 62

L

Latent heat, 6, 14
   of fusion, 8

Leakage, of Refrigerant 12, 206
  at a hose fitting, how to correct, 235
  away from a hose fitting, how to correct, 236
Leak-testing, 154, 157–160
  during vacuum-pumping, 174
  GM compressors, 241, 254
Liquid-charging, into the high side, 177
  into the low side, 176
Liquid line, 28, 141
  test fitting on, 146
Low-pressure side, 28, 63
Low-pressure switch, 84, 112

M

Manual test fittings, 148
Microprocessor, in automatic temperature control, 122
Mode door, in air distribution system, 107
Moisture, as a cause of system malfunction, 196–199
  external freezeup of, on evaporator, 198
Motor, as a device to power fan, 36

O

O-rings, service, 223
Ohms, measure of resistance, 40
Oil, compressor, collecting and measuring, 170, 172
  adding to Chrysler C-171, 263
  adding to Chrysler V-2, 292
  adding to GM axial six-cylinder, 255
  adding to GM radial four-cylinder, 255
  adding to Nippondenso, 268
  adding to Sankyo, 274–276
  adding to system, 172–173
  adding to Tecumseh two-cylinder, 280–281
  adding to York two-cylinder, 280–281

Oil, compressor, collecting and measuring (*Contd.*)
  adding to York rotary vane, 293, 298–299
Ommeter, hookup of, 41
One-pound can, of Refrigerant 12, 166
Orifice tube, in cycling clutch system, 92–95
  replacement of, 227–228
Outside air door—see Fresh air flap door

P

Parallel circuit, 37
Perspiration, 19
Pressure, 8
  atmospheric, 8, 13
  barometric, 8
  decreasing, 12
  gauges, 8
  increasing, 9
  in cooling system, 10
  temperature relationship, 28, 168
  testing system, 144–154
  troubleshooting chart, 189
  type cycling clutch switch, 92
Potentiometer, 117
  feedback type, 122
Programmer, in automatic temperature control, 117
  with solenoid valves, 123
Propane, as leak detector, 158

R

Radiator cap, 10, 131
Receiver-dryer, 54
  replacement, 228
  servicing Valves-in-Receiver type, 228–235
Recharge, system with Refrigerant 12, 169
  using gas method, 175
  using gauge manifold, into low side, 179–181

Recharge, system with Refrigerant 12 (*Contd.*)
   using gauge manifold, liquid into high side, 182
   liquid into high side, 182
   with sight glass, 182
Recirculation door—see Fresh air flap door
Reed valves, operation of, 46
Refrigerant 134A, 22
Refrigerant 12, 21
   containers and tap (dispensing) valves, 164-168
   multi-can adapters, 167
   safe handling, 165-166
Relay, operation of, 34-35
   high-blower type, 115
   time-temperature delay type, 88, 112
   vacuum-checking type, 118, 127
Reservoir, vacuum, 104, 116
Resistance, 40
   at connections, 40
Resistors, 40
   variable, 117
ROVAC, air conditioning system, 22, 301-304

S

Saturated vapor, 30
Schrader test fittings, 148
Scotch yoke, modified type in compressor, 51
Semi-automatic temperature control, 125
   all-vacuum system, 126
   bi-metal sensor in, 126
   with electric motor-operated blend door, 126
Sensors, temperature, 112
   bi-metal, in semi-automatic temperature control, 126
   in-car, basic check on systems with automatic temperature control, 143
   temperature, in automatic temperature control, 117
Series circuit, 38
Short circuit, 38
Skivving, 24
Soap solution, as leak detector, 157
Solenoid, 36
Starving the evaporator, 59
Suction accumulator, 87
Suction side, of system, 28
Suction throttling valve
   cable type, 69
   location of, 73
   operation of, 67-76
   Pilot-operated-absolute (POA) type, 71
   POA type in Valves-in-Receiver, 71
   testing, 194-195, 208-212
   vacuum diaphragm type, 69-70
Superheat, 11
Superheat spring, in expansion valve, 59
Superheat switch, in thermal limiter circuit, 84
Swash plate, in compressor, 49
Switches, types of, 33-36
   acceleration cutout type, 88
   ambient-low pressure type, 84, 112
   pressure type for cycling clutch system, 92
   themostatic type for cycling clutch system, 92

T

Temperature, 1
   and heat transfer, 4
   differential, 5-6
   drop from refrigerant vaporization, 25
   effect of pressure, 8, 25
   when heat is taken away, 7
   sensor, 112, 117, 126, 143
   vs. heat, 2
Test fittings (service or test ports)
   adapter, 148
   connecting to, 153
   locations, 144-147
   types of fittings, 148
Test lamp, hookup of, 42
   battery-powered type, 42

Thermal grease, on capillary tube, 97
Thermal limiter, operation of, 84
    testing circuit, 203–204
    troubleshooting system with, 194–195
Thermistor, 117, 127
Thermostatic expansion valve, operation of, 55
    criteria for calibration, 62
    H-type, 62, 97
    how equalized, 59
    service, 225
    troubleshooting, 198, 206–208
Thermostatic-type cycling clutch switch, 92
Time-temperature delay relay, 88, 110, 112
Transducer, in automatic temperature control, 117

V

Vacuum, 12
    actuator, 104
    diaphragm unit, 101–104
    checking for problems, 217
    checking relay, 118, 120, 127
    check valve, 104, 116
    diaphragm unit, 101–104
    from engine, 100
    motor, 104, 118
    pump, function in air distribution system, 101
    pumping system after discharge, 172–174

Vacuum (Contd.)
    reservoir, 104, 116
    signal, in automatic temperature control, 117
    supply hose, 101
Valves
    cable types, 69, 107
    check, vacuum type in air distribution system, 104
    expansion—see Thermostatic expansion valve
    high pressure relief, 86
    in-Receiver design, 61, 198
    reed, in compressor, 46
    suction throttling type—see Suction throttling valve
    water control (for heater), 100
Vane-type rotary compressor, 51
Vapor, 6
    compressing to raise temperature, 25
    saturated, 30
Variable resistor, 117
    in semi-automatic temperature control, 126
Voltmeter, hookup of, 41
Volts, 40

W

Water, 6
    boiling point, 6
    control valve, for heater, 100